GAME PROGRAMMING
WITH PYTHON

GAME PROGRAMMING WITH PYTHON

SEAN RILEY

CHARLES RIVER MEDIA, INC.
Hingham, Massachusetts

Publisher: Jenifer Niles
Production: Publishers' Design and Production Services
Cover Design: The Printed Image

CHARLES RIVER MEDIA, INC.
10 Downer Avenue
Hingham, Massachusetts 02043
781-740-0400
781-740-8816 (FAX)
info@charlesriver.com
www.charlesriver.com

This book is printed on acid-free paper.

Sean Riley. *Game Programming with Python*.
ISBN: 1-58450-258-4

Library of Congress Cataloging-in-Publication Data

Riley, Sean.
    Game programming with Python / Sean Riley.
        p.   cm.
    ISBN 1-58450-258-4 (pbk. : alk. paper)
    1. Computer games—Programming. 2. Python (Computer program language) I. Title.
    QA76.76.C672R55 2003
    794.8'15262—dc22
                                        2003017136

Printed in the United States of America
05 7 6 5 4 3 2

Contents

Preface   **xvii**

1   Overview   **1**

What This Book Is About   1

What Is Python?   1

What Is Game Development?   2

Can Python Be Used for Games?   3

The Contents of This Book   4

Prerequisites   4

SECTION I   Introduction   **5**

2   Game Architecture   **7**

2.1 Architecture Diagram   8

2.2 Physical Simulations   9

2.3 Data Drivers   10

2.4 Graphics Engines   11

2D Engines   11

3D Engines   12

Graphics Engine Subcomponents   12

Competing APIs   12

2.5 Audio Systems   13

2.6 Game Simulations   14

2.7 User Interfaces   15

2.8 Network Layers   17

Summary   18

3   Python Game Architectures   **19**

3.1 Performance Characteristics of Python   19

3.2 Pure Python   20

3.3 Python Programming   21

3.4 Python Scripting   22

3.5 Python Data   22

3.6 Other Languages   23

The Lua Programming Language   23

The Tcl Programming Language   23

The Java Programming Language   24

Summary   24

SECTION II   Game Infrastructure   **25**

4   Python Game Framework   **27**

4.1 Infrastructure Technology   27

4.2 Initialization   28

4.3 The Main Module   29

4.4 The Main Loop   31

4.5 Cleanup   32

4.6 Running the Example Code   34

Summary   34

5   Simulation Concepts   **35**

5.1 The Physical Simulation   36

5.2 Components of the Physical Simulation   36

5.3 Implementing Simulations with Python   37

5.4 Reactive Simulation   37

5.5 Controlled Simulation   39

5.6 Parallel Simulation   40

5.7 Simulation Conventions   41

5.8 Variable Rate Updating   43

5.9 The Base Simulation Class   44

5.10 The Simulation World   47

5.11 Updating the Simulation   49

Summary   52

6   Data-Driven Simulations   **55**

6.1 Benefits of Data-Driven Systems   56

6.2 Data Sources   57

Text Files   57

XML   57

Relational Databases   58

Scripting Languages   58

6.3 Implementing a Data Repository   58

Summary   67

7   Collision Detection   **69**

7.1 Classifying Objects for Collision   70

7.2 Partitioning the World for Collision Detection   72

7.3 Methods of Collision Checking   74

Per Polygon   74

Per Pixel   75

Bounding Boxes   75

Bounding Spheres   75

Tiles   76

7.4 Coordinate Spaces   77

Coordinate Spaces for Collision Detection   77

Coordinate Spaces and Bounding Boxes   78

7.5 Axially Aligned Bounding Boxes   79

7.6 Bounding Spheres   82

7.7 Dealing with Moving Objects   84

7.8 Implementing a Collision Grid in Python   87

7.9 Making a Module   94

Summary   95

SECTION III   Game Technologies   **97**

8   Graphics   **99**

8.1 Art Pipeline   100

8.2 Using Python for Graphics Programming   101

Minimize the Number of Elements Exposed in the Interface   102

Minimize the Amount of Python Code Executed at Runtime   102

Keep Graphics-Specific Data in the Graphics Engine   102

Hide Implementation Details   102

8.3 High-Level Graphics Interface   103

Module Interfaces versus Object Interfaces   103

The Graphics Engine Interface   103

8.4 Python Graphics Engine   107

The Module Interface   107

The Graphics Object Interface   116

Integrating with the Simulation   123

Example Application   127

8.5 Visualizing the Collision System   129

Summary   131

9   Audio   **133**

9.1 Audio Concepts   134

Amplitude   134

Frequency   134

Channels   134

Sample Rate   134

Pulse Code Modulation   135

9.2 Playing Sound Effects   135

9.3 Ambient Sounds   138

9.4 Playing Music   141
Summary   142

10   Input   143
10.1 Message Handling   144
10.2 Keyboard Input   146
10.3 Mouse Input   148
10.4 Joystick Input   149
Summary   150

11   Unit Testing   151
11.1 Introduction to Unit Testing   152
11.2 Setup for Testing   152
11.3 Testing the DataManager   154
11.4 Testing the Simulation   155
Summary   159

SECTION IV   Game Programming   161
12   Game Simulations   163
12.1 Players and Avatars   164
    The PongBallGame Class   165
    The PongPlayer Class   167
    The Simulation Objects   169
12.2 Game Modes   172
    Mode Classes   172
    The Breakout Example   174
12.3 The Entity Class   185
12.4 Object Identification   185
12.5 Game Events   188
Summary   195

13   Game Levels   197
13.1 Game Levels   197

13.2 Level Data   198

13.3 Level Data in Python   199

13.4 Game Modes for Levels   202

The Pre-Level Mode   205

The Post-Level Mode   207

13.5 Managing Resources with Levels   209

Summary   211

14   User Interfaces   213

14.1 Game User Interfaces   214

UI Drawing   214

Coordinate Systems   214

User Interface Optimizations   217

14.2 PyUI Introduction   217

14.3 PyUI Concepts   218

The Desktop   218

Widgets   218

Panels   219

Windows   219

Frames   219

Dialogs   219

Layout Managers   219

Themes   220

Renderers   220

Fonts   221

Events   221

14.4 Using PyUI   221

CanvasPanel Class   222

CanvasFrame Class   224

SaveDialog Class   227

14.5 Interacting with the Simulation   230

14.6 Drawing Text   235

Bitmap Fonts   235

Dynamic Fonts   236

Summary   237

15 Artificial Intelligence   **239**

15.1 Basic State Machines   240

15.2 State Machine Enhancements   244

Transition Validation   244

State Inputs   245

Parallel State Machines   246

15.3 Pathfinding Concepts   253

World Representations for Pathfinding   253

15.4 The A* Algorithm   256

15.5 Implementing A* in Python   258

15.6 Visualizing the Pathfinder   264

Summary   268

16 Procedurally Generated Game Content   **269**

16.1 Predictable Random Numbers   270

Random Number Distributions   271

Predictable Random Numbers   272

Using the random Module   272

16.2 Terrain Generation   274

Height Maps   274

Mid-Point Displacement   275

16.3 Terrain Generation in Python   279

16.4 Name Generation   287

Summary   293

SECTION V   Multiplayer Games   **295**

17 Network Concepts   **297**

17.1 Network Identification   298

Internet Names   298

IP Addresses   299

Name Translation   300

Port Numbers   301

Subnets   302

17.2 TCP/IP   303

17.3 UDP/IP   304

17.4 Blocking and Nonblocking I/O   305

17.5 Bandwidth   305

17.6 Latency   306

17.7 Byte Ordering   307

Summary   309

18   Network Layers   **311**

18.1 Socket Basics   313

18.2 Sending and Receiving Data   315

18.3 TCP/IP Server Models   317

Connection Management   317

Simple Iterative Server   318

Concurrent Forking Server   321

Concurrent Threaded Server   324

Concurrent Asynchronous Server (Reactor Pattern)   326

18.4 Introduction to Twisted   328

The Twisted Reactor   329

Twisted Protocols   330

18.5 Game Protocol Design   330

Static and Dynamic Protocols   330

Streams and Packing   331

Network Packets   333

Summary   339

19   Clients and Servers   **341**

19.1 Multiplayer Game Architectures   342

Peer-to-Peer Architecture   342

Client/Server Architecture 344

Massively Multiplayer 345

19.2 Code Organization 347

19.3 A Game Server 348

19.4 A Game Client 356

The LobbyFrame class 364

Summary 366

20 Multiplayer Game Example **367**

20.1 Code Organization 368

20.2 The Tic-Tac-Toe Game 369

20.3 The Game Server 370

The TicTacGame Class 372

The TicTacServerProtocol Class 376

The TicTacServer Class 377

Running the Server 377

20.4 The Tic-Tac-Toe Game Client 378

The Client Protocol 378

The Client Application 380

The TicTacWindow Class 381

Running the Client 385

Summary 388

SECTION VI Advanced Topics **389**

21 Using the Python C API **391**

21.1 The Abstract Object Layer 392

The Object Protocol 393

The Number Protocol 394

The Sequence Protocol 394

The Mapping Protocol 395

Other Protocols 395

21.2 Reference Counting 395
  Heap vs. Stack Memory 396
  Reference Counting Macros 397
21.3 Exception Handling 398
21.4 Data Conversion 399
  Extracting Parameter Values 399
  Building Return Values 401
21.5 Concrete Object Layer 402
  Fundamental Objects 403
  Numeric Objects 404
  Sequence Objects 404
  Mapping Objects 405
  Other Objects 405
Summary 406

22 **Extending Python** 407
22.1 Writing Extension Modules 408
  Using Extension Modules 409
  Creating an Extension Module 410
  Extension Module Example 413
22.2 Writing Extension Types 422
  Type Structures 423
  Instance Creation and Deletion 426
  Member Function of Extension Types 428
22.3 Compiling Extension Code 432
22.4 Automating Interface Generation 435
  SWIG 437
  Boost.Python 439
  Psyco 440
Summary 442

23 Embedding Python **443**

23.1 Embedding the Interpreter 444

Python Context 446

Executing Python Code 448

23.2 Communicating with the Host Application 449

23.3 Example Application 451

23.3 Project Setup 454

Summary 455

Preface

As I was writing this book, a number of people asked me why I chose to write a book about Python game programming. The unspoken subtext of this question is that the choice of programming language used for development is not important, so why would programmers choose to use Python when their last game project was in C++? There are many ways to answer this question, depending on who is asking it. It was usually professional C++ game programmers with no Python experience who asked this question, so for this book's audience of programmers, I'll try to answer that question here.

The choice of programming languages for a project is *very important*. Programming languages have different characteristics that drastically affect the time it takes to develop programs with them. Python is at the far end of the spectrum of programming languages that allow rapid development of systems. It is literally possible to develop programs in Python in a fraction of the time it takes to develop programs with equivalent functionality in most other languages.

The impact of rapid development in the area of game development is easy to underestimate. With strict frame-rate requirements and memory budgets, game programming has traditionally focused on runtime performance and memory use in favor of ease of development. This is characterized by hyper-optimized systems that take a long time to develop and are difficult to change and maintain. The real problem with this type of development is that the programmers don't find out if their solution actually works until they are far down an implementation path that could take months to change. Python offers an alternative by allowing systems to be developed and evaluated quickly, so that feedback can be incorporated into the game development process at a much earlier stage. It allows the implementation of optimized versions of a system to be deferred until the fundamental concepts have been proven, and their flaws discovered. In the long run, this leads to better programs, and better games.

The ability to develop quickly gives programmers the confidence to abandon dead-end implementation strategies. If a programmer takes six months to develop a system in C++, his (and his manager's) attachment to it might be so strong that he might be unable and unwilling to consider an alternative and superior implementation that suddenly presents itself. The horror of another six months to re-implement the new solution could be infeasible. In Python development, the initial implementation would progress much more quickly, which would lead to the discovery of the superior implementation in weeks instead of months. With this information in hand, the programmer (who is still mentally fresh) would have the courage to tackle the re-implementation.

This type of refactoring and courage are discussed in the Extreme Programming (XP) methodology. Aspects of this methodology work very well with Python and very much apply to game development. There is often no tangible customer in game development; it tends to call for requirements gathering through discovery rather than specification. This makes prototyping and refactoring even more important than in non-game application development.

So, when people ask me why they should use Python for a game project, I tell them that it will reduce their development time, improve their technical designs, and make their programmers much happier.

Sean Riley

1 Overview

WHAT THIS BOOK IS ABOUT

Game Programming with Python is about building games using the Python programming language. It deals with general concepts of game development and specifics that apply when using Python for game development. Some of the general topics covered in this book are simulations, game architectures, graphics, networking, and user interfaces. The Python-specific topics covered include Python development strategies, using Python for data-driven systems, performance tuning, modules and packages, and interfaces between Python and other programming languages. Additionally, a series of increasingly complex examples are developed throughout the book using Python.

As Python is a high-level language, this book is less focused on implementation details than other game programming books, and more focused on technical design and architecture. In Python development, many low-level tasks are taken care of by the language itself, by libraries that are part of the standard distributions, or other available components. This allows developers to spend more time concentrating on their real goals—in the case of this book, making games.

This book discusses the issues that arise when building large-scale, commercial-quality games. It does not show trivial examples of the technologies of game development; it shows how to build real game components and systems using these technologies as the underlying framework.

WHAT IS PYTHON?

Python is a high-level programming language that combines a clean syntax with powerful built-in data structures and a large standard library. It is used in a variety of areas, including user interface development, Web-based content delivery systems, and computer games. According to the official Python FAQ, Python is "an interpreted, interactive, object-oriented programming language."

From a programming language perspective, Python is a relatively modern, interpreted language that compiles to byte code in a similar way to Java. It has been around since 1997, and unlike many popular languages such as Java and C++, it is a dynamically typed language, which gives it great flexibility. Python uses built-in reference counting and an incremental garbage collection system for memory management that largely removes the burden of object lifecycle tracking from application programmers. Although Python has a reputation in some circles as a *scripting* language similar to Perl or PHP, it is a fully functional programming language with object-oriented capabilities, and debugging and profiling tools.

Python's source code is freely available under an open-source license and is portable to many different hardware platforms. This has led to the growth of a large community of developers around the world who use Python and contribute to its development. This is a great strength of Python; there is always someone available in an online chat room or a mailing list that can help with problems. Because of this large community of developers, Python has a feature-rich standard library that includes such versatile capabilities as an HTML parser, HTTP and other Internet servers, object serialization services, threading, and a user interface library.

Python has a robust and easy-to-use interface to the C programming language. It is possible to build extensions to Python with C, and to embed the Python interpreter into programs written in C. This has led to Python being used as a "glue" language. In this role, it acts as a control language for systems written in other languages and makes it possible for disparate systems to communicate with each other. This aspect of Python makes it useful for game development where some components such as graphics engines have high performance requirements that require them to be written in C or C++, and other components have different requirements relating to flexibility and rapid development.

Above all, Python is a programming language that is fun and easy to use. *Game Programming with Python* applies this attitude to the field of game development.

WHAT IS GAME DEVELOPMENT?

Game development is the practice of taking ideas, designs, and concepts and turning them into finished products that can be enjoyed by the ultimate end users—people who play games. It is a technology-driven process comprised of several disciplines, including art, programming, design, audio, production, and quality assurance. However, this book focuses mainly on the programming stage of the game development process. It strays into the areas of design, art, and production, but only enough to give the core programming topics context.

Games have grown to be large projects in terms of the amount of content, the scope of the designs, the number of players participating, and the number of technologies involved. A modern commercial game includes hundreds, perhaps thousands, of art assets and many thousand lines of code. These projects deal with a broad range of technologies, including networking, 3D graphics, asset management, animation systems, user interfaces, audio, input devices, data persistence, and physics. We discuss some of these topics in later chapters of this book.

Since game technology covers such a broad scope of topics, it is too costly for developers to start from scratch on each new game project—they must reuse code from previous projects, use third-party libraries, or even purchase commercial components. Game development is a combination of writing software and integrating existing software. Python enables this reuse and accelerates the rate at which game developers can work.

CAN PYTHON BE USED FOR GAMES?

Python is already being used by professional game developers! A number of popular commercial games including Totally Games' award winning *Star Trek® Bridge Commander™*, Irrational Games' *Freedom Force™*, and Electronic Arts' *Earth & Beyond™* have already been released that use the Python programming language in varying degrees.

Python has found a niche in game development because it has characteristics that are very different from traditional game development languages. It allows developers to quickly build systems that are flexible and can be easily driven by data. Systems written in traditional game development languages (usually C or C++) take much longer to write, and although they might execute faster, are more difficult to change. Python has found a place in the dynamic environment of game development as a tool that allows developers to implement ideas quickly and provides flexibility during the development process. Programmers who switch from C and C++ to Python find that their productivity rises dramatically.

Python is being used in three major ways in game development. It is used as a full-fledged programming language to develop real software systems; it is used as a scripting language to control and interface between systems written in other languages; and it is used as a data language to describe game rules and game objects. In this book, we discuss each of these major ways to use Python and the differences between them.

THE CONTENTS OF THIS BOOK

This book consists of six parts that transition from introductory overviews at the beginning, to advanced topics toward the end of the book:

Section I: Introduction

Section II: Game Infrastructure

Section III: Game Technologies

Section IV: Game Programming

Section V: Multiplayer Games

Section VI: Advanced Topics

PREREQUISITES

To get the most out of this book, the reader should have some programming background. *Game Programming with Python* is not an introduction to programming. It assumes the reader has a basic grasp of software engineering principles. Some useful areas of technical knowledge include:

- Python programming
- Object-oriented programming and design
- Geometry and trigonometry
- TCP/IP networking
- C/C++ programming
- Design patterns

This book also assumes some knowledge of the game development process and game architectures. With the focus on Python programming, it is beyond the scope of this book to examine the entire process of game development, but enough is covered—especially in the early chapters—that most readers should be able to cope.

Introduction

2 | Game Architecture

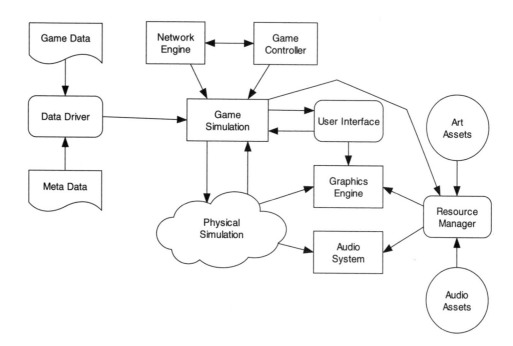

This chapter describes the components that make up a generalized game architecture. It describes each of the components, the relationships between components, and the relevance of using Python for their development. It also explains the applicability of Python for developing each of these components, and discusses potential solutions related to Python.

Most games share certain common infrastructure components. These include *physical simulations, game simulations, graphics engines, audio systems, user interfaces, network layers,* and *data drivers.* These components and the relationships between them comprise the architecture of the game. Each game's architecture is

7

different, but these common components provide an overview of how games work on the inside.

This architectural description is general background information that is relevant to the Python-specific architecture and implementation issues in the next chapter.

2.1 ARCHITECTURE DIAGRAM

Figure 2.1 shows all of the components that will be discussed in this chapter and some of the relationships between them.

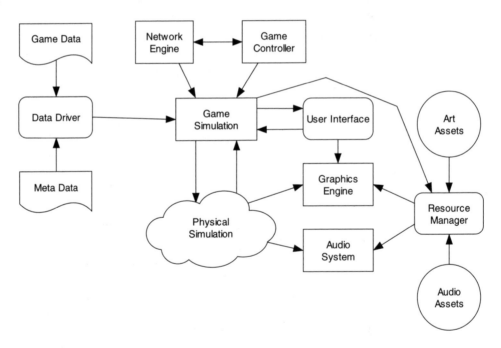

FIGURE 2.1   Logical game architecture.

The components shown in Figure 2.1 are discussed at a high level in the remaining sections of this chapter, and in more detail throughout the rest of the book. The chapters that correspond to the components in Figure 2.1 are shown here:

- Physical Simulations (Chapters 5 and 7)
- Data Drivers (Chapter 6)
- Graphics Engines (Chapter 8)
- Audio Systems (Chapter 9)
- Game Simulations (Chapters 12 through 16)
- User Interfaces (Chapter 14)
- Network Layers (Chapters 17 through 20)

2.2 PHYSICAL SIMULATIONS

A *physical simulation* is a representation of a situation that includes objects with characteristics that approximate the real world. In this book, we distinguish between physical simulations and game simulations. Physical simulations include tangible attributes of object behavior, such as motion and collision. In contrast, game simulations cover more abstract concepts that might have no counterpart in the real world, such as the way magic inflicts damage on players, or rules for scoring points.

In the real world, objects have physical attributes such as position, velocity, acceleration, and orientation. As objects in a physical simulation are an approximation of these real objects, they tend to have attributes that are similar to real world objects.

Physical simulations have rules and conventions that all the objects within them must obey. These rules usually emulate the rules of the real world, but can sometimes differ in interesting ways. Some physical simulations allow time to be slowed down, resulting in *bullet time* from the game *Max Payne*™. Others allow objects to pass through other objects for specific game-play reasons. The rules of a physical simulation do not need to exactly model the real world, but whatever the rules of the simulation are, they must be applied to the simulation with the same conviction that physics applies to objects in the world in which we live.

Having a robust and efficient physical simulation is a very important part of any game. Any discrepancies or errors that occur in this component can produce problems that are glaringly obvious to players, which can ruin the play experience. Players have expectations from the real world concerning how objects in a physical simulation should behave. One of the worst sins that game developers can commit is to shatter these expectations with misbehaving physical simulation objects.

Physical simulations are a core component of the game architecture, and interface with game simulations, graphics engines, and sound systems.

Suitability of Python

Although not appropriate for the internals of complex physical simulations, Python is an excellent vehicle for controlling rather than implementing physical simulations. The dynamic features of Python are very useful when writing code that deals with simulations from the outside. In game development, it is often game simulations that are the layer above physical simulations. This game simulation layer is often the driving component that controls the physical simulations. As we will demonstrate, game simulations are a very appropriate place for Python code.

Physical simulations are an area of game development that involves a great deal of math, and potentially, a large number of objects. Running physical simulations requires specific functions to be performed at a high frequency, and potentially a large amount of data to represent the physical objects. This means that writing complex physical simulations is a very performance-sensitive area in any language.

Fortunately, there are libraries and extension modules for Python that can be used to encapsulate some of the inner workings of physical simulations. These make it possible to develop some physical simulations in Python, but still, the most complex physical simulations are better suited to languages such as C and C++.

In This Book

Chapters 5 and 7 of this book cover physical simulations in Python in great detail. Chapter 5, "Simulation Concepts," implements a two-dimensional (2D) physical simulation in Python, and Chapter 7, "Collision Detection," implements a collision system in Python that enhances the physical simulation.

2.3 DATA DRIVERS

The *data driver* is the component that handles the management of data within the game—both metadata and game data. There are many different approaches to data-driven systems in game development. They range from hard-coding the data into the source code, to using a relational database to store large volumes of metadata. In some of these approaches, there is no data driver, or it is so small that it is implicit in some other system, but in systems that are very data driven, the data driver can be a significant amount of infrastructure.

Data drivers have close relationships with game simulations, as the two components often work very closely together.

Suitability of Python

Python is an excellent language for almost all data-related tasks. Its dynamic nature and flexibility make it easy to drive Python systems with data, or even to construct Python classes and objects from data sources.

In This Book

The example code uses a `DataManager` class as a manager of metadata, and uses Python files to store this data. In this example system, the game reads data in at startup by executing the Python files and creating "category" objects. This topic will be explained in detail in Chapter 6, "Data-Driven Simulations."

2.4 GRAPHICS ENGINES

Graphics engines are components for drawing output to the screen. Images on the screen are the primary form of feedback that users receive during gameplay, so the component that produces these images—the graphics engine—is one of the most critical portions of any game.

Graphics engines come in a vast number of forms, from simple text placement routines to mathematically complex libraries that render three-dimensional (3D) objects. However, in most modern games, they can be classified into two main categories: 2D graphics engines, and 3D graphics engines.

Graphic engines are another core piece of game architecture that can have relationships to almost any component, but their most important interfaces are to physical simulations and resource managers.

2D Engines

Two-dimensional graphics engines have been around for a long time. Before the advent of hardware-accelerated 3D graphics, almost all games relied on this type of graphics engine to display their game worlds. Games that use 2D graphics engines are restricted to displaying the game from a fixed set of viewpoints—sometimes only a single viewpoint. They use sprites to draw individual game objects and usually employ sophisticated routines to copy rectangular pieces of memory around to render these sprites.

Although 2D graphics engines are now considered "old school" by most game programmers, many of the most popular games on the shelves still use this type of engine. One reason for this is that the hardware requirements for 2D graphics engines are often lower than those for 3D engines, so people with lower-end computers can play games built with them.

3D Engines

Three-dimensional graphics engines are probably the most volatile technology of game development. The latest console machines from Sony, Nintendo, and Microsoft have 3D capabilities, and the latest video cards for desktop computers have astounding 3D capabilities. Modern graphics engines are complex. Their performance is accelerated by interfacing with special hardware that is optimized for rendering 3D graphics.

In contrast to 2D graphics engines, one of the defining characteristics of 3D graphics engines is their ability to display the world or scene from any viewpoint. This allows much more interactive simulations where the player's presence can move around freely and the player can view the world from any position within it. This flexibility makes games that use 3D technology much more realistic looking to players.

Almost all of the latest games use 3D technology—sports games, car racing games, fighting games, and flight simulators all use 3D worlds that require 3D graphics engines to render them.

Graphics Engine Subcomponents

Treating a graphics engine as a single component of a game architecture is an ambitious categorization. By themselves, graphics engines are a large topic and can be made up of many subsystems. Some of the subsystems that fall within graphics engines include:

- Particle systems
- Animation systems
- User interface rendering
- Culling
- Clipping
- Terrain

Competing APIs

There are two competing application programming interfaces for 3D graphics: OpenGL, which is an open standard, and Direct3D, which is produced and controlled by Microsoft. Both of these libraries provide access to 3D rendering hardware, provide high-performance routines for developers to use, and are used for commercial game development. There is also a library called the Simple Directmedia Library (SDL) that can be used as an application framework for graphics engine development in both OpenGL and Direct3D.

Suitability of Python

Graphics engines are very performance-sensitive components—possibly even more so than physical simulations. They are extremely mathematically intense components that perform many low-level operations such as sorting, list iterations, and comparisons. In addition, they often have to manage large amounts of data for the visual representation of objects such as mesh and animation data.

These characteristics of graphics engines mean that pure Python is not an appropriate language for the development of complex graphics engines. However, similar to physical simulations, Python can be an appropriate language for controlling the behavior of graphics engines. Moreover, there are libraries and extension modules for Python that make the development of graphics engines in Python somewhat feasible.

In This Book

The examples in this book use the OpenGL library for rendering. They also use a library called PyOpenGL that provides an interface for the Python language to the OpenGL libraries. The book uses a library called PyGame (which is an interface to SDL) to aid in the development of graphics examples.

Chapter 8, "Graphics," deals with graphics engine and rendering with Python and PyOpenGL.

2.5 AUDIO SYSTEMS

An *audio system* is a component for making sound effects and music that is integrated with a game. Sound effects and music are important to the atmosphere and interactivity of games. They can reinforce the game's mood and style, and provide additional context-sensitive feedback to heighten the drama at critical times.

Audio systems must be able to load sound files from disk, manage playing and stopping sound effects, and are often required to handle music that streams from disk or CD. Audio assets can be quite large; therefore, audio systems must be able to unload them when they are not in use to conserve memory.

Audio is a hardware-dependent area of game programming. Different audio cards in computers can have different advanced features that are dependent on the manufacturer of the card. Consequently, games often use third-party libraries for audio functionality. It is actually relatively rare in recent times for game developers to write low-level audio system code, because the existing libraries in the field are well established and feature rich.

In addition to commercial audio packages, there are a number of freely available libraries for developing audio systems. The Direct Sound API from Microsoft can be used to deal with audio in a hardware-independent way on Windows platforms, and the SDL that was mentioned previously also provides a library for developing audio systems that works—which additionally works across multiple platforms.

Audio systems are usually driven by game simulations and/or physical simulations, and have interfaces to resource managers.

Suitability of Python

Python interfaces to libraries used for audio system development are common. As sound is a mature area of game development with existing libraries, developing new systems in Python to perform low-level sound functionality is uncommon.

In This Book

Chapter 9, "Audio," examines using audio with Python in detail, and the example code uses the Python interface to the SDL sound system found in PyGame.

2.6 GAME SIMULATIONS

Game simulations are more abstract simulations that are often built on physical simulations. They often deal with objects and concepts that have no exact correlation in the real world, or have no physical presence in the real world. Game simulations are the core of what makes games interesting and fun, rather than mundane like a spreadsheet or a finance application. It is in the game simulation that dragons, space ships, magical swords, and princesses live. This is where the creative content produced by game designers resides.

Like physical simulations, game simulations have very strict rules that govern how objects within them can behave and interact, but unlike physical simulations, these rules are often wildly different from how objects act in the real world.

Game simulations are an area where data-driven systems are a key element. Data-driven systems are important for game simulations because of the sheer number of game objects that exist in large, modern games, and the necessity for game systems that can be extended easily and quickly both during development and after they are shipped.

Game simulations are a core component that can have relationships with almost all other components of a game. Most importantly, they interface with physical simulations, user interfaces, data drivers, and resource managers.

Suitability of Python

Game simulations are probably the most volatile of the components discussed in this chapter. They tend to change often during the development of a game, and are often required to change after games ship as expansion packs, patches, and add-ons become available. This volatility requires game simulations to be able to be developed and modified quickly, which makes Python an ideal language for this component. Python's capacity for rapid development and the ease at which Python code can be changed and refactored makes it a good match for game simulations.

Game simulations tend to have less complex mathematical requirements and fewer objects than physical simulations. For example, a flock of birds might be represented as a single game object with relatively few operations that can be performed on it. Yet, it might require dozens of simulation objects that require their positions and orientations to be constantly updated. The more lightweight nature of game simulation eases the performance issues that make writing physical simulations in Python problematic.

Python also excels at data-driven systems. Its language features that allow classes and objects to be built from data, and its suitability as a data language are more reasons why Python is very appropriate for game simulations.

Game simulations are probably the most common place where Python has been used in the commercial game industry. It has found a role where game simulations written in Python are used to control physical simulations and renderers written in C or C++.

In This Book

All of the game simulation code in this book is in Python. In particular, Chapters 12 through 16 deal with game simulations as we build a series of example games with Python.

2.7 USER INTERFACES

The *user interface* of a game is the component that interacts with the user. It displays information in the form of widgets or *head-up display* (HUD) elements, and accepts input from the user via a mouse, keyboard, or joystick.

User interfaces for games have one requirement that make it impossible to use mainstream user interface libraries—the user interface elements must be drawn on the game window, and the game window is usually a special surface that doesn't allow regular drawing to be performed on it. Most games require special access to video memory or 3D surfaces and have optimized or special-purpose drawing functionality that is incompatible with most user interface libraries.

Many user interface libraries claim that they support 3D surfaces such as OpenGL Contexts, but in reality, the widgets in the library usually can't be drawn on these 3D surfaces. This is especially important when games run in full-screen mode. The difference is illustrated in Figure 2.2.

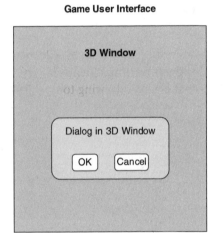
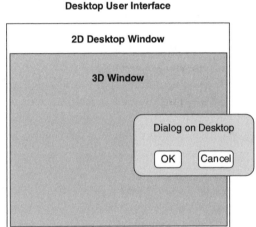

FIGURE 2.2   User interfaces for games.

The *desktop user interface* in Figure 2.2 is contained within a desktop window and can't have dialogs or widgets drawn on it. The *game user interface* takes over the responsibilities of drawing both the game world and the user interface widgets.

The unique requirements that user interfaces for games possess mean that they are closely tied to graphics engines. In some games, the user interface might actually be part of the graphics engine. In addition, user interfaces in games must interface with the game simulation.

Suitability of Python

There are many Python user interface libraries available; however, many of them are wrappers around popular libraries written in other languages that are used for regular, non-game application development. Some of the user interface libraries that are accessible through Python wrappers are Microsoft's win32 API and Microsoft Foundation Classes (MFC), the open-source GTK toolkit, the Tk toolkit, and Trolltech's QT toolkit. These libraries are appropriate for certain types of application development, but are less useful for game development.

Python is an extremely good language for user interface development, as its object-oriented features map well to the widget paradigm. In game development, Python is very appropriate for the higher-level pieces of user interface implementation, but the lower-level rendering aspects of rendering sophisticated user interfaces exhibit many of the same characteristics as graphics engines and require careful performance considerations.

The PyUI user interface library is an interesting hybrid approach to game user interfaces. Its higher-level functions and widgets are implemented in Python, and it exposes a rendering interface that allows the actual drawing to be performed in any language.

In This Book

For the examples in this book, we will use the open source PyUI user interface library, which provides a widget set that can be drawn on 3D surfaces. In Chapter 14, "User Interfaces," we will examine user interfaces with Python for games.

2.8 NETWORK LAYERS

The *network layer* is a component that deals with communicating with other computers during multiplayer games. There are two aspects of network engines: low-level issues that are at or near the level of systems programming, and more game-oriented high-level issues.

The low-level issues that network layers deal with include protocols, connection management, byte ordering, data buffers, and handling network events from operating systems. These tasks can require an in-depth knowledge of operating systems and platforms, but fortunately, there are libraries available that handle many of the operating-system specific issues.

At the high level, network layers provide the interface between game simulations and the lower-level services. This includes areas such as object serialization, networked observation, message and command processing, and tracking players who are participating in games.

Network layers have close relationships with game simulations, and must often interface with game controllers.

Suitability of Python

There are many networking libraries available for Python that provide services at different levels of abstraction. Even Python's standard library provides a number of network services that can be used for game development.

Python is an excellent language for sophisticated games that require persistent connections and distributed objects. The ease in which object serialization services can be implemented, and Python's available network libraries make developing and using network layers with Python much easier than with many other languages.

In This Book

Chapters 17 through 20 of this book deal with network layers and multiplayer games in great detail. These chapters cover developing network layers from a socket level and up, as well as using existing libraries and frameworks that provide network services for Python.

SUMMARY

Games are made of components that can be quite complex. The range of technologies included in game development is very broad, which makes game development both an interesting field, and a field that requires a wide range of skills to be successful.

The different components that make up a game vary, but this chapter is an overview of the most common, and a preface to many of the areas that are covered in this book.

3 Python Game Architectures

This chapter describes a number of game architectures for games using Python. These architectures cover a spectrum from using *only* Python, to using *no* Python. In between these two extremes are two major architectures that are labeled *Python scripting* and *Python programming*. Figure 3.1 shows the spectrum of use of Python in games.

FIGURE 3.1 Spectrum of use of Python in games.

Each of these architectures is described in this chapter and their strengths and weaknesses are examined. The examples mostly fall into the category of Python programming.

3.1 PERFORMANCE CHARACTERISTICS OF PYTHON

Before examining the different Python game architectures, let's examine the performance characteristics of Python in relation to games. This is also a quick guide to writing efficient Python code—a topic that will be elaborated on in later chapters.

Since Python is not a fully compiled language, there is a greater overhead in executing Python statements when compared to executing statements in a fully compiled language such as C or C++. One consequence of this overhead is that code that performs small or simple tasks many times—either with many lines of code or by looping over a small section of code or function—will be affected. An example of this type of code is a function that performs a long series of simple operations and conditional checks.

Python's powerful and dynamic type model represents every piece of data as a Python object—even simple types such as integers and floats are objects in Python. A consequence of this representation is that operations on simple data types can take longer in Python than they would in a statically typed language. Consider adding two integers—this is an operation between two full objects in Python, where in C, this can be optimized to a single add operation.

Therefore, when looking for code that probably *shouldn't* be written in Python, we will be on the lookout for series of many instructions that need to be executed, and many operations between simple data types. Nevertheless, don't despair about the performance of Python. As we will demonstrate, with a little care, Python is fast enough to be used for game development, and its strengths easily outweigh these performance issues.

3.2 PURE PYTHON

It is possible to develop games entirely in Python! This statement might be a little misleading, as these games still require libraries written in other languages to perform tasks such as rendering and audio, but all of the game application code is written in Python.

Advantages of pure Python:

- Free
- High programmer productivity
- Easy to distribute
- No language interface issues
- Many libraries available
- Almost entirely platform independent
- Can use standard language tools—debugger, profiler

Disadvantages of pure Python:

- Interpreted instead of compiled
- Memory overhead for Python objects
- Might not be able to interface to certain libraries

3.3 PYTHON PROGRAMMING

This architecture uses Python for the majority of development tasks, but also uses other languages such as C or C++ for some portion of development. This is called *extending Python* in the Python community, as the main program is still a Python program and the language is *extended* by writing extension modules using the Python C API that interact with the Python code.

This architecture keeps the object model in Python and manages to maintain almost all the advantages of developing purely in Python, but allows modules that require high performance or use large amounts of memory to be converted to C or C++.

Advantages of Python programming:

- High programmer productivity
- Can optimize modules into C/C++
- Access to libraries in all languages
- Mostly platform independent
- Can use standard language tools—debugger, profiler

Disadvantages of Python Programming:

- Some memory overhead for Python objects
- Some runtime overhead of Python
- Language interface issues
- Management of multiple language environment

When using the Python programming architecture, it is mainly the game components that have strict performance requirements—such as graphics engines and physical simulations—that are written in languages other than Python.

3.4 PYTHON SCRIPTING

This architecture uses some other language for much of the development and uses Python as a *scripting* language. This is called *embedding Python* in the Python community, as the Python interpreter is embedded into a program written in another language, and an interface developed with the Python C API is used to communicate between Python *scripts* and the host application.

This architecture often has the object model in the language of the host application and uses only small, simple pieces of Python code for behavioral or data-driven functionality. A variation of this architecture is to keep all of the game state information in the host application, and have the Python code that is executed maintain no state of its own.

Advantages of Python scripting:

- Fast and easy to write scripts
- Low runtime overhead
- Low memory overhead
- Access to libraries in all languages

Disadvantages of Python scripting:

- Difficult to use standard Python tools
- Less powerful Python code
- Language interface issues
- Less platform independent
- Management of multiple language environment

When using the Python scripting architecture, it is often the game simulation and data-driver components that are controlled by or written in Python.

3.5 PYTHON DATA

This architecture uses Python for data representation, and uses other languages for all of the runtime code. In this architecture, Python source code is used to store information—usually game metadata that describes the rules or types of objects in the game. The data is loaded at startup into some type of data repository, and no more Python code is executed while the game is running.

Python is a good language for metadata, as its syntax is simple and concise. In addition, it is also powerful enough to represent complex data structures. It is easy to generate Python data with tools, and there is no need to write a parser to read it in—the interpreter can be used to execute the Python source code that contains the metadata.

Advantages of Python data:

- No runtime overhead
- Simple syntax
- Can represent complex data structures
- Easy to generate

Disadvantages of Python data:

- No access to Python code during execution
- Need a data repository in another language

3.6 OTHER LANGUAGES

Other languages can be used for game development, and some of them have characteristics similar to Python. This section lists some of these languages, but doesn't go into great detail, as the purpose of this book is to focus on Python game development.

The Lua Programming Language

Lua is a lightweight programming language designed to be embedded into applications. Using the vocabulary in this chapter, it fits more into the *scripting* category than the *programming* category. Lua has some basic object-oriented features, and because of its simplicity, Lua can provide decent performance. It has also been used in commercial game programming, but not as extensively as Python.

Lua has a smaller developer community than Python and there are fewer libraries available for it. It is free to use and the source code is freely available. Lua is portable to many platforms, as its core is quite small.

The Tcl Programming Language

Tcl is a simple language that has been around for a long time. It is often referred to as Tcl/Tk or the *Tk Toolkit*, which is a popular user interface library closely tied to Tcl. Even more so than Lua, Tcl is more of a scripting language rather than a real programming language. It is lightweight and embeddable, and so has been used in game development—often as a data language.

Tcl has a large developer community, and there are many libraries available for it. It is freely available and has been ported to many platforms. However, Tcl lacks some features such as real data types and object-oriented functionality that make it less suited for real game programming.

The Java Programming Language

Java™ is an object-oriented programming language that was created by Sun Microsystems. It has a colorful and very public history and has become a popular language for business development. Java is a fully featured language—it might even have too many features and libraries associated with it. Java has been used in game development for both programming and scripting.

Java has a very large developer community, many of whom are professional programmers in business environments building e-commerce applications. The number of developers using Java for games appears to be rather less.

SUMMARY

Python can be used in a variety of different ways in game development. The ways in which Python are used can even vary within projects, as different portions of projects can have varying performance and flexibility requirements. For any particular project, the questions of where Python should be used, and how Python should be used must be answered on a case-by-case basis. The information in this chapter can be used in helping to make these decisions.

Game Infrastructure

4 | Python Game Framework

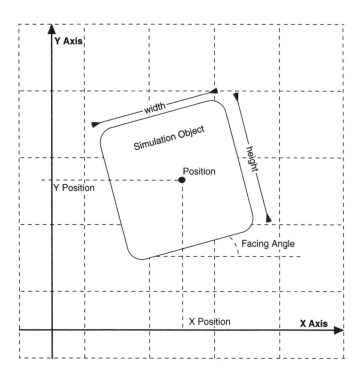

In this chapter, we get to our first actual Python source code. We describe the infrastructure required in Python to create a game window, to get the game application running, and to close the game down properly. By the end of this chapter, we will have a simple but stable framework that will be the basis for further development.

4.1 INFRASTRUCTURE TECHNOLOGY

Building an interesting game in Python requires more technology than the core Python language distribution provides. Access to graphics, audio, user-input events, and the windowing system are all required for games. To interface to these technologies, it would be possible to write custom code in C or C++, but there are existing libraries available that provide these interfaces.

Probably the most mature and widely used piece of infrastructure for Python games is the *PyGame* library. PyGame is a very useful component that itself uses the SDL as its underlying framework. It gives access to the windowing system, to user events, and to audio, all through the SDL. PyGame also works with the OpenGL graphics library that we will use in later chapters, so it is the perfect choice for the example code in this book.

In addition to PyGame, the examples in this book also use the PyUI user interface library that can act as a layer above PyGame. We discuss this in more detail in later chapters, especially Chapter 14, "User Interfaces."

4.2 INITIALIZATION

The simplest possible Python game framework is a game window that displays itself, and runs until it gets an event to shut itself down. This sounds easy, but is complicated by the choices that have to be made at initialization time. What capabilities should the created surface have? What color depth should the surface have? How big should the window be?

In the world of computer graphics, the word *capabilities* has a special meaning. When applied to a window or surface, it refers to the types of operations that can be performed on the surface, and the characteristics of that surface. Some typical capabilities are alpha blending or Z buffering. The set of capabilities of the game window is usually tightly coupled to the video card of the computer and the drivers that the video card uses. Capabilities are important because they allow a game to query its environment (the computer and video card on which it is running), and adjust itself to work well in that environment. With some graphics libraries such as Microsoft's Direct3D, this can be a difficult task as the number of different video cards and different capabilities represent a combinatorial explosion.

Luckily, with PyGame, most of the low-level capabilities are taken care of for us, and all we have to worry about is screen resolution and color depth.

Most modern PCs have relatively powerful video cards that allow them to run at screen resolutions of 1024x768 or higher. To be conservative, our first examples will run at a screen resolution of 800x600. This means that the game window is 800 pixels wide and 600 pixels high. The larger the game window, the slower the game is going to run because it has more screen space to update. The size of 800x600 should be small enough that most machines can handle it, but large enough to see a reasonable portion of the game world.

Color depth is a measure of how much color information is stored for each pixel on the screen. This value ranges from a low of 8 bits (which is usually palletized) per pixel to a high of 32 bits for the best color resolution. When running full screen, games have absolute control over color depth and screen resolution, but when running in a window, games must conform to the existing color depth of the desktop. Our example code defaults to using the same color depth as the desktop. This might result in some degradation in the quality of the display, but means that the game window is less likely to have conflicts with video cards.

The following is the Python source code to initialize PyGame with a screen resolution and some appropriate capabilities:

```
import pygame
pygame.init()
pygame.display.init( (800,600), OPENGL | DOUBLEBUF | HWSURFACE )
```

Notice that the second parameter is a Python tuple that consists of two elements separated by a comma. This is a common Python idiom. The second parameter is a bitmask of three capabilities. Technically, the "|" character (known as the *pipe*) performs a *bitwise OR* between the values. Practically, the three capabilities OPENGL, DOUBLEBUF, and HWSURFACE are all applied to the window that is created.

The OPENGL capability allows OpenGL drawing calls to be performed on the surface (we discuss this in more detail in Chapter 8, "Graphics." The HWSURFACE means that the surface is created in *video hardware memory* as opposed to system memory. This increases its performance, as video hardware memory is actually on the graphics card instead of being in the main memory of the computer.

To simplify things even further, the examples in this book use the PyUI library, which provides a layer above PyGame that includes user interface and event handling features. When PyUI is initialized, it actually executes something very similar to the initialization code shown previously. Here is the code to initialize PyUI:

```
import pyui
pyui.init(800,600)
```

4.3 THE MAIN MODULE

Before getting to the implementation of a main loop, let's look at some initialization Python language issues. A file that contains Python code is referred to as a *module*. Modules are an implementation unit of Python that can be executed, loaded at runtime, and used as libraries. Unlike statically compiled languages such as C++, in Python, module information is available at runtime. This can be useful for creating dynamic systems and even choosing between different versions of code while the program is running.

When a file containing Python code is executed, the built-in variable __name__ is populated with the name of the module being executed. If the value of __name__ is __main__ , then that file is the original file that was used to invoke the application from a command line or an icon. This is useful, as it allows code to know the difference between when it is invoked and when it is imported by another Python program. It also provides a convenient place to provide one-time startup code.

There is a common Python idiom of putting the executable code for a file in a function and then invoking that function if the file is invoked as the main file. With this structure, there can be code in the main.py file to define classes and functions, and then a run function to kick things off, as shown in Listing 4.1:

Listing 4.1   First application.

```python
import pyui

class Application:
    def __init__(self, width, height):
        self.width = width
        self.height = height

    def run(self):
        """I am called to begin the game.
        """

def run():
    width = 800
    height = 600
    pyui.init(width, height)
    app = Application(width, height)
    app.run()

if __name__ == '__main__':
    run()
```

This code declares an Application class, and then invokes a run method that creates an instance of that class. This application object then has its run method called to start the main loop. If this particular module were imported by another Python module, the top-level run method wouldn't be called as it is conditional on this module being the main module.

Notice that the initialization of the PyUI library happens before the application object is created.

4.4 THE MAIN LOOP

The main loop is a central feature of almost all games. This is different from the way in which most non-game applications work. Most applications draw their user interface and then go to sleep until they receive some input from the user, from a device, or from the network. This works fine for applications like word processors or e-mail programs, but games are much more dynamic. Even when the user isn't interacting with a game, the game simulation continues to run and the display must be updated. To achieve this continuous experience, games use a *main loop* that is always running.

The main loop is literally a loop that runs until it is told to shut down. It is responsible for updating other systems such as input, simulation, and the renderer; and it controls when the game exits. The main loop can also track statistics such as frame rate and other timing information.

A side effect of the main loop when compared to non-game applications is that games tend to use all of the available processing power of the machine on which they are running. This can make game applications less friendly to the desktop or other applications. One way to compensate for this is to have games run their main loop at a fixed rate, or to add a small delay or *sleep* in the main loop to allow other applications a chance to run.

The following is an example of a simple main loop in Python:

```python
def run(self):
    """I am called to begin the running of the game.
    """
    running = 1
    frames = 0
    counter = 0
    lastFrame = 0
    while running:
        pyui.draw()
        if pyui.update():
            pass # update world here
        else:
            running = 0

        # track frames per second
        frames += 1
        counter += 1
        now = pyui.readTimer()

        # calculate FPS
        if now - lastFrame > 1.0:
```

```
FPS = counter
counter = 0
lastFrame = now
print "FPS: %2d " % FPS
```

There are some things to point out in this piece of code. First, below the definition of the function `run` is a *documentation string* that gives some information about the function. Documentation strings (often called *doc strings*) are a common style of documentation in Python that we use throughout this book. In Python, doc strings are different from comments, as they can be made available on objects at runtime. Python objects have a __doc__ attribute that contains their documentation information.

The call to `pyui.draw` invokes the renderer to draw the display. This currently does nothing but show a black screen, but eventually will draw the game world and user interface elements. We discuss rendering the game world in Chapter 8.

The call to `pyui.update` processes any incoming events from the user or the OS. Notice that the return value of this call is checked. If this method returns false (a zero value), then the `running` flag is set to false so that the next time through, the main loop will exit.

The code also tracks the frames per second (FPS) that the application is processing. This is the measurement of how fast the game is running. The higher the FPS, the better! A constant FPS value of about 24 or more makes the game world appear to flow smoothly. In comparison, films and television use frame rates of around 24 FPS.

Timing is an area where games have different requirements than most applications. Because games operate in real time, they require accurate, high-resolution timers. Most non-game applications work perfectly well when relying on Python's built-in `time` module, but the more time-sensitive nature of games means that the accuracy supplied by that module is not sufficient. Python's built-in `time` module relies on system calls, but the accuracy and resolution of these can vary widely depending on the hardware and software platform. This code uses PyUI's `readTimer` function, which, in this case, calls in to PyGame, which in turn calls in to SDL, which actually provides accurate timing functionality.

4.5 CLEANUP

When a game is ready to exit, the control flow must break out of the main loop, and any cleanup operations must be performed. Exiting can be triggered by in-game events, or by the user interface. By default, the PyUI library will return false from its `update` method when its internal `quit` flag has been set. If that happens, the application should call `pyui.quit` before it exits to clean up the renderer and user interface. By default, the Escape key quits the application.

The amount of cleanup and shutdown that needs to be performed in Python programs is generally less than many other languages, as Python has a garbage collector that cleans up unused objects without the programmer having to do it explicitly.

Listing 4.2 is the full example code for this chapter that includes the cleanup code.

Listing 4.2 First full application.

```python
import pyui

class Application:
    def __init__(self, width, height):
        self.width = width
        self.height = height

    def run(self):
        """I am called to begin the running of the game.
        """
        running = 1
        frames = 0
        counter = 0
        lastFrame = 0
        while running:
            pyui.draw()
            if pyui.update():
                pass # update world here
            else:
                running = 0

            # track frames per second
            frames += 1
            counter += 1
            now = pyui.readTimer()

            # calculate FPS
            if now - lastFrame > 1.0:
                FPS = counter
                counter = 0
                lastFrame = now
                print "FPS: %2d " % FPS
```

```
def run():
    width = 800
    height = 600
    pyui.init(width, height)
    app = Application(width, height)
    app.run()
    pyui.quit()

if __name__ == '__main__':
    run()
```

4.6 RUNNING THE EXAMPLE CODE

To run the examples, the following software packages must be installed:

- Python 2.2 or later
- PyGame 1.5 or later
- PyUI 1.0 or later

ON THE CD

The final code from this chapter is on the accompanying CD-ROM as chapter4/main.py. To run this example from a command line, use the command:

```
python main.py
```

The executable python.exe must be in the path, and the installed libraries must be available in the Python path.

SUMMARY

This is just about the simplest game application framework that can be made with Python. It is heartening to note that this framework is less than 50 lines of code! Python code is very compact, but still easy to read.

Running this code should create an empty game window with a black background that stays visible until the Escape key is pressed. The console from which the code was invoked will print out the FPS value at one-second intervals.

Since there isn't anything going on, the FPS value for this application should be quite high.

5 Simulation Concepts

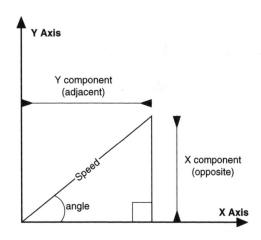

A *simulation* can be defined as an "imitation or representation of a potential situation." At their core, all games are simulations. The worlds that they simulate can be abstract (e.g., puzzle games), fantastical (e.g., fantasy role-playing games), or as close to the real world as technology allows (e.g., military combat games), but all of these types of games have a simulation at their core.

Physical simulations are an area of game development in which performance is a key factor. For this reason, building extremely complex or computationally challenging simulations in pure Python is quite a daunting task. However, it is possible to build quite powerful simulations in Python, and the language's modular structure can allow these simulations to be optimized with small pieces of code in other languages that handle key pieces of functionality.

This chapter discusses different simulation architectures that use varying amounts of Python code in Sections 5.2 through 5.6. Section 5.7 discusses simulation conventions, and Section 5.8 discusses variable rate updating of simulation objects. Sections 5.9 and 5.10 introduce Python implementations of the key simulation concepts of the simulation object and the simulation world.

5.1 THE PHYSICAL SIMULATION

In game development, there are conceptually two simulations that are closely related. The first is the *physical simulation* of the world. This deals with the physical nature of the world and objects within it with respect to the rules, such as position, size, and velocity. The second is the *game simulation*, which deals with the specific properties of objects in the world in regard to the actual game, such as hit points, magic, or experience.

The proportion of each type of simulation varies enormously between different types of games. Some games are almost entirely physical simulations that deal with cars racing down tracks or tanks firing guns. Some games are almost entirely game simulations that deal with points or virtual cash. Most games fall somewhere in between.

Since the game simulation sits on top of the physical simulation, there should be a robust physical simulation in place before implementing the game simulation. In this chapter, we primarily discuss physical simulations and build groundwork for the example game.

5.2 COMPONENTS OF THE PHYSICAL SIMULATION

Physical simulations are made up of rules, information about the game world, and objects that inhabit the game world. From an implementation point of view, physical simulations also often include a collision system.

Rules are the information that describes how the simulation works and how the objects in the simulation interact with each other. Simulation objects are the entities that exist within the physical simulation. These entities must behave within the rules, but within that constraint, they might have wildly varying characteristics and behaviors that can be driven by higher-level systems such as artificial intelligence and player input.

Simulations can be 3D (e.g., first person shooters and flight simulators), or 2D (e.g., many arcade games and puzzle games). In each case, many of the underlying concepts are the same. The examples in this book use a 2D simulation. For the sake of simplicity and accessibility, some concepts that are more relevant for 3D simulations than for 2D simulations (e.g., vectors and matrix math) are deliberately avoided in this section.

5.3 IMPLEMENTING SIMULATIONS WITH PYTHON

Physical simulations tend to have characteristics that make them somewhat inappropriate for development in Python. They require much iteration through sets of objects, and many math operations to update the state of the simulation—both areas where the overhead of Python is significant. Python is fine for small or simple simulations, but for large complex simulations involving thousands of objects, and running at many FPS, Python can be too slow.

For this reason, games that use Python often have a physical simulation written in a lower-level language and use Python to control, but not to actually run, the simulation.

There are a number of different approaches for dealing with simulations in different languages. These approaches have different trade-offs that are appropriate for different types of games. The next sections describe a number of game simulation architectures using Python, and define terminology associated with each of these architectures.

5.4 REACTIVE SIMULATION

In a *reactive simulation*, both the simulation and the simulation objects are built in a low-level language. Python is used for decision making and behavior as the simulation is running, but no state actually resides on the Python side—Python is only used to describe the behavior of objects that already exist in the physical simulation.

This is called a *reactive* simulation, as Python code is called from the simulation to allow it to react to events that occur as the simulation runs. For example, when a particular door in the simulation world is opened, some Python code could be called to determine what happens. This Python code could set other high-level events in motion in the simulation, such as spawning a monster to attack the player, but the simulation would then run without any other Python code until some other event happens and a decision has to be made (see Figure 5.1).

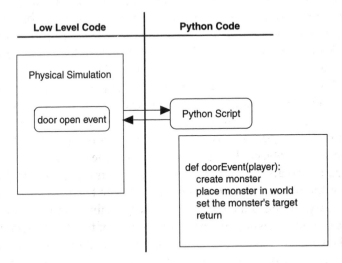

FIGURE 5.1   Reactive simulation.

This type of simulation is more in the Python scripting than the Python programming model. This approach is appropriate in a number of situations:

- When there are large numbers of objects that would require too much memory to represent in Python
- When the simulation requires complex math to be performed that would be too expensive to perform in Python
- When there is an existing physical simulation, and Python is being added to the system to provide greater flexibility
- Where a limited set of functionality is being supplied to nonprogrammers

This approach uses a Python interface to the physical simulation so that Python code segments can interact with the physical simulation. It corresponds to *embedding Python*, which we discuss in Chapter 23, "Embedding Python."

5.5 CONTROLLED SIMULATION

In a *controlled simulation*, the simulation is a hybrid of Python code and low-level code that combine to provide a full simulation. The information that controls the simulation resides in Python code, and the simulation objects are Python objects that might have representations in the lower-level code. In this type of simulation, the Python code does not include all of the information required to actually run the simulation.

For example, there is a Python object in a physical simulation that represents a door. This object has methods that are invoked on it when operations such as opening and closing are performed. The door could contain references to other game or simulation objects and is able to interact with them directly. In addition to the Python door object, there is a door object in the low-level code that tracks more detailed information about the object, such as its exact open angle, its current swinging velocity, and its 3D representation. These two simulation objects interact, but decision making and control are the responsibility of the Python object. As a specific example, it would be the responsibility of the Python simulation to decide exactly when to start and stop swinging the door when it is opened, but the responsibility of the low-level simulation to swing the door each frame when it is moving (see Figure 5.2).

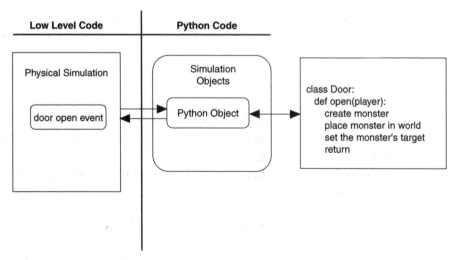

FIGURE 5.2 Controlled simulation.

This type of simulation is closer to the Python programming than the Python scripting model, and is appropriate in a number of situations:

- When the simulation requires a high degree of flexibility
- When the application is in Python and the simulation must interact with it
- When all or part of the simulation is simple enough to be easily represented in Python
- When there needs to be very close interaction between the physical and the game simulations

This approach has a higher proportion of functionality in Python and therefore requires a smaller Python interface to the physical simulation.

5.6 PARALLEL SIMULATION

In a *parallel simulation*, two simulations run in parallel. One simulation in a low-level language runs very accurately at a fine level of granularity. This low-level simulation is used for things that must be run in real time and be updated accurately every frame, such as rendering and animation. A second simulation runs in Python at a more course level of granularity, but is sufficient for making certain decisions required for the game simulation. This approach does require interaction between the simulations to ensure that they stay in sync, and includes elements of reactive and controlled simulations. In this approach, the Python code has all the information to run the simulation at a level required to make game level decisions, but probably doesn't have all the information required to render the world.

For example, in this approach, there are door objects in two simulations. Both objects are capable of opening and closing, and the objects communicate with each other to ensure that they keep their states synchronized. In some cases, such as on a server, the low-level door object might not exist, as the type of simulation it is performing is not needed. In these cases, the higher-level door object is still able to act function because it can act independently (see Figure 5.3).

This type of simulation is more in the Python programming than the Python scripting model, and is appropriate in a number of situations:

- When the simulation is simple enough that a version of it can be run entirely in Python
- When the simulation is to be run on a server and on a client
- When the game simulation doesn't require real-time interaction with the physical simulation

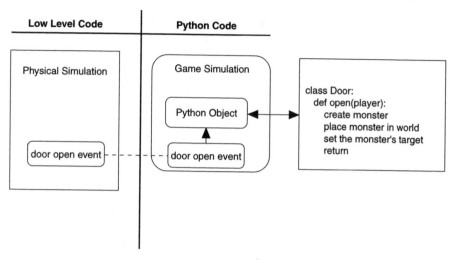

FIGURE 5.3 Parallel simulation.

This approach has the advantage that the Python version of the simulation can be run without the low-level version of the simulation. This means that the Python version could be run on a server, or on a low-end client that doesn't have graphical capabilities. It can also mean that development on the Python version of the simulation can be performed independently of the low-level simulation—or even before the low-level simulation has been developed! This separation between the simulations can allow progress to be made on game systems before the low-level simulation is in place.

5.7 SIMULATION CONVENTIONS

When defining any simulation, it is important to specify any parameters that could have multiple values. Trying to integrate systems that have different underlying assumptions about how the physical world works is very difficult and can lead to obscure bugs. It is best to identify any potential ambiguities and resolve them before writing any simulation code.

In a 2D simulation, the properties of the physical world that can vary include which directions the X and Y axes run, and whether positive turnRate is clockwise or counterclockwise. In a 3D world, there is an additional Z axis to deal with.

The examples in this book use a standard set of rules for 2D simulations called the *Cartesian coordinate system*. In this system, the positive X direction is to the right, the positive Y direction is up, and positive turnRate is counterclockwise. This has some implications to the simulation code. In a traditional 2D computer screen and in most user interface programming, the upper left of the screen is the origin, and the positive Y direction is down the screen. This is different from the Cartesian coordinate system our simulation uses, so there are some cases where the Y value will be reversed in the code. Moreover, most math functions that deal with rotation assume that the positive rotation direction is clockwise, which is again different from the Cartesian coordinate system. To deal with this difference, the simulation code will use *360 - angle* in some situations to reverse the rotation direction. The utility function toRadians has this conversion built in. Figure 5.4 illustrates the conventions.

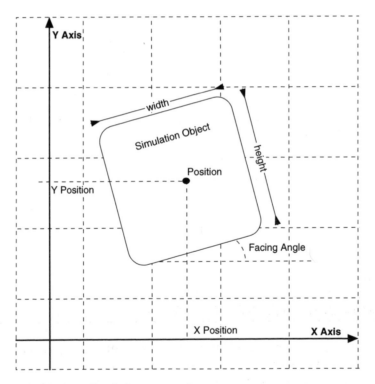

FIGURE 5.4   Simulation conventions.

In addition to just the axis, Figure 5.4 shows a simulation object. Moreover, some conventions must be decided on for simulation objects. In Figure 5.4, we can see that the center of the object is the object's position, rather than the position being at the top-left corner as in some simulations.

We can also see that the object rotates around its center. It would be possible for the object to rotate around a corner, but this would make it move as it rotates (see Figure 5.5). Having the rotation point in the center of the object puts it in exactly the same position as the object and allows the object to rotate in place without moving.

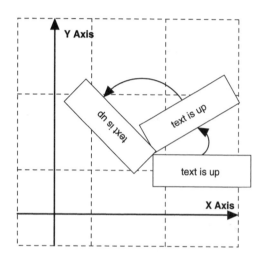

FIGURE 5.5 Rotation around a corner.

5.8 VARIABLE RATE UPDATING

Updating objects in the simulation is computationally expensive, so techniques exist in game development to minimize the number of object updates that are performed. One such technique is to vary the frequency at which objects are updated based on the magnitude of their movement. Fast-moving or spinning objects must be updated every frame, but slower-moving objects and stationary objects can be updated less often without any loss in fidelity of the simulation. In some circumstances, this technique can lead to a large reduction in the processing time required for updating sets of simulation objects.

The problem of determining the optimal threshold of exactly when to reduce the frequency of updates for simulation objects is a complex one that can be affected by many factors. However, decent results can be obtained by using extremely simple tests on just the velocity and rotation of simulation objects.

The strategy for variable rate updating used in the example code sets the maximum time between updates for any simulation object to be one second. It allows a threshold to be set on each object, which controls how sensitive that object is to variations of speed and turnRate. If an object's speed or turnRate is greater than the object's threshold, it will be updated every frame. Otherwise, the ratio of the object's speed and turnRate, and the threshold, is used to calculate an interval of less than one second that will pass between updates.

For example, if an object has a threshold of 10 and has a velocity of 6 units, then an interval will be calculated of 0.4 seconds (1.0 – 6 / 10 * 1 second). If the object accelerates to a velocity of 8, the interval will be 0.2 seconds (1.0 – 8 / 10 * 1 second), and if it accelerates to a velocity of 10 or more, it will be updated every frame. This threshold system allows game code to tune the sensitivity of objects with relation to performance.

If the threshold for an object is 0, then it is updated every frame regardless of its speed and turnRate. If the threshold is set to 1, the effective behavior will be to update the object every frame when it is moving, and then update it once per second when it is stationary. Setting thresholds should be done carefully, as the consequences of varying the update rate of critical game objects can be non-obvious.

5.9 THE BASE SIMULATION CLASS

The basis of a physical simulation system is a simulation class that behaves according to the rules of the simulation. This class embodies the physical properties of entities that exist in the physical simulation. There will be a relationship between this class and the classes used in the game simulation, but this relationship will vary depending on the type of simulation used.

For the example game, a 2D simulation is used, so the simulation objects must fit into this 2D world. The following is the beginning of a simulation class in Python:

```
class SimObject:
    """A Simulation object in a two-dimensional space.
    """

    def __init__(self, width, height, mobile=1, threshold=0, life=0):
        self.width = width    # width of object
```

```
self.height = height   # height of object
self.mobile = mobile   # is this object mobile
self.life = life       # lifetime for object (seconds)
self.alive = 1         # flag for staying alive
self.posX = 0          # current X position
self.posY = 0          # current Y position
self.velocityX = 0     # current X velocity
self.velocityY = 0     # current Y velocity
self.facing = 0        # current facing (degrees)
self.turnRate = 0      # degrees / second
self.accel = 0         # speed / second
self.threshold = threshold # threshold for update frequency
self.uDelay = 0        # update delay
self.uTimer = 0        # update timer
self.removeCallback = None # callback when removed from the world
```

This initializes a simulation object with information to describe its nature (the width, height, and mobility, and its current state in the world), the position, facing and velocity information, and the changes in its state in the world (the turnRate and acceleration). Simulation objects have a `life` member attribute that can be used to make objects remove themselves from the world after a period of time. If set, this `life` value is updated as the simulation runs, and when it falls below 0, the object's `alive` flag is set to 0, which will cause it to be removed from the world.

Initially, the physical state of the object is undefined. To set the physical state, we'll use another method that is usually only called when an object is added to a simulation.

```
def setState(self, posX, posY, facing, speed = 0):
    """Set the simulation state of the object.
    """

    self.posX = posX
    self.posY = posY
    self.facing = facing
    self.calculateVelocity(speed, facing)
```

This method bypasses any collision tests or other validations in the world, so shouldn't be called for objects that are already interacting in the world. Notice that this method uses a helper method to calculate the object's velocity. While this object's external interface exposes speed and facing, internally this object uses velocity for its calculations. This is the first example of simulation math so far, and as such requires some explanation.

The `calculateVelocity` method calculates the X and the Y components of the object's speed based on its current speed and facing. It uses high-school-level trigonometry theory, and the Python math library. Figure 5.6 shows how the speed is broken down into the two components.

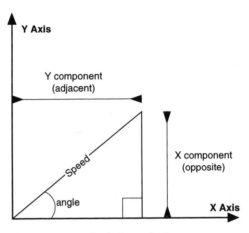

FIGURE 5.6   Calculating velocity.

The math to perform the actual calculation is derived from the formulas:

$$sin(angle) = opposite \,/\, hypotenuse$$

and

$$cos(angle) = adjacent \,/\, hypotenuse$$

In these formulas, the hypotenuse is replaced by the object's speed, the angle is replaced by the object's facing, and they are rearranged to the form of:

```
def calculateVelocity(self, speed, facing):
    radians = toRadians(self.facing)
self.velocityX = math.cos(radians) * speed
self.velocityY = math.sin(radians) * speed
```

Notice that first, the object's facing is converted from degrees into radians by another helper method. Radians are the measure of angle that are used by Python's math functions (and almost all other math libraries).

A common operation for simulation objects in the example games we will build is finding a position with a specific offset from the center of a simulation object.

This can be used when adding bullets to the world, or creating smoke trails behind objects. The following method is a convenient addition to the SimObject class that allows application code to find positions relative to a SimObject instance. This code uses trigonometry to calculate the desired position.

```
def findOffset(self, direction, distance):
    """find a position in a direction a distance from my center
    """
    radians = toRadians(direction)
    dx = math.cos(radians) * distance
    dy = math.sin(radians) * distance
    return (self.posX + dx, self.posY - dy)
```

We now have a simulation object with state that is ready to add to the simulation world. There is one more interesting thing about this class. Simulation objects have the capability to have a method called when they are removed from the world. The removeCallback member is a callback function that will be invoked by the world when the object is removed from the world. It can be set with this function:

```
def setRemoveCallback(self, callback):
    self.removeCallback = callback
```

This callback provides a way for simulation objects to perform cleanup operations or release resources when they are removed from the world.

5.10 THE SIMULATION WORLD

The simulation world is the container of all the simulation objects and the world information. It controls when simulation objects are updated.

```
class World:
    """Simulation world.
    """
    def __init__(self, width, height):
        self.width = width
        self.height = height
        self.mobiles = []     # the set of mobile simObjects
        self.immobiles = []      # the set of immobile simObjects

    def addToWorld(self, sim, x, y, facing, speed=0, force=0):
        sim.posX = x
        sim.posy = y
```

```
            if force==0 and self.canMove(sim, x, y, facing) == 0:
                return 0
        if sim.mobile:
            self.mobiles.append(sim)
        else:
            self.immobiles.append(sim)
        sim.setState(x, y, facing, speed)
            return 1

    def removeFromWorld(self, sim):
        if sim.mobile:
            self.mobiles.remove(sim)
        else:
            self.immobiles.remove(sim)
        if sim.removeCallback:
            sim.removeCallback(self)
        return 1
```

The simulation objects are placed into two lists—one for mobile objects and another for immobile objects. The distinction between the two is useful for optimization. Immobile objects don't need to be updated every frame and can be drawn differently, so they are kept in a separate list.

The addToWorld method is where the state of the simulation object is set for it in the world. This state is applied to the object as it is added to the world. Linking the acts of setting the object's state and adding it to the world ensures that objects being added to the world always have valid state information. This method also checks that the object can be placed in the specified position by using the canMove method, although this can be overridden by specifying the force argument.

The removeFromWorld method performs the opposite of addToWorld, and in addition invokes the removeCallback of the object if one is set. This method is passed self, which in this case is the world object itself.

The simulation world has a final method to remove all of the objects from it. This method iterates through all mobile and immobile objects and removes them from the world. Notice that this code doesn't use the more common for obj in objects: syntax for accessing the items in the lists. This is because the removeFromWorld method removes the object from the list. This could cause problems if the loop is iterating though the list while the objects are removed from that same list. The solution is to reference the first item in the list and remove it until the list is empty.

```
    def removeAll(self):
        while len(self.mobiles):
            obj = self.mobiles[0]
            self.removeFromWorld(obj)
        while len(self.immobiles):
```

```
        obj = self.immobiles[0]
        self.removeFromWorld(obj)
```

5.11 UPDATING THE SIMULATION

Once we have a simulation world, and simulation objects in it that have valid state information, the simulation can be run. Some code must be added to the main loop of the application to call the update method of the world and to pass the interval value into it.

```
def run(self):
    """I am called to begin the running of the game.
    """
    running = 1
    frames = 0
    counter = 0
    lastFrame = pyui.readTimer()
    endFrame = pyui.readTimer ()

    while running:
        pyui.draw()
        if pyui.update():
            # update world here
            interval = pyui.readTimer () - endFrame
            endFrame = pyui.readTimer ()
            if self.world.update(interval) == 0:
                running = 0
        else:
            running = 0

        # track frames per second
        frames += 1
        counter += 1

        # caluclate FPS
        if endFrame - lastFrame > 1.0:
            FPS = counter
            counter = 0
            lastFrame = endFrame
            print "FPS: %2d " % FPS
```

This code calculates the time that passes between each call to world.update() and passes that time into the method as the interval parameter.

While the game is running, each simulation object in the world will be processed in turn to update its state to allow for the passing of time. To accommodate this, the world has a very important update method. This method will be called on the world, which then calls update on simulation objects. As an optimization, only simulation objects that have the mobile flag set are updated. Here is the simple update method for the world:

```python
def update(self, interval):
    """update the simulation world for an interval
    """
    deleteList = []
    for sim in self.mobiles:
        if sim.update(interval, self) == 0:
            deleteList.append(sim)
    for sim in deleteList:
        self.removeFromWorld(sim)
    return 1
```

Notice that the world checks for the update method of the simulation object returning a zero value. This is used to cleanly remove simulation objects from the world. In a similar manner, the world update method returns a non-zero value to indicate to the main loop that it should continue running.

The following is an update method for simulation objects in our 2D space:

```python
def update(self, interval, world):
    """update an object's physical state for an interval.
    """
    if self.threshold and self.uDelay:
        self.uTimer += interval
        if self.uTimer < self.uDelay:
            return
        else:
            interval = self.uTimer
            self.uTimer -= self.uDelay

    radians = toRadians(self.facing)
    if self.accel:
        dx = math.cos(radians) * self.accel
        dy = math.sin(radians) * self.accel
        self.velocityX += dx
        self.velocityY += dy

    newPosX = self.posX + (self.velocityX * interval)
    newPosY = self.posY - (self.velocityY * interval) # use negative Y!
```

```
if self.turnRate:
    newFacing = self.facing + self.turnRate*interval
    newFacing = newFacing % 360
else:
    newFacing = self.facing

if world.canMove(self, newPosX, newPosY, newFacing):
    self.posX = newPosX
    self.posY = newPosY
    self.facing = newFacing

if self.life:
    self.life -= interval
    if self.life <= 0:
        self.alive = 0

# calculate the variable delay
if self.threshold:
    value = max( abs(self.velocityX),
                 abs(self.velocityY), abs(self.turnRate) )
    if value < self.threshold:
        self.uDelay = 1.0 - (value / self.threshold)
    else:
        self.uDelay = 0

return self.alive
```

There is an argument called `interval` that is passed into this method. This is a floating-point value in seconds that is used to make sure that the simulation runs at a constant rate that is independent of the frame rate of the application. If the game is running at a frame rate of 10 FPS, then the interval parameter will have a value of 0.1. In practice, the interval passed in will be the time in seconds since the last time `update` was called.

Notice that when the simulation calculates the new Y position of the object, it applies the negative of the Y value:

```
newPosY = self.posY - (self.velocityY * interval) # use negative Y!
```

This reversing of the Y value makes the simulation conform to the conventions described earlier in this chapter.

The change in velocity of the object is computed from the acceleration in a very similar way to how the velocity was computed earlier. Then, a new position is calculated by adding the object's velocity to its current position. It is critical to note that the velocity and acceleration are multiplied by the interval that was passed into the update method. The new facing is calculated using the turnRate and is again modified by the interval.

Once the new position and facing have been calculated, the simulation object checks with the world whether it can move to the new location and facing. At this stage, the world's canMove method only checks for the object passing outside the extents of the world, but eventually, this will perform more sophisticated collision detection.

```python
def canMove(self, sim, newPosX, newPosY, newFacing):
    if newPosX < 0 or newPosY < 0:
        return 0
    if newPosX + sim.width >= self.width or
        newPosY + sim.height >= self.height:
        return 0
    return 1
```

If the world responds that the position is valid, then the object's actual position and facing are updated with the new values.

Notice that this update method decreases the value of the SimObject's life attribute and switches the alive flag when the value of life becomes less than zero. This will be useful later for temporary objects such as bullets and explosions that have a finite lifespan in the simulation world.

The update method also includes code to handle variable frequency updating. If the object has an update threshold, at the beginning of the method, it checks the update timer to decide whether it should skip the current update call by returning early. Then, at the end of the method, it recalculates the object's update timer based on the object's latest velocity and turnRate.

SUMMARY

This chapter described components of physical simulations that are common in many different types of games. It included example implementations of each component in Python, and examples of their use with short Python applications. The components discussed were simulation architectures and conventions, variable rate updating, and the simulation object and simulation world concepts.

The base simulation class and the world simulation class developed in this chapter will be contained in the hoop library that is put together at the end of Chapter 8. These are useful and generic classes that could be used in a variety of applications. Note that the SimObject class created in this chapter is not the final version of that class. It will be extended to include more functionality in the next few chapters.

The code from this chapter will be the basis for the functionality that is developed for collision detection and will interact with the graphics and game simulation code that is developed in later chapters. There will be some modifications to this simulation as those features are integrated with it, but the same structure will remain.

Physical simulations have been the topic of a huge amount of research and writing. Advanced simulations include concepts such as friction, gravity, and wind that can generate realistic and interesting environments for games. This chapter serves as a starting point to demonstrate the basic principles of physical simulations, but there is much more out there on this topic.

6 Data-Driven Simulations

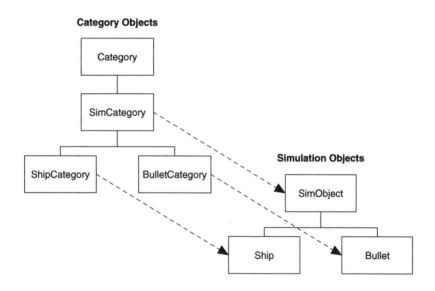

Category Objects

Category

SimCategory

ShipCategory   BulletCategory

Simulation Objects

SimObject

Ship   Bullet

*D*ata-driven systems* are an architectural design characterized by a separation of data and code. They consist of a relatively small core of code that can behave in many different ways based on the data used to configure it. Data-driven systems require a *data source* to draw data from, and have a runtime *architecture* to apply the data to the system as it executes. They also often have a *data repository* that tracks all the data in the system and allows access to it. Data-driven systems are becoming a standard tool for game developers. They are used to provide flexibility and extensibility during development and even after games ship.

Data can drive many aspects of games. A common example is using data to define the types of objects in the game world and the variations of these objects. Instead of hard-coding into the game engine many different types of swords with different damage values, a single sword could be coded, and then data used to define variations of it with different characteristics. Weapons, armor, monsters, space ships, and terrain are all examples of game objects that can be driven by data.

Python is especially good for data-driven systems. The language's built-in reflection capability can be used to remove a layer of indirection between data and code, and its dynamic typing can make these systems generic and reusable while remaining compact and elegant. Python is also appropriate as a data language because its syntax is simple but powerful. In some cases, the data that drives these systems can actually be in Python source code.

The chapter discusses some of the benefits of data-driven systems in Section 6.1, and different types of data sources in Section 6.2. Section 6.3 shows the implementation of the core of a data-driven game architecture in Python.

6.1 BENEFITS OF DATA-DRIVEN SYSTEMS

Data-driven systems are popular because they have tangible benefits to the game development process, both during development and after a title ships.

Data-driven systems lower the cost of developing games by increasing the productivity of programmers and designers, and allowing iterations of game content to take place faster.

Not having to compile code to make changes opens the game development environment so that nonprogrammers can have interactive feedback earlier in the development cycle. The ability for designers to experiment with configuration data and try out new ideas without relying on programmers can dramatically increase their productivity. This creates a level of feedback that is hard to match when there is an additional level of communication and delay added by having programmers involved. Game designers thrive on feedback, and data-driven systems provide them with a means of getting it.

Data-driven systems allow game content to be added without adding or changing code. This means that changes can be made with greater confidence, as there is less chance that they will introduce bugs. It also means that testing cycles can be minimized, and in live environments, it means that patches can be data only—not requiring any changes to executables. The increased rate of content development provided by data-driven systems can lower the cost of game development.

Combining data-driven systems with Python or another higher-level language can multiply the advantages of either of these approaches.

6.2 DATA SOURCES

Different mediums can be used to store the data used for data-driven systems. These mediums are referred to as *data sources*.

Text Files

Text files can be used as a data source to drive data-driven systems, but they are a primitive medium that lacks structure and tools. For serious game development, data is probably better off being stored in a more structured medium so that it can be validated, cross-referenced, and processed more efficiently. Text files are, however, very simple and can be appropriate for smaller sets of data.

XML

XML, which stands for *eXtensible Markup Language* is a standard language for storing data in a structured and platform-independent way. XML files are similar to HTML; text files that consist of tags that can be nested to specify data. As XML is very flexible, it can be used as a data source for games.

XML is, however, verbose, and although there are tools and libraries available to parse it (including Python libraries), it can take a long time to parse large quantities of XML data. It can also be difficult to manage large amounts of XML data, lacks good management tools, and doesn't scale well to deal with hundreds or thousands of items of data.

The following is an example of XML that could be used as a data source:

```
<object name="rocking chair">
    <property name="texture" value="rocker1.jpg">
    <property name="width"   value="100">
    <property name="height"  value="60">
    <property name="icon"    value="rocker_icon.jpg">
    <property name="cost"    value="40">
</object>

<object name="bar stool">
    <property name="texture" value="barstool.jpg">
    <property name="width"   value="40">
    <property name="height"  value="40">
    <property name="icon"    value="barstool_icon.jpg">
    <property name="cost"    value="20">
</object>
```

Relational Databases

Relational databases are the heavyweights of the data source world. They provide unique capabilities for storing and retrieving large amounts of data, and have robust, scalable runtime engines. They, however, also come with a significant overhead.

Unless you plan to ship a relational database with each copy of your game, the databases can only be used as data repositories during development or on the server-side of online games. This might require an alternative approach for the runtime portion of the game when it comes time to deploy, such as exporting data from the database into data files.

Relational databases also introduce a large overhead of management and integration. They require the use of proprietary libraries to access them. Sometimes, databases and the tools required to use them can be very expensive. Usually, only projects with extremely large amounts of data and large budgets are willing to take on the overhead and potential headaches of using a relational database as a data source for game development. This has changed to some extent recently, with the emergence of inexpensive open-source databases running primarily on the Linux OS.

Scripting Languages

Scripts in a number of languages (including Python) can be used as data sources. Scripts have the advantage that they are already structured data that can be loaded just by executing them. There is no need to write a special, game-specific parser for most scripting languages. They are also good as a data source, as they can represent relatively complex data in compact and concise ways.

Of course, if your programming language is already Python, the idea of using scripts as a data source is practically redundant. The example code in this book uses this technique.

6.3 IMPLEMENTING A DATA REPOSITORY

This section implements a data repository that is used to data-drive some of the examples in this book. This implementation uses Python source code as its data source and has a central `DataManager` object that keeps sets of *category objects* to represent variations of types of objects.

The goals of this data repository are:

- Load the data from its source at initialization
- Allow access to the data when the program is running
- Allow major categories of object types with many variations
- Provide a way to create objects of any category

This data repository is also a factory that can be used to create objects of any of the categories that reside within it. The interface to create objects looks like this:

```
newObject = dataManager.createInstance("mobile rectangle", "sims")
```

This code creates a SimObject with the characteristics that are defined by the "mobile rectangle" category. The two arguments to the createInstance method of the DataManager are the name of the category that controls the actual data used to populate the create object, and the name of the *meta category* that controls what type of object to create.

The data repository uses *category classes* to represent variations of types of objects. There is a base Category class from which all of the category classes in the system inherit.

```
class Category:
    """ base class for all Category classes that describe
    simulation objects in the game.
    """
    def __init__(self, name):
        self.name = name
```

The SimCategory class is then derived from the Category class. The SimCategory class is used to represent different types of SimObjects. Notice that the data members of the SimCategory class match the data members of the SimObject class (see Listing 6.1).

Listing 6.1   Simulation category class.

```
class SimCategory(Category):
    """I am a category class for simulation objects. Each sim category
    has data that allows it to create a different type of actual
    simObject."""
    def __init__(self, name, width, height, mobile, life, threshold):
        Category.__init__(self, name)
        self.width = width
        self.height = height
        self.mobile = mobile
        self.life = life
        self.threshold = threshold
```

```
def create(self):
    """Create a SimObject using my data as a template.
    """
    newSim = SimObject(self)
    return newSim
```

The SimCategory also contains a create method that allows it to act as a *factory*. It can create actual simulation objects using its data as a template. This change requires that the constructor of the SimObject class be changed to accept a category object instead of individual parameters for each piece of data. The updated SimObject constructor is show here:

```
class SimObject:
    """A Simulation object in a two-dimensional space.
    """
    def __init__(self, category):
        self.category = category
        self.width = category.width        # width of object
        self.height = category.height      # height of object
        self.mobile = category.mobile      # is object mobile
        self.life = category.life          # lifetime (seconds)
        self.threshold = category.threshold # variable update frequency

        self.posX = 0            # current X position
        self.posY = 0            # current Y position
        self.velocityX = 0       # current X velocity
        self.velocityY = 0       # current Y velocity
        self.facing = 0          # current facing (degrees)
        self.rotation = 0        # degrees / second
        self.accel = 0           # speed / second
        self.alive = 1           # flag for staying alive
        self.uDelay = 0          # update delay
        self.uTimer = 0          # update timer
        self.removeCallback = None # callback when removed from the world
```

The difference between this version of the constructor and the previous version is that the data used to populate the SimObject's members is taken from the category object that is passed in, rather than from individual arguments. It would have been possible to reduce the memory usage of the object by just storing the category object in this object and referencing the data members of that object when information is required. This would be an example of the *FlyWeight* design pattern. However, in this situation, the convenience of being able to access the data members on the object directly wins out.

The relationship between `SimCategory` and `SimObjects` classes in the data repository and classes in the simulation is used throughout the example applications in this book. These two types of classes form a tightly coupled parallel hierarchy of classes (see Figure 6.1).

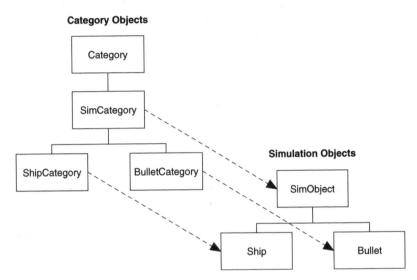

FIGURE 6.1   Parallel class hierarchy.

This parallel class hierarchy provides a separation of code and data that facilitates the data-driven nature of the system. `Category` objects can be created from data independently of the creation of actual simulation objects—even when the simulation is not running, such as during the initialization of the program.

The next piece of the data repository is a class to act as a container for the category classes and manage them while the program is running. In the example game framework, this is called the `DataManager`.

```
class DataManager:
    """Repository of category objects that define the types
    of simulation objects in the game.
    """

    def __init__(self):
        self.categories = {}     # lists of category objects
```

The DataManager is a very data-driven class. It keeps a dictionary of lists of category objects to store all the category information. This is the type of high-level data structure that Python is very good at dealing with. Figure 6.2 illustrates how the structure works.

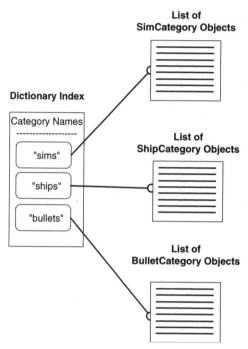

FIGURE 6.2 Category objects in the DataManager.

Each entry in the dictionary uses the name of the category as its key, and the list of category objects for that category as its value. It would be possible to represent this data as member variables on the DataManager class:

```
class InflexibleDataManager:
    def __init__(self):
        self.simCategories = []
        self.shipCategories = []
        self.bulletCategories = []
```

However, this structure hard-codes the set of categories into the DataManager and makes it less flexible. Storing the categories in a dictionary makes it easy to look up categories by their name, and allows categories to be added to the DataManager at runtime.

At program startup, the DataManager must be initialized. This is done by calling the initCategory method to load the data for each category and add it to the DataManager. This method is designed to be independent of the format of the data that loads. The code uses some features of Python to able to load data for many different types of category objects all with the same function. This method uses some Python techniques that are uncommon for programmers used to C/C++ code.

The arguments to the function are:

- label: A string to identify the meta-category being loaded
- rawData: A list of tuples of data to load
- categoryClass: The class to associate with the meta-category

The rawData list contains one item for each of the categories within the meta-category. Each item is a tuple that contains the data to construct a category object to represent that particular variation. Note that the number of items in the tuple corresponds to the number of arguments that the constructor of the SimCategory class accepts. The data looks like this:

```
initialSimCategories = [
    # name                 width height mobile  life threshold
    ("mobile square",       10,    10,    1,     0,   0),
    ("mobile rectangle", 50,     4,     1,     0,   6),
    ("static square",       10,    10,    0,     0,   1)
]
```

This is an example of using Python source code as a data source. This particular piece of code doesn't have to reside in the same source file as the DataManager or Category classes. It can be moved into a separate source file—possibly in a different directory or module. This "code" is designated as a data file rather than a code file. Although it is technically still Python source code, it is conceptually data for the purposes of this application.

The initCategory method loops through each of the items in the list and uses Python's built-in apply function to construct an object with the categoryClass argument. Usually, the apply function is used to invoke a function with a set of arguments by using a callable object. However, it can also be used to construct an object instance. This is performed by using a class object instead of a function or method object. When this is done, the new object's __init__ method is invoked with the additional arguments that were passed to the apply call. The following code demonstrates using apply to construct an object. This code will print the string "test = 1".

```
class Test:
    def __init__(self, value, text):
        self.value = value
        self.text = text

newTestObject = apply(Test,1, "test")
print "%s = %d " % (newTestObject.text, newTestObject.value)
```

This use of a class as a parameter to a function can seem unusual to programmers who are more familiar with C or C++, but it a common technique in Python programming. This type of generic programming allows code to be written that deals with many different types of objects. It is similar to template programming in C++, but more powerful, as it can be extended at runtime rather than at compile time.

The initCategory method uses this technique to allow it to construct category objects of the class object that was passed into the function. The code for the method is:

```
def initCategory(self, label, rawData, categoryClass):
    newCatList = []
    for categoryTuple in rawData:
        newCatObj = apply( categoryClass, categoryTuple)
        newCatList.append( newCatObj )
    self.categories[label] = newCatList
```

When the apply function is invoked, the values in the categoryTuple are mapped to the arguments to the constructor of the categoryClass. In this case, the SimCategory class is constructed with name, width, height, mobile, life, and threshold arguments. However, this code can be used to construct any class with any number and type of arguments in the same way.

The following code initializes the only category that is in the DataManager in this chapter. Later in this book, the set of categories in the DataManager will grow as the application becomes more complicated. Notice that the class object SimCategory is imported from another module before it is passed to the method. This is another example of using a class as data that can be confusing at first.

```
from world import SimCategory
dataManager.initCategory("sims", initialSimCategories, SimCategory)
```

Once this data is in the DataManager, it can be accessed and used to create instances of objects. The DataManager uses two methods when it creates objects. It uses the findCategory method to look up a category object based on a given name and category name, and the createInstance method to actually call the create method on the appropriate category object. The createInstance uses another Python programming technique to make the system more flexible. The third argument to createInstance is "*args". The asterisk before that argument means that it will not be a single argument, but a tuple that contains all of the remaining arguments to the method that have not already been assigned. The following Python code demonstrates its use:

```
def myFunc(name, *values):
    print "Name = %s" % name
    count = 0
    for value in values:
        print "   Value #%d: %s" % (count, value)
        count += 1

myFunc("test", 34, 10, "a string", 3.333)
```

This code loops though each of the items in the values tuple and prints them out. It doesn't matter what types of objects are in the arguments or how many objects are supplied, they will all end up in the *values tuple. This is similar to the way varargs work in C programming. This code will print out the result:

```
Name = test
   Value #1: 34
   Value #2: 10
   Value #3: a string
   Value #4: 3.333
```

The createInstance method uses this technique to allow arguments to be passed through to the constructor of the object created. Since the variable args is a tuple, it can be passed directly to the apply method, which passes the values to the constructor of the new object it creates.

```
def findCategory(self, name, categoryName):
    category = self.categories.get(categoryName, None)
    if not category:
        return None
    for cat in category:
        if cat.name == name:
            return cat

def createInstance(self, name, categoryName, *args):
    category = self.findCategory(name, categoryName)
```

```
        if category:
            return apply(category.create, args)
```

These methods allow application code to lookup `category` objects by their name and category name, and to create instances of objects based on a name. This binding between textual name and types of simulation objects allows the `DataManager` to act as a data-driven factory for simulation objects. This functionality will be useful later when populating a level from a data source.

Listing 6.2 is the full source code for the `DataManager` class.

Listing 6.2   The DataManager.

```python
class DataManager:
    """Repository of category objects that define the types
    of simulation objects in the game.
    """
    def __init__(self):
        self.categories = {}    # lists of category objects
        self.initCategory("sims", initialSimCategories, SimCategory)

    def initCategory(self, label, rawData, categoryClass):
        newCatList = []
        for categoryTuple in rawData:
            newCatObj = apply( categoryClass, categoryTuple)
            newCatList.append( newCatObj )
        self.categories[label] = newCatList

    def findCategory(self, name, categoryName):
        category = self.categories.get(categoryName, None)
        if not category:
            return None
        for cat in category:
            if cat.name == name:
                return cat

    def createInstance(self, name, categoryName, *args):
        category = self.findCategory(name, categoryName)
        if category:
            return apply(category.create, args)
```

The `DataManager` class is implemented in fewer than 50 lines of code. This again shows Python's capability to express powerful design ideas in a very compact way.

SUMMARY

This chapter described data-driven systems, different types of data sources, and an implementation of a data-driven game core that used the `DataManager` as a data repository and `category` objects as templates for creating game objects in a data-driven way.

The `DataManager` and `category` objects discussed in this chapter were designed to be both generic and extensible. They will be used in many of the further chapters in this book as the basis for data-driven game examples, and are added to the hoop library that is packaged at the end of Chapter 8.

Data-driven systems have been the subject of many articles and portions of books in the game industry. As a key architectural component of many games, there have been many implementations of data-driven architectures and much discussion of their merits and how to implement and use them effectively.

7 Collision Detection

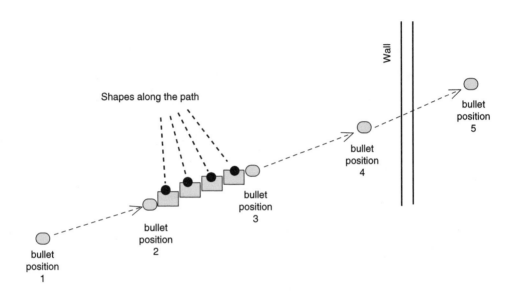

This chapter discusses collision systems and how to implement them in Python. Collisions are one of the most common ways that objects interact, and are certainly one of the most visible portions of a game. Inaccuracies or inconsistencies in the collision detection in any game are very noticeable and can ruin the experience for the player. Players expect objects in physical simulations to behave in predictable ways that mirror the real world—balls should bounce and bullets should not go through walls. If the collision system of a game does not behave the way players expect it to, frustration and annoyance can ensue.

Collision detection is a math-intensive area of game programming, and sophisticated, 3D collision detection systems are beyond the scope of this book. The examples in this chapter are 2D, but deal with the same concepts as 3D collision systems do.

Collision detection can be computationally expensive, especially when there are many objects involved. In the most naive collision detection systems, every object in the physical simulation would check whether it collides with every other object in the simulation every frame. This leads to an enormous number of calculations and isn't a feasible solution for any but the most trivial games. There are some common strategies for collision detection to address this problem, such as collision grids and quad trees. A collision grid is implemented in Python in this chapter.

Collision detection with Python is a particularly sensitive area, considering the performance requirements of collision systems. Python can be used to build collision systems, but this is another area where the optimization of hotspots with a language such as C or C++ might be appropriate.

Section 7.1 discusses how to classify different types of objects for optimal collision detection, and Section 7.2 discusses a technique to partition the game world for optimal collision detection. Section 7.3 discusses a number of techniques for detecting collisions, Section 7.4 discusses coordinate systems, and Sections 7.5 and 7.6 discuss some collision shapes that are used by collision systems. Section 7.7 deals with the difficult problem of handling collisions with moving objects, Section 7.8 shows an implementation of a collision grid system in Python, and Section 7.9 wraps up the infrastructure code implemented to this point into the *hoop* library that we use throughout the rest of this book.

7.1 CLASSIFYING OBJECTS FOR COLLISION

It is possible to classify objects in the game world so that collision detection only needs to be performed on a subset of them, and so that some objects only need to be updated some of the time. Since the updating and collision detection code for simulation objects is expensive in terms of CPU time, this is a good area to focus on techniques for optimization. The classification system described in this chapter will enable optimal decisions to be made by the simulation when performing collision detection.

Stationary objects are unable to initiate collisions with other objects. Although it might be possible for moving objects to collide with them, they cannot actually run into other objects themselves. These are classified as *immobile* objects, and the simulation knows not to run proactive collision checks for them. Walls and trees are examples of immobile objects.

Certain other objects might never collide in any way with other objects in the game world. These objects are never checked for collisions and are not added to the collision system. These are classified as *noncollidable* objects. Smoke trails, fog, and certain particles are examples of noncollidable objects.

In games that have terrain in addition to simulation objects, there might be another type of collidable object—the terrain itself. We don't discuss this type of collision in this chapter.

Table 7.1 lists some examples of classifying game objects.

TABLE 7.1 Examples of Classifying Objects

Type of Object	Mobile	Collidable
Space Ship	x	x
Tree	–	x
Bullet	x	x
Explosion	x	–
Block	x	x

SimObjects in the example code already have a mobile attribute. This can be extended by adding the collidable attribute to SimObject, and extending the SimCategory in the DataManager so that categories of objects can be classified with data. The following code shows the SimCategory class with the new attribute added to it.

```
class SimCategory(Category):
    def __init__(self,name,width,height,mobile,life,threshold,collidable):
        Category.__init__(self, name)
        self.width = width
        self.height = height
        self.mobile = mobile
        self.life = life
        self.collide = collide
        self.threshold = threshold
```

The data in the structure initialSimCategories must also be extended to include collidable data:

```
initialSimCategories = [
    # name              width height mobile life collide  threshold
```

```
("mobile square",    10,    10,    1,    1,    1,    0),
("mobile rectangle", 50,     4,    1,    1,    1,    6),
("static square",    10,    10,    0,    0,    0,    1) ]
```

Finally, the `SimObject` class must be extended to support the collidable attributes. This is handled nicely by the `category` object. Notice that no new arguments are added to the constructor of `SimObject`. We are already benefiting from the data-driven architecture.

```python
class SimObject:
    """ A Simulation object in a two-dimensional space.
    """
    def __init__(self, category):
        self.category = category
        self.width = category.width          # width of object
        self.height = category.height        # height of object
        self.mobile = category.mobile        # is object mobile
        self.life = category.life            # lifetime (seconds)
        self.collide = category.collide      # collision flag
        self.threshold = category.threshold  # variable update frequency
```

7.2 PARTITIONING THE WORLD FOR COLLISION DETECTION

Even with the number of colliding objects reduced by classification, the number of objects in a simulation is still a problem. When every object must check for collisions with every other object, the total number of collision calculations is the number of objects in the system squared. This number goes up very rapidly as Figure 7.1 indicates.

Even with a relatively small number of simulation objects, the number of calculations gets very high. When a simulation contains hundreds of simulation objects, this becomes infeasible.

The common solution to this problem is to partition the world into a set of smaller spaces that each contain a lesser number of simulation objects. With this system, the simulation only needs to perform collision detection between objects that are in the same spaces. This set of smaller spaces is often called a *collision grid*, as it partitions the 2D world space into a grid of smaller spaces. Figure 7.2 shows a space partitioned into a collision grid.

This space is broken down in four segments on each side, giving it 16 grid squares. Implementations of collision grids usually keep a list of each of the simulation objects in each grid square and update this information as objects move.

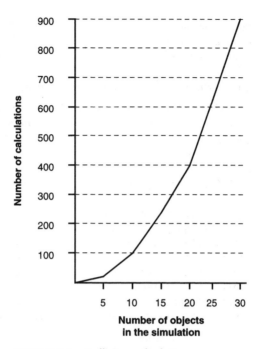

FIGURE 7.1 Collision calculations.

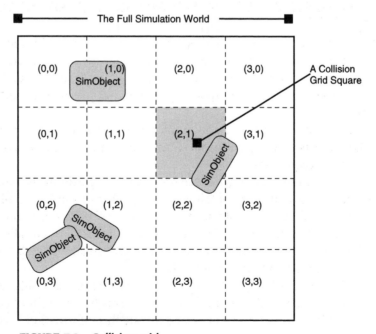

FIGURE 7.2 Collision grid.

Notice that the objects in this space sometimes cross the borders of grid squares. This overlap means that objects cannot just check for collisions with other objects in the grid square. That would lead to some collisions being missed when objects lay across grid boundaries. There are a couple of solutions to this problem.

The first solution is to have the simulation check for collisions with objects in adjacent grid squares and the current grid square. This would not be a great solution for our example in Figure 7.2, as eight of the total 16 squares adjacent each square, but it can work well with larger grids. This has the limitation that objects cannot be larger than the size of a grid square, as they could poke out of the set of adjacent squares.

The second solution is to have each object in the simulation reside in multiple squares if objects cross grid boundaries. This makes the grid system a little more difficult to manage and adds some overhead to each movement, but it solves the problem without the object size limitation. This solution can also work better for smaller grids such as the one in Figure 7.2.

Collision grids are a common feature of real-time strategy games. There is also a variation of the collision grid called a *quad tree* that allows dynamic partitioning of spaces. This variation can be made to adjust itself while it is running to better handle congregations of many objects in areas of the grid.

7.3 METHODS OF COLLISION CHECKING

A number of methods can be used for collision checking in games. The one that is appropriate for a particular game depends on factors such as the number and complexity of the objects in the game, the amount of real-time feedback, and the pace of the actions.

Per Polygon

Per-polygon collisions are very accurate collisions that can be performed in 2D or 3D simulations. In this method, the actual geometry of the simulation objects is used to calculate intersections. Each polygon in the geometry of the objects is compared, which can make it very expensive for complicated objects. This must take into account rotation, translation, and animation of the polygons so that they are in their actual position when the intersection tests take place.

This method of collision is math-intensive and can use a large amount of CPU resources. This level of accuracy is only needed in games that have real-time feedback requirements and where accurate collision testing is essential to gameplay.

First-person shooters are the most common users of per-polygon collision testing, because this type of game must be certain whether a bullet or a rocket hits its target—the gameplay consequences of collisions are dramatic.

Per Pixel

Per-pixel collisions are another very accurate method of collision detection used in games. This method uses the actual pixels that are drawn for objects to determine intersections. This method is common in 2D games that have rectangular objects with transparent portions. The collision system takes into account the transparent portions of the objects at a pixel level to ensure that the collisions appear to be realistic. This method is also sometimes used to determine the exact object under the mouse cursor—a process called "mouse picking."

This method is quite expensive and requires access to the final drawn pixels of objects, which can make it complicated if that information is difficult to access in real time.

Bounding Boxes

Bounding boxes are a collision detection method in which a conceptual box is drawn around each object in the simulation, and collision checks are performed between the boxes rather than the object themselves. It can be used in 2D or in 3D and provides a fairly good approximation of collisions, especially for simple objects.

This method of collision checking uses a moderate amount of math and CPU resources. It is often used in games as a first-pass or crude check to determine if a more expensive check needs to be made. It is also often used for server-side collision detection in online games, as it doesn't require the full geometry data for objects to be present. For game servers that use large worlds with many objects, keeping only a bounding box in memory for each object rather than the full object's geometry can greatly reduce the game servers' memory requirements.

Python can be used for simple bounding box systems. We discuss bounding boxes in more detail later in this chapter.

Bounding Spheres

Bounding spheres are a method of collision checking similar to bounding boxes. A sphere or circle is created around the objects in the simulation, and intersection tests are performed between the spheres rather than the actual objects.

This method uses simple math and a low amount of CPU resources. Its main drawback is that it can be very inaccurate for oddly shaped objects—a sphere drawn around a long thin object such as a cylinder isn't a very good approximation of its shape. Bounding spheres are used in places similar to where bounding boxes are used. Figure 7.3 shows bounding spheres for some objects.

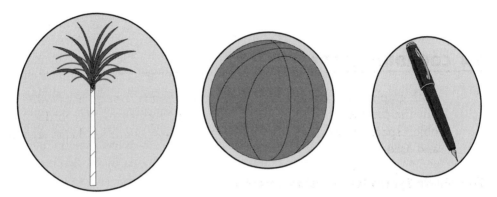

FIGURE 7.3   Bounding spheres.

As bounding spheres are relatively inexpensive to calculate and compare to each other, Python can be used for bounding sphere systems.

Tiles

Collision checking can be performed in 2D systems by dividing the world into small tiles and enforcing that each tile can only be occupied by one object at a time. Tile systems usually use square tiles, but some tile systems such as war games use hexagonal tiles. This method of collision checking is very simple and light on CPU utilization. It can be ideal for games where accurate or real-time collision testing isn't a requirement. Role-playing games often used tile-based collision systems.

However, tile systems can restrict the objects in the game to the size of a single tile, or objects can have a *mask* of tiles that they take up. They impose restrictions or limitations on game objects and art resources so that they conform to the tile grid—a limitation that can impact gameplay or game designers' ability to innovate.

Tile based collision systems can be implemented in Python—the characteristics of tile-based collision systems fit well with Python development, and the runtime requirements are low.

7.4 COORDINATE SPACES

Both graphics and simulation programming use the concept of *coordinate spaces*. For the purposes of collision detection, there are two useful coordinate spaces: object space and world space. These impact the way bounding shapes are generated and used.

Coordinate Spaces for Collision Detection

Object space is the context where geometry that makes up objects is defined. Positions defined in this space are relative to objects' local origins and remain the same distance from each other no matter where in the simulation world the object is located. Simulation objects have independent object spaces so that their geometry can be defined in absolute positions.

World space is the space where simulation objects interact with each other. All positions in world space are relative to the origin of the world, not the local origins of simulation objects. This is the space that positions must be in to be compared to each other; therefore, this is the space that bounding boxes must be in to check for intersections between them. The process of moving from one coordinate space to another is known as a *transformation*.

As an example, consider a set of points in a diamond formation around a center. The center can be designated as the (0,0) position of the diamond object's coordinate space; it is the origin of the space. This system is sufficient to specify the diamond object, but it can't deal with the idea of *another* object in the same space! This other object with its center at somewhere other than the origin would have the information that defines its points corrupted by the offsets from the origin. To give it the same clean definition that the diamond object has, it must be defined in its own coordinate space with its points offset from its own origin. To determine if these two example objects collide with each other, they must be transformed into world space so that they share the same origin.

Coordinate Spaces and Bounding Boxes

Coordinate spaces are important to know about when generating bounding boxes and when intersecting bounding boxes.

Generating bounding boxes for collision objects can be expensive. The simulation objects used in this book are relatively simple, but the simulation objects in commercial games can be made up of hundreds or even thousands of vertices, which makes calculating bounding shapes for them expensive. Consequently, calculating bounding boxes should be done as infrequently as possible. Doing this calculation in object space and keeping the bounding box itself in object space means that the bounding box does not have to be recalculated when the object moves. If a bounding box were calculated from an object's geometry in world space, the box would have to be recalculated from scratch every time the object moved, which would be wastefully inefficient.

It is a common practice to generate bounding boxes for simulation objects when they are loaded, or even in an external tool that saves the bounding information so that it can be loaded with the object, and no calculations have to be performed at runtime.

However, the process of comparing the bounding boxes of two objects still requires the bounding boxes to be in the same coordinate space. One technique is to transform each bounding box into world space before the comparison between them can be made. This is an acceptable overhead, as transforming bounding boxes is relatively inexpensive when compared with transforming entire simulation objects. A bounding box can be described with much less information than the actual geometry they bound, so fewer points need to be transformed. This is much less expensive than transforming all the points of a simulation object and then generating a new bounding box for them in world space.

7.5 AXIALLY ALIGNED BOUNDING BOXES

There are two types of bounding boxes: *axially aligned* and *arbitrarily aligned*. Axially aligned bounding boxes (AABBs) have the property that their sides must be perpendicular to the principle axes. Arbitrarily aligned bounding boxes can be aligned in any direction with no regard for the principle axes. The example code uses axially aligned bounding boxes, as they are simpler to calculate and operate on.

Figure 7.4 shows both types of bounding boxes.

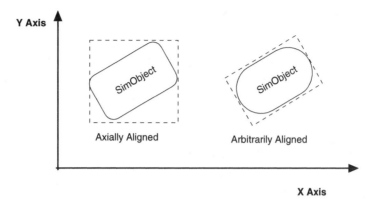

FIGURE 7.4 Bounding boxes.

Calculating bounding boxes for simulation object is straightforward and does not require any fancy mathematics. For a 2D system, AABBs are made up of the minimum and maximum X and Y values for the points that make up an object. To compute this, the minimum and maximum values for an AABB are reset, and then each of the points for the simulation object are *added* to the bounding box. With each point added, the AABB expands to enclose the point so that once all of the points are added, the bounding box encloses all of the points that make up the simulation object.

Listing 7.1 is Python code for a 2D AABB that computes itself in object space from a simulation object. For convenience, the AABB class holds another AABB instance within it (called worldAABB) that holds their AABB in world coordinates. It uses the transform method to transform the AABB into world space using a specified position and orientation.

Listing 7.1 Axially aligned bounding box.

```
bigNumber = 99999999

class AABB:
    """Axially Aligned Bounding Box.
    """
```

```
    def __init__(self, world=0):
        self.reset()
        if not world:
            self.worldAABB = AABB(1) # avoid recursive creation

    def reset(self):
        self.minX = bigNumber
        self.minY = bigNumber
        self.maxX = -bigNumber
        self.maxY = -bigNumber

    def add(self, x, y):
        self.minX = min(self.minX, x)
        self.minY = min(self.minY, y)
        self.maxX = max(self.maxX, x)
        self.maxY = max(self.maxY, y)

    def computeFor(self, obj):
        """Compute the axially aligned bounding box for the simObject.
        Computes it in object space.
        """
        self.reset()
        self.add(-obj.width/2, -obj.height/2)
        self.add(obj.width/2, -obj.height/2)
        self.add(obj.width/2, obj.height/2)
        self.add(-obj.width/2, obj.height/2)

    def transform(self, x, y, facing):
        """transform the AABB into world space.
        """
        self.worldAABB.reset()
        radians = toRadians(facing)

        # transform upper left
        newX = x+(self.minX* math.cos(radians)+self.minY *
math.sin(radians))
        newY = y+(-self.minX*math.sin(radians)+self.minY *
math.cos(radians))
        self.worldAABB.add(newX, newY)

        # transform upper right
        newX = x+( self.maxX*math.cos(radians)+self.minY *
math.sin(radians))
        newY = y+(-self.maxX*math.sin(radians)+self.minY *
math.cos(radians))
        self.worldAABB.add(newX, newY)
```

```
        # transform lower left
        newX = x+( self.maxX*math.cos(radians)+self.maxY *
math.sin(radians))
        newY = y+(-self.maxX*math.sin(radians)+self.maxY *
math.cos(radians))
        self.worldAABB.add(newX, newY)

        # transform lower right
        newX = x+( self.minX*math.cos(radians)+self.maxY *
math.sin(radians))
        newY = y+(-self.minX*math.sin(radians)+self.maxY *
math.cos(radians))
        self.worldAABB.add(newX, newY)
```

This class uses a large number of math operations and executes a relatively high number of Python statements to perform its calculations. This type of code executes faster in lower-level languages such as C or C++, so it is an example of code that should probably not be in Python. The powerful dynamic capabilities of Python are not useful in this circumstance, and the overhead they impose on this code is probably unacceptable for a large game.

The checkWorld method of the AABB class determines if the object collides with the extents of the world and returns a direction that tells the code the side of the world with which it collided. As this method works in world space, the *bottom* of the world is zero and the *top* is the largest Y value.

```
def checkWorld(self, left, right, bottom, top):
    """check if the aabb collides with the edges of world.
    """
    if self.worldAABB.minX < left:
        return WEST
    elif self.worldAABB.maxX > right:
        return EAST
    elif self.worldAABB.minY < bottom:
        return SOUTH
    elif self.worldAABB.maxY > top:
        return NORTH
    return 0
```

The checkPoint method of the AABB class determines if a single point in world space collides with the object. This is useful for checking if the mouse position is over an object.

```
def checkPoint(self, x, y):
    """check if a point collides with me. in world space.
    """
    if x > self.worldAABB.minX and x < self.worldAABB.maxX:
        if y > self.worldAABB.minY and y < self.worldAABB.maxY:
            return 1
```

To complete the class, a `checkCollide` method determines if two bounding boxes intersect with each other. This method uses the `worldAABB` member that contains the AABB's representation in world space.

```
def checkCollide(self, aabb):
    """check if another aabb collides with this one.
    """
    if self.worldAABB.minX > aabb.worldAABB.maxX:
        return 0
    if self.worldAABB.maxX < aabb.worldAABB.minX:
        return 0
    if self.worldAABB.minY > aabb.worldAABB.maxY:
        return 0
    if self.worldAABB.maxY < aabb.worldAABB.minY:
        return 0
    return 1
```

7.6 BOUNDING SPHERES

As bounding spheres are the least expensive type of collision shape in terms of CPU resources, they are a good candidate for the most granular checks in a collision system. This section shows a Python implementation of bounding spheres. This class has an identical external interface to the AABB class in the previous section, so the two classes can be used almost interchangeably.

Listing 7.2 is the Python code for the `BoundingSphere` class.

Listing 7.2 Bounding spheres.

```
class BoundingSphere:
    """Bounding Sphere for a sim object.
    """
    def __init__(self, world=0):
        self.reset()
        if not world:
            self.worldSphere = BoundingSphere(1)
```

```python
def reset(self):
    self.posX = 0
    self.posY = 0
    self.radiusSq = 0
    self.radius = 0

def add(self, x, y):
    r = x**2 + y**2
    self.radiusSq = max(r, self.radiusSq)

def computeFor(self, obj):
    """Compute the bounding sphere for the object in object space.
    """
    self.reset()
    self.add( -obj.width/2, -obj.height/2)
    self.add( obj.width/2, -obj.height/2)
    self.add( obj.width/2, obj.height/2)
    self.add( -obj.width/2, obj.height/2)
    self.radius = math.sqrt(self.radiusSq)

def transform(self, x, y, facing):
    self.worldSphere.posX = x
    self.worldSphere.posY = y
    self.worldSphere.radius = self.radius
    self.worldSphere.radiusSq = self.radiusSq

def checkCollide(self, sphere):
    dx = self.worldSphere.posX - sphere.worldSphere.posX
    dy = self.worldSphere.posY - sphere.worldSphere.posY
    distance = dx**2 + dy**2
    if distance < self.radiusSq + sphere.radiusSq:
        return 1
    else:
        return 0

def checkWorld(self, left, right, bottom, top):
    """check if the sphere collides with the edges of world.
    """
    if self.worldSphere.posX - self.radius < left:
        return WEST
    elif self.worldSphere.posX + self.radius > right:
        return EAST
    elif self.worldSphere.posY - self.radius < bottom:
        return SOUTH
    elif self.worldSphere.posY + self.radius > top:
        return NORTH
    return 0
```

```
def checkPoint(self, x, y):
    """check if a point collides with me. in world space.
    """
    dx = x - self.worldSphere.posX
    dy = y - self.worldSphere.posY
    distance = dx**2 + dy**2
    if distance < self.radiusSq:
        return 1
    else:
        return 0
```

This code is very similar to the AABB code. The bounding sphere is calculated in object space and uses an internal bounding sphere called worldSphere to track its state in world space. The radius of the bounding sphere is calculated in the computeFor method, which is very similar to the computeFor method for AABBs. As an optimization, the computeFor method doesn't run the square root function until all of the points have been added.

7.7 DEALING WITH MOVING OBJECTS

Performing collision tests for moving objects in a simulation is more complicated than dealing with just stationary objects. Since the simulation is running at a variable rate, it is possible that the distance that objects move during one frame could be large enough that they skip over some area of the simulation world where they should have found a collision! The classic example of this in game development is fast-moving bullets going through walls (see Figure 7.5).

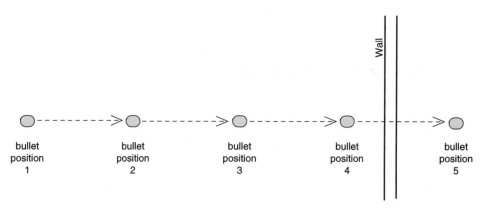

FIGURE 7.5 Bullet moving through a wall.

This shows a bullet moving a relatively large distance each frame. At the fourth position, it is on the left side of the wall, and at the fifth position, it is on the right side of the wall but it never actually collides with the wall. This type of behavior can produce strange anomalies in simulations and can be very difficult to track down.

One solution to this problem is to draw a line from the object's starting position to the object's final position, and check whether the line collides with any other objects. This works for the case of the wall in Figure 7.5, but does not handle all cases. It only deals with objects that overlap the exact center of the path between the positions. A more sophisticated version of this is to create a single box or cylinder that covers the entire space that the object would move through to reach the final point (see Figure 7.6).

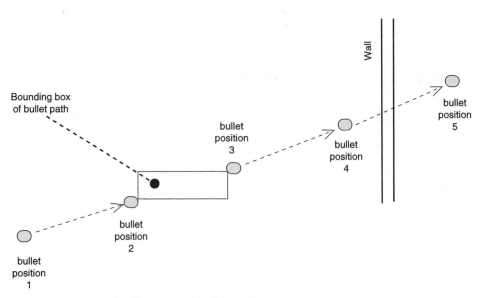

FIGURE 7.6   Bounding box around bullet path.

While this solution is accurate at detecting the wall in its path, in a system that uses AABBs or bounding spheres, the bounding shape for this path can be much larger than the actual path. This could cause incorrect collisions in situations where the bullet should have passed harmlessly by. To counteract this problem, another solution is to walk the bounding shape for the object along the path until it reaches the final position (see Figure 7.7).

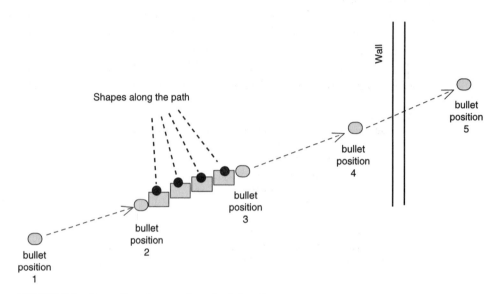

FIGURE 7.7   Bounding shapes along bullet path.

While this method is more expensive because it requires multiple bounding boxes to be calculated and checked, it provides a more accurate result in both the positive and negative cases.

Dealing with moving objects can become even more complex when there are multiple moving objects crossing a space during the same frame. The skipping problem becomes more difficult when there are multiple moving objects involved. Dealing with these advanced cases is beyond the scope of this book.

7.8 IMPLEMENTING A COLLISION GRID IN PYTHON

This section implements a collision grid in Python. This collision grid is integrated with the simulation world and simulation objects from the previous chapter.

A collision grid has some similar properties to the simulation world, and in this case, it is contained in the world object. The grid is a container of simulation objects that must be notified when objects are added or removed, and when objects move. The collision grid contains a set of grid squares. Each grid square contains a list of simulation objects that are in the grid square.

The GridSquare class represents a collision grid square. This class has methods for adding simulation objects to it and removing simulation objects from it.

```python
class GridSquare:
    def __init__(self, posX, posY, width, height):
        self.posX = posX
        self.posY = posY
        self.width = width
        self.height = height
        self.sims = []

    def addSim(self, sim):
        self.sims.append(sim)
    def removeSim(self, sim):
        self.sims.remove(sim)
```

Next, we define a class to represent the collision grid itself. It contains a number of grid squares in a dictionary that allows the grid to be accessed quickly based on their location (see Listing 7.3).

Listing 7.3 Collision grid.

```python
class CollisionGrid:
    """grid that manages collision of simulation objects.
    """
    def __init__(self, width, height, ratio):
        self.width = width
        self.height = height
        self.squareWidth = width / ratio
        self.squareHeight = height / ratio
        self.numSquaresX = width / self.squareWidth
        self.numSquaresY = height / self.squareHeight
        self.squares = {} # dictionary of grid squares by location

        # initialize grid squares
```

```
        for y in range(0,self.numSquaresY+1):
            for x in range(0,self.numSquaresX+1):
                self.squares[ (x,y) ] = GridSquare(
                        x*self.squareWidth, y*self.squareHeight,
                        self.squareWidth, self.squareHeight)

    def addSim(self, sim):
        location = ( (int)(sim.posX/self.squareWidth),
                     (int)(sim.posY/self.squareHeight) )
        sq = self.squares.get( location )
        sim.location = location
        sim.aabb.transform(sim.posX, sim.posY, sim.facing)
        sq.addSim(sim)

    def removeSim(self, sim):
        sq = self.squares.get(sim.location)
        sq.removeSim(sim)

    def moveSim(self, sim, newX, newY, newFacing):
        """This does not update the aabb as that should have been
        done in checkCollide before this was called.
        """
        newLocation = ( (int)(newX/self.squareWidth),
                        (int)(newY/self.squareHeight) )
        if newLocation != sim.location:
            oldSq = self.squares.get(sim.location)
            oldSq.removeSim(sim)
            newSq = self.squares.get(newLocation)
            newSq.addSim(sim)
            sim.location = newLocation
```

This class uses two new attributes in the SimObject class. The location data member is a tuple of the X and Y position of the grid square in which the object resides. The aabb data member is an axially aligned bounding box for the object. This is calculated in object space when the sim is created using the following code, and is then transformed into world space when the object is added to the world and when it moves so that it is always valid.

```
        self.aabb = AABB()
        self.aabb.computeFor(self)
```

The collision grid has another method that actually performs the work of checking for collisions. The checkCollide method is called when an object is added to the world and when an object in the world attempts to move. The checkCollide method has to perform these functions:

- Calculate an AABB for the position the object is attempting to move to
- Calculate AABBs for other objects that don't have up-to-date AABBs
- Compare the AABBs to determine collisions
- Invoke the `hit` method to determine if the objects can hit each other
- Return the object that was collided with

It has the added complication of dealing with the object moving from one position to another. The issues described in Section 7.9 are covered by this code to ensure that fast-moving objects collide correctly with other objects.

The `hit` method is another new addition to the `SimObject` class. It is called when there is a potential collision between two objects, and its result determines whether the actual collision occurs. This functionality can be useful for enforcing the order of collisions between different types of objects, such as to ensure that bullets always collide with ships, rather than the other way around. It is also a hook for game objects to react to collisions by overriding the default implementation with their own.

The `checkCollide` method uses two helper methods. The first method is `checkCollideAABB`. This is used to check if an AABB in world space collides with any of the other objects in the world. In the `checkCollide` method, this method is called to see if the final position that the object is moving to is empty. This method is shown here:

```
def checkCollide(self, sim, newX, newY, newFacing):
    """Check if the sim can move to the new position and facing.
    If it would collide with another sim, then return that sim.
    On success return None.
    """
    sim.aabb.transform(newX, newY, newFacing)

    # check for any skipped space
    result = self.checkSkip(sim, newX, newY, newFacing)
    if result:
        return result

    # check for collision at final position
    return self.checkCollideAABB(sim.aabb, sim, newX, newY, newFacing)
```

The `checkCollideAABB` method finds the grid square that the object is in and checks for colliding objects in that square and all of the surrounding squares. This covers the case of objects that are overlapping the edges of grid squares. This method also checks for collisions with the extents of the world. If the box is outside the world, the method returns a constant from the AABB's checkWorld method that tells the application which side of the world extents were hit (see Listing 7.4).

Listing 7.4   The checkCollideAABB method.

```
def checkCollideAABB(self, aabb, sim, newX, newY, newFacing):
    """check the collision for a AABB in world space.
    """
    # check for edges of world
    edge = sim.aabb.checkWorld(0,self.width, 0,self.height)
    if edge:
        sim.hit(None, newX, newY, newFacing)
        return edge

    gridX = (int)(newX/self.squareWidth)
    gridY = (int)(newY/self.squareHeight)

    # iterate through local and adjacent squares
    for y in range( gridY-1, gridY+2):
        for x in range( gridX-1, gridX+2):
            if x<0 or y<0 or x>=self.numSquaresX or
y>=self.numSquaresY:
                continue
            sq = self.squares.get( (x,y) )
            for other in sq.sims:
                if other == sim:
                    continue
                # check for collision
                if aabb.checkCollide(other.aabb):
                    hitResult = sim.hit(other, newX, newY, newFacing)
                    if hitResult:

other.hit(sim,other.posX,other.posY,other.facing)
                        sim.aabb.transform(sim.posX,sim.posY,sim.facing)
                        return other
```

If a collision does occur, the bounding box of the simulation object is transformed back to its original state, as the object will not complete the requested move. The strategy of transforming the object's bounding box before the collision is an optimization that assumes that more collision checks will return true rather than false. If a check is not a collision—the most common case—then only a single transformation is required.

When objects do collide with each other at this level, the collision code calls the hit method of the object. This is a hook that game objects can implement to perform actions or to "opt out" of collisions based on some other state. The hit method of SimObject is very simple. This simple hit method stops the motion of the simulation object that has collided.

```
def hit(self, other, newPosX, newPosY, newFacing):
    """Called when I hit another object.
    """
    self.velocityX = 0
    self.velocityY = 0
    self.accel = 0
    return 1
```

The second helper method used by the checkCollide method is checkSkip. This method determines if the object is moving fast enough to skip any space (as described in Section 7.9), and then walks a bounding box down the skipped path to ensure that it is empty (see Listing 7.5).

Listing 7.5 The checkSkip method.

```
def checkSkip(self, sim, newX, newY, newFacing):
    """check if this displacement skips any space
    """
    if abs(sim.posX-newX)-sim.width>0 or abs(sim.posY-newY)-
sim.height>0:
        # create a bounding box to fit in the skipped area
        skipBox = AABB()
        skipBox.computeFor(sim)

        # calculate skip box values
        dx = newX - sim.posX
        dy = newY - sim.posY

        if dx > 0:
            xMultiplier = 1
        else:
            xMultiplier = -1
        if dy > 0:
            yMultiplier = 1
        else:
            yMultiplier = -1

        if dy == 0:
            skipWidth = sim.width * xMultiplier
            skipHeight = 0
        elif dx == 0:
            skipWidth = 0
            skipHeight = sim.height * yMultiplier
```

```
else:
    ratio = float(abs(dx)) / float(abs(dy))
    if ratio > float(sim.width)/sim.height:
        skipWidth = sim.width * xMultiplier
        skipHeight = (sim.height / ratio) * yMultiplier
    else:
        skipWidth = (sim.width * ratio) * xMultiplier
        skipHeight = sim.height * yMultiplier

# move the skipBox to the first position
skipPosX = sim.posX + skipWidth
skipPosY = sim.posY + skipHeight

# move the skipbox along the path
while 1:
    skipBox.transform(skipPosX, skipPosY, newFacing)
    result =
    self.checkCollideAABB(skipBox,sim,skipPosX,skipPosY,
    newFacing)
    if result:
        return result
    skipPosX += skipWidth
    skipPosY += skipHeight
    if abs(newX-skipPosX) < sim.width and abs(newY-skipPosY)<
    sim.height:
        break
        return 0
```

This method calls the `checkCollideAABB` helper method defined previously to check the bounding box at each location.

To implement this collision system in the simulation world, the world object must be modified to use the `CollisionGrid`. When objects are added and removed from the world, the collision grid must be notified. Additionally, when objects within the world move, a new method `move` must be called on the world.

```
def move(self, sim, newPosX, newPosY, newFacing):
    if sim.collide or sim.blocking:
        self.grid.moveSim(sim, newPosX, newPosY, newFacing)
```

This ensures that the position of objects in the collision is kept up to date as objects in the world move. In the update method of `SimObject`, the code to move now looks like:

```
if world.canMove(self, newPosX, newPosY, newFacing):
    self.posX = newPosX
```

```
self.posY = newPosY
self.facing = newFacing
world.move(self, newPosX, newPosY, newFacing)
```

Detecting collisions between objects is most useful if we can tell in which direction the collision has occurred. The code so far has only been able to detect that a collision happened, not any more detailed information about the collision. In the interests of keeping the collision detection code fast, it is a good tactic to only calculate this additional information when the initial, cheaper operation has already determined that a collision did indeed occur. Therefore, we will add a method to the SimObject class to determine the collision direction once we know a hit has occurred.

This method returns a tuple of (hitX,hitY) that tells us if the collision took place on each of the X and Y axes (see Listing 7.6).

Listing 7.6 The findHitDirection method.

```
def findHitDirections(self, other, newPosX, newPosY, newFacing):
    """Determine what direction(s) an object should bounce.
    This should only be called from within the "hit" method of
    this class.
    """
    hitX = 0
    hitY = 0

    # test for world extents first
    if not isinstance(other, SimObject):
        if other == collision.WEST or other == collision.EAST:
            hitX = 1
        if other == collision.NORTH or other == collision.SOUTH:
            hitY = 1
        return (hitX, hitY)

        aabb = copy.copy(self.aabb)

    # test if collide if just X is changed
    aabb.transform(newPosX, self.posY, newFacing)
    hitX = aabb.checkCollide(other.aabb)

    # test if collide if just Y is changed
    aabb.transform(self.posX, newPosY, newFacing)
    hitY = aabb.checkCollide(other.aabb)

    # set both if neither hits alone
    if not hitY and not hitX:
```

```
        hitY = 1
        hitX = 1
    return (hitX, hitY)
```

This type of information can be used to make simulation objects bounce correctly off walls or other objects. It should only be called from within the `hit` method of a simulation object. The following code is an example of using the results from the preceding method to make an object bounce.

```
def hit(self, other, newPosX, newPosY, newFacing):
    (hitX, hitY) = self.findHitDirections(other, newPosX, newPosY,
    newFacing)
    if hitY:
        self.velocityY = -self.velocityY
    if hitX:
        self.velocityX = - self.velocityX
    return 1
```

The collision grid also has the functionality of determining if a single point collides with any of the objects it is tracking. The `checkPoint` module method uses the `checkPoint` methods of the AABBs to check if the point actually collides with anything.

```
def checkPoint(self, x, y):
    """Check if a point collides with any sims
    """
    location = ( (int)(x/self.squareWidth), (int)(y/self.squareHeight)
)
    square = self.squares.get( location )
    if square:
        for sim in square.sims:
            if sim.aabb.checkPoint(x, y):
                return sim
```

7.9 MAKING A MODULE

All of the code developed up to this point forms a layer of infrastructure that could be applied to many different game situations. To make this code into a reusable component, it is a good idea to compartmentalize it into a Python module.

Making modules in Python is very simple—we just move all of the code into a directory and add a file called __init__.py to the directory. This file is an actual

Python file and will be invoked when the module is loaded. Although this file can be useful for performing module-level initializations, it isn't actually required to contain any code.

We will name the code developed so far the *hoop* library and move the following files into the hoop directory along with an empty __init__.py file:

```
aabb.py
collision.py
datamanager.py
sim.py
utils.py
world.py
engine.py
```

Accessing the classes in these files is now slightly different. Instead of using the syntax:

```
from sim import SimObject
```

code that uses classes from within the module must include the module name:

```
from hoop.sim import SimObject
```

The hoop game library is now ready to use! Note that it also includes the file engine.py that we will develop in Chapter 8, "Graphics."

SUMMARY

This chapter described a broad range of topics related to the theory and implementation of collision detection systems in games with Python. The concepts discussed in this chapter included object classification, world partitioning, coordinate spaces, collision shapes, and collisions with moving objects. This chapter also presented a Python-based collision system that uses axially aligned bounding boxes. This collision system will be sufficient for the example games in this book, but it only handles simple rectangular shapes and probably would not scale to handle the number of objects in large games.

This chapter is the end of the infrastructure section of this book and wraps up the code developed so far into the *hoop* library. The collision module developed in this chapter is a generic component that is part of that library.

Collision detection is an area of game development that has been the subject of many articles and research. Advanced collision detection systems that are much more sophisticated than the code presented in this chapter are used in certain types of games. There are many topics for further investigation into collision systems, such as oct-trees, walkable surfaces, multi-resolution maps, and more complex collision shapes.

Game Technologies

8 Graphics

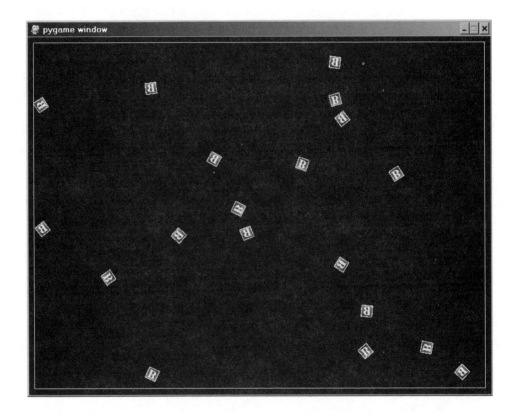

Graphics programming is one of the most demanding and specialized aspects of the game industry. High-quality, impressive visuals sell games, so game developers devote time and energy to having the latest and greatest graphics technology in their products. Graphics engine development is a leading-edge quest for performance and functionality that is driven by the competitive nature of the game market. It relies on APIs and hardware that change rapidly when compared to other technologies, so keeping up with the state of the art in graphics is a great deal of work.

Graphics programming also has stringent performance requirements. With the amount of data they process, the coordination with hardware, and the frame rates that players expect, graphics engines are very sensitive to performance issues. Graphics programmers are notorious for being performance experts and are probably the most likely of all game programmers to resort to assembly language programming to squeeze out the greatest possible performance from their code.

Python graphics programming in games has mostly been restricted to an overseeing role rather than an implementation role. Most graphics engines are written in C/C++, and the interactions with Python are usually to control the engine, rather than as part of the implementation of the engine. However, it possible to do graphics programming with Python, and it is especially possible to develop functional prototypes of game concepts in Python. The scientific community uses Python for scientific visualization software, and the PyOpenGL library provides a interface to OpenGL from Python. This chapter implements a graphics infrastructure that demonstrates some of the principles of graphics programming that is used by the examples in this book.

In this chapter, Section 8.1 discusses the art pipeline process, and Section 8.2 discusses some of the issues involved with using Python for graphics programming. Section 8.3 defines a high-level interface to a graphics engine, and Section 8.4 goes on to provide an implementation of this interface in Python. Finally, Section 8.5 shows an example of using this graphics engine to visualize the inner workings of the collision system from Chapter 7, "Collision Detection."

8.1 ART PIPELINE

Graphics engines are very data intensive. In commercial game projects, the amount of information that it takes to define a single object for a graphics engine can be enormous. This information can include geometry data, texture data, animation data, effects, particles, connection points, and more! Often, some of this information is generated by artists using tools such as Discrete's *3d max*® or custom tools built by game developers. The data is exported from the tools into files that the graphics engine reads. This process is sometimes known as the *art pipeline*, and Figure 8.1 shows how it works.

Art pipelines are crucial for game projects, as they can have a huge impact on the productivity of both artists and programmers. They can be very complicated, as the different components of a piece of art might require multiple tools to develop, need collaboration between different artists with different talents, and also require input from graphics programmers.

Although the graphics code in this book is in two dimensions, it does *not* use the strategies of sprites and bit blitting. With the advent of OpenGL and DirectX as

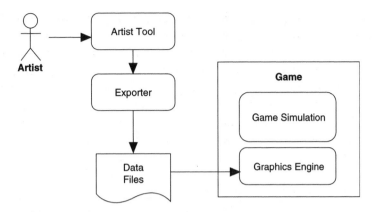

FIGURE 8.1 The art pipeline.

mature 3D graphics APIs, and the proliferation of hardware-accelerated graphics cards, modern games don't use the concept of sprites as often as games from the 1980s and early 1990s. This book describes a hardware-accelerated graphics strategy that is a better representation of the graphics engines in modern games than a sprite-based strategy would be. Games that use 2D graphics techniques do still exist—even some of the highest selling titles such as *RollerCoaster Tycoon*® and *The Sims*™ use 2D graphics. However, as 3D graphics technology becomes more established and hardware support for it becomes more widespread, it is essential for game developers to be familiar with 3D graphics techniques.

8.2 USING PYTHON FOR GRAPHICS PROGRAMMING

Python game programming and graphics engine programming have very different philosophies. Graphics programming is hardware specific, low level, works best with static data structures, and involves iteration and math. Python is more dynamic and flexible—it is better suited to *controlling* graphics engines than it is to *writing* graphics engines.

To achieve the performance requirements of commercial game development, Python can be used as a controlling layer on top of graphics engines written in lower-level languages. This technique of using Python to control graphics engines (and in a similar way, to control simulations) has been used successfully for commercial games.

To achieve the goal of separating graphics engine code from Python code, there must be an interface between the two sides. This interface is where graphics functionality is exposed to Python and is the interface that simulation code and game application code will use to control the graphics engine from Python. There are many possible ways to implement an interface of this type, so to narrow the options, we will describe some of the requirements for the interface.

Minimize the Number of Elements Exposed in the Interface

It is a general rule of interface design to make interfaces complete and minimal (see *Effective C++* by Scott Meyers). This is particularly true for cross-language interfaces and applies to the graphics engine interface as much as any other. The graphics engine interface should be as small as it can be to remain effective.

Minimize the Amount of Python Code Executed at Runtime

This is a consideration because of the performance requirements of graphics engines and the potentially large amount of data used by them. The interface should minimize the runtime overhead of Python. As an example, if many graphics objects must be drawn each frame, the graphics engine should expose a single API call to render them all, rather than requiring the Python application code to iterate through the objects and render each.

Keep Graphics-Specific Data in the Graphics Engine

The large amount of data that graphics engines use and the nature of that data make it inappropriate to process in Python. Python's built-in data structures such as dictionary and lists are flexible and dynamic—very different from the requirements of the types of data used within a graphics engine. It is very expensive to convert vertex data, texture coordinate data, and other graphics engine-related data types from their native representation into Python, and vice versa.

To minimize this overhead, the interface to the graphics engine should keep the graphics engine's data within the graphics engine. As an example, when loading animation data from files, the engine should expose an API call to load the data from the file directly rather than to require the application code to load the data and then pass it to the graphics engine.

Hide Implementation Details

There are a number of different low-level libraries for performing graphics operations, including OpenGL and Direct3D. This interface should provide an abstraction that buffers application code from dealing with low-level graphics APIs. It should hide the implementation details from the game application code.

8.3 HIGH-LEVEL GRAPHICS INTERFACE

With the preceding requirements in mind, this section defines an interface to a graphics engine. This graphics engine component could be implemented in any language—in fact, in this chapter, a graphics engine is implemented in Python that conforms to this interface, and later in this book, a Python extension module is implemented in C/C++ that also conforms to the interface.

Module Interfaces versus Object Interfaces

The interface to a Python module can expose methods at the module level, or it can expose classes within the module that themselves expose methods. Implementing interfaces that only expose module methods is much simpler due to the nature of the Python API. However, module method interfaces are not appropriate for some situations. They are fine when the module acts as a *singleton* object and there is only one instance of it, but when the module allows creation of actual object instances, it is more natural to use an object-based API.

The graphics engine interface in this chapter uses a combination approach. As the graphics engine object itself is a singleton, the interface to it is at the module level, but the module also exposes a `GraphicsObject` class that is an object-level interface.

The Graphics Engine Interface

The graphics engine module is responsible for high-level operations and object management operations. This portion of the interface consists of only five methods, conforming to the requirement of a complete but minimal interface.

```python
def initialize(width, height):
    """initialize the graphics engine.
    """

def addObject(object, x, y, facing):
    """Add a graphics object to the engine to be renderered.
    """

def removeObject(object):
    """remove a graphics object from the engine
    """

def render():
    """Draw all of the objects in the engine.
    """
```

```
def setView(posX, posY):
    """set the origin of the viewport.
    """
```

These basic operations are all module-level operations. They are invoked on the module that implements the graphics engine regardless of the language in which the module is implemented. For example:

```
import engine
engine.initialize(800,600)
```

These methods should be self-explanatory except for the setView method. This method sets the position of the viewport in the world. This allows the screen to be a moving window onto a world that is larger than the area of the screen. This is similar but simpler than the camera metaphor that is common in 3D graphics engines.

Since this is a 2D graphics engine, there are also some 2D drawing utility methods at the module level:

```
def drawLine( x1, y1, x2, y2, color):
    """Draw a line from (x1,y1)(x2,y2)
    """

def drawRect( x, y, width, height, color):
    """Draw a rectangle.
    """

def drawText(text, position, color):
    """Draw text at a position.
    """

def drawImage( x, y, width, height, image ):
    """Draw a texture at x, y
    """

def clear():
    """Clears the background.
    """
```

Note that these utility functions are very similar to functions provided by PyUI's renderer class. They are included here to make the graphics engine interface complete and so that they can be implemented within the graphics engine for high performance.

The GraphicsObject is a class that is defined within the graphics engine interface. This complicates the implementation of the interface in languages other than

Python, but it is a more natural way for the interface to expose this functionality. The GraphicsObject interface is also quite small to conform to the complete but minimal interface requirement.

```python
class GraphicsObject:
    def __init__(self, source, image=None):
        """Create an object from a source of data.
        """

    def getSimData(self):
        """called by simulation to get data required to use
        this object in the simulation.
        returns (centerX, centerY, width, height)
        """

    def setState(self, x, y, facing):
        """updates the state of the object.
        """

    def setFrame(self, frame):
        """Set the animation frame.
        """

    def nextFrame(self):
        """go to the next animation frame, implicitly cycle.
        """

    def destroy(self):
        """Destroy the object and release resources.
        """
```

This interface assumes that it is working with an art pipeline system. When objects are created, the details relevant to the graphics engine are loaded from a data file rather than being included in the DataManager. The DataManager is still used to store game simulation-level information about objects, but the graphics data for objects is stored in data source files. However, the DataManager does contain the information that specifies which data source file is associated with each object.

When an object is created, it passes a source that it uses to load graphics data. The graphics engine is entirely responsible for loading data from sources and managing that data. This strategy means that much of the data associated with objects in the graphics engine bypasses the *game* layer entirely and is loaded directly from data source files into the graphics engine. This fits well with the strategy of graphics data in the graphics engine. The GraphicsObjects can also be passed an image at creation time. This allows different objects with the same geometry to use different images as textures.

The graphics objects that are loaded by this object could be 3D models, 2D sprites, or even just lines of descriptive text. The interface has no visibility into the internal representation of objects within the graphics engine. This is an ideal situation for interface design, but when actually developing the example games in this book, the data that defines graphics objects must be specified. This is detailed in the next section where the Python version of the graphics engine is implemented.

The next two methods are for interaction between the graphics engine and the physical simulation. The getSimData method is used to pass information about the nature of the object from the graphics engine to the physical simulation. Since the collision detection system exists on the Python side, it must know the physical attributes of objects. Previously, this information was stored in the DataManager, but with the definition of objects being moved into data source files within the graphics engine, there must be a way for the physical simulation to access this data. The getSimData method is called by the physical simulation when a graphics object is created to get the information required to use the object in the simulation.

The setState method is the interface in the other direction. As the state of objects exists in the physical simulation, when that state changes, the GraphicsObjects must be informed so that they are drawn in the correct locations. This method is called by the physical simulation when the state of objects changes. This separation of state is important. If both the graphics engine and the physical simulation could change the state of objects, then the possibilities for conflicts and bugs increases. It is best to place the responsibility for this data with a single system.

The GraphicsObject interface also includes two methods for dealing with animated textures. Objects in the graphics engine might have multiple animation frames, and the setFrame and nextFrame methods are available to control the animation of these objects. Figure 8.2 shows how multiple animation frames can be included in a single image file for use with the animation system in this graphics engine.

FIGURE 8.2 Animation frames in a single image.

A discussed in Chapter 3, "Python Game Architectures," the system that is responsible for physical state data does vary in different game architectures. Although this particular architecture has elements of a controlled simulation, it doesn't fit neatly into any of the types of simulations lists in Chapter 3.

8.4 PYTHON GRAPHICS ENGINE

In this section, we will develop a 2D graphics engine in Python that conforms to the interface in the previous section and uses the OpenGL library for low-level graphics. As far as graphics engines go, this one is very simple, but it will be used to demonstrate interactions between game application code and graphics engine code. It includes components that are analogous to those that exist in more sophisticated graphics engines, but are simpler because of the 2D nature of this engine and the simplicity of the objects it uses.

This chapter uses the PyOpenGL library for low-level graphics operations. PyOpenGL is a Python wrapper around the standard OpenGL graphics library that allows these operations to be performed from Python. Although this method is fine for simple graphical applications, it would be inappropriate to use it for large 3D scenes, or very complex worlds or complex objects. Some of the characteristics of graphics engines are lots of looping behavior and math calculations—areas in which the overhead of Python can be an issue.

This is not a book about OpenGL, so this section only includes a minimal amount of detail about the OpenGL code being used. For more detail on OpenGL programming, there are many other resources available both in books and online.

The Module Interface

To implement the module-level interface for the graphics engine, pass-through methods are used to refer to a global instance of the Engine class. This class keeps a list of all the graphics objects that are currently in the engine to be drawn (see Listing 8.1)

Listing 8.1 Engine class.

```
class Engine:
    def __init__(self, w, h):
        self.mobileObjects = RenderBucket()
        self.staticObjects = RenderBucket(dynamic = 0)
        self.width = w
        self.height = h
        self.posX = w/2
        self.posY = h/2

        glEnable(GL_TEXTURE_2D)
        glDisable(GL_DEPTH_TEST)
        glOrtho( 0, w, 0, h, -1, 0)

    def add(self, obj, x, y, facing):
```

```
        """adds a graphics object to the engine.
        """
        obj.setState(x, y, facing)
        if obj.mobile:
            self.mobileObjects.addObject(obj)
        else:
            self.staticObjects.addObject(obj)

    def remove(self, obj):
        """removes a graphics object from the engine.
        """
        if obj.mobile:
            self.mobileObjects.removeObject(obj)
        else:                       .
            self.staticObjects.removeObject(obj)

    def dirty(self, obj):
        """dirties an object and it's bucket.
        """
        if obj.mobile:
            self.mobileObjects.dirtyObject(obj)
        else:
            self.staticObjects.dirtyObject(obj)

    def render(self):
        """Draw all of the objects.
        """
        glPushMatrix()
        glTranslate(self.width/2-self.posX, self.height/2-self.posY, 0)
        self.staticObjects.render()
        self.mobileObjects.render()
        glPopMatrix()

    def setView(self, posX, posY):
        self.posX = posX
        self.posY =
```

This class is an internal class used by the graphics engine. Application code only interacts with this through these shadow methods that are defined on the module itself that conform to the specified graphics engine interface (see Listing 8.2).

Listing 8.2 Engine module interface.

```
gEngine = None   # graphics engine singleton

def initialize(width, height):
```

```
        """initialize the graphics engine.
        """
        global gEngine
        gEngine = Engine(width, height)

    def addObject(object, x, y, facing):
        """Add a graphics object to the engine to be renderered.
        """
        gEngine.add(object, x, y, facing)

    def removeObject(object):
        """remove a graphics object from the engine
        """
        gEngine.remove(object)

    def render():
        """Draw all of the objects in the engine.
        """
        gEngine.render()

    def setView(posX, posY):
        """set the origin of the viewpoints.
        """
        gEngine.setView(posX, posY)
```

Notice that this piece of code also includes a module-level variable that is used to hold the single instance of the Engine class. These pass-through methods add a layer of overhead to interacting with the engine, but as these are not high-frequency methods, the performance difference should not be noticeable. This overhead could be alleviated by promoting methods of the engine instance to the level of the module. The following code shows how this is done.

```
addObject = gEngine.addObject
removeObject = gEngine.removeObject
```

As methods are objects in Python, they can be operated on like any other data. The method objects of the module-level engine instance can be added to the module as top-level data variables also. These methods could then be called directly on the module. While this technique does eliminate the function call overhead, it does have some drawbacks. There is an extra level of management to be considered, as the methods on the module must be updated if the global graphics engine object is replaced. Moreover, the arguments to the module methods must be the same as the class methods.

The graphics engine object uses two other internal classes, TextureBucket and RenderBucket. These classes are used for optimized management and drawing of graphics objects within the engine. When drawing with OpenGL, swapping between textures is an expensive operation, so the graphics engine groups the graphics objects into TextureBuckets that can be drawn without changing textures. Each TextureBucket object is a container that holds graphics objects that use the same texture. This class is optimized further by the use of OpenGL *display lists*. These are batches of drawing calls that can be compiled once and then drawn quickly with a single call later. Display lists are an effective optimization technique for static objects, as a group of objects can be batched together and drawn very quickly. This is the functionality the TextureBucket provides (see Listing 8.3).

Listing 8.3 TextureBucket.

```
class TextureBucket:
    """I am a container of objects with the same texture.
    I am responsible for rendering my objects.
    """
    def __init__(self, texture, dynamic):
        self.texture = texture
        self.objects = []
        self.dynamic = dynamic
        self.displayList = 0
        self.dirty = 1

    def addObject(self, object):
        self.objects.append(object)
        self.dirty = 1

    def removeObject(self, object):
        self.objects.remove(object)
        self.dirty = 1

    def render(self):
        """Draws the objects using display lists if enabled.
        """
        if self.dynamic:
            # render objects outside of display list
            self.renderObjects()
        else:
            # recreate display list if required
            if self.dirty:
                if self.displayList:
                    glDeleteLists(self.displayList, 1)
                self.displayList = glGenLists(1)
```

```
            glNewList(self.displayList, GL_COMPILE)
            self.renderObjects()
            glEndList()
            self.dirty = 0

        # always draw the display list
        glCallList(self.displayList)

    def renderObjects(self):
        """actually renders the objects.
        """
        texture = loadImage(self.texture)
        glBindTexture(GL_TEXTURE_2D, texture)
        for object in self.objects:
            glColorub(255,255,255,255)
            object.render()
```

The code in Listing 8.3 is the first time in this book that actual PyOpenGL is exposed. The lines of code beginning with *gl* are calls to OpenGL.

The TextureBucket can be configured with a *dynamic* flag to specify whether it is intended to hold static or dynamic objects. Since there is some overhead to creating and maintaining display lists, using them for sets of objects that change every frame uses resources without providing any performance improvement. In these cases, the TextureBucket should be created with the *dynamic* flag set, and it will not incur the overhead of using a display list.

The TextureBucket calls out to the render method of the GraphicsObject class for the actual drawing of objects. When not in dynamic mode, it only does this when its contents have changed. In most cases, static TextureBuckets can be drawn with a single OpenGL call that is many times faster than iterating through the objects in Python and calling across the PyOpenGL language boundary for each object.

The RenderBucket class contains a number of TextureBucket objects that hold the actual GraphicsObject instances. This class is responsible for managing the TextureBuckets and putting graphics objects into the correct TextureBuckets so that they can be drawn quickly. It is also a convenient unit for separating static and dynamic objects. The Engine class has a RenderBucket for mobile objects that has its *dynamic* flag set, and another for static objects (see Listing 8.4).

Listing 8.4 RenderBucket.

```
class RenderBucket:
    """sorts objects by texture to minimize texture swapping.
    """
    def __init__(self, dynamic = 1 ):
```

```
            self.buckets = {}
            self.dynamic = dynamic

        def addObject(self, object):
            bucket = self.buckets.get(object.image, None)
            if not bucket:
                bucket = TextureBucket(object.image, self.dynamic)
                self.buckets[object.image] = bucket
            bucket.addObject(object)

        def removeObject(self, object):
            bucket = self.buckets.get(object.image, None)
            if not bucket:
                raise GraphicsException("Unable to find image:
%s"%object.image)
            bucket.removeObject(object)

        def render(self):
            """Calls each texture bucket to render the objects.
            """
            glEnable(GL_TEXTURE_2D)
            for bucket in self.buckets.values():
                bucket.render()
```

The remaining methods of the engine module are the utility methods for drawing basic primitives. The simplest of them is a line.

```
def drawLine( x1, y1, x2, y2, color):
    """Draw a line from (x1,y1)(x2,y2)
    """
    glDisable(GL_TEXTURE_2D)
    glBegin(GL_LINES)
    glColor4ub( color[0], color[1], color[2], color[3] )
    glVertex2i(x1, y1)
    glVertex2i(x2, y2)
    glEnd()
    glEnable(GL_TEXTURE_2D)
```

This method draws a single line from the position (x1,y1) to the position (x2,y2). It uses the OpenGL call glBegin to designate the beginning of a set of vertices to be drawn, and that the drawing mode GL_LINE should be used. It uses glColor4ub to specify the color to use for the line, and then it calls glVertex2i to supply the actual vertex information.

The glVertex OpenGL call is an important function that will be used often in these examples. This function is the way the vertex data is passed to the OpenGL drawing library. All of the primitives that this graphics engine can draw use glVertex to pass information to OpenGL. The suffix of "2i" at the end of the glVertex method designates the number of parameters and the type of data being passed. In Python code, this might seem superfluous, but it is a standard OpenGL convention that should be adhered to.

Drawing lines does not use a texture, so the use of textures is turned off before drawing the line, and re-enabled after the line is drawn. This is done with the glEnable and glDisable OpenGL calls. This graphics engine assumes that the use of textures is *on* by default. Switching from textured mode to nontextured mode is quite expensive for OpenGL. Therefore, since most of the objects that will be drawn will use textures, the graphics engine keeps texturing enabled as its default state.

The next utility method draws a colored rectangle. This method draws an axially aligned rectangle of a specified color. This is very similar to the code to draw a line, except that it uses the mode GL_QUADS instead of GL_LINES.

```python
def drawRect( x, y, width, height, color):
    """Draw a rect with it's upper left at x,y
    """
    glDisable(GL_TEXTURE_2D)
    glBegin(GL_QUADS)
    glColor4ub( color[0], color[1], color[2], color[3] )
    glVertex2i(x, y)
    glVertex2i(x+width, y)
    glVertex2i(x+width, y+height)
    glVertex2i(x, y+height)
    glEnd()
    glEnable(GL_TEXTURE_2D)
```

The clear method is very simple. It just calls straight to the OpenGL library function to clear the screen. It can accept a color to clear the screen with, but it defaults to black.

```python
def clear(color=None):
    if color:
        apply(glColor,color)
    else:
        glColor(0,0,0,255)
    glClear(GL_COLOR_BUFFER_BIT|GL_DEPTH_BUFFER_BIT)
```

The drawText method draws text on the screen at a specific position. This method uses the built-in text drawing functionality of the OpenGL GLUT library to draw simple text. Again, this is done with texturing turned off.

```
def drawText(text, position, color):
    """Draw text at position.
    """
    glDisable(GL_TEXTURE_2D)
    glColor4ub( color[0], color[1], color[2], color[3] )
    glRasterPos2f(position[0], position[1]+13)
    for char in text:
        glutBitmapCharacter(GLUT_BITMAP_HELVETICA_12, ord(char))
    glEnable(GL_TEXTURE_2D)
```

This is a very simple text drawing function. It doesn't allow features such as multiple fonts, bold, italics, or scaling. Drawing text in OpenGL can get quite complicated, so this example will stay away from more advanced text features to remain simple. This amount of functionality in text drawing is not sufficient for game displays, so later examples will use PyUI's text rendering capabilities that include True Type font rendering with multiple fonts at any size. We discuss this in more detail in Chapter 14, "User Interfaces."

The final utility method is the drawImage method to draw an image to the screen in a specified rectangle. This method uses OpenGL *texture coordinates* to map an image to a 2D quad. The gTextureCoords structure is allocated statically outside of the method so that it can be used each time without being reallocated.

```
gTextureCoords = [[0.0,1.0],[1.0,1.0],[1.0,0.0],[0.0,0.0]]

def drawImage( x, y, width, height, image ):
    """Draw a texture
    """
    global gTextureCoords

    glColor4ub(255,255,255,255)
    texture = loadImage(image)
    glBindTexture( GL_TEXTURE_2D, texture)

    glBegin(GL_QUADS)
    glTexCoord2f(gTextureCoords[0][0], gTextureCoords[0][1])
    glVertex2i( x, y)
    glTexCoord2f(gTextureCoords[1][0], gTextureCoords[1][1])
    glVertex2i( x+width, y)
    glTexCoord2f(gTextureCoords[2][0], gTextureCoords[2][1])
    glVertex2i( x+width, y+height)
    glTexCoord2f(gTextureCoords[3][0], gTextureCoords[3][1])
    glVertex2i( x, y+height)
    glEnd()
```

This method requires the internal `loadImage` method, which we explain later in this chapter.

With the functionality implemented so far, for the first time in this book it is possible to display something on the screen. As an example, the following code draws yellow lines around the outside of the screen, draws a blue box, and some white text in the center.

```
def drawStuff(width, height):
    engine.clear()
    color = pyui.colors.yellow
    engine.drawLine(10,10, width-10,10, color)
    engine.drawLine(width-10,10, width-10,height-10, color)
    engine.drawLine(width-10,height-10, 10,height-10, color)
    engine.drawLine(10,height-10, 10,10, color)

    engine.drawRect(50, 50, 300, 200, pyui.colors.blue)
    engine.drawText("First Graphics Test", (100,100),
pyui.colors.white)
```

This method uses the module-level drawing methods to perform some simple drawing. To keep the display current, this method must be called every frame. This seemingly simple task is complicated by the interaction between different types of objects that must be drawn. User interface elements must be drawn *above* the view of the world so that the world appears at the back and the user interface is floating over it. This affects the order in which different types of objects must be drawn. Fortunately, PyUI provides a hook to draw the world in the correct order.

```
self.renderer.setBackMethod(drawStuff, width, height)
```

The `setBackMethod` method of the PyUI renderer registers the `drawStuff` to be called each frame in the correct time to draw the background. Notice that the additional arguments to `setBackMethod` correspond to the arguments to `drawStuff`. When `setBackMethod` is called, the additional arguments are tracked by PyUI and passed to the registered function each time it is called. The `setBackMethod` must be called before the main loop begins to run, so in this case, it is called from within the `__init__` method of the game application.

To complete this first graphics example, the graphics engine must be initialized. This is also in the `__init__` method of the application:

```
engine.initialize(width, height)
```

The full listing to this example is the file chapter8/firstGraphics.py on the accompanying CD-ROM. Figure 8.3 shows the output that it produces.

FIGURE 8.3 First graphics screenshot.

The Graphics Object Interface

The graphics object interface is more complicated than the module-level interface. It requires some more graphics infrastructure to be developed before it can be implemented. To support graphics objects, the engine must be able to load image files as textures and load definitions of graphics objects from data files.

To load textures, the engine uses a combination of PyGame and OpenGL functionality. This functionality resides in an internal utility method of the graphics engine called `loadImage`. PyGame provides a facility to load image files from disk as Python objects. The actual pixel data is then extracted from the image object and passed to PyOpenGL to create an OpenGL texture. The graphics engine is responsible for managing which textures are loaded and ensuring that textures are only loaded once. To manage textures, the engine module has a module-level dictionary keyed on the name of the texture file:

```
gTextures = {} # textures that have been loaded
```

Listing 8.5 shows the `loadImage` function.

Listing 8.5 The `loadImage` function.

```
def loadImage(filename):
    """load or lookup an image and return the OpenGL Handle to it.
    *** this is in internal method ***
    """
    if gTextures.has_key(filename):
        return gTextures[filename]
```

```
    # Load the texture into memory
    surface = pygame.image.load(filename)
    surface = pygame.transform.flip(surface,0,1)
    data = pygame.image.tostring(surface, "RGBA", 1)
    ix = surface.get_width()
    iy = surface.get_height()

    # Create the OpenGL Texture
    texture = glGenTextures(1)
    glBindTexture(GL_TEXTURE_2D, texture)
    glPixelStorei(GL_UNPACK_ALIGNMENT,1)
    glTexImage2D(GL_TEXTURE_2D,0,4,ix,iy,0,GL_RGBA,GL_UNSIGNED_BYTE,
data)
    glTexParameterf(GL_TEXTURE_2D, GL_TEXTURE_MAG_FILTER, GL_NEAREST)
    glTexParameterf(GL_TEXTURE_2D, GL_TEXTURE_MIN_FILTER, GL_NEAREST)

    # add the texture to global dictionary
    gTextures[filename] = texture
    return texture
```

Notice that the image is flipped on its Y axis by the line:

```
surface = pygame.transform.flip(surface,0,1)
```

This must be done to put the pixel data into the correct format to be drawn in world coordinates. Pixel data in files is in screen space with the origin at the upper-left corner. If this data were used as a texture in our graphics engine without flipping it, the images would appear upside down, as the positive Y direction in the world is up, not down.

At the end of the function, the texture is added to the global gTextures dictionary and the method returns the new texture handle. The next time loadImage is called for the same image, it will be found in the gTextures dictionary and the handle will be returned without loading the texture from disk. This prevents images from being loaded multiple times.

Some restrictions apply to images loaded into this system. The first restriction is that only images of certain formats can be loaded. The PyGame library that is used for image loading supports a variety of formats, including GIF, PNG, JPG, and TGA, so images used by the graphics engine must be in one of these formats. The images used in the examples in this book are PNG images. The second restriction is the size and shape of the images. OpenGL requires that images that are used as textures have widths and heights that are multiples of powers of two. This means that images can be 32 pixels by 64 pixels, but not 57 pixels by 31 pixels. Developers must use image files that meet these criteria, or the engine will not be able to use those files.

This is a good example of using libraries that are available for Python instead of writing everything from scratch. It would have been possible to write Python code to read images from disk, and to parse out the header information for the different types of image file formats. However, since there is already an available library that performs this task, it makes no sense to do the work ourselves. In addition, the image-loading library is written in C and is much faster than a library written in Python would be!

The graphics engine also has to be able to load graphics object definitions from data files. This data is managed in a similar way to the way images are managed. There is module-level variable called gSources that tracks the source objects that have been loaded.

```
gSources = {}  # imported source objects
```

Up to this point, the details of how graphics objects are defined have not been discussed. Since this is where the data files for graphics objects are being defined, this is a good place to also define the data that makes up graphics objects for this engine. The data files for the engine are Python files. The following is the graphics source data file for a rectangular object from the file sourceQuad.py.

```
name = "quad"
image = "basic.png"
centerX = 0
centerY = 0
numFrames = 1
points = ( (-10,-10), (10,-10), (10,10), (-10,10) )
primitives = [ (GL.GL_QUADS, (0,1,2,3)) ]
```

The information is Python code, so there is no need to write any parsing code to extract it. The geometry information in the file consists of a set of points, and a set of primitives. The points are 2D locations in object space that define the vertices used by the object. The primitives are a list of OpenGL primitives that make up the object. Each primitive has a type and a set of indices that are offsets into the points of the object. This data structure allows vertices to be shared between multiple primitives and is a convenient format to use when rendering the object using OpenGL.

This particular object is a rectangle with four vertices and a single GL_QUAD that is bounded by the four vertices. This is about the simplest graphics object we can construct with this system.

To load and manage graphics object source data, the graphics engine uses an internal class called GraphicsSource. These objects are created and managed by the getSource method of the engine module. This internal method is invoked when the first GraphicsObjects is created that uses a particular source (see Listing 8.6).

Listing 8.6   The getSource function.

```
def getSource(source):
    """Load or find a modules based on the source.
        *** this is in internal method ***
    """
    if gSources.has_key(source):
        return gSources[source]

    # load and store the module
    sourceDict = {}
    execfile(source, globals(), sourceDict)
    sourceObject = GraphicsSource(sourceDict)
    gSources[source] = sourceObject
    return sourceObject
```

This class uses the gSources module variable to determine if a source has already been loaded, and returns a GraphicsSource object to the caller. It uses the built-in Python function execfile to load the Python file by its name. This executes the code in the specified file, and any variables that are set in the code's local scope are used to populate the dictionary passed as the third argument. Using the execfile method is similar to importing a module, but instead of the resulting Python object being added to Python's list of modules, it is returned to the caller as a dictionary. Using execfile instead of the built-in function __import__ in this case means that Python's module administration isn't invoked for our data files that are not actually modules.

In the getSource function, the sourceDict variable is populated with one entry for each of the variables set in the source file. For the sourceQuad.py file shown previously, the resulting dictionary contains:

```
{ 'name': 'quad',
  'image': 'basic.png',
  'centerX': 0,
  'centerY': 0,
  'numFrames': 1,
  'points': ( (-10,-10), (10,-10), (10,10), (-10,10) ),
  'primitives': [ (GL.GL_QUADS, (0,1,2,3)) ]
}
```

This dictionary is used to populate the members of a GraphicsSource object. Listing 8.7 shows the code for the GraphicsSource class.

Listing 8.7 The GraphicsSource class.

```
class GraphicsSource:
    def __init__(self, sourceDict):
        # set the attributes on this object
        self.__dict__.update(sourceDict)

        # calculate the aabb, width and height for this source
        self.aabb = aabb.AABB()
        for (x,y) in self.points:
            self.aabb.add(x,y)
        self.width = self.aabb.maxX - self.aabb.minX
        self.height = self.aabb.maxY - self.aabb.minY

        # calculate animation offset
        if self.numFrames:
            self.frameOffset = self.width / self.numFrames
        else:
            self.frameOffset = 0

        # calculate texture coordinates for this source
        self.coords = []
        frameOffset = 0
        frameWidth = 1.0 / self.numFrames
        for i in range(0, self.numFrames):
            frameCoords = []
            for x,y in self.points:
                tx =
(((x+float(self.width)/2.0)/self.width)/self.numFrames)
                ty = 1 - ((y+float(self.height)/2.0) / self.height)
                frameCoords.append( (tx+frameOffset,ty) )
            self.coords.append( frameCoords )
            frameOffset += frameWidth
```

This class stores the data from the source dictionary as members of the class. The following line sets the attributes of the class from the dictionary.

```
self.__dict__.update(sourceDict)
```

This line sets the update method of Python's dictionary object to populate the dictionary object with the values in another dictionary object. In this case, the GraphicsSource object's internal dictionary (__dict__) is populated with the values from the source dictionary that were loaded from the source file. This is an example of using the built-in dynamic functionality of the Python language for a useful game-related purpose.

The initialization also performs some pre-processing to generate the data for the simulation and to generate texture coordinates that are used when objects of this type are rendered. The generation of texture coordinates for source objects is complicated by supporting multiple frames of animation. Instead of the coords attribute containing a single set of texture coordinates, it contains a list of sets of co-ordinates—one for each frame of animation.

With this infrastructure in place, the final step is the implementation of the GraphicsObject class. Remember that this class represents an individual instance of an object in the graphics engine rather than a definition of a type of object in the graphics engine like the GraphicsSource class.

The initialization of the GraphicsObject class invokes the getSource module method to load the graphics data, and sets up the member variable of the class. Notice that an image can be passed into the constructor for this class. This image can be used to override the image specified in the data file so that different object instances that use the same geometry data can use different images. It also includes a drawCallback argument that can be used to perform customized drawing when the object is rendered. This method will be called by the engine after the object has been rendered so the application can perform any special drawing it requires for the object. For example, this could be used to draw health bars or character names beside objects on the screen.

```
class GraphicsObject:
    def __init__(self, source, mobile, image=None, drawCallback=None):
        """Create an object from a source of data.
        """
        self.posX = 0
        self.posY = 0
        self.facing = 0
        self.frame = 0
        self.animOffset = 0
        self.mobile = mobile
        self.sourceName = source
        self.sourceObject = getSource(source)
        self.drawCallback = drawCallback
        if image:
            self.image = image
        else:
            self.image = self.sourceObject.image
```

The methods of the class to interact with the physical simulation are straight-forward. The following methods get and set member variables of the graphics object.

```
def getSimData(self):
    """called by simulation to get data required to use
    this object in the simulation.
    """
    return (self.sourceObject.centerX,
            self.sourceObject.centerY,
            self.sourceObject.width,
            self.sourceObject.height)

def setState(self, x, y, facing):
    """updates the state of the object.
    """
    self.posX = x
    self.posY = y
    self.facing = facing

def setFrame(self, frame):
    """Set the animation frame.
    """
    if frame < self.sourceObject.numFrames:
        self.frame = frame

def nextFrame(self):
    """go to the next animation frame, implicitly cycle.
    """
    self.frame += 1
    if self.frame >= self.sourceObject.numFrames:
        self.frame = 0
```

The most interesting part of the GraphicsObject class is the functionality to actually render the object using OpenGL. The following code draws a graphics object at its location with its orientation by iterating through the primitives and drawing each of them with OpenGL calls.

```
def render(self):
    """draw this object.
    *** this is an internal method ***
    """
    glPushMatrix()
    glTranslate( self.posX, self.posY, 0)
    glRotate(360-self.facing, 0, 0, 1)
    for prim, indicies in self.sourceObject.primitives:
        glBegin(prim)
        for i in indicies:
            apply(glTexCoord2f,
self.sourceObject.coords[self.frame][i])
            apply(glVertex, self.sourceObject.points[ i ])
```

```
        glEnd()
    glPopMatrix()
    if self.drawCallback:
        self.drawCallback()
```

This code uses the points, the indices, and the texture coordinates from the source object. The `glBegin` OpenGL call starts the drawing of primitives, and the `glEnd` OpenGL call ends the set of primitives and causes the actual draw to be executed. Notice that the object drawing is wrapped by calls to `glPushMatrix` and `glPopMatrix`. The initial `glPushMatrix` call pushes a new value onto the OpenGL state stack that allows operations to be performed in a local scope. This is significant because the vertex data for the objects is stored in the object's local coordinate space, but it must be drawn in the world coordinate space. The OpenGL translation and rotation calls that occur after `glPushMatrix` makes the drawing operations for the objects occur in world coordinate space, but we don't want this transformation to persist for all of the objects in the world, as each object's position and orientation could be different. Luckily, the reciprocal `glPopMatrix` call is available to pop the state of the OpenGL stack back to the state it was in before `glPushMatrix` was called. This allows each object to be rendered independently.

The OpenGL methods `glTranslate` and `glRotate` are used put OpenGL into the proper state for drawing.

Integrating with the Simulation

Some changes must be made to the simulation code to cater to the graphics engine. This integration will be implemented so that there is minimal impact on the game application code.

With the relationship between simulation objects and graphics objects, each `SimObject` instance now has a corresponding `GraphicsObject` instance. This is implemented as a compositional relationship rather than an inheritance relationship—the `SimObject` *contains* a `GraphicsObject` instead of the `SimObject` being derived from the `GraphicsObject`. Using composition instead of inheritance is common in Python programming. Composition is a more flexible relationship and requires less code dependencies between the classes involved. Listing 8.8 is the updated initialization code for the `SimObject` class.

Listing 8.8   Simulation object.

```
class SimObject:
    """ A Simulation object in a two-dimensional space.
    """
    def __init__(self, category, drawCallback = None):
```

```
        self.category = category
        self.mobile = category.mobile       # is object mobile
        self.life = category.life           # lifetime (seconds)
        self.collide = category.collide     # collision flag
        self.threshold = category.threshold # variable update frequency

        # create my graphics object
        self.graphicsObject = engine.GraphicsObject(
            category.source, self.mobile, category.image, drawCallback)

        # find out the size of my graphics object
        result = self.graphicsObject.getSimData()
        (self.centerX, self.centerY, self.width, self.height) = result

        self.posX = 0           # current X position
        self.posY = 0           # current Y position
        self.velocityX = 0      # current X velocity
        self.velocityY = 0      # current Y velocity
        self.facing = 0         # current facing (degrees)
        self.rotation = 0       # degrees / second
        self.accel = 0          # speed / second
        self.alive = 1          # flag for staying alive
        self.uDelay = 0         # update delay
        self.uTimer = 0         # update timer
        self.aabb = AABB()
        self.aabb.computeFor(self)
        self.removeCallback = None # callback when removed from the
world
        self.handle = 0
```

The major differences are the creation of the graphics object and that the width and height are now acquired from the graphics object rather than being passed into the method. This change to the creation of simulation objects also affects the DataManager. It must be updated to reflect the changes here, and the initial data must be changed to conform to the new data required for simulation objects. Listing 8.9 shows the new code for the SimCategory class.

Listing 8.9 Simulation category.

```
class SimCategory(Category):
    """I am a category class for simulation objects. Each sim category
    has data that allows it to create a different type of actual
    simObject."""
    def __init__(self,name,mobile,life, collide, threshold, source,
image):
        Category.__init__(self, name)
```

```
                self.mobile = mobile
                self.life = life
                self.collide = collide
                self.threshold = threshold
                self.source = source + ".py"
                self.image = image

        def create(self):
            """Create a SimObject using my data as a template.
            """
            newSim = SimObject(self)
            return newSim
```

This updated code includes the source and the image for the category. Notice that the source has ".py" added to it so that it corresponds to a Python file. The data used to initialize the SimCategories is:

```
initialSimCategories = [
    # name                mobile life collide thresh source   image
    ("mobile square",     1,    0,   1,      5,   "sourceQuad", "basic.png"),
    ("mobile rectangle",  1,    0,   1,      0,   "sourceSkinny",
    "basic.png"),
    ("static square",     0,    0,   0,      0,   "sourceQuad",   "basic.png")
]
```

This data is very similar to the initialization data from Chapter 5, "Simulation Concepts," but it includes data for the source file and the image file for the category.

The SimObject instance must also delete the graphics object when it is itself deleted.

```
def __del__(self):
    self.graphicsObject.destroy()
```

This overriding of the built-in __del__ method of the SimObject class ensures that the graphics object is destroyed when the simulation object is destroyed.

As the simulation is the system that owns the state of objects, when the state of objects in the simulation changes, the graphics engine must be informed. This is handled by adding code to the setState method of the SimObject class to push that state into the corresponding graphics object.

```
def setState(self, posX, posY, facing, speed = 0):
    """Set the simulation state of the object.
    """
    self.posX = posX
    self.posY = posY
```

```
    self.facing = facing
    self.calculateVelocity(speed, facing)
    self.graphicsObject.setState(posX, posY, facing)
```

However, this is not the only place that the state of simulation objects is changed. The setState method is used when objects are added to the world, but the update method is where the state of simulation objects is changed once they are within the world. At the end of the update method where collision checking has already been performed, the state of the graphics object is updated.

```
if world.canMove(self, newPosX, newPosY, newFacing):
    self.posX = newPosX
    self.posY = newPosY
    self.facing = newFacing
    world.move(self, newPosX, newPosY, newFacing)
    self.graphicsObject.setState(newPosX, newPosY, newFacing)
return 1
```

Finally, in the world object, when simulation objects are added to and removed from the world, their corresponding graphics objects must be added to and removed from the graphics engine. The following is update code for the world:

```
def addToWorld(self, sim, x, y, facing, speed=0, force=0):
    if force==0 and self.canMove(sim,x, y, facing) == 0:
        return 0
    if sim.mobile:
        self.mobiles.append(sim)
    else:
        self.immobiles.append(sim)
    sim.setState(x, y, facing, speed)
    if sim.collide or sim.blocking:
        self.grid.addSim(sim)

    engine.addObject(sim.graphicsObject, x, y, facing)
    return 1

def removeFromWorld(self, sim):
    if sim.mobile:
        self.mobiles.remove(sim)
    else:
        self.immobiles.remove(sim)
    if sim.collide or sim.blocking:
        self.grid.removeSim(sim)
    engine.removeObject(sim.graphicsObject)
    return 1
```

Example Application

In the example application in the previous chapter, only a single simulation object was created. Now that there is something to see, this example creates a number of simulation objects and places them randomly in the world. The following is the new version of the __init__ method of the game Application object with this functionality:

```
from random import randint

class Application:
  def __init__(self, width, height):
    self.width = width
    self.height = height
    self.renderer = pyui.desktop.getRenderer()

    self.dm = datamanager.DataManager()
    self.world = world.World(width, height)

    self.renderer.setBackMethod(drawStuff, width, height)
    engine.initialize(width, height)

    for i in range(0,20):
        sim1 = self.dm.createInstance("basic mobile", "sims")
        sim1.rotation = randint(-200,200)
        x = randint(0,width-20)
        y = randint(0,height-20)
        facing = randint(0,360)
        speed = randint(0,200)
        self.world.addToWorld(sim1,x, y, facing, speed)
```

This code used the DataManager to create 20 simulation objects and adds the objects to the world with randomly determined positions, rotations, and speeds. A change to the hit method of SimObject will make them bounce off each other and the edges so they spin and float around the screen.

```
def hit(self, other, newPosX, newPosY, newFacing):
    """Called when I hit another object.
    """
    self.velocityX = -self.velocityX
    self.velocityY = -self.velocityY
    self.accel = 0
    self.rotation = -self.rotation
    return 1
```

Finally, the `drawStuff` method must call the `render` method of the engine so that the objects are drawn.

```
def drawStuff(width, height):
    engine.clear()
    color = pyui.colors.yellow
    engine.drawLine(10,10, width-10,10, color)
    engine.drawLine(width-10,10, width-10,height-10, color)
    engine.drawLine(width-10,height-10, 10,height-10, color)
    engine.drawLine(10,height-10, 10,10, color)
    engine.render()
```

Once this is all in place, for the first time we are able to see the objects in the simulation world moving around in real time. Figure 8.4 is the first screen shot using the code in the file firstObjects.py.

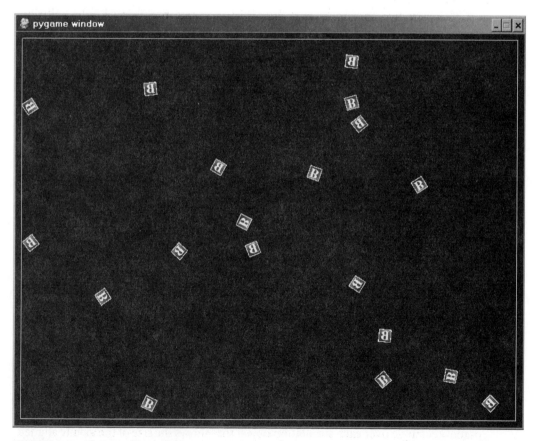

FIGURE 8.4 First graphics objects.

Notice that the frame rate of this application slowly goes up over time. As the objects collide with each other and are slowed by each collision, the variable update threshold kicks in and the update methods of the objects are called less and less often. This shows visually that simulating a static world can be done faster than simulating a world with moving objects.

8.5 VISUALIZING THE COLLISION SYSTEM

In this section, we use the graphics engine to show the workings of the collision system. This is a good exercise that reinforces our knowledge of how to use the graphics engine, and also helps us to visualize exactly how the collision systems works in real time.

There are two components of the collision system represented—the collision grid, and the bounding boxes that surround the simulation objects.

To represent the collision grid, we draw lines for the borders of the grid squares, and text in each square that shows the number of simulation objects inside it. The utility method drawGrid is implemented to draw the collision grid. This will be set as PyUI's backMethod so it is called each frame. Note that it also calls the render method on the engine to invoke the drawing of the simulation objects.

```
def drawGrid(grid):
    """Draw the collision grid
    """
    engine.clear()
    for x in range(0,grid.numSquaresX):
        engine.drawLine( x * grid.squareWidth, 0,
                    x * grid.squareWidth, grid.height,
pyui.colors.grey)
    for y in range(0,grid.numSquaresY):
        engine.drawLine( 0, y * grid.squareHeight,
                    grid.width, y * grid.squareHeight,
pyui.colors.grey)
    for square in grid.squares.values():
        pyui.desktop.getRenderer().drawText( "%d" % len(square.sims),
                    (square.posX+40, square.posY+30),
pyui.colors.white)
    engine.render()
```

To represent the bounding boxes of simulation objects, we will draw a transparent rectangle over each simulation object that shows the size of the axially aligned bounding box for that object. To do this, a new class is created that is derived from the SimObject class and a corresponding category class is defined. The CollisionSim class has a method drawAABB, which is registered as its drawCallback so the bounding box rectangle is drawn each frame.

```
class CollisionSim(SimObject):
    def __init__(self, category):
        SimObject.__init__(self, category, self.drawAABB)

    def drawAABB(self):
        engine.drawRect(
            self.aabb.worldAABB.minX,
            self.aabb.worldAABB.minY,
            self.aabb.worldAABB.maxX - self.aabb.worldAABB.minX,
            self.aabb.worldAABB.maxY - self.aabb.worldAABB.minY,
            (255,255,255,100) )

class CollisionCategory(SimCategory):
    def __init__(self):

SimCategory.__init__(self,"collision",1,0,1,0,"sourceQuad",None)
```

Then, in the setup of the application, a number of these objects are created and set loose in the world with random directions and rotations.

```
cat = CollisionCategory()
for i in range(0,40):
    collisionSim = CollisionSim(cat)
    collisionSim.rotation = randint(-200,200)
    x = randint(0,width-20)
    y = randint(0,height-20)
    facing = randint(0,360)
    speed = randint(0,200)
    self.world.addToWorld(collisionSim,x, y, facing, speed)
```

The resulting output is interesting to watch. As the objects in the simulation rotate, their bounding boxes shrink and grow. As the objects move between grid squares, the numbers that show the population of each square change in real time. This is a good way to understand exactly how the collision system works.

Figure 8.5 is a screenshot of the collision system in action.

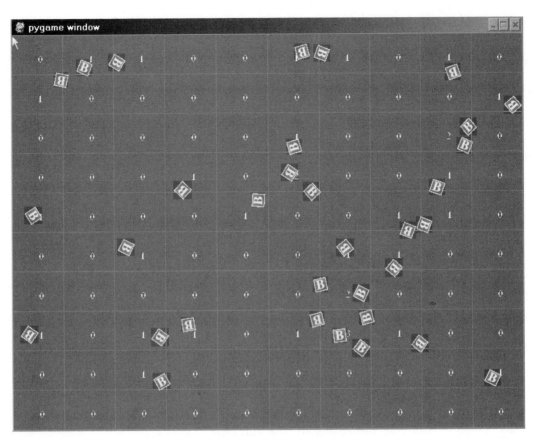

FIGURE 8.5 Visualizing the collision system.

SUMMARY

This chapter discussed issues involved with doing graphics programming in Python, and showed an implementation of a 2D graphics engine in Python using the OpenGL graphics library. This engine demonstrated a number of aspects of graphics engine implementation, and while it is not fast enough for a large commercial game, it will be used for the game examples in the rest of this book.

As an example, this chapter included a visualization of the collision system from Chapter 7. This example demonstrates how to use the functionality of the graphics engine, and serves as an interesting look into the internal workings of the collision system.

The graphics engine developed in this chapter is general enough in its applicability, and was added to the hoop library. Some additions to this engine will be made in later chapters, but the majority of the code developed in this chapter will exist unchanged in the hoop library.

The information about graphics programming in this chapter is by no means complete. This topic is the subject of continuing development and research in the game industry and in academia. There is a great deal of published information available about graphics programming, including many books that specifically deal with both the OpenGL and DirectX libraries that are commonly used in game development.

9 Audio

Graphics are only part of the sensory experience associated with games. Audio is an important component that gives games their immersive qualities and draws the player into the game world. There are a number of ways that audio is used in games. The most apparent is sound effects that are tied to game events. For example, when a player hits a monster with a sword, a *thunk* sound is played and the monster might scream. These types of sound effects are used in almost every type of game on every platform, and provide synchronization between the visual and audio experience. They are tied closely to the game simulation and are usually triggered by specific in-game events.

Another use of audio in games is ambient sounds. These are sounds that are related to the environment rather than to specific, discrete game events. For example, when a player is by an ocean, the game might play watery wave sounds, and when the player is in a scary dungeon, the game might play torturous screaming sounds in the distance. This type of audio is often associated with areas of the game world, or proximity to specific game objects.

Yet another use of audio in games is music. It has become almost compulsory for games to have interesting and relevant music soundtracks that draw the player into the game's mood. Game music has evolved to include dynamic elements so that the music can match the player's current situation to further the urgency of game play.

In this chapter, Section 9.1 discusses how to use PyGame to play sound effects. Section 9.2 talks about ambient sounds and integrating them with simulation objects, and Section 9.3 discusses playing music using PyGame.

9.1 AUDIO CONCEPTS

Sounds are played by specific hardware called *sound cards*. Although in many modern computers, the sound card is actually a built-in component of the motherboard, the name is still common. To interact with the sound card, games use sound library software. There are commercial sound libraries such as the Miles Sound System, operating system libraries such as Microsoft's Direct Sound, and freely available libraries such as the SDL Mixer library that is incorporated into PyGame. These libraries provide varying capabilities and access to more advanced sound processing effects such as positioning sounds in 3D space, and environmental effects. This section uses PyGame's mixer and sound modules for audio.

Let's now review some basic audio terms.

Amplitude

Amplitude is the volume of a sound as measured by the distance between the highest and lowest points of its waveform. When sounds are stored digitally, the relative amplitude is usually encoded into an 8-bit, 16-bit, or 32-bit value. The higher this number, the more space the audio file takes up, and the higher the quality of a recorded sound.

Frequency

Frequency is the number of sound waves that pass a given point in one second. This determines the pitch of a sound wave at any time. When sounds are stored digitally, the combination of frequency and amplitude at each point of the wave determines the sound's pitch and volume at that point in time. Hertz (Hz) is the unit for measuring frequency.

Channels

Sounds can be stored with multiple *channels* of information. Sounds with single channels are called *mono* sound, and sounds with two channels are called *stereo* sounds. Very high-quality digital sounds can have more channels, up to five or six for theater-quality sounds.

Sample Rate

Sample rate is a measure of how often a recording device measures the frequency and amplitude of a sound as it is recorded. The frequency of the sample rate has a large impact on the quality of a recorded sound. CD-quality sound is sampled at a rate of 44.1 kHz.

Pulse Code Modulation

Pulse code modulation is a method that is used to store sounds in a digital format. It is used by some of the common sound file formats, including the wave (.wav) format.

Before any sounds can be played, the audio system must be initialized. The code to initialize the mixer module is:

```
pygame.mixer.init(frequency, size, stereo, buffersize)
```

All of the arguments to this method are optional. The default values are 22050 for frequency, −16 for signed 16-bit data, stereo on, and a buffer size of 1024 samples. It is a good idea to ensure that the playback format specified by these values matches the format of the sound files that are used. If these formats do not match, the audio data must be converted before it is played, resulting in a loss of sound quality and the use of unnecessary CPU processing time.

Like most pieces of hardware, sound cards have limitations. They are limited in the number of sounds they can play simultaneously, the type and size of the sounds stored in their on-board memory, and the advanced processing effects that they can apply to sounds. The limit on the number of simultaneous sounds is implemented by the concept of *channels*. Each channel is an entity that can play a single sound at a time. Each sound card has a maximum number of channels that can be active at once, so games must manage their sounds to achieve a consistent audio environment.

The PyGame mixer module provides functionality to manage sound channels. The mixer defaults to eight channels, but this value can be changed. It provides methods to operate on all of the channels at the same time. This is useful when the game is changing modes or important in-game events occur. The mixer modules provides the capabilities of fading out the sounds on all the active channels over a period of time, temporarily stopping playback of sounds on all channels, resuming the paused playback of sounds on all channels, and querying the mixer for the number of active or currently busy channels.

9.2 PLAYING SOUND EFFECTS

The PyGame mixer module provides Sound and Channel objects to use when playing sound effects. The easiest way to play sounds is to create a Sound object from a sound file and call the object's play method, as shown here:

```
sound = pygame.mixer.Sound("hit.wav")
sound.play()
```

This plays the sounds on an available channel, and does nothing if there are no channels available. In a game with many events occurring in a short period of time, it is possible that more sound could be triggered than can be played on the number of available channels. In that situation, the preceding code will simply fail to play sounds that cannot find available channels. The `play` method returns the `channel` object that the sound is played on, and if the return value is None, the application can tell that there were no available channels, and potentially try the sound again later.

In addition to just playing a sound once, sounds can be played in looping mode. The `play` method takes two arguments that enable sounds to begin playing again from the start when they finish playing. This is useful for background sounds, small pieces of music, or any other sound that must play continuously. The following code shows how to loop a sound five times. Passing a–1 as the loop value makes the sound loop forever.

```
sound = pygame.mixer.Sound("hit.wav")
sound.play(5)
```

Sounds can also be made to stop automatically after a certain amount of time. This is useful when the sound is coordinated with some other type of game activity that takes a specific amount of time. This can be combined with a looping sound. The following code shows how to make a sound stop after 500 milliseconds. If the sound is shorter than the specified time value, the loop value of –1 makes it loop until that time is reached.

```
sound = pygame.mixer.Sound("hit.wav")
sound.play(-1, 500)
```

Stereo sound effects are another feature of audio systems that are easy to use. In PyGame, the stereo parameters are set on the `channel` object, not the `sound` object. Multi-speaker stereo functionality is controlled by the volume setting on the channel. When the volume of a channel is set, an additional parameter to control the stereo ratio can also be passed. Both of these values are floating-point numbers in the range 0.0 to 0.1. Listing 9.1 shows a class derived from the `simulation` object that plays a sound in stereo when it collides with anything.

Listing 9.1   NoiseMaker class.

```
class NoiseMaker(sim.SimObject):
    def __init__(self, worldWidth):
        sim.SimObject.__init__(self, NoiseMakerCategory())
        self.sound = pygame.mixer.Sound("hit.wav")
```

```
                    self.worldWidth = float(worldWidth)

          def hit(self, other, newPosX, newPosY, newFacing):
              channel = pygame.mixer.find_channel()
              if channel:
                  channel.set_volume(1.0, self.posX/self.worldWidth)
                  channel.play(self.sound)
              return sim.SimObject.hit(self, other, newPosX, newPosY,
      newFacing)
```

Notice that the play call is performed on a `channel` object rather than on a `sound` object. Each time a collision occurs, a free `channel` object is requested from the mixer, the stereo volume ratio is set on the channel, and the sound is played on the channel. The horizontal position of the simulation object is used to calculate the stereo ratio as a ratio of the width of the world. This means that when the position of the object is close to zero at the left of the world, the sound emanates from the left speaker, and when the position of the object is close to the width of the world, the sound emanates from the right speaker.

However, there is something seriously wrong with the code in Listing 9.1. Each instance of the `NoiseMaker` class creates a `sound` object from the sound file, so each has a full copy of the data of the sound! This is extremely wasteful of memory. To alleviate this problem, sounds can be managed by a singleton `SoundManager` class that ensures that only one instance of each sound file is loaded at a time. This approach is similar to the way texture instances are managed by the graphics engine in Chapter 8, "Graphics." Listing 9.2 shows the code for a simple `SoundManager` class.

Listing 9.2   SoundManager class.

```
class SoundManager:
    """I manage sound data to ensure there are no duplicate
    sound files loaded into memory.
    """
    def __init__(self):
        self.soundMap = {}
        pygame.mixer.init()

    def loadSound(self, filename):
        """load a sound file or return the existing instance
        of the loaded sound data.
        """
        newSound = self.soundMap.get(filename, None)
        if newSound:
            return newSound
        newSound = pygame.mixer.Sound(filename)
```

```
            self.soundMap[filename] = newSound
            return newSound
```

The `NoiseMaker` class can easily be modified to use this class by changing the constructor to the following:

```
class NoiseMaker(sim.SimObject):
    def __init__(self, worldWidth, soundManager):
        sim.SimObject.__init__(self, NoiseMakerCategory())
        self.sound = soundManager.loadSound("hit.wav")
        self.worldWidth = float(worldWidth)
```

ON THE CD The full code to the example that uses `NoiseMaker` objects is on the accompanying CD-ROM in chapter9/noisemakers.py.

9.3 AMBIENT SOUNDS

Ambient sounds are different from the sound effects described in the previous section, as they are conceptually playing all the time. These sounds are continuous sounds that provide environmental effects or background audio for the game world. Conceptually, these sounds are *on* as long as the object or location with which they are associated continues to exist. However, in practical terms, these sounds must be started and stopped just like other sounds effects to conserve the use of channels and memory.

The `SoundManager` class from the previous section can be extended to have a reserved channel for an ambient sound. Listing 9.3 shows the modified `SoundManager`.

Listing 9.3   `SoundManager` with ambient sound channel.

```
class SoundManager:
    def __init__(self):
        """I manage sound data to ensure there are no duplicate
        sound files loaded into memory.
        """
        self.soundMap = {}
        pygame.mixer.init()
        pygame.mixer.set_reserved(1)
        self.ambientChannel = pygame.mixer.Channel(0)
        self.ambientSound = None

    def loadSound(self, filename):
```

```
        """load a sound file or return the existing instance
        of the loaded sound data.
        """
        newSound = self.soundMap.get(filename, None)
        if newSound:
            return newSound
        newSound = pygame.mixer.Sound(filename)
        self.soundMap[filename] = newSound
        return newSound

    def playAmbient(self, filename, volume=1.0, stereo=0.5):
        """Play the ambient sound.
        """
        self.ambientSound = self.loadSound(filename)
        self.ambientChannel.stop()
        self.ambientChannel.set_volume(volume, stereo)
        self.ambientChannel.play(self.ambientSound, -1, -1)

    def stopAmbient(self):
        """Stop the ambient sound.
        """
        self.ambientChannel.stop()

    def setAmbientProperties(self, volume, stereo):
        """set the volume properties on the ambient
        sound channel.
        """
        self.ambientChannel.set_volume(volume, stereo)
```

This class has a channel reserved for playing the current ambient sound. It uses mixer module's set_reserved method to reserve channel zero for the ambient sound. It provides methods to start and stop the ambient sound, and to change the properties of the ambient sound channel. Listing 9.3 shows that having a channel object for the ambient sound is useful. The setAmbientProperties method allows the properties of the ambient sound channel to be changed while a sound is being played on it. Notice that while the ambient sound is playing, it loops continuously. This means that the sound files used as ambient sounds must be properly constructed to loop smoothly. This code allows a single ambient sound to be active at any time.

Listing 9.4 shows a helper class that can be used to wrap the lower-level ambient sound functionality. This class can be used to attach ambient sounds to simulation objects.

Listing 9.4 AmbientSound class.

```
class AmbientSound:
    def __init__(self, posX, worldWidth, filename, sm):
        self.posX = posX
        self.worldWidth = float(worldWidth)
        self.filename = filename
        self.sm = sm
        self.volume = 1.0

    def start(self):
        self.sm.playAmbient(self.filename, self.volume,
                            self.posX / self.worldWidth)

    def update(self, posX):
        self.posX = posX
        self.sm.setAmbientProperties(self.volume, self.posX/
self.worldWidth)
```

The AmbientSound class can be embedded in a simulation object so the position of the simulation object changes the parameters of the ambient sound. The following code shows how to add an ambient sound to a simulation object.

```
sim1.ambient = AmbientSound(0, width, "wind.wav", self.sm)
sim1.ambient.start()
```

This code works in conjunction with a modified update method of the object. This method is shown here:

```
def update(self, interval, world):
    if self.ambient:
        self.ambient.update(self.posX)
    return sim.SimObject.update(self, interval, world)
```

In each frame, the update method sets the position of the ambient sound, which in turn sets the properties of the ambient sound channel in the SoundManager. This makes the sound follow the simulation object as it moves across the screen. This simple sound integration could be extended with checks for visibility or proximity to a player object that stop or start the sound when appropriate.

9.4 PLAYING MUSIC

Music is different from other types of sound effects, as the data for songs is usually so large, it is not feasible to load it all into memory at once. In games, music is usually streamed from disk or the game CD-ROM. Fortunately, PyGame provides facilities to do this very easily

To play music from a music CD-ROM, PyGame's cdrom module can be used. This module allows games to interrogate the computer's CD drive to determine if an audio CD is present, and the number of tracks on the CD. It can then make the CD drive play the CD to provide background music. The interface to this module is very easy to use. The following code shows how to play a track from the CD-ROM disc.

```
pygame.cdrom.init()
self.cd = pygame.cdrom.CD(0)
self.cd.init()
numTracks = self.cd.get_numtracks()
print "CD has %d tracks." % numTracks
for i in range(0,numTracks):
    if self.cd.get_track_audio(i):
        self.cd.play(i)
        print "Playing Audio Track #%d" % (i)
        break
```

This code begins playing the first audio track on the CD that it finds and skips non-audio tracks. The application must be careful to explicitly stop playing the CD when it exits, or the music will continue to play.

Playing streams of music from files is also very easy to do with PyGame. The PyGame mixer.music module provides an interface to allow music to be streamed from files on disk. This module allows the music to be started, stopped, paused, and faded out. The following code simply loads and begins playing music from a very large wave file.

```
pygame.mixer.music.load("superman.wav")
pygame.mixer.music.play()
```

Unlike music from CD-ROMs, this music is being controlled by the application and will stop when the application exits.

SUMMARY

This chapter described basic concepts in audio for games, and how to use PyGame to integrate audio functionality into games. It showed how to play sound effects that are triggered by events in a physical simulation, play ambient sounds with dynamic stereo control, and how to play music from CD-ROM discs and files.

The topics described in this chapter can be used to make games more immersive by appealing to the ears as well as the eyes. The SoundManager class developed in this chapter can be used to manage and control multiple sound effects and ambient sounds to give games complex audio properties.

This chapter only scratched the surface of audio programming in games. Advances in audio hardware now allow environmental effects, Dolby digital quality sounds, and real-time voice to be available for game developers to experiment with. In addition, techniques such as dynamic music and context-sensitive music are making audio a more integral and responsive part of game development.

10 Input

As games are interactive simulations, they require input from their users. This chapter looks at the ways that games accept input from players and adds functionality to the example code to handle input from a number of difference sources. The primary methods of input into games are the keyboard, the mouse, and the joystick.

Handling input in a game application is different from other types of applications. Unlike many other types of applications, games often require real-time input. Since the game simulation is running in real time, the player must be able to interact with it at the same pace. The way that most non-game applications receive input events is as window messages from the OS. Sometimes, this is not sufficiently accurate for games.

In the examples in this chapter, input is used to control the movement of a simple `player` object in the simulation. This `player` object is just another simulation object, and is subject to the same simulation rules as every other object, but it will also be manipulated by code that responds to user input. The `player` object is created and added to the world in the initialization of the `application` object.

```
self.player = self.dm.createInstance("mobile rectangle", "sims")
    self.player.setImage("ship.png")
```

This object has a different image from the other `simulation` objects so it is immediately obvious which object represents the player. We discuss player and avatar objects in more detail in Chapter 12, "Game Simulations."

Games might use different methods of input processing for different purposes. For example, while the simulation might use direct mouse position information as in the preceding example, the user interface might use a message-based approach for mouse handling as that fits better with its design. There is no reason why different types of user input cannot coexist in a single application. This chapter covers input events, keyboard input, joystick input, and mouse input.

10.1 MESSAGE HANDLING

The simplest way to receive input from users is by listening for messages or events from the OS. Within the game framework in this book, there are a number of different levels at which events can be captured. The lowest level is OS itself. It is possible to implement a Windows message loop using the Python win32 extensions that receives messages directly from the OS. The example code in this book does not use this method; it receives OS input via the SDL library that is wrapped by PyGame. SDL has an event system that captures OS events, and PyGame translates those events into Python objects. The next layer is the PyUI library. PyUI has an event framework that is integrated with its user interface system. This event framework captures events from its renderer—in this case, PyGame—so it has access to events propagating up from the OS. This might seem like many layers, but in practice, it is easy to use (see Figure 10.1).

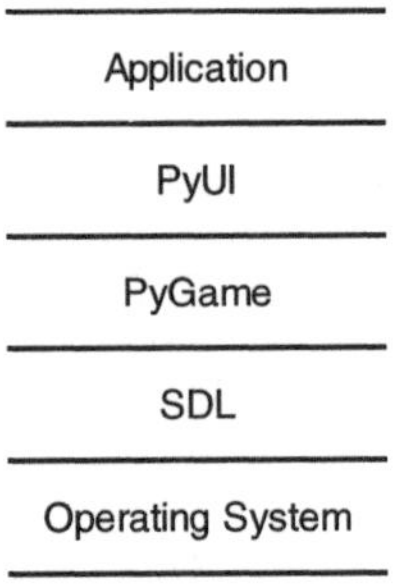

```
 _____
 Application
 _____
 PyUI
 _____
 PyGame
 _____
 SDL
 _____
 Operating System
 _____
```

FIGURE 10.1 Input layers.

To make the game respond to messages, the application must register for particular message types. In PyUI, this can be done at the application level or for individual widgets. User interface programming with PyUI is covered in Chapter 14, "User Interfaces," so this section focuses on application-level message handling.

Registering for a PyUI message uses the `registerHandler` method of the PyUI desktop object, and some of the event types that are defined in pyui.locals include:

```
MOUSEMOVE              = 0x1000
LMOUSEBUTTONDOWN       = 0x1001
LMOUSEBUTTONUP         = 0x1002
RMOUSEBUTTONDOWN       = 0x1003
RMOUSEBUTTONUP         = 0x1004
MMOUSEBUTTONDOWN       = 0x1005
MMOUSEBUTTONUP         = 0x1006
MOUSEWHEEL             = 0x1007
LMOUSEDBLCLICK         = 0x1008
RMOUSEDBLCLICK         = 0x1009
MMOUSEDBLCLICK         = 0x100A
EVENT_KEYBOARD         = 0x2000
CHAR                   = 0x2000
KEYDOWN                = 0x2001
KEYUP                  = 0x2002
```

The `registerHandler` method takes an event type as its first argument and a Python method as its second argument. This method will be called when an event occurs and the `event` object will be passed to it. The following is an example of registering for an event.

```
def onMouseMove(event):
    print "Mouse moved (%d,%d)" % (event.pos[0], event.pos[1])
    return 0
desktop = pyui.desktop.getDesktop()
desktop.registerHandler( pyui.locals.MOUSEMOVE, onMouseMove)
```

The return value of the `handler` function determines whether other registered handlers will get a chance to process an event. If a non-zero value is returned by a `handler` method, the system assumes that the handler has fully processed the event and it shouldn't be passed to any other handlers. Returning a null value allows other handlers a chance to process it.

The `event` object that is passed to the `handler` method is a PyUI `guiEvent` object whose class is defined in the file pyui.desktop.py. The `guiEvent` is a very simple class; its entire definition is listed here:

```
class guiEvent:
    """an event that can be processed by the system.
    """
    def __init__(self, type, id = 0, x = 0, y = 0, key = 0, mods = 0):
        self.type = type
        self.id = id
        self.pos = (x,y)
        self.key = key
        self.mods = mods
```

This class can be this simple because of Python's dynamic nature. If an application wants to add some information to an event, it can just assign a new attribute to the instance of the event object! In Python, there is no need to have different classes for different types of events.

To create events in the PyUI library, the postUserEvent method of the desktop object is used. The signature of this method is:

```
def postUserEvent(self, type, x = 0, y = 0, key = 0, mods = 0)
```

This can be used to post events into the PyUI event system. This can be useful to control the framework or to schedule actions to take place in the next frame. Since the processing of events is asynchronous, any events submitted during one frame will not actually be processed until the next time PyUI's update method is called.

The postUserEvent method conveniently returns the event object that is passing into the system. This gives application code the opportunity to set any additional data attributes on the event, as the asynchronous processing ensures that it won't be accessed by any other code until the next frame. The following example demonstrates this.

```
def onMyEvent(event):
    print "event data ", event.newStuff

MY_EVENT = 5022
desktop.registerHandler(MY_EVENT, onMyEvent)
event = desktop.postUserEvent(MY_EVENT)
event.newStuff = "added to the event"
```

The newStuff attribute is added to the event object after it is created and is then available to the handle method on the next frame.

10.2 KEYBOARD INPUT

For most non-game applications, the standard way to receive keyboard input in a Windows application is to listen for window messages such as WM_KEYDOWN, WM_KEYUP, and WM_CHAR. This is sufficient for some types of applications, and even for most portions of game development. These events are available through the PyUI event system as the KEYDOWN, KEYUP, and CHAR events.

Unfortunately, there is some inherent latency in window messages. When a game is running in fullscreen mode and using all of the CPU resources on a machine, there can be a small delay in receiving window messages from the OS. In addition, when a key is held down, the OS might generate window messages for the key at a frequency that varies on different machines, and it can be complicated to manage the states of multiple keys when relying on events. These issues can make depending on window messages for real-time input problematic. To bypass these issues, games sometimes use keyboard polling to receive keyboard input.

Keyboard polling is the process of checking the current state of keyboard keys without waiting for the OS to generate events for changes in key state. This polling is performed every frame so that changes in the state of the keyboard are reflected in the game simulation immediately.

At the OS level, Microsoft's DirectInput library provides functionality to poll for keyboard status, and the Win32 API has a built-in GetKeyState function that retrieves the status of the specified virtual key. At the Python level, the PyGame library provides methods to poll keyboard state that uses the keyboard polling facilities of SDL.

Using PyGame's keyboard polling is simple. The method pygame.key.get_pressed returns a tuple of Booleans that represents the status of all of the keys on the keyboard. This tuple is ordered so that constants can be used as offsets into it to find the status of individual keys.

To demonstrate keyboard polling, this example allows the user to move the player object around with the arrow keys. The following code is called from the main loop of the example application to update the velocity of the player object every frame.

ON THE CD

The full example is in chapter10/keyboard.py on the accompanying CD-ROM.

```python
def processKeys(self):
    pressed = pygame.key.get_pressed()
    vx = 0
    vy = 0
    if pressed[pyui.locals.K_LEFT]:
        vx -= 50
    if pressed[pyui.locals.K_RIGHT]:
        vx += 50

    if pressed[pyui.locals.K_UP]:
        vy += 50
    if pressed[pyui.locals.K_DOWN]:
        vy -= 50
    self.player.velocityX = vx
    self.player.velocityY = vy
```

This might seem overly complex just to process four keys, but remember that multiple keys might be down at any time. If both the left and right keys are down at the same time, this code ensures that there are no ordering issues that give keys priority over one another. When experimenting with this example, you will notice that it behaves correctly with any combination of keys up or down.

Another feature to notice about the preceding code is that it sets the velocity on the `player` object rather than changing the object's position directly. This is done because movement in the simulation must be tracked and verified by the collision system. If this code changed the actual position of the object, it would become discordant with the data stored about the object in the collision system. Setting the velocity solves this problem by allowing movement to occur in the proper manner and be integrated with the collision system. Notice that the "up" direction is the positive Y direction. This movement is in world space, not in screen space, so positive Y is up rather than down.

10.3 MOUSE INPUT

Most applications use messages from the OSs such as the Windows WM_MOUSE-MOVE, WM_LBUTTONDOWN, and WM_MBUTTONUP messages to receive mouse input information. This approach suffers from some of the same issues as message processing for keyboard input; in particular, there can be some latency involved in receiving messages from the OS.

In a similar way that polling for keyboard messages eliminates latency for keyboard events, it is possible to poll for the location of the mouse and the status of mouse buttons. PyGame provides an interface to poll for mouse status that is very similar to the interface for polling for keyboard status. The method `pygame.mouse.get_pos` returns the current position of the mouse, and the method `pygame.mouse.get_pressed` returns the state of the mouse buttons.

When in windowed mode rather than in fullscreen mode, the default behavior for mouse input is to ignore mouse events that happen outside of an application's window. This behavior might not be desirable for some games that rely on mouse input. To alleviate this issue, it is possible for an application to register with the OS to receive all mouse events. PyGame conveniently provides a method to access this functionality. The `pygame.event.set_grab()` method makes the application receive all mouse events, not just those that occur over its drawable area of the screen.

The following example shows how to make the `player` object in the simulation move toward the mouse cursor.

The full example is in chapter10/mouse.py on the accompanying CD-ROM.

```
def processMouse(self):
    (mx, my) = pygame.mouse.get_pos()
    dx = mx - self.player.posX
    dy = my - self.player.posY
    self.player.velocityX = dx
    self.player.velocityY = -dy
```

Notice again that the `player` object's velocity is modified rather than its position. This keeps the object obeying the rules of the collision system. This example uses the absolute position of the mouse cursor to calculate the velocity. For some purposes, it might be more appropriate to use the relative movement of the mouse rather than the absolute position. PyGame also supplies a way to access this information. The following example shows how to implement similar functionality using relative mouse movement.

```
def processMouseRelative(self):
    (dx, dy) = pygame.mouse.get_rel()
    if dx or dy:
        self.player.velocityX = dx*100
        self.player.velocityY = -dy*100
    else:
        self.player.velocityX = self.player.velocityX*0.8
        self.player.velocityY = self.player.velocityY*0.8
```

Using the exact values for relative mouse movement leads to very jerky movement of the `player` object. The preceding code makes the velocity of the object decay over time to smooth the jerky effect, leaving a smoothly controlled player object. Notice again that the value of Y is positive in the up direction.

ON THE CD
The full code to this example is in chapter10/mouse.py on the accompanying CD-ROM.

10.4 JOYSTICK INPUT

Because the joystick is an input device that is used almost solely for games, there is not the same support for joysticks in OSs that there is for more common devices such as mice and keyboards. Because of this, joystick input cannot rely on messages from the OS; it must use a polling interface.

PyGame includes a polling joystick interface that provides access to all the joystick functionality required for games. It is slightly more complex than the interfaces for mouse devices and keyboards.

The first step when receiving input from a joystick with PyGame is to create a `joystick` object and initialize it. Once a `joystick` object exists, you can call a number of methods on it to poll for its current state, including `get_button` and `get_axis` and `get_hat`. This API doesn't have functionality for joystick calibration, but this is usually handled outside of games in separate applications.

The following example shows how to make the `player` object in the simulation move around with the joystick and to drop simple `simulation` objects into the world with the fire button. The first piece of initialization code is from the constructor of the `Application` object.

The full example is in chapter10/joystick.py on the accompanying CD-ROM.

```
self.j = pygame.joystick.Joystick(0)
    self.j.init()
```

This code is then called from within the main loop each frame. Again, it sets the Y value to be negative to conform to the world space movement convention.

```
def processJoystick(self):
    x = self.j.get_axis(0)
    y = self.j.get_axis(1)
    self.player.velocityX = x*1000
    self.player.velocityY = -y*1000
    if self.j.get_button(0):
        drop = sim.SimObject("quadSource", "basic.png")
        self.world.addToWorld(drop, self.player.posX,
                                    self.player.posY+50,0)
```

The `player` object's velocity is set based on the status of the axis of the joystick, and the status of the joystick button is checked to trigger dropping objects into the world.

The full code to this example is in chapter10/joystick.py on the accompanying CD-ROM.

SUMMARY

This chapter provided us with enough user input infrastructure to control objects in the physical simulation. It covered input events from the user interface and the OS, keyboard input handling, joystick input handling, and mouse input handling.

This chapter included runnable Python examples of each type of input that allows the user to control an object in the physical simulation.

More input devices are available than were mentioned in this chapter, and some of them are much more sophisticated. Force feedback joysticks, gloves, light guns, game controllers, and even customized control devices are used in some games—all of which require input handlers. Although the implementation details for more advanced input devices might be different, the basic principles described in this chapter should be a good basis for further work.

11 Unit Testing

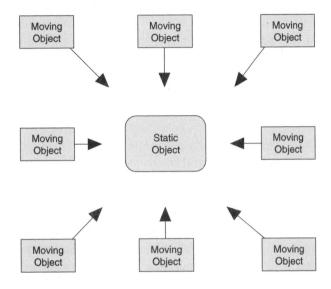

U nit testing is the practice of verifying the behavior of a unit of code by interacting with its external interface. It is a useful tool for programmers whose use has become widespread over the last five years. Unit testing has been partially driven by the notoriety of the *Extreme Programming(XP)* movement.

Unit testing is as applicable to game development as it is to any other field of software development. As games have increased in size and scope, their lifespans have been extended by expansion packs and online play. The need for stable, maintainable code in game development has grown, and unit testing provides a way for game developers to achieve these goals.

This chapter discusses the concept of unit testing and its terminology. Section 11.2 shows how to set up to run unit tests for some of the code developed earlier in this book, Section 11.3 show unit tests for the DataManager from Chapter 6, "Data-Driven Simulations," and Section 11.4 shows unit tests for the simulation from Chapter 5, "Simulation Concepts," and Chapter 7, "Collision Detection."

11.1 INTRODUCTION TO UNIT TESTING

Unit testing partitions code into small, cohesive pieces called *units*. Each unit has a specific external interface and behavior that can be reproduced to determine if it is functioning correctly. To verify the behavior of units, *test cases* are developed that execute and evaluate units of code. These test cases exercise particular facets of a unit of code to ensure that it continues to behave in an expected way. Test cases are grouped into *test suites* so that they can be run as a single operation that tests all of the facets of a unit of code. There might be infrastructure or other common setup tasks that must be performed for each test case of a suite. These are called *fixtures,* and can be built into the suite so they are performed automatically when the tests are run.

Unit testing allows developers to make changes to code with greater confidence. It allows them to quickly and easily find bugs in new code, and breakages introduced by changes in code. Unit testing provides a way to deal with large projects and longer lifecycles by increasing the quality of code and helping to ensure that it stays stable as ongoing changes are made to it.

There are unit-testing *harnesses* for many languages, including *CppUnit* for the C++ programming language, *JUnit* for the Java programming language, and *PyUnit* for use with Python. Unit-testing harnesses provide infrastructure for writing, managing, and running unit tests. With some languages, this task can introduce a high degree of overhead into the development process, but Python's introspection and reflection capabilities make writing unit tests with PyUnit very easy. PyUnit can be found online at *http://pyunit.sourceforge.net*. It includes full documentation and examples.

As Python is a dynamic language that cannot be completely checked for syntax errors at compile time, syntax errors can creep into Python code that would have been caught by the compiler in statically typed languages. With Python, unit testing can act as a replacement for compile-time error checking. Running the unit tests for a program can expose errors that the compiler would have found.

Unit testing is included at this stage of this book because it forms part of the infrastructure that is used to build the examples in later chapters. The example code developed up to this point of the book includes a world, a simulation, and collision detection. This code provides enough substance to apply unit testing to.

11.2 SETUP FOR TESTING

This section builds test cases for the example code from the previous chapters. These tests use the PyUnit testing framework. They verify the correctness of the game infrastructure code, and are used as a basis for further tests throughout this chapter.

The skeleton for the unit tests for the infrastructure code is a standard skeleton for PyUnit.

```
import unittest

from datamanager import DataManager
from world import World, SimObject

# test cases go here

suite1 = unittest.makeSuite(DataManagerTest, "test")
suite2 = unittest.makeSuite(WorldTest,       "test")

if __name__ == "__main__":
    unittest.main()
```

Some operations can be tested for almost all types of objects. Testing creation and deletion are the most basic tests. The following code shows these tests for the World and DataManager classes.

```
class DataManagerTest(unittest.TestCase):
    def setUp(self):
        self.dm = DataManager()
    def tearDown(self):
        self.dm = None

    def testExists(self):
        assert self.dm != None, "data manager doesnt exist!"

class WorldTest(unittest.TestCase):
    def setUp(self):
        self.world = World(500,500)
    def tearDown(self):
        self.world = None

    def testExists(self):
        assert self.world != None, "world doesnt exist!"
```

This most basic level of testing is in the example file chapter11/firstTest.py on the CD-ROM. Its output is shown here:

```
$ python firstTest.py
  ..
----------------------------------------------------------------
```

```
Ran 2 tests in 0.000s

OK
```

With the basic testing framework in place, we can move on to actually testing the functionality of the infrastructure systems that have been built so far.

11.3 TESTING THE DataManager

The DataManager is a special case when it comes to testing. As a highly data-driven class, there is a fine line between testing the functionality of the code, and testing the validity of the data it uses. These are both worthy goals, but in this case, we are interested in testing the DataManager itself.

To isolate the DataManager from its data, the set of test data does not use any actual game code. This data is guaranteed to remain constant as the game evolves, and can be used as a reference for the functionality of the DataManager over time. Combining tests of infrastructure components and game components is a pitfall of data-driven systems. Tests of each of these components should be isolated from each other so that it is always clear which components are working, and which are not.

First, we will define some test data to use. This data defines a variety of categories of test objects that can be used to test the DataManager.

```python
initialSimCategories = [
    # name               mobile life collide threshold source       image
    ("mobile square",    1,   0,   1,      5,        "sourceQuad",   None),
    ("mobile rectangle", 1,   0,   1,      0,        "sourceSkinny", None),
    ("static square",    0,   0,   0,      0,        "sourceQuad",   None)
    ]
```

Second, we can write some unit tests that use the data and verify the results.

```python
def testInitCategory(self):
    self.dm.initCategory("test", initialSimCategories, SimCategory)
    assert len(self.dm.categories) == 2, "not enough categories"

def testInstances(self):
    self.dm.initCategory("test", initialSimCategories, SimCategory)
    o1 = self.dm.createInstance("mobile square", "test")
    o2 = self.dm.createInstance("mobile rectangle", "test")
    o3 = self.dm.createInstance("static square", "test")
    assert isinstance(o1, SimObject), "basic not a simObject"
```

```
    assert isinstance(o2, SimObject), "skinny not a simObject"

def testAttributes(self):
    self.dm.initCategory("test", initialSimCategories, SimCategory)
    o1 = self.dm.createInstance("static square", "test")
    assert o1.mobile == 0, "mobile not correct"
    assert o1.collide == 0, "collide not correct"
    assert o1.category.source == "sourceQuad.py", "source not correct"
```

The first test just loads the test data into the DataManager and verifies that the appropriate category was created. The second test creates instances of each of the test objects, and the third test creates an instance and checks that its attributes are correct. These three tests form an increasingly more complex suite that covers a high percentage of the functionality of the DataManager class.

The early tests might appear to be redundant to the later ones, but this is a deliberate strategy. Starting with simple tests and gradually increasing the complexity of the tests makes it easy to pinpoint exactly where problems occur. If a suite has a single complex test, when this test breaks, it can be difficult to track down where the problem occurred. When a problem manifests itself in a suite of tests varying from simple to complex, usually some of the tests pass, and some of the tests fail. This can be very helpful in pinpointing the source of the problem.

We can finish the coverage of the DataManager by adding one more test. This test exercises the findCategory method.

```
def testFindCategory(self):
    self.dm.initCategory("test", initialSimCategories, SimCategory)
    category = self.dm.findCategory("mobile rectangle", "test")
    assert category != None, "didnt find category!"
    assert category.name == "mobile rectangle", "found wrong category"
```

11.4 TESTING THE SIMULATION

The following is example output from PyUnit when a test fails.

```
$ python testDatamanager.py
.....F.
======================================================================
FAIL: testContainment (__main__.WorldTest)
----------------------------------------------------------------------
Traceback (most recent call last):
  File "testDatamanager.py", line 55, in testContainment
```

```
     assert len(self.world.mobiles) == 2, "adding to world failed"
AssertionError: adding to world failed
----------------------------------------------------------------
Ran 7 tests in 0.010s

FAILED (failures=1)
```

This output shows the file and the test case in which the failure occurred. This particular failure occurred while the example test code was being developed. It was caused by the simulation objects being added to the world in the same position—which caused the second object to collide with the first and therefore fail to be added. This is an excellent example of how useful test cases are!

Following is the actual test that failed. Notice that it has an assert in it to test that objects added at the same position do actually collide with each other. This was only added after the failure shown previously. Adding tests for failure conditions that occur is a very good practice. If the failure happens once, it could happen again, and it is always best to catch it in test code rather than in real application code.

```
def testContainment(self):
    obj1 = self.dm.createInstance("mobile square", "test")
    obj2 = self.dm.createInstance("mobile square", "test")
    self.world.addToWorld(obj1, 50, 50, 0)
    self.world.addToWorld(obj2, 50, 50, 0)
    assert len(self.world.mobiles) == 1, "objects should collide"
    self.world.addToWorld(obj2, 100, 100, 0)
    assert len(self.world.mobiles) == 2, "adding to world failed"
    self.world.removeFromWorld(obj1)
    self.world.removeFromWorld(obj2)
    assert len(self.world.mobiles) == 0, "removing failed"
```

Testing the simulation is again different from testing a simple interface. Often, simulations must actually run for some period to exercise much of their functionality. This requires test cases to run the simulation. Although the simulation is linked to real time with the interval parameter that is passed to the update method of the World class, this can be tricked into thinking that time is running faster than it really is by passing artificial interval values.

The implementation of testMove illustrates this technique.

```
def testMove(self):
    startPosX = 60
    speed = 10
    numUpdates = 8
    obj1 = self.dm.createInstance("mobile square", "test")
```

```
        self.world.addToWorld(obj1, startPosX, 50, 0, speed)
        for i in range(0,numUpdates):
            self.world.update(1)
        assert obj1.posX == startPosX + numUpdates*speed, "moved to wrong
position"
```

A value of 1 is passed to `world.update` that expects an interval in seconds. Notice that the constant values used in the test are defined as variables, not just used as *magic numbers* in the code. This makes the test much more readable. It is poor practice to hard-code obscure numbers into test cases. Imagine coming back to read this and the previous test case if the last line was written as:

```
    assert obj1.posX == 50 + 10*10, "moved to wrong position"
```

or even worse:

```
    assert obj1.posX == 150, "moved to wrong position"
```

Unit tests that use well-named variables instead of *magic numbers* are much easier to read and maintain over time.

The next piece of the simulation to test is collision detection. Testing the collision grid is a tricky problem that can best be illustrated with a diagram (see Figure 11.1).

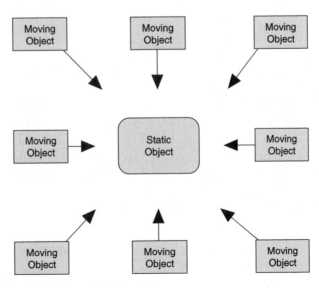

FIGURE 11.1 Collision tests.

Figure 11.1 shows the possible collision tests that can be performed. There are eight tests—left, right, top, bottom, plus the four corners. In each case, there is a starting state where the two objects are not colliding with each other, and a finishing state where the objects have collided. In between, the Static object stays stationary and the Test object moves from its starting position toward the Static object until the collision occurs.

To test all of these combinations, this test case will itself be data driven. Following is the code for the eight situations in a single test case:

```python
def testCollisions(self):
        startPosX = 100
        startPosY = 100
        speed = 7
        numUpdates = 6
        obj1 = self.dm.createInstance("mobile square", "test")
        obj2 = self.dm.createInstance("mobile square", "test")
        self.world.addToWorld(obj1, startPosX, startPosY, 0, 0)

        directions = [ (-1,-1,  45),
                       ( 0,-1,  90),
                       ( 1,-1, 135),
                       (-1, 0,   0),
                       ( 1, 0, 180),
                       (-1, 1, 315),
                       ( 0, 1, 270),
                       ( 1, 1, 225) ]

        for (dx, dy, facing) in directions:
            self.world.addToWorld(obj2,
                                    startPosX + dx*25,
                                    startPosY + dy*25,
                                    facing,
                                    speed)
            beginVelocityX = obj2.velocityX
            beginVelocityY = obj2.velocityY

            for i in range(0, numUpdates):
                self.world.update(1)
                print obj1.posX, obj1.posY, obj2.posX, obj2.posY,
    obj2.velocityX, obj2.velocityY

            assert obj2.velocityX != beginVelocityX or
                    obj2.velocityY != beginVelocityY, ("didnt collide:
    %s %s %s" % (dx, dy, facing))
            self.world.removeFromWorld(obj2)
```

This test case uses the list of tuples `directions` to store the starting positions and facings for each of the situations. Inside the inner loop, the simulation is run for enough time for the objects to collide. When they do collide, the velocity of `obj2` is reversed so the actual velocity no longer matches the beginning velocity that was stored after the object was added to the world.

As this example shows, using data to drive unit tests can greatly reduce the time required to write comprehensive unit test suites and reduce the amount of code that makes them up. It might seem pointless for this chapter to write unit tests for code that is already working, but these tests can now provide a regression suite to ensure that the code continues to work after changes are made to it.

SUMMARY

This chapter described the concept of unit testing and the terminology it uses. We used the PyUnit testing framework to demonstrate unit testing and developed unit tests for some of the code from previous chapters. The components we tested in this chapter were the simulation world, simulation objects, the collision system, and the `DataManager`.

Further information on unit testing with Python can be found in the documentation for the PyUnit package. In addition, there are many books and online articles devoted to the subject of unit testing in general.

IV Game Programming

12 Game Simulations

Game simulations are the core part of a game application that control how game objects behave and how they interact with each other. Game simulations are different from physical simulations in that the objects contained in them might have no correlation with physical objects, and might not even have physical characteristics. They are more abstract simulations that exist as a controlling layer above the physical simulation.

Game simulations are an area in which Python excels. Building game simulations in Python is fast and easy due to the powerful built-in features of the language. Python's object model is well suited to developing the types of systems used in game simulations, and its dynamic typing can make these systems generic and reusable while remaining compact and elegant.

This chapter examines some components of game simulations that are common in many different types of games. Section 12.1 discusses players and avatars, and includes the first working game example in this book. Section 12.2 discusses game modes and includes another working game example. Section 12.3 introduces the Entity class, Section 12.4 discusses object identification, and Section 12.5 discusses the concept of game events.

12.1 PLAYERS AND AVATARS

In game development, there is a subtle distinction between the person in the real world who actually plays the game and the representation of the player in game world. To avoid confusion, and to establish a standard vocabulary, this book designates the real person as the *player*, and the physical manifestation of the player as the *avatar*.

An avatar is the player's remote presence inside of the game. Avatars in games come in many forms. From the simple paddle in *Pong* to the highly detailed, 3D models in first-person shooters, almost all games include an object that represents the player in the game's virtual world. Avatars are the focus of the player's attention while they are playing and are the objects that are directly influenced by their input. Because of this, games often put a lot of emphasis on making the avatar highly detailed and interesting.

The object in the physical simulation that represents the player might not be the same object as the player itself. It can actually be useful to separate the player from the player's physical presence. A loose coupling between them makes it easier to implement functionality such as possessing another body or changing the appearance of the avatar. It can also be convenient to separate the storage of data related to the player and data related to the player's avatar. This is especially important in online environments where certain data about the player and his account might be persistent beyond the scope of individual game play sessions.

It might initially seem appropriate to make the relationship between player classes and avatar classes an inheritance relationship, with the player being a special class derived from the avatar, which itself derived from a simulation object. However, this structure creates an inflexible binding between the physical object (the avatar) and the abstract object (the player) that can cause problems when implementing more advanced functionality. This structure does not allow the avatar for a player to be changed, and ties the lifetime of the avatar object to the player object.

A more flexible model is a *compositional* relationship where the player object *contains* an avatar object that can be created and destroyed or even replaced without impacting the existence of the player object (see Figure 12.1).

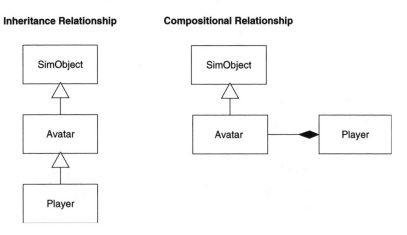

FIGURE 12.1 Inheritance and composition relationships.

In games, player objects might not always represent the actual player at the local machine. Players might be opponents that are controlled by the computer, or in multiplayer games, players might be other real people playing the same game from different computers.

To illustrate the player concept, this section implements one of the simplest possible games, a paddle-and-ball game we will call *PongBall*. This game uses the hoop library that was built in earlier chapters.

The `PongBallGame` **Class**

The core of the PongBall game is the `PongBallGame` class. This class holds all of the game objects and handles some global drawing and input handling functionality (see Listing 12.1).

Listing 12.1 PongBallGame class.

```
class PongBallGame:
    """A game of pong.
    """
    def __init__(self, world):
```

```
            self.world = world
            self.ball = None
            self.message = ""

            self.player = PongPlayer(0, self, "The Player", posX=100)
            self.computer = PongPlayer(1, self, "The Computer", posX=700)

            pyui.desktop.getDesktop().registerHandler(pyui.locals.KEYDOWN,
                                                      self.onKey)
            self.renderer = pyui.desktop.getRenderer()
            self.renderer.setBackMethod(self.draw)

    def update(self, interval, world):
        if self.player.update() == 0:
            self.message = self.player.message
        if self.computer.update() == 0:
            self.message = self.computer.message

    def draw(self):
        engine.drawImage(0,0,800,600, "pongBack.png")
        engine.render()
        engine.drawText("Player Score: %d" % self.player.score,
                                        (180,10),
pyui.colors.yellow)
        engine.drawText("Computer Score: %d" % self.computer.score,
                                        (480,10),
pyui.colors.yellow)
        if self.message:
            engine.drawText(self.message, (300,300),
                                              pyui.colors.white)
            engine.drawText("press escape to exit", (300,360),
                                              pyui.colors.white)
        elif self.ball == None:
            engine.drawText("press space to start", (300,300),
                                              pyui.colors.white)

    def destroyBall(self):
        self.ball.alive = 0
        self.ball = None

    def onKey(self, event):
        if event.key == pyui.locals.K_SPACE:
            if self.ball == None and self.message == "":
                self.ball = self.player.shootBall()
                self.computer.followBall(self.ball)
                return 1
        return 0
```

A single instance of this class is created by the main application when it starts up. The initialization of PongBallGame creates instances of the PongPlayer class for the player and the player's computer-controlled opponent. This class is discussed later in this chapter. The initialization also registers a handler to trap keyboard events, caches PyUI's renderer for drawing text, and sets its draw method to be called by PyUI each frame. Notice that the class has an attribute for the ball, and an attribute called message that is used to hold the currently displayed message and for some primitive state control. We discuss a more generalized game state control system using game modes later in this chapter.

Each frame, the main application calls the PongBallGame update method, which in turn updates each player object. Most times, these update methods will return a non-None value, but if something important happens during the execution of that method, they will return None and the game's message attribute is set.

The PongBallGame's draw method is also invoked each frame. This method draws a background image and then calls the render method of the engine to draw the simulation objects—in this case, the paddles and the ball. Finally, it draws some text on the screen to display the current score and the game state.

The destroyBall method simply makes the current ball disappear and removes the game's reference to it. This will be called by game objects when they need the ball to be destroyed.

The final method of the PongBallGame class is the onKey method. This was registered during the initialization as the handler for keyboard events, so it is invoked when the player presses a key. This method makes the player shoot out a ball object if the game is in the correct state. Notice that it also makes the computer-controlled opponent follow the new ball.

The PongPlayer **Class**

The next class is the PongPlayer class. This class is used to represent the real player and the computer player (see Listing 12.2).

Listing 12.2   PongPlayer class.

```
WIN_SCORE = 3
class PongPlayer:
    """A player in a game of pong. May or may not be
    controlled by an actual user.
    """
    def __init__(self, followMouse, game, name, posX):
        self.followMouse = followMouse
        self.game = game
        self.message = "%s wins!!!" % name
        self.paddle = PongPaddle()
```

```
        self.game.world.addToWorld(self.paddle, posX, 300, 90)
        self.score = 0

    def followBall(self, ball):
        self.paddle.followBall(ball)

    def update(self):
        if not self. followMouse:
            self.processMouse()
        if self.score >= WIN_SCORE:
            return 0
        return 1

    def processMouse(self):
        (dx, dy) = pygame.mouse.get_rel()
        if dy:
            self.paddle.velocityY = -dy*100
        else:
            self.paddle.velocityY *= 0.8

    def shootBall(self):
        ball = PongBall(self.game)
        self.game.world.addToWorld(ball, self.paddle.posX+40,
                                   self.paddle.posY, 15, 600)
        return ball

    def losePoint(self):
        self.score += 1
```

The two types of players behave similarly, the difference being that the computer's paddle must follow the ball automatically, and the real player's paddle must move with the mouse. To deal with this distinction, the constructor is passed an argument called followMouse that tells it whether the object's paddle should be affected by mouse movements. This is implemented in the update method where the processMouse method is only called if followMouse is set. Notice that the velocity of the paddle is negative to convert it from screen space into world space.

This class contains a simulation object for the paddle that is used to hit the ball when the game is running. In this case, the paddle is the player's avatar in the physical world of the game. This example follows the strategy of making the relationship between the player and the avatar a compositional one rather than an inheritance relationship. Notice that the player does not call the update method on the player's paddle. This is because the paddle is a simulation object and its update method will be called by the world during the world's update method.

The shootBall method of the PongPlayer creates a ball object and adds it to the world so that it fires from the position of the player's paddle.

The Simulation Objects

Next are the two types of simulation objects in the game. Since this game only has two types of simulation objects, the example code does not use the DataManager for object creation. Even without the DataManager, simulation objects still require category classes to be initialized from, so we must create two category classes.

```
class PaddleCategory:
    def __init__(self):
        self.mobile = 1
        self.collide = 1
        self.life = 0
        self.threshold = 0
        self.image = "pongPaddle.png"
        self.source = "sourcePaddle.py"

class BallCategory:
    def __init__(self):
        self.mobile = 1
        self.collide = 1
        self.threshold = 0
        self.life = 0
        self.image = "pongBall.png"
        self.source = "sourceBall.py"
```

These simple classes hold the information about how the paddle and the ball behave in the simulation, and how the graphics engine should draw them. They are used in the construction of PongPaddle and PongBall objects. These classes could have been derived from the Category class defined in the DataManager module, but this is not necessary in Python. Unlike in C++, as long as the objects expose an appropriate interface, they don't require a common base class.

In this simple game, the PongPaddle class represents the player's avatar. This class's only real functionality is the ability to follow the vertical component of a specific ball object. To follow the ball, the paddle could snap perfectly to the position of the ball, but that would make it impossible for the player to actually beat the computer. Instead, the paddle changes its velocity so that it moves in the direction of the ball. This gives the player a chance to sneak the ball past.

```
class PongPaddle(SimObject):
    """A Paddle that the user can control or that follows
    the ball.
    """
    ACCURACY = 5
    def __init__(self):
        SimObject.__init__(self, PaddleCategory())
```

```
        self.ball = None
        self.follow = 0

    def followBall(self, ball):
        self.ball = ball
        self.follow = 1

    def hit(self, other, newPosX, newPosY, newFacing):
        if not isinstance(other, SimObject):
            self.setState(self.posX, self.posY, 270, 0)
        return 1

    def update(self, interval, world):
        if self.follow:
            self.velocityY=(self.ball.posY-
self.posY)*PongPaddle.ACCURACY
        return SimObject.update(self, interval, world)
```

Notice that the variable ACCURACY is used as a multiplier on the difference between positions in the update method. The value of this variable can be tuned to make the paddle move faster or slower toward the ball. The higher the ACCURACY, the harder it will be for the real player to beat the computer-controlled opponent.

The final class in the PongBall game is the ball itself. This class is a simulation class that implements a complex hit method to deal with collisions in the game.

```
class PongBall(SimObject):
    """A Bouncing ball.
    """
    def __init__(self, game):
        self.game = game
        SimObject.__init__(self, BallCategory())

    def hit(self, other, newPosX, newPosY, newFacing):
        if not isinstance(other, SimObject):
            if other == collision.WEST:
                # player missed!
                self.game.computer.losePoint()
                self.game.destroyBall()
                return 1

            if other == collision.EAST:
                # computer missed!
                self.game.player.losePoint()
                self.game.destroyBall()
                return 1
```

```
    if other == collision.SOUTH or other == collision.NORTH:
        self.velocityY = - self.velocityY
        return 1

# hit a paddle
self.velocityY = (self.velocityY  + other.velocityY)/2
self.velocityX = -self.velocityX
return 1
```

A number of types of collisions are important for the ball in this game, and the hit method covers them all. A collision with the west (or left) side of the screen means that the real player loses a point and the ball disappears. A collision with the east (or right) side of the screen means that the computer player loses a point and the ball disappears. A collision with the top or bottom of the screen simply makes the ball bounce, and a collision with a paddle makes the ball bounce, but adds some of the velocity of the paddle to the velocity of the ball.

That is it for the PongBall game. Figure 12.2 shows it in action.

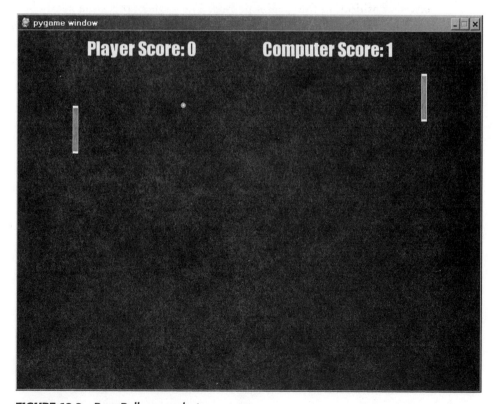

FIGURE 12.2 PongBall screenshot.

ON THE CD

The full code for this game is in the files pongMain.py and pongGame.py on the accompanying CD-ROM.

12.2 GAME MODES

The structure of game applications means that they must operate in different ways at different times. For example, when a game application starts, it might display an introduction sequence and then move into a sequence to attract players until a key is pressed or it detects some activity from the user. This particular type of activity is called an "attract mode" and is common in arcade machines that reside in public places. This is just one of many modes that a game application might be in. Some other possible game modes include:

- Startup mode
- Game Introduction mode
- Level mode
- Game Over mode
- Multiplayer Lobby mode
- High Score Entry mode

Game modes and the transition between them are used for high-level control of what game code is executed at any time. Modes can have standard hooks that are invoked when the game enters a mode, exits a mode, or when the game is running in a mode.

In the example code up to this point, the main Application object has handled ownership of the world object. However, modes can also hold game data, especially game data whose lifetime corresponds to the game staying in a particular mode. This allows explicit cleanup and resource management to be performed when a game exits a mode. With the introduction of modes and a game object (like the PongBallGame class in the previous section), there are more choices about where to store game data. Data that exists for the lifetime of the program should reside in the Application object, data that exists for the duration of a game should reside in the Game object, and data that only exists while the game is in a particular mode should reside in the corresponding mode object.

Mode Classes

The following code is the base class for game modes. It defines a very simple interface for mode classes to implement. Game mode classes in the example code do not necessarily inherit from this as a base class—they might just implement the same interface. In Python programming, this type of loose coupling of interfaces is a common method of reducing dependencies between modules. The code for this class is shown here:

```python
class GameMode:
    """A mode within a game.
    """
    def __init__(self, game):
        self.game = game

    def enterMode(self):
        """invoked when the game enters the mode"""

    def exitMode(self):
        """invoked when the game exits the mode"""

    def update(self, interval, world):
        """invoked each frame"""
```

This class works in conjunction with a Game class. The PongBallGame class in the previous section was an example of a class to represent a game object, and Game class in the following code defines a generalized game class that uses modes for state management. The code for the Game class is shown here:

```python
class Game:
    """A game.
    """
    def __init__(self, displayWidth, displayHeight):
        self.dm = dataManager
        self.mode = None
        self.world = None

    def update(self, interval):
        self.mode.update(interval, self.world)

    def enterMode(self, newMode):
        if self.mode:
            self.mode.exitMode()
        self.mode = newMode

    def setWorld(self, newWorld):
        if self.world:
            self.world.removeAll()
        self.world = newWorld
```

The Breakout Example

To demonstrate the use of game modes, this section implements a game similar to the classic Atari game *Breakout*. This game has an attract mode, a playing mode, and a game-over. It uses the DataManager extensively to manage the different types of simulation classes and even mode classes, so the game is extremely data-driven.

The DataManager for this game is populated with category objects for game modes and for the different types of blocks used in the game. Listing 12.3 shows the code for the data portion of the game.

Listing 12.3

```python
from hoop import datamanager

def initialize(dm):
    dm.initCategory("modes",   initialModeCategories,
BreakModeCategory)
    dm.initCategory("blocks",  initialBlockCategories,
BreakBlockCategory)


############### modes ###################
from breakModes import AttractMode, PlayMode, GameOverMode

class BreakModeCategory(datamanager.Category):
    def __init__(self, name, modeClass):
        datamanager.Category.__init__(self, name)
        self.modeClass = modeClass

    def create(self, *args):
        newMode = apply(self.modeClass, args)
        return newMode

initialModeCategories = [
    # name         modeClass
    ("attract",   AttractMode),
    ("play",      PlayMode),
    ("gameover",  GameOverMode)
    ]


############### blocks ###################
from breakObjects import BreakBlock

class BreakBlockCategory(datamanager.SimCategory):
    def __init__(self, name, mobile, hits, source, image):
        datamanager.SimCategory.__init__(self, name, mobile,
                                    life=0, collide=1, threshold=0,
                                    source=source, image=image)
        self.hits = hits
```

```
    def create(self, game):
        newBlock = BreakBlock(game, self)
        return newBlock

initialBlockCategories = [
    # name  mobile hits  source          image
    ("simple", 0, 1,   "sourceBlock",
"breakImages/breakBlockSimple.png"),
    ("double", 0, 2,   "sourceBlock",
"breakImages/breakBlockDouble.png"),
    ("static", 0, -1,   "sourceBlock",
"breakImages/breakBlockStatic.png"),
    ]
```

The initialize method of the breakData module adds the data for modes and blocks to the DataManager. This allows mode and block objects to be created by game code using the factory method of the DataManager while the game is running. The game object invokes this during its own initialization:

```
self.dm = datamanager.DataManager()
breakData.initialize(self.dm)
```

The BreakModeCategory classes act as a mapping between category names and mode classes that are imported from the breakModes.py file. These classes implement the detailed functionality of each mode and are discussed later in this section. The BreakBlockCategory classes each describe a different type of block object in the game. The most interesting thing about the block types is the different number of hits they can withstand before being destroyed. This is stored as the hits attribute.

Although there are only a small number of block types defined here, it would be easy to define many types of blocks here that have different sizes, images, and lifetime. This type of data-driven definition of game object types is a very powerful tool.

The block itself is a simple object that is derived from the SimObject. The code for this class is shown here:

```
class BreakBlock(SimObject):
    """A block that balls bounce off.
    """
    def __init__(self, game, category):
        SimObject.__init__(self, category)
        self.game= game
        self.hits = category.hits

    def hit(self, other, newPosX, newPosY, newFacing):
```

```
                    if self.hits > 0:
                        self.hits -= 1
                        if self.hits == 0:
                            self.game.mode.removeBlock(self)
                    return 1
```

`Block` objects count the number of times they have been hit and remove themselves from the game when they run out of hits. Notice, however, that blocks with
a hits value of –1 are completely invulnerable to being hit by balls.

The other types of objects in this game are balls and paddles. Since there is only
one type of each of these objects, they are not defined in the `DataManager`. These
classes are defined in the file breakObjects.py on the accompanying CD-ROM, and
their code is shown in Listing 12.4.

ON THE CD

Listing 12.4   breakObjects.py.

```
from hoop import collision
from hoop.sim import SimObject

############### ball ####################
class BreakBallCategory:
    def __init__(self):
        self.name = "ball"
        self.mobile = 1
        self.collide = 1
        self.threshold = 1
        self.life = 0
        self.image = "breakImages/breakBall.png"
        self.source = "sourceBall.py"

############### paddles ####################
class BreakPaddleCategory:
    def __init__(self):
        self.name = "paddle"
        self.mobile = 1
        self.collide = 1
        self.threshold = 0
        self.life = 0
        self.image = "breakImages/breakPaddle.png"
        self.source = "sourcePaddle.py"

class BreakPaddle(SimObject):
    def __init__(self):
        SimObject.__init__(self, BreakPaddleCategory())
```

```
class BreakBall(SimObject):
    MAXSPEED = 250
    def __init__(self, game):
        SimObject.__init__(self, BreakBallCategory())
        self.game = game

    def hit(self, other, newPosX, newPosY, newFacing):
        if other == collision.SOUTH:
            self.game.mode.removeBall(self)
            return 1

        if isinstance(other, SimObject):
            if other.velocityX:
                self.velocityX = (self.velocityX+other.velocityX)/2

        (hitX, hitY) = self.findHitDirections(other,newPosX,newPosY,
newFacing)

        if hitY:
            # hit vertical
            self.velocityY = -self.velocityY
        if hitX:
            # hit horizontal
            self.velocityX = - self.velocityX

        if abs(self.velocityX) < 5:
            self.velocityX *= 5
        if self.velocityX > BreakBall.MAXSPEED:
            self.velocityX = BreakBall.MAXSPEED
        if self.velocityX < -BreakBall.MAXSPEED:
            self.velocityX = -BreakBall.MAXSPEED
        return 1
```

This file defines `category` objects for balls and paddles and defines the `SimObject` derived classes for balls and paddles. The `BreakBall` class defines a `hit` method to handle the ball colliding with the walls and other objects. This `hit` method uses the `findHitDirections` method that was implemented in Chapter 5, "Simulation Concepts," to determine which way to bounce, and it has a special case to remove itself from the world if it hits the south or bottom wall of the screen. The ball also ensures that its speed is capped to the value of the constant `MAXSPEED`. This keeps the ball from traveling at speeds that the player would be unable to keep up with.

The most significant portions of this example are pieces that implement the `Game` class and the various modes that the game uses. The `BreakGame` class implements the `Game` interface that was specified earlier in this section. The code for the `BreakGame` is shown in Listing 12.5.

Listing 12.5   breakGame.py.

```
import breakData

class BreakGame:
    """A game.
    """
    def __init__(self, displayWidth, displayHeight):
        self.mode = None
        self.displayWidth = displayWidth
        self.displayHeight = displayHeight
        pyui.desktop.getRenderer().setBackMethod(self.draw)

        # initialize data
        self.dm = datamanager.DataManager()
        breakData.initialize(self.dm)

        # create the world
        self.world = world.World(displayWidth, displayHeight)

        # enter starting mode
        startMode = \
self.dm.createInstance("attract","modes",self,"welcome")
        self.enterMode(startMode)

    def update(self, interval):
        result = self.world.update(interval)
        self.mode.update(interval, self.world)
        return result

    def draw(self):
        self.mode.draw()

    def enterMode(self, newMode):
        if self.mode:
            print "Exiting mode:", self.mode.name
            self.mode.exitMode()
        self.mode = newMode
        print "Entering mode:", newMode.name
        self.mode.enterMode()

    def setWorld(self, newWorld):
        if self.world:
            self.world.removeAll()
        self.world = newWorld
```

The game is responsible for the creation of the DataManager, the world, and the starting mode. The game class handles switching modes with its enterMode method. This takes a mode object and replaces the current mode with it while calling enter-Mode and exitMode on the appropriate mode objects. There is one issue to be aware of in this case. Because the new mode object is constructed and passed into this method, the order in which the constructors and enter/exit mode calls might not be obvious. The sequence is:

1. The new mode is constructed.
2. exitMode is called on the old mode object.
3. enterMode is called on the new mode object.

This is significant because any work performed in the constructor of the new mode that deals with the world might conflict with work performed in the exitMode call of the old mode! Code needs to be careful to defer any operations that affect the game world to the enterMode call rather than the constructor.

The Attract mode is the mode that the game starts in. This mode displays some moving text over a simple field of stars and waits for the user to press the space bar to start the game. Listing 12.6 shows the code for the AttractMode class.

Listing 12.6 AttractMode.

```
class AttractMode:
    """Attract mode. just sits until the user presses the
    space bar.
    """
    def __init__(self, game, message):
        self.name = "Attract Mode"
        self.game = game
        self.message = message
        self.stars = []
        for i in range(0,100):
            self.stars.append( (randint(0,800), randint(0,600)) )
        self.textY = 30
        self.dy = 200
        self.renderer = pyui.desktop.getRenderer()

    def enterMode(self):
        """Enter the attract mode."""
        pyui.desktop.getDesktop().registerHandler(pyui.locals.KEYDOWN,
self.onKey)

    def exitMode(self):
        """Exit the attract mode"""
```

```
            pyui.desktop.getDesktop().unregisterHandler(pyui.locals.KEYDOWN)

    def update(self, interval, world):
        """move the title text up/down"""
        self.textY += self.dy*interval
        if self.textY < 10:
            self.dy = -self.dy
            self.textY+=self.dy*interval
        if self.textY > 400:
            self.dy = -self.dy
            self.textY+=self.dy*interval

    def onKey(self, event):
        if event.key == pyui.locals.K_SPACE:
            playMode=self.game.dm.createInstance("play", "modes",
self.game)
            self.game.enterMode(playMode)
            return 1
        return 0

    def draw(self):
        engine.clear()
        for (x,y) in self.stars:
            engine.drawRect(x, y, 3, 3, pyui.colors.white)
        engine.drawText("BreakGame Example", (200,self.textY),
                            pyui.colors.red)
        engine.drawText(self.message, (200,self.textY+80),
                            pyui.colors.white)
        engine.drawText("Press SPACE to begin", (200,self.textY+160),
                            pyui.colors.yellow)
```

Notice that the registration and unregistration for PyUI messages is performed
in the enter and exit methods rather than in the constructor. This is to ensure that
there are no conflicts between other modes that also register message handlers.

The main work of the game is performed in the Play mode. This class is responsible for creating all of the game objects and managing the state of the game as it is
running. It also handles user input to move the paddle in response to the mouse.
Listing 12.7 shows the code for the PlayMode class.

Listing 12.7 PlayMode.

```
class PlayMode:
    """Play mode. play the game.
    """
    def __init__(self, game):
```

```
        self.name = "Play Mode"
        self.game = game
        self.world = game.world
        self.dm = game.dm
        self.numBalls = 10
        self.numBlocks = 0
        self.balls = []
        self.renderer = pyui.desktop.getRenderer()

    def enterMode(self):
        """Enter the game play mode. This populates the world with objects.
        """
        pyui.desktop.getDesktop().registerHandler(pyui.locals.KEYDOWN,
self.onKey)

        # create the paddle
        self.paddle = BreakPaddle()
        self.world.addToWorld(self.paddle, 400, 50, 0)

        # create the blocks
        for i in range(0,20):
            simpleBlock1=self.dm.createInstance("simple","blocks", self.game)
            simpleBlock2=self.dm.createInstance("simple","blocks", self.game)
            simpleBlock3=self.dm.createInstance("simple","blocks", self.game)
            doubleBlock=self.dm.createInstance("double","blocks", self.game)
            self.world.addToWorld(simpleBlock1, i*40+20, 520, 0, force=1)
            self.world.addToWorld(simpleBlock2, i*40+20, 240, 0,  force=1)
            self.world.addToWorld(simpleBlock3, i*40+20, 400, 0,  force=1)
            self.world.addToWorld(doubleBlock,  i*40+20, 330, 0, force=1)
            if i % 4 == 0:
                staticBlock = self.dm.createInstance("static", "blocks",
self.game)
                self.world.addToWorld(staticBlock,  i*40+60, 460, 0, force=1)
            self.numBlocks += 4

        # reset relative mouse movement
        (dx, dy) = pygame.mouse.get_rel()

    def exitMode(self):
        """Exit the game. Remove any balls, but leave the blocks.
        """
        pyui.desktop.getDesktop().unregisterHandler(pyui.locals.KEYDOWN)

    def onKey(self, event):
        if event.key == pyui.locals.K_SPACE:
            if self.numBalls > 0:
                self.addBall()
```

```
            return 1
        return 0

    def addBall(self):
        ball = BreakBall(self.game)
        ballX = self.paddle.posX+self.paddle.width/2
        if self.world.addToWorld( ball, ballX, 70, 95, 400):
            self.balls.append(ball)
            self.numBalls -= 1

    def removeBall(self, ball):
        self.world.removeFromWorld(ball)
        self.balls.remove(ball)

    def removeBlock(self, block):
        self.world.removeFromWorld(block)
        self.numBlocks -= 1

    def update(self, interval, world):
        self.processMouse()
        if self.numBalls == 0 and len(self.balls) == 0:
            newMode = self.dm.createInstance("gameover",
                            "modes", self.game, "You Lose!")
            self.game.enterMode(newMode)
        if self.numBlocks == 0:
            newMode = self.dm.createInstance("gameover",
                            "modes", self.game, "You Win!")
            self.game.enterMode(newMode)
        self.paddle.velocityX *= 0.8

    def processMouse(self):
        (dx, dy) = pygame.mouse.get_rel()
        if abs(dx)>0:
            self.paddle.velocityX = dx*100
        else:
            self.paddle.velocityX *= 0.9

    def draw(self):
        engine.clear()
        engine.render()
        engine.drawText("Remaining Balls: %d" % self.numBalls,
                            (20, 20), pyui.colors.green)
        engine.drawText("Remaining Blocks: %d" % self.numBlocks,
                            (570, 20), pyui.colors.green)
        if len(self.balls) == 0:
            engine.drawText("Press space to launch a ball",
                            (260, 280), pyui.colors.yellow)
```

The enterMode method of the play mode sets up the game and simulation for the game to be run. It creates a paddle object, and five lines of block objects that represent each of the types of blocks defined in the DataManager. All of these game objects are added to the simulation world.

The PlayMode object tracks the balls and blocks in the world so it can tell when the game is over. If the player destroys all of the blocks that are destroyable, the player wins. If the player runs out of balls, the player loses. These checks are performed in the mode's update method, which also processes mouse movements. The creation of balls is performed in the addBall method. Notice that the return code of the addToWorld method is checked. This ensures that if a ball cannot be added to world because of a collision with another ball, then the numBalls counter and balls list will not be updated with an erroneous ball.

Finally, the mode's draw method performs the standard engine clear and render, and then draws some text to display status information to the user.

The GameOver mode is invoked when the play mode determines that the game has ended. This mode continues to display the blocks in the simulation world, but only for five seconds. At the end of that time, it switches the game back into the attract mode. Listing 12.8 shows the code for the GameOverMode.

Listing 12.8 GameOverMode.

```python
class GameOverMode:
    """Displayed when the game is finished.
    """
    def __init__(self, game, message):
        self.name = "Game Over Mode"
        self.game = game
        self.message = message
        self.timer = 5
        self.renderer = pyui.desktop.getRenderer()

    def enterMode(self):
        pyui.desktop.getDesktop().registerHandler(pyui.locals.KEYDOWN,
self.onKey)

    def exitMode(self):
        self.game.world.removeAll()
        pyui.desktop.getDesktop().unregisterHandler(pyui.locals.KEY-
DOWN)

    def draw(self):
        engine.clear()
        engine.render()
        engine.drawText("Game Over", (220,200), pyui.colors.red)
        engine.drawText(self.message, (200,260), pyui.colors.white)
```

```
            engine.drawText("Press SPACE to play again", (180,320),
    pyui.colors.yellow)

        def onKey(self, event):
            if event.key == pyui.locals.K_SPACE:
                playMode=self.game.dm.createInstance("play", "modes",
    self.game)
                self.game.enterMode(playMode)
                return 1
            return 0

        def update(self, interval, world):
            self.timer -= interval
            if self.timer <= 0:
                newMode=self.game.dm.createInstance("attract",
                                    "modes", self.game, "Play Again!")
                self.game.enterMode( newMode )
```

This mode's `timer` attribute is decremented each frame until it reaches zero, which causes the `attract` mode to be invoked.

The full code to the Breakout game is in the chapter12/break directory on the accompanying CD-ROM (see Figure 12.3).

ON THE CD

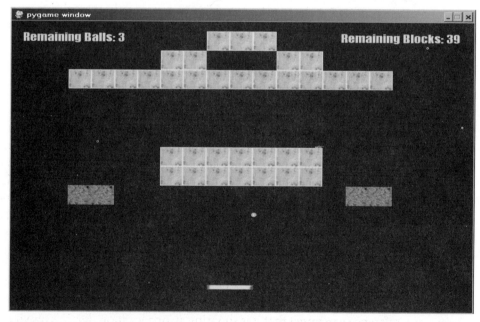

FIGURE 12.3 Breakout screenshot.

12.3 THE ENTITY CLASS

In many game architectures, there is a class that is the main interface between game systems and infrastructure systems. This class is known by various names, including GameObject, GOB, GameEntity, or Entity; or more concretely as Actor, Body, or SimObject. This class pulls together functionality from different infrastructure systems and integrates them into a useful and flexible class from which other game-level classes are derived. It is also used to define the set of common functionality that exists in all game objects so that game objects can interact with each other and make assumptions about the behavior of other game objects.

This section introduces this book's version of that class. We call it the Entity class. As we progress through the next few chapters, functionality is added to this class until it is a powerful and flexible base class for game classes to use.

The initial definition of the Entity class is derived from the Sim class, but doesn't add any new functionality. This acts as a template to which functionality is added throughout this chapter. The initial Entity class is shown here:

```
class Entity(SimObject):
    """Game Entity.
    """
    def __init__(self, category, drawCallback = None):
        SimObject.__init__(self, category, drawCallback)
```

12.4 OBJECT IDENTIFICATION

The idea of object identification might seem at first glance to be trivial, but it can be an important part of a game architecture. The basic concept is that every game object is assigned a unique token that allows it to be identified. A central broker that could be an object factory, or some other class, assigns these identifiers to objects. In addition to giving out identifiers and ensuring that they don't clash, this broker is usually able to look up an identifier and return the object that corresponds to it. In this book, the unique object identifier is called a Game Object Identifier, or GID.

The ability to reference objects by a GID rather than by a direct reference can be very useful. Sometimes, keeping a reference or a pointer to an object is not possible, and in these situations, the GID can be used. For example, when objects are written out to disk for a save game, the disk medium does not support storing pointers or references. If an object has a reference to another object inside it, such as a reference to a target that it is shooting at, or a location that it is moving toward, the GID of this other object can be written out instead of the object itself. When it comes time to load the object back in, the GID can be turned back into a reference, and the game can continue. Multiplayer games can benefit from object identifiers in a similar way. Instead of sending object references over a network, it can be useful to send just GIDs.

Another benefit of object identifiers over references is that in Python, they do not increment the reference count of the corresponding object. There are situations in which this is useful, such as the event system described in the next section.

GIDs can also be used to test if two objects are actually the same game object. This can be a fast and reliable method of determining if two references actually refer to the same or different objects. In cases where the references have been created from different mediums, such as from a save file, or in response to a network message, this might be the only reliable way to tell if they are the same object.

Unique identification is the first piece of functionality that will be added to the Entity class. Listing 12.9 shows how GIDs are generated and how they are assigned to entities as the entities are created. Listing 12.9 shows how the entity manager that controls GIDs are created. Listing 12.10 shows the Entity class that using the entity manager to obtain a unique ID.

Listing 12.9   entityManager.py.

```
import weakref
from hoop.sim import SimObject

## Entity GID management
gLastId = 1000
gAllEntities = weakref.WeakValueDictionary()

def lookupGID(gid):
    return gAllEntities.get(gid,None)

def nextGID(entity):
    global gLastId, gAllEntities
    gid = gLastId
    gAllEntities[gid] = entity
    gLastId += 1
    return gid
```

Listing 12.10   entity.py.

```
from hoop.sim import SimObject
import entityManager

class Entity(SimObject):
```

```
"""Game Entity with unique ID
"""
def __init__(self, category, drawCallback = None):
    SimObject.__init__(self, category, drawCallback)
    self.gid = entityManager.nextGID(self)

def isSame(self, other):
    if isinstance(other, Entity):
        return self.gid == other.gid
    else:
        return 0
```

There are a couple of interesting things about this code. First, it uses global variables! Although the variables gLastId and gAllEntities look like global variables, they are actually module-level variables of the entityManager module. There will only ever be one instance of each of these variables for the lifetime of the entity module, so these variables act like globals, but their scope is defined by the module in which they reside. These are *private* variables that are not intended to be accessed by user code. The lookupGID and nextGID functions should be used instead of accessing them directly.

The second interesting thing about this code is the use of Python's weakref module. The variable gAllEntities is a special type of dictionary that holds *weak* references to the value rather than regular references. The difference between a weak reference and a regular reference is that the weak reference does not increment the reference count of the object, and so does not prevent the object from being garbage collected. This is useful in situations such as the gAllEntities that contains references to all of the Entity instances in existence. If this dictionary were to keep real references to each of these objects, the objects would never be garbage collected and would continue to hold memory even after they should have been released. The weak reference dictionary is a useful technique to avoid this potential problem. When the game releases its last reference to an object, it will be removed from the weak value dictionary automatically.

The isSame method that the Entity class implements can be used when comparing two instances of the class. In this case, we can compare the GIDs of the objects so that uniqueness will be maintained even if there are multiple instances referring to a single game object. There is a built-in Python method called __cmp__ for classes that Python uses as a comparison operator, but that method is used in many cases, some where the customized comparison of GIDs would not be appropriate.

With this code, entities have a unique GID that can be used for many purposes. An example of the use of this code is shown here:

```
import entity
import entityManager

entity1 = entity.Entity(category)
entity2 = entity.Entity(category)

print "GIDs are %d and %d" % (entity1.gid, entity2.gid)
print "Not Equal:", entity1 == entity2

gid = entity1.gid
otherEntity = entityManager.lookupGID(gid)
print "Equal:", entity1.isSame(otherEntity)
```

This code creates two `Entity` instances and confirms that they have different GIDs. It then looks up the GID of one of the instances and makes sure that the GIDs are the same. Notice that the `lookupGID` function is called on the `entity` module, not on an instance of an `Entity`. The output of this code is:

```
$ python entityTest.py
GIDs are 1000 and 1001
Not Equal: 0
Equal: 1
```

It is possible for objects other than `Entities` to also use the unique identifiers system. Any class that includes the line:

```
self.gid = entityManager.nextGID(self)
```

in its constructor can be managed by the entity manager and found by its GID. Game code must be careful when doing this, as the objects that are returned from `lookupGID` might not always be the type of object that the code was expecting.

12.5 GAME EVENTS

Events are a common strategy used in many types of systems, from user interfaces to network servers. They are often used to introduce a layer of indirection between components of systems, to make systems responsive to extensible sets of different inputs, or to make systems that can be easily data-driven. Events can be used to make actions in games occur asynchronously, which can be a powerful tool and can eliminate an entire class of bugs related to object destruction while games are running. The simplest implementation of deferred events is to delay execution of events to the end of the current frame.

Consider the situation in the breakout game where a block is removed from the world. Because that game is very simple, blocks can be removed from the world from within the `hit` method of the ball without causing any problems. However, in more sophisticated games, removing an object from the simulation in the middle of a frame update can cause problems. If another object is using the first object as a target or is path-finding to it, removing the first object from the world could cause the `update` methods of the other object to fail.

To prevent corrupting the current frame with major changes to the state of the world, games often use events to make these changes asynchronous. Instead of removing an object immediately, the object could post a `remove` event for itself, which would be invoked at the end of the frame—after all of the `update` methods for other objects in the simulation have been completed.

A logical extension of delaying events to the end of the current frame is to allow events to be delayed for a specified time before they are invoked. This technique associates a delay with each event and at the end of each frame, only events whose time has expired are invoked. The remaining events stay active until their own time delay expires. This technique can be a very powerful way to control game objects. To implement it in an efficient way, the list of events kept by the system can be sorted in the order in which they are to be called. This allows the system to quickly determine when the remaining events in the list are not ready to be called.

Event-driven game architectures are also appropriate for multiplayer games. Events are a convenient unit for passing information to other computers involved in a multiplayer game. This will be covered in more detail in Chapter 20. Event systems are also useful, as they route all actions through a single channel where they can be logged or recorded for debugging purposes or for playback at a later time.

Event systems in Python are very easy to develop in comparison to many other languages. Python's built-in reflection capabilities make it easy to map types of events to method calls without any intermediary layer. The example code uses Python's built-in `getattr` function to find methods on objects based on event names.

Listing 12.11 is a class for game events. This class encapsulates actions that can be invoked on a specific target object. The `GameEvent` class stores the GID of the `target` object rather than a reference to the object. This reduces the number of dependencies in `event` objects and simplifies operations on events such as saving them or sending them across network boundaries.

Listing 12.11   `event.py`.

```
from hoop import entityManager

class GameEvent:
```

```
"""A game event that is invoked on an object.
"""
def __init__(self, gid, action, callTime, args):
    self.gid = gid
    self.action = action
    self.callTime = callTime
    self.args = args

def __cmp__(self, other):
    return cmp(self.callTime, other.callTime)

def __call__(self):
    """Execute the event's action on the target."""
    target = entityManager.lookupGID(self.gid)
    if target:
        meth = getattr(target, "event_%s" % self.action)
        if meth:
            return apply(meth, self.args)
    else:
        print "ERROR: unable to find object <%d>" % self.gid
```

This class allows events to invoke methods that begin with the prefix "event_" on game objects. It uses the built-in Python function getattr to find the method of the target object that corresponds to the action name passed in, and executes that method with the supplied arguments when the event is invoked. Using an explicit prefix for methods that are callable by events serves a couple of purposes. It provides a degree of security in the code that prevents events from calling methods that should only be invoked in particular circumstances. It also provides an explicit event interface to classes that is highly visible when reading the code. When a developer sees a method with the name event_destroy, it is immediately obvious that this method will be invoked by an event rather than by game code directly.

This class implements two of Python's built-in class methods, __cmp__ and __call__. The __cmp__ method is like a comparison C++ operator and is used by the eventManager class to sort event objects by their call time. In this case, it makes comparisons between event objects use the callTime method. The __call__ method is like a C++ () operator and is used to make GameEvent instances into callable objects—just like built-in functions and methods.

Finally, the GameEvent class uses the entityManager to find the target object to invoke the action on. Since it doesn't keep a direct reference to the target, it supplies the GID to the entityManager, which looks up the Entity object. Not keeping a direct reference to the target object means that the reference count of the target object is not effected by events that are pending on it. In the situation in which the target object is deleted before an event on it is invoked, the lookupGID method will return an empty target and the event will be ignored.

Events are managed by the eventManager module. This module includes functionality to process events and to allow objects to post events. It keeps a list of all the pending events sorted by the call time of each event, and invokes them when the processEvents method is called. Listing 12.12 shows the eventManager code.

Listing 12.12 eventManager.py.

```
from bisect import insort_right
from hoop.event import GameEvent

gEvents = []     # list of events sorted by time
gEventTimer = 0  # current event time (not the real time!)

def postEvent(gid, action, delay, args):
    """Post an event to be processed. insert in sorted order
    """
    event = GameEvent(gid, action, gEventTimer+delay, args)
    insort_right(gEvents, event)
    print event
    return event

def processEvents(interval):
    """process all of the pending events up to the current time.
    """
    global gEvents, gEventTimer
    gEventTimer += interval

    while len(gEvents) > 0:
        # grab the next event
        event = gEvents.pop(0)
        if event.callTime < gEventTimer:
            # time to call it
            event()
        else:
            # not time to call it yet, put it back in the list.
            gEvents.insert(0, event)
            break

def clearEventsFor(gid):
    """clear all pending events for a game object ID.
    """
    global gEvents
    gEvents = filter(lambda e: e.gid != gid, gEvents)
```

The eventManager module uses Python's built-in bisect module to keep the list of events in sorted order. The insort_right method of the bisect module is used to insert new events into the event list in sorted order without resorting the list. It uses a binary search algorithm to find the correct place to insert the new event and is much faster and more convenient than managing the list of event objects manually.

If the list of events wasn't sorted by the event call times, the eventManager would have to iterate through every event in the list and compare their times to the current time each frame. As a general rule of game programming performance, you should avoid performing any operations on a per-frame basis that are not absolutely essential. In this case, moving the event time identification from per-frame to a one-time cost is a worthwhile optimization.

The clearEventsFor method uses Python's built-in filter method to remove entries from the events list that correspond to the GID passed in.

To use this infrastructure, the Entity class can be extended to allow it to conveniently post events. This addition to the Entity class makes it easy for code to post an event to an object. Listing 12.13 shows the updated Entity class.

Listing 12.13   Entity class with event posting.

```python
from hoop.sim import SimObject
import eventManager
import entityManager

class Entity(SimObject):
    """Game Entity with event posting
    """
    def __init__(self, category, drawCallback = None):
        SimObject.__init__(self, category, drawCallback)
        self.gid = entityManager.nextGID(self)

    def isSame(self, other):
        if isinstance(other, Entity):
            return self.gid == other.gid
        else:
            return 0

    def postEvent(self, action, delay, *args):
        return eventManager.postEvent(self.gid, action, delay ,args)

    def clearEvents(self):
        eventManager.clearEventsFor(self.gid)
```

The newly added postEvent method can be invoked to post an event to the object. Internally, this calls the postEvent method on the eventManager to get the event into the system. With this addition, there are two ways to call events: directly on the eventManager, or through an Entity object. Examples of using each of these methods to invoke the event *jump* with a single argument are shown next. These calls will both invoke the method `event_jump` on the target object.

```
# posting event through the event manager
eventManager.postEvent(someObject.gid, "jump", 20)

# posting event with an Entity object
self.postEvent("jump", 20)
```

To demonstrate events in action, the next example application makes simulation objects change their direction and turn rate with events. The `Turner` class is a new class derived from the `Entity` class that posts events to itself once a second. It understands two events: a `turn` event to make it spin, and a `straight` event to make it change direction and travel without spinning. Listing 12.14 shows the code for the `Turner` class.

Listing 12.14   Turner example event class.

```
class TurnerCategory:
    def __init__(self):
        self.name = "turner"
        self.mobile = 1
        self.collide = 1
        self.threshold = 0
        self.life = 0
        self.image = "basic.png"
        self.source = "sourceQuad.py"

class Turner(Entity):
    def __init__(self, category):
        Entity.__init__(self, category)

    def begin(self):
        self.postEvent("turn", random())

    def event_turn(self):
        if self.turnRate > 0:
            self.turnRate = 200
        else:
            self.turnRate = -200
        self.postEvent("straight", 1.0)

    def event_straight(self):
        self.turnRate = 0
        tmp = self.velocityX
        self.velocityX = self.velocityY
```

```
            self.velocityY = tmp
            self.postEvent("turn", 1.0)

    def hit(self, other, newPosX, newPosY, newFacing):
        if isinstance(other, Turner):
            other.clearEvents()
            other.postEvent("turn", 0.1)
        self.velocityX = -self.velocityX
        self.velocityY = -self.velocityY
        return 1
```

When the Turner's `begin` method is called, it schedules a `turn` event for a random time up to one second in the future, and then each time an event is called, it schedules another event for a whole second in the future. This makes the `Turner` alternatively spin, and then switch directions and travel straight. If it collides with another instance, it posts a `turn` event to that instance, which is then processed after a short interval. This causes some erratic but interesting behavior in the objects on screen. To watch the internals of the `eventManager`, the `drawStuff` method of this application displays on the screen the currently active events. The `drawStuff` method is shown here:

```
def drawStuff(width, height):
    engine.clear()
    engine.render()
    y = 10
    engine.drawText( "Time: %.2f Number of Events: %d" %
                        (eventManager.gEventTimer,
len(eventManager.gEvents)),
                        (20, y), pyui.colors.white)
    for e in eventManager.gEvents:
        y += 20
        engine.drawText( "%d %s %.2f" % (e.gid, e.action, e.callTime),
                        (20, y), pyui.colors.white)
```

ON THE CD

The full code for this example is on the accompanying CD-ROM in chapter12. Figure 12.4 is a screenshot of the event test application in action. The list of active events can be seen at the lower left of the screen.

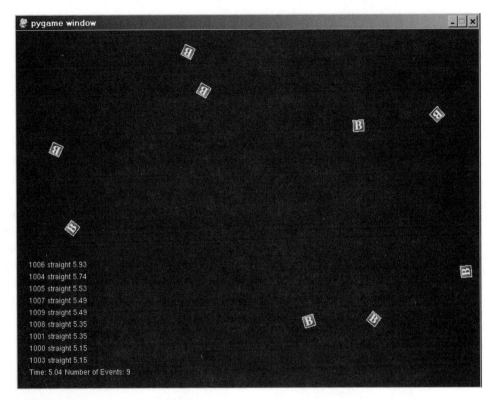

FIGURE 12.4   Event test example.

SUMMARY

This chapter described components of game simulations that are common in many different types of games. It included example implementations of each component in Python and examples of their use with short Python applications. The components discussed were players and avatars, game modes, the Entity class, object identification, and game events.

As examples, this chapter included a working game similar to the old game of Pong that demonstrated the concepts of player and avatars, and a working game similar to the old game of Breakout that demonstrated the concept of game modes. The final example was a test application that showed how events can be used to control game objects. These examples used portions of the hoop library code that has been developed in this book. The main pieces of the hoop library used in these examples were the `DataManager`, the simulation system, the collision system, and the graphics engine.

Some of the code developed in this chapter is general enough in its applicability that it was added to the hoop library. The `Event` class, the `eventManager`, the `Entity` class, and the `entityManager` from this chapter were all added to the hoop library. Note that the `Entity` class created in this chapter is not the final version of that class; it will be extended to include more functionality in the next few chapters.

The topics described in this chapter and the functionality developed in this chapter are some of the key areas where game application differ from other types of applications. These concepts can be used to add structure and extensibility to game applications, and to build a game simulation to be the groundwork for complex and interesting games.

The information about the topics in this chapter is by no means complete. These topics are the subject of continuing development and research in the games industry and in academia. There is great deal of published information available on the topic of event-based systems, and some information about class hierarchies for games. The game mode system described in this chapter is a special case of the finite state machine concept that is covered in more detail in Chapter 15, "Artificial Intelligence."

13 Game Levels

Levels are a common method used in game development to partition the world and the play experience into manageable pieces. Levels serve many purposes in game development, both in terms of design and programming. Levels are used in many types of games, from RTS games to adventure games, and exist on almost all game-development platforms.

Python can be used in conjunction with data-driven systems to make it easy to implement level systems. Python source files can be used as level data, which conveniently eliminates some of the need for custom-level file formats, although it might not be appropriate for large amounts of binary data.

This chapter discusses game levels in general and how to implement a level system in Python. Section 13.1 is a general discussion of levels, and Section 13.2 talks about level data. Section 13.3 shows how to use Python source files as data for levels, Section 13.4 discusses integrating levels and game modes, and Section 13.5 discusses how to use levels for resource management. This chapter also shows how levels can be added to the Breakout game developed in the previous chapter.

13.1 GAME LEVELS

As game worlds can be very large, it is not usually possible to fit the entire world into memory at once. To overcome this limitation, levels can be used to break large worlds into smaller chunks that can be held in memory. This is usually done by having separate *level files* on disk that each contain the data for a particular level. At any stage of the game, the player is always considered to be within one of these levels, so the game only needs to keep the data for that particular level in a quickly accessible form. When a player moves to a new level, the game stops the action and pauses while the data for the new level is loaded. This pause is often disguised by clever game design and by adding additional activities for players to perform between levels, such as shopping or assigning skill points. This strategy allows games to unload objects and resources when a level is completed. It applies to both game objects in the simulation and data resources such as textures and models. In console development, this aspect of levels is especially important because of the restricted memory environments of console machines.

Although levels are a convenient unit of data management, they are usually not the only data used in games. There will often be some data that is persistent across level changes. For example, the player object usually exists for the lifetime of an entire game, not just a single level.

Levels also provide a convenient point for saving games. Some games only save the highest level that the player has achieved instead of the state of all of the objects in the game. This shortcut can significantly reduce the size of save games and the amount of work it takes to save and load games. This is useful optimization for console development where the amount of space available for save games can be very small.

A common addition to the level concept is the concept of tile-sets or texture groups. This is the tactic of grouping media assets into groups of assets that are used in similar situations so that they can be operated on as a larger unit. For example, a game might have multiple levels set in snowy terrain and multiple levels in desert terrain. The developer could define a snow tile-set and a desert tile-set, and then designate each level as either snow or desert. This prevents duplication of assets in level files, and allows the snow-related assets to be reused in multiple levels.

13.2 LEVEL DATA

Almost any type of data can be stored in level files. Some common types include:

- Terrain data
- Mission objectives or level goals
- Starting positions and status of game objects
- Behavioral data (scripts)

Level files are often stored in optimized format so that they can be loaded quickly. These files are sometimes created by special level-editing tools that allow designers or level-builders to create levels with little or no input from programmers.

Python can be used as medium for storing level data. Although not very appropriate for storing large amounts of binary information such as geometry or detailed terrain height-fields, Python can be a good solution for most types of level data. It has a number of advantages over custom file formats:

- Human readable
- Can be compiled to byte-code for fast loading
- No requirement to write a parser or loader
- Easily generated by tools
- Integrates with the programming or scripting language without translation
- Can be used to embed behavioral data
- Can easily be loaded and manipulated outside of the game

13.3 LEVEL DATA IN PYTHON

This section shows how to add levels to the Breakout game example. It uses Python code as the data files, similar to the way in which the graphics engine uses Python code as the source for graphics master objects. This example uses levels to manage the different arrangements of blocks at each stage of the game, to determine how many balls are available at each level, and to control the flow through the levels.

Listing 13.1 shows the contents of a level data file used by the game. This is Python source code that will be loaded by the BreakLevel class.

Listing 13.1 Level data.

```
### second level ###

name = "Medium Level"
blockWidth = 40
blockHeight = 40
legend = { 's': ("simple", "blocks"),
           'd': ("double", "blocks"),
           'x': ("static", "blocks"),
           '.': (None, None)
           }
numBalls = 4
nextLevel = "level3"
data =[
    ".................",
    ".........sss........",
    ".......ss...ss......",
```

```
"...sssssssssssssss...",
"....................",
"....................",
"....................",
".......sssssss......",
".......sssssss......",
"...dd..........dd...",
"....................",
"....................",
"....................",
"....................",
"...................."
]
```

Figure 13.1 is a screenshot of this level from the Breakout game.

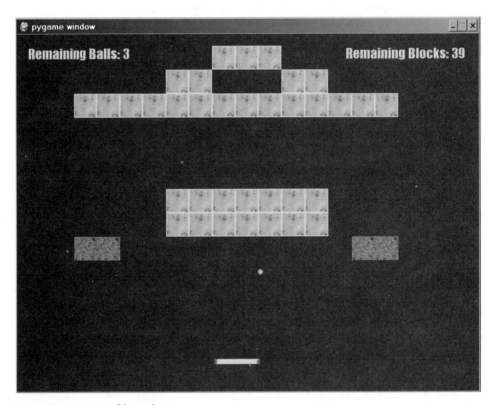

FIGURE 13.1   Level in action.

This data file has a number of elements that are used by the BreakLevel class to populate the game world with objects and for use when drawing. The nextLevel attribute is the name of the level to switch to when this level is completed, and the numBalls attribute is the number of balls available to the player to complete the level. The data attribute specifies which blocks to add to the world and what types those blocks are. The characters in the data attribute of the level module are used by the BreakLevel class to look up category names in the legend that is supplied. These category names are then used to construct objects with the DataManager. Listing 13.2 shows the BreakLevel class.

Listing 13.2 BreakLevel class.

```
class BreakLevel:
    """a level in the breakout example game.
    """
    def __init__(self, game, dataModuleName):
        self.game = game
        levelDict = {}
        execfile(dataModuleName, globals(), levelDict)
        self.__dict__.update(levelDict)

    def populate(self, world):
        """Load the blocks for the level into the world.
        """
        numBlocks = 0
        y = 0
        for line in self.dataModule.data:
            x = 0
            for character in line:
                (categoryName, metaCatName) = self.legend[character]
                if not categoryName:
                    x += 1
                    continue
                newObj = self.game.dm.createInstance(categoryName,
                                          metaCatName, self.game)
                world.addToWorld(newObj, x*self.blockWidth,
                                          world.height-
y*self.blockHeight,
                                          facing=0,force=1)
                if newObj.hits > 0:
                    numBlocks +=1
                x+=1
            y += 1
        return numBlocks
```

The constructor of the `BreakLevel` class uses Python's built-in execfile method to load the data from the file into a dictionary. This is the same method of loading used for graphics source objects in Chapter 8, "Graphics." It also uses the dictionary `update` function to populate the object from the dictionary that was just loaded. In this case, all of the variables that were defined in the level file are set as attributes on the `BreakLevel` object. This conveniently eliminates the need for special code to load data from the level file.

The `populate` method is the core of the `BreakLevel` class. It performs the lookups of characters in the legend, constructs game objects, and adds the objects to the world using the coordinates it keeps track of as it walks though the data. The Y position of each block is subtracted from `world.height` to transform it into world space. Since the data in the module has its origin at the upper left, objects must be transformed like this when they are added to the world so they appear to correspond with the data in the module. Notice that the period character is used to show an empty space that has no block in it. The values in the legend for this character are None so that the `populate` method can know to skip these characters when it is processing the data.

The `level` object itself, which is an instance of the `BreakLevel` class, is held by the `Game` object. The object is held by the game, as its lifetime can span multiple game modes. Similar to a `player` object, it is a game-scoped, rather than a mode-scoped object. In this game, there can only be one `level` object active at a time.

13.4 GAME MODES FOR LEVELS

The modes in the game must be modified to handle levels. This section describes the process of adding more modes to the example game to deal with levels and modifying the main play mode. Two new modes are added to the game to deal with the state before a level starts, and the state after a level is completed. This code also replaces the `playMode` mode from the previous chapter with the `playLevel` mode. Each of these modes is a separate class that is associated with a category in the `DataManager`. The set of modes in the `DataManager` for this section is:

```
initialModeCategories = [
    # name        modeClass
    ("attract",   AttractMode),
    ("preLevel",  PreLevelMode),
    ("playLevel", PlayLevelMode),
    ("postLevel", PostLevelMode),
```

```
("gameover", GameOverMode)
]
```

The new modes are the pre-level mode and the post-level mode. The pre-level mode is entered from the attract mode to begin the game, and then again at the start of each level. It is an opportunity for the player to examine the block layout, and to prepare himself before starting the level. The post-level mode is entered when the player successfully completes a level. It is a place to show summary information about how the player fared in the just completed level before he switches to the next level.

Although the information presented in this example application in these modes is trivial, and very similar for each mode, this does serve to illustrate the concept of associating modes with the level transition process. In a more sophisticated game such as a first-person shooter where each level represents a round in a tournament, the information presented in each of these modes would be more relevant. The pre-level mode could give the player the opportunity to fly through the level to locate the positions of weapons and power-ups, and it could show information such as the team members, opponents, and the victory conditions for the level. The post-level mode could show statistics on numbers of kills, accuracy, and number of deaths for each team member and allow the player to choose to save his progress, or play the level again.

To add some interesting statistics, the example game tracks the number of spare balls at each stage, the number of times the player hits the ball with the paddle, and the total time taken for the level. To contain this information, the example game uses a simple Player class. This class tracks the statistics described previously for the last level played, and for the entire game (see Listing 13.3).

Listing 13.3   Player class.

```
class Player:
    def __init__(self):
        # totals for entire game
        self.totalTime = 0
        self.totalBalls = 0
        self.totalHits = 0
        # totals for last level
        self.levelTime = 0
        self.levelBalls = 0
        self.levelHits = 0

    def addLevelInfo(self, levelTime, levelBalls, levelHits):
        self.totalTime += levelTime
```

```
        self.totalBalls += levelBalls
        self.totalHits += levelHits
        self.levelTime = levelTime
        self.levelBalls = levelBalls
        self.levelHits = levelHits

    def reset(self):
        self.totalTime = 0
        self.totalBalls = 0
        self.totalHits = 0
        self.levelTime = 0
        self.levelBalls = 0
        self.levelHits = 0
```

The PlayMode class implements a method to populate the player data at the end of each level. The following is the code for this updateStats method.

```
def updateStats(self):
    """update the player's stats for this level.
    """
    interval = self.renderer.readTimer() - self.startTime
    winningBalls = self.numBalls + len(self.balls)
    player = self.game.player
    player.addLevelInfo(interval,winningBalls,self.paddle.bounces)
```

The time taken for the level is calculated by using the startTime attribute that is stored when the enterMode of the mode object is invoked. The number of balls still alive is calculated by adding the number of balls left and the number of balls still in play, and the hits attribute is tracked by the BreakPaddle class whenever it is hit by a ball.

The PlayMode class also implements a method to finish the current level and switch to the post-level mode.

```
def finishLevel(self):
    """finish the current level.
    """
    self.updateStats()
    for ball in self.balls:
        self.world.removeFromWorld(ball)
    newMode = self.dm.createInstance("postLevel", "modes", self.game)
    self.game.enterMode(newMode)
```

This is called from the mode's update method that is modified to call finishLevel or gameOver event depending on how the level ends.

```
def update(self, interval, world):
    self.processMouse()

    # check if player has run out of balls
    if self.numBalls == 0 and len(self.balls) == 0:
        self.gameOver("You Lose!")

    # check if all blocks are destroyed
    if self.game.level and self.numBlocks == 0:
        self.finishLevel()

    self.paddle.velocityX *= 0.8
```

The Pre-Level Mode

The pre-level mode is where the level instance is created. This mode is passed the name of a level when it is created. It uses this name to create a BreakLevel instance that populates the world with objects. In a game that uses a large number of game resources in its levels, loading the level data can take a nontrivial amount of time. In situations like this, the pre-level mode can be augmented by a *loading* mode where the user sees a progress bar or splash screen while the level data is loaded into memory. Listing 13.4 shows the code for the PreLevelMode.

Listing 13.4 PreLevelMode.

```
class PreLevelMode:
    """Before a level is started.
    """
    def __init__(self, game, levelName):
        self.name = "Play Level Mode"
        self.game = game
        self.world = game.world
        self.dm = game.dm
        self.renderer = pyui.desktop.getRenderer()
        self.levelName = levelName
        self.numBlocks = 0
        self.numBalls = 0

    def update(self, interval, world):
        pass

    def enterMode(self):
        """Enter the game play mode. This populates the world with
objects.
        """
```

```
        pyui.desktop.getDesktop().registerHandler(pyui.locals.KEYDOWN,
self.onKey)
        self.world.removeAll()
        level = breakLevel.BreakLevel(self.game, name)
        self.numBlocks = level.populate(self.world)
        self.numBalls = level.numBalls
        self.game.setLevel(level)

    def exitMode(self):
        """Exit the game.
        """

pyui.desktop.getDesktop().unregisterHandler(pyui.locals.KEYDOWN)

    def onKey(self, event):
        if event.key == pyui.locals.K_SPACE:
            playMode = self.game.dm.createInstance("playLevel","modes",
                                                    self.game,
self.numBlocks)
            self.game.enterMode(playMode)
            return 1
        return 0

    def draw(self):
        engine.drawImage(0,0,800,600, self.game.level.image)
        engine.render()
        self.renderer.drawRect( (255,255,255,150), (220,150,300,150) )
        engine.drawText("Level: %s" % self.levelName, (280,160),
                                pyui.colors.red)
        engine.drawText("Num Blocks: %d" % self.numBlocks, (280,190),
                                pyui.colors.red)
        engine.drawText("Num Balls: %d" % self.numBalls, (280,220),
                                pyui.colors.red)
        engine.drawText("Press SPACE to begin", (280,250),
                                pyui.colors.yellow)
```

This class is similar to the mode classes defined earlier. The most interesting method is the enterMode method that populates the game world. The draw method of this class draws a background image, renders the simulation objects, and displays some text that describes the level the player is about to play.

Notice that at this stage, there is no paddle in the world and no player input is being processed. Although the game world has been loaded with the objects for the level, the player cannot interact with the game in this mode, as there is no input handling in this mode.

The Post-Level Mode

The post-level mode shows the player's statistics from the current level and for the entire game so far. Listing 13.5 shows the code for the PostLevelMode.

Listing 13.5   PostLevelMode.

```python
class PostLevelMode:
    """Before level is started.
    """
    def __init__(self, game):
        self.name = "Post Level Mode"
        self.game = game
        self.world = game.world
        self.dm = game.dm
        self.renderer = pyui.desktop.getRenderer()

        if game.level.nextLevel != None:
            self.message = "Press SPACE to go to the next level"
        else:
            self.message = "Press SPACE to end the game"

    def update(self, interval, world):
        pass

    def enterMode(self):
        """Enter the post-level mode.
        """
        pyui.desktop.getDesktop().registerHandler(pyui.locals.KEYDOWN,
self.onKey)

    def exitMode(self):
        """Exit the game.
        """
        self.world.removeAll()
        pyui.desktop.getDesktop().unregisterHandler(pyui.locals.KEY-
DOWN)

    def onKey(self, event):
        if event.key == pyui.locals.K_SPACE:
            if self.game.level.nextLevel:
                mode = self.game.dm.createInstance("preLevel", "modes",
                                self.game, self.game.level.nextLevel)
            else:
                mode = self.game.dm.createInstance("gameover", "modes",
                                self.game, "You Win!")
```

```
            self.game.enterMode(mode)
            return 1
        return 0

    def draw(self):
        engine.drawImage(0,0,800,600, self.game.level.image)
        engine.render()
        engine.drawText("Finished Level < %s >"%self.game.level.name,
                        (220,20), pyui.colors.white)

        player = self.game.player

        self.renderer.drawRect( (255,255,255,150), (200,80,300,340) )

        engine.drawText("Total Time:  %d seconds" % player.totalTime,
                        (240,100), pyui.colors.red)
        engine.drawText("Total Balls: %d" % player.totalBalls,
                        (240,130), pyui.colors.red)
        engine.drawText("Total Hits:  %d " % player.totalHits,
                        (240, 160), pyui.colors.red)

        engine.drawText("Level Time:  %d seconds" % player.levelTime,
                        (240,250), pyui.colors.blue)
        engine.drawText("Level Balls: %d" % player.levelBalls,
                        (240,280), pyui.colors.blue)
        engine.drawText("Level Hits:  %d " % player.levelHits,
                        (240, 310), pyui.colors.blue)

        engine.drawText(self.message,(180,520),pyui.colors.yellow)
```

This mode is again very similar to the previous modes. The most interesting piece of it is the draw method. This method displays the player's statistics for the last level, and the statistics for the entire game.

The full code for the Breakout example using levels is in chapter13/break on the
ON THE CD   accompanying CD-ROM.

Figure 13.2 is a screenshot of the second level of the Breakout game.

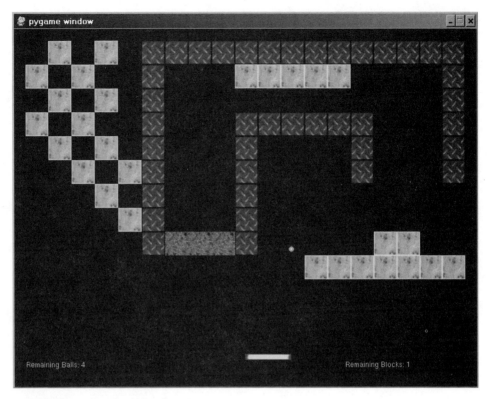

FIGURE 13.2   Breakout level.

13.5 MANAGING RESOURCES WITH LEVELS

Levels can be used as units of resource management to partition large game worlds into manageable pieces. The types of resources that can be managed by this system include textures, models, sounds, and any other kind of level data. A common strategy used by games is to create a manifest of all the resources that are used during a level, and load these resources before the level begins. This avoids hitches in frame rate due to asset loading as the player plays the level. When the level is completed, the game can unload the previous level's set of resources and load the resources for the next level. This granularity can be broken down further into associating resources with game modes within levels, especially if memory is limited on the platform.

To perform this type of loading and unloading, the objects that manage resources must expose an interface to allow game code to load bulk sets of resources, and to flush resources. In the graphics engine described in this book, the GraphicsSource objects and texture objects can be flushed in this way. GraphicsSource objects are kept in the dictionary gSources within the graphics engine so that GraphicsObject instances can be created from them quickly. They should only be removed when the game is flushing all resources, or the game knows that the source object will not be used again—such as when switching to a new level where the types of objects are completely different. The code in the graphics engine to flush all of the source objects is shown here:

```
def flushSources():
    global gSources
    gSources = {}
```

This code clears the dictionary that holds all the source objects. This will cause the reference count on those objects to drop the zero so that they are garbage collected by Python.

Textures are slightly different from source objects. As OpenGL manages textures, the engine only has handles to them. This means that Python's reference counting cannot be used to clean up the textures; it requires an explicit call to the OpenGL function glDeleteTextures. The code to flush all of the textures from the graphics engine is shown here:

```
def flushTextures():
    global gTextures
    if gTextures:
        glDeleteTextures( gTextures.values() )
    gTextures = {}
```

The glDeleteTextures function takes a list of texture IDs. This list is extracted from the values of the gTextures dictionary, and that dictionary is cleared.

Although the example game only uses a handful of resources, these cleanup facilities can easily be added to it. In the pre-level mode, the game calls the flush functions of the engine to clear out the textures and source objects that were created by the previous level:

```
def enterMode(self):
    """Enter the game play mode. This populates the world with objects.
    """
    pyui.desktop.getDesktop().registerHandler(pyui.locals.KEYDOWN,
                                                    self.onKey)
    self.world.removeAll()
    engine.flushTextures()
    engine.flushSources()
```

```
level = breakLevel.BreakLevel(self.game, self.levelName)
self.numBlocks = level.populate(self.world)
self.numBalls = level.numBalls
self.game.setLevel(level)
```

Notice that the flush methods are *after* the code to remove all the objects from the world. If there were objects in the world being rendered when the flush was performed, the textures those objects are using would be deleted and the results of drawing those objects in the next frame would be undefined.

In addition to the capability to flush resources, it is sometimes useful for the game to query the objects that manage resources to find out how many resources are in use. Therefore, corresponding to functions that clear resources, engines often provide functions to retrieve the resources that are in use. In the case of the graphics engine in this book, these functions simply return the keys from the dictionaries that track source objects and textures. The code for them is shown here:

```
def getSources():
    return gSources.keys()

def getTextures():
    return gTextures.keys()
```

SUMMARY

This chapter showed that levels are a useful technique for partitioning game worlds and managing the resources that are used at different times. This chapter described game levels, how they are used in games, how to use levels for resource management, and how to implement a level system in Python using a data-driven game architecture. It included an example application that added level support to the Breakout game developed in Chapter 12.

There has been experimentation in games recently with a concept called *continuous worlds* that make games appear to the player as if they were not segmented into levels. This is intended to give the player a feeling of a large and immersive game world and to prevent the play experience from being broken up by level load screens. Although these systems might appear to be without levels, often, the underlying implementation system still uses something analogous to levels, and the concepts described in this chapter can still be useful background.

14 User Interfaces

ser interfaces (UIs) display information and accept user input. In games, the UI consists of the visual components that are not part of the game or physical simulation. This includes menus, status displays, dialogs, heads-up displays, buttons, and toolbars. Some games have much more complex UIs than others. PC games in particular tend to have complex interfaces due to their larger screen resolutions and combination of mouse and keyboard input.

UIs are an area in which Python excels. Its dynamic typing and loose coupling of interfaces can make it easy to write powerful, generic user code. With a UI library that is written in, or exposes to Python, building game interface components becomes fast and easy. Python UI code also integrates easily with game code and other infrastructure code. Python is also good for rapid development or prototyping of UIs, since it can be written quickly and can integrate with other systems with minimal knowledge of them.

This chapter examines issues involved in developing and using UIs for games. Section 14.1 is a general discussion of game UIs, and Sections 14.2, 14.3, and 14.4 discuss using the PyUI library. Section 14.5 discusses integrating UIs with game simulations, including the observer design pattern, and includes an example. Section 14.6 talks about the issues with rendering text.

14.1 GAME USER INTERFACES

In the area of UIs, games are different from other types of applications. Games often run in exclusive, full-screen mode rather than within a window on the desktop. Moreover, most game windows are special surfaces that use OpenGL, DirectX, or other hardware accelerated drawing. This makes them inaccessible to most UI libraries. These differences mean that most existing UI libraries cannot be used for game development. Games tend to use their own UIs that are tied closely to the game's graphics engine. This was briefly discussed in Chapter 2, "Game Architecture."

UI Drawing

UIs in games are made up of primitives that can be drawn by the graphics engine. These primitives are very similar to the ones in the graphics engine that was developed in Chapter 8, "Graphics." These similarities are not surprising, as they are both concerned with 2D graphics.

The types of drawing primitives used by UIs include:

- Colored rectangles
- Textured rectangles
- Gradient rectangles
- Text
- Clipping areas
- Other geometric primitives (lines, circles, etc.)

Higher-level UI objects such as windows, dialog boxes, menus, and toolbars are constructed from these low-level primitives. The primitives are drawn in a back-to-front order so that the display order is correct on the screen. For example, a dialog box could be constructed from primitives as in Figure 14.1.

Coordinate Systems

UIs tend to exist in screen space where the origin of their coordinate system is the upper-left corner of the screen. This is different from the coordinate system of the graphics engine and simulation in this book. Both the graphics engine and simulation use quadrant one of the Cartesian coordinate system where the origin is at the lower left of the screen. In addition, the simulation world can be larger than the screen when the view window scrolls around the simulation world, but the UI is locked to the size and position of the screen. These differences can make translation between screen space and world space tricky. Code that deals with these differences

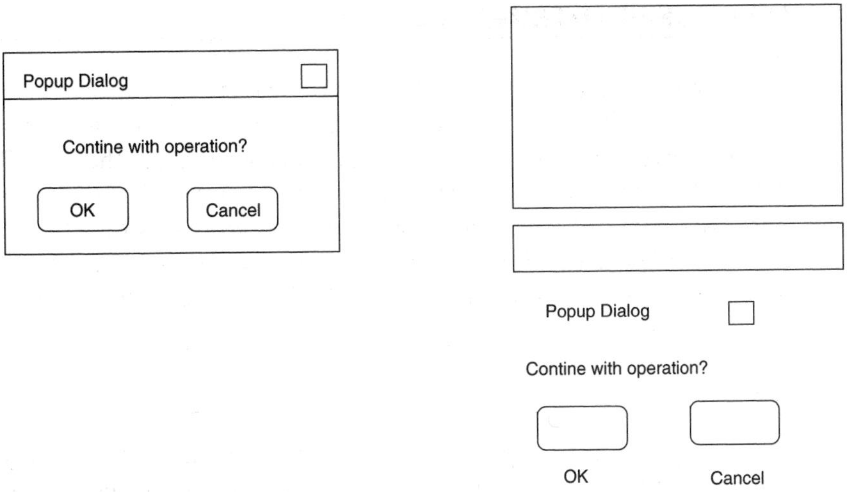

Popup Dialog

Contine with operation?

OK   Cancel

Popup Dialog

Contine with operation?

OK   Cancel

FIGURE 14.1   UI primitives for a dialog box.

must be very careful not to misuse coordinates in the wrong circumstances. Figure 14.2 shows a view port and game object.

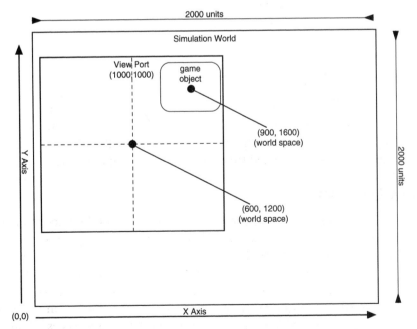

FIGURE 14.2   Screen space and world space.

In Figure 14.2, the game object is at position (900,1600) in the simulation world, and the player's view of the world (1000x1000 units in size) is centered at the position (600,1200) in world space. To transform the game object into screen space, we must find the difference between the position of the view port and the object; in this case, (300,400). Since the position of the view port is actually the center of the screen, we must add to this half of the dimensions of the view port—in this case (500,500)—which gives a position of (800,900). Finally, we must take into account the difference in the Y directions in each of these coordinate systems and subtract the Y value from the Y dimension of the view port. This places the game object at the correct position of (800,100) in screen space. Note that this position might not actually be within the boundaries of the screen.

The reverse of this process is to translate a position on the screen to a position in the game world. This is useful when the user clicks on a location on the screen, and this position must be used as a game world position. In 3D worlds, this is a much more complex problem and is referred to as "picking." In our 2D scenario, we can calculate the position in a similar way to how the reverse translation was done.

First, the Y component of the position is reversed. If the player clicked on the game object that we know is at position (800,100), the Y component of 100 would be subtracted from the height of the screen to give the position (800,900). Then, the half dimensions of the screen are subtracted from it to give (300,400), and then the position of the center of the screen is added to it to give (900,1600). Not coincidentally, this is the original position of the game object in world space.

It is often useful to provide utility functions to transform positions from world space to screen space, and vice versa. Listing 14.1 shows two methods on the graphics engine to perform these translations.

Listing 14.1 UI translation functions.

```
def worldToScreen(self, posX, posY):
    """transform position from world space into screen space.
    """
    screenX = (posX - self.posX) + self.width/2
    screenY = self.height - ((posY - self.posY) + self.height/2)
    return (screenX, screenY)

def screenToWorld(self, posX, posY):
    """transform position from screen space into world space.
    """
    worldX = (posX - self.width/2) + self.posX
    worldY = ((self.height - posY) - self.height/2) + self.posy
    return (worldX, worldY)
```

User Interface Optimizations

The concepts of UIs in games are the same as in non-game applications, but the implementations are quite different. Since games use a continuously running main loop and redraw the screen every frame, the UI must also be redrawn each frame. This is different from non-game applications where the UI is only redrawn when it changes or the user interacts with it. This difference means that game UIs have much more stringent performance requirements than other types of UIs. In some desktop applications such as office suites, it can take literally seconds to redraw the entire window from scratch. This type of performance is not acceptable in games, as it would conflict with the real-time simulation. To allow complex UIs, games use certain techniques to minimize the amount of UI drawing.

Even though the game window is redrawn each frame, many UI elements don't actually change every frame. Status displays such as hit points or gold change much less frequently than each frame, so game UIs can cache optimized versions of these types of elements and redraw them very quickly each frame. When the elements do change, the game can regenerate the optimized version of the element so that it only takes the performance hit infrequently.

There are a number of methods of caching version of UI elements. One way is to render the element to a texture in memory each time it changes, and to draw that texture to the screen each frame. It is much faster to draw a single texture than to build and draw a complex UI element. Another method is to cache the drawing instructions as data in the form of a vertex buffer or a display list. This also allows the interface elements to be drawn very quickly when they are static.

14.2 PYUI INTRODUCTION

Writing a UI library that can draw these primitives, can construct higher-level elements that use these primitives, and is fast enough to be useable in games can be very time consuming. Luckily, the PyUI library exists to provide this piece of functionality. PyUI is an open-source library that was primarily developed by the author of this book. It provides a set of widgets and UI infrastructure for game development in Python and is available for no cost under the LGPL license.

Although PyUI is not as feature rich as commercially available UI libraries, it has most of the features that games require. It is written entirely in Python, so it is easy to use and extend, and it is capable of rendering on OpenGL surfaces. Even if PyUI doesn't meet the UI requirements of a particular game, its source code is fully available, and can be used as inspiration for your own UI system. Figure 14.3 shows PyUI's interactive Python console in use.

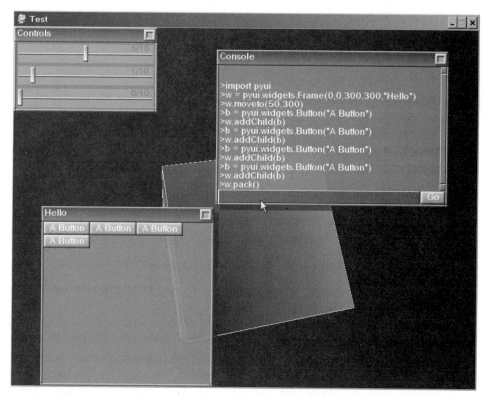

FIGURE 14.3   PyUI screenshot.

14.3 PYUI CONCEPTS

All of the types of components described in this section are implemented completely in Python in PyUI. As such, they can all be subclassed by user code to be extended and have their functionality customized by Python code. While the vocabulary of these concepts is in terms of PyUI, none of these concepts are unique to PyUI, and many are common concepts that exist in many UI libraries.

The Desktop

In any PyUI application, there is single space in which everything is drawn. This is known as the *desktop*. It is a rectangular 2D plane that hosts all the other UI components. In most renderers, the desktop is opaque—it has a background that can contain an image, a fill color, or a view into 3D world. There is a single desktop object, which can be retrieved by calling pyui.desktop.getDesktop().

Widgets

Widgets are interactive UI objects that provide specific functionality. This includes list boxes, edit boxes, scroll bars, buttons, and labels. There are many types of widgets, all derived from the `pyui.widgets.Base` class. Widgets can be contained in other widgets. In some UI libraries, widgets are known as *controls*.

Panels

Panels are a special type of widget that is designed to contain other widgets in an organized fashion. *Layout managers* place widgets within a panel procedurally. There are also special types of panels such as the `TabbedPanel` and `SplitterPanel` for more direct control over the layout of widgets within the panel.

Windows

Windows are higher-level UI objects that also contain widgets. Windows differ from widgets and panels, as they are top-level interface elements that cannot be embedded within other widgets or windows. They are managed by the desktop and can overlap each other, but are still drawn in the correct order. Each window contains a default panel that in turn contains widgets and other panels. Most user code will use frames rather than windows.

Frames

Frames are a special type of Window that has a title bar, a frame border, and functionality for resizing and moving. Similar to windows, frames have a default panel within them, but it is enclosed within the title bar and frame borders. Frames can also have menus within them.

Dialogs

Dialogs are special types of frames that provide specific functionality. For example, there is a `ConsoleDialog`, which is an interactive Python console—it allows text to be entered and executed as Python code, and then displays the resulting output in a scrolling area. Dialogs can be *modal*—they might require that the user interact with them before any other UI interactions can take place. Other types of dialogs that come with PyUI include a Color Picker dialog, a File dialog, and a Standard dialog for simple Boolean responses.

Layout Managers

Layout managers are objects that control the placement of widgets within panels. There are a number of built-in layout managers, such as the GridLayoutManager and BorderLayoutManager that do common types of widget placement. The most powerful layout manager is the TableLayoutManager. This allows widgets to be placed in a grid and to span multiple rows and columns of the grid. Layout managers will position all of the child widgets for their panel when the panel's pack method is called.

Themes

Themes are tools for specifying how the various interface elements are drawn. Each theme has a particular look and feel that makes it appear unique. Themes in PyUI are procedural rather than just data-driven, so themes are able to perform varying and interesting visual implementations.

Renderers

Renderers are components that implement PyUI's renderer interface for drawing and input handling. These are used to interface the generic PyUI core to a specific implementation built on lower-level libraries. The renderer used in all of the examples in this book is the PyGame OpenGL renderer, which is the most fully featured of all the renderers (see Figure 14.4).

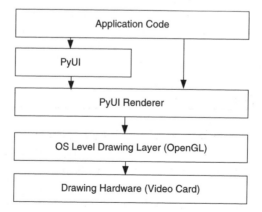

FIGURE 14.4 PyUI renderer architecture.

Fonts

Fonts are the capability to draw text with different character sets, sizes, and effects. Font support in PyUI is delegated to the renderer components. The most robust font support is in the PyGame OpenGL renderer using the built-in FreeType-based font functionality of PyGame/SDL. This renderer allows relatively fast, quality rendering of True-Type fonts under OpenGL.

Events

PyUI event handling was discussed briefly in Chapter 10, "Input." In addition to global event handlers, PyUI allows event handlers to be attached to widgets with the registerEvent method. PyUI events are generated by the renderer and passed to each of the top-level windows. The windows propagate events down their hierarchy of widgets until a handler method returns a positive value to specify that it has consumed the event. Event registration for widgets looks like:

```
self.registerEvent(pyui.locals.LMOUSEBUTTONDOWN, self.onDown)
self.registerEvent(pyui.locals.LMOUSEBUTTONUP, self.onMouseUp)
self.registerEvent(pyui.locals.MOUSEMOVE, self.onMouseMotion)
```

PyUI is just one example of a UI architecture for a game. Many games use a different separation of UI and rendering than PyUI. Instead of doing high-level UI operations *and* low-level widget construction and drawing both in Python, some games develop a UI library in their underlying language (usually C/C++) and expose a wrapper to the scripting language to allow it to control and interact with the UI. While both of these approaches are valid, the UI library in the low-level language provides higher performance, and the pure Python solution provides more flexibility and better integration with the game code that is also in Python.

14.4 USING PYUI

This chapter shows how to use PyUI by implementing an application that allows the user to draw strokes on a canvas. This application allows the user to draw in a number of colors within a frame with the mouse. It uses PyUI's built-in Color Picker dialog to let the user pick custom colors to draw in, and uses PyUI's built-in File dialog to allow the user to load and save sets of strokes. Figure 14.5 is a screenshot of the drawing application in action.

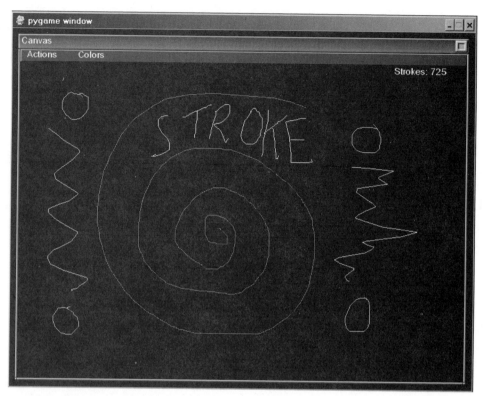

FIGURE 14.5 Stroke application.

This application uses a main loop that is similar to the previous game examples and includes three main classes: CanvasPanel, CanvasFrame, and SaveDialog.

CanvasPanel **Class**

The CanvasPanel class is derived from PyUI's Panel class. It is the area of the screen that can be drawn on and has handlers for mouse operations. It keeps the set of lines that the player has drawn in the *strokes* list. Although this is just a list of straight segments, most of them are so short that they appear to form rounded shapes on the screen. Each entry in the strokes list is a tuple of the start position, the end position, and the color of the stroke. Listing 14.2 show the code for the CanvasPanel class.

Listing 14.2   CanvasPanel class.

```
class CanvasPanel(pyui.widgets.Panel):
    """Panel to track mouse operations and draw strokes.
    """
    def __init__(self):
        pyui.widgets.Panel.__init__(self)
        self.registerEvent(pyui.locals.LMOUSEBUTTONDOWN,
self.onMouseDown)
        self.registerEvent(pyui.locals.LMOUSEBUTTONUP, self.onMouseUp)
        self.registerEvent(pyui.locals.MOUSEMOVE, self.onMouseMotion)

        self.strokes = []
        self.drawing = 0
        self.strokePos = None
        self.color = (255,255,255,255)

    def setColor(self, color):
        self.color = color

    def clear(self):
        self.strokes = []
        self.setDirty()

    def onMouseDown(self, event):
        if self.hit(event.pos):
            self.drawing = 1
            self.finishStroke(event.pos)
            return 1
        else:
            self.drawing = 0

    def onMouseUp(self, event):
        if self.hit(event.pos) and self.drawing:
            self.finishStroke(event.pos)
            self.strokePos = None
            self.drawing = 0
            return 1
        else:
            self.drawing = 0

    def onMouseMotion(self, event):
        if self.hit(event.pos) and self.drawing:
            self.finishStroke(event.pos)
            return 1

    def finishStroke(self, pos):
        """finish a single stroke and add it to the
```

```
            list of strokes.
            """
            windowX = pos[0] - self.window.rect[0]
            windowY = pos[1] - self.window.rect[1]
            endPos = (windowX, windowY)
            print self.windowRect
            if self.strokePos:
                self.strokes.append( (self.strokePos, endPos, self.color) )
                self.setDirty()
            self.strokePos = endPos

        def draw(self, renderer):
            """Draw the strokes and the stroke count.
            """
            renderer.drawRect(pyui.colors.black, self.windowRect)
            engine.drawText("Strokes: %d" % len(self.strokes),(650,50),
                                                        pyui.colors.white)
            for start, end, color in self.strokes:
                renderer.drawLine(start[0], start[1], end[0], end[1],
color)
```

The method `finishStroke` is where the main work of the `CanvasPanel` is performed. In this method, the position of the mouse is converted into coordinates relative to the top-level window with the code:

```
windowX = pos[0] - self.window.rect[0]
windowY = pos[1] - self.window.rect[1]
```

In PyUI objects, the variable `self.rect` holds the object's size and position in absolute screen coordinates. Since drawing for PyUI objects is performed relative to the object's top-level window, these are the coordinates that strokes are stored in so that they match the position of the mouse when they were created.

CanvasFrame **Class**

The `CanvasFrame` class is derived from PyUI's `Frame` class. This class is the container of the `CanvasPanel` and has menus for performing application-level actions. It is the container for the `CanvasPanel` and the menu of operations. It is this class that invokes the dialogs to allow saving and loading of stroke files, and changing the drawing color. Listing 14.3 shows the code for the `CanvasFrame` class.

Listing 14.3   CanvasFrame class.

```
# Colors for color menu
colorData = [
    ("Red",   (255,0,0,255) ),
    ("Green", (0,255,0,255) ),
    ("Blue",  (0,0,255,255) ),
    ("White", (255,255,255,255) ),
    ("Grey",  (128,128,128,255) )
    ]
class CanvasFrame(pyui.widgets.Frame):
    """Frame with a menu that contains the draw canvas.
    """
    def __init__(self):
        pyui.widgets.Frame.__init__(self, 10, 10, 780, 580, "Canvas")
        self.canvas = CanvasPanel()
        self.replacePanel(self.canvas) #replace default panel with
canvas panel
        self.createMenus()

    def frameResize(self, w, h):
        """dont allow resizing"""
        return

    def frameMove(self, x, y):
        """dont allow moving"""
        return

    def frameClose(self):
        """dont allow closing"""
        return

    def createMenus(self):
        self.menubar = pyui.frame.FrameMenuBar()
        self.actionMenu = pyui.frame.FrameMenu("Actions")
        self.colorMenu = pyui.frame.FrameMenu("Colors")
        self.menubar.addMenu(self.actionMenu)
        self.menubar.addMenu(self.colorMenu)
        self.setMenuBar(self.menubar)

        # add color menus
        for title, color in colorData:
            menuItem = self.colorMenu.addItem(title, self.onColorMenu)
            menuItem.color = color
        self.colorMenu.addItem("Custom", self.onCustomColorMenu)

        # add actions
        self.actionMenu.addItem("Open", self.onOpenMenu)
```

```
        self.actionMenu.addItem("Save", self.onSaveMenu)
        self.actionMenu.addItem("Clear", self.onClearMenu)

    ## Menu Handler Functions ##
    def onColorMenu(self, item):
        """this uses the color set on the menu item previously
        """
        self.canvas.color = item.color
        return 1

    def onCustomColorMenu(self, item):
        """this dispays a dialog to choose a color"""
        self.dialog = pyui.dialogs.ColorDialog(self.customColorChosen)
        self.dialog.doModal()
        return 1

    def onClearMenu(self, item):
        """Clears the strokes on the canvas panel."""
        self.canvas.clear()
        return 1

    def onSaveMenu(self, item):
        """Shows a dialog to save the strokes to"""
        self.dialog = SaveDialog()
        self.dialog.doModal(self.onSaveChosen)
        return 1

    def onOpenMenu(self, item):
        """Shows a dialog to load files from"""
        self.dialog = pyui.dialogs.FileDialog(os.getcwd(),
                                    self.onOpenChosen, ".*stk")
        self.dialog.doModal()
        return 1

    def customColorChosen(self, color):
        self.canvas.setColor(color)
        self.dialog.destroy()
        self.dialog = None

    def onSaveChosen(self, filename):
        if filename:
            saveFile = file(filename, 'w')
            pickle.dump(self.canvas.strokes, saveFile)
            saveFile.close()
        self.dialog.destroy()
        self.dialog = None
```

```
def onOpenChosen(self, filename):
    loadFile = file(filename, 'r')
    strokes = pickle.load(loadFile)
    loadFile.close()
    self.canvas.strokes = strokes
    self.setDirty()
    self.dialog.destroy()
    self.dialog = None
```

The `CanvasFrame` class implements the methods `frameResize`, `frameMove`, and `frameClose`. These are methods from the base `Frame` class that allow classes to customize the behavior of the object when it is resized, dragged, or closed with the mouse. In this case, custom implementations prevent the user from performing any of these operations on the `CanvasFrame`.

The `createMenus` method sets up the menus within the frame. It creates a `FrameMenuBar` object and two menus that are attached to it. The Action menu is populated with the actions that users can perform on the application. These actions each invoke a different method on the object. The Color menu is populated from the data in the `colorData` list. This list is used to create five menu items. The loop that creates these menu items adds a "color" attribute to each of the items as they are created. The code:

```
menuItem.color = color
```

actually creates a `color` attribute on the menu item object that was returned from the `addItem` method call on the menu. This would be impossible in C++, but Python allows attributes to be added to objects at runtime! This shortcut means that we don't have to create a special type of menu item that extends PyUI's menu item class, but it does mean that we must be careful to only use the `color` attribute of menu items when we are sure it exists. In this case, the `onColorMenu` method is the only place the `color` attribute of the menu item is accessed.

In addition to the colors from the `colorData` list, the Color menu also has an item to open the built-in Color Picker dialog to allow the user to select a custom color.

SaveDialog **Class**

The next class in the strokes application is the `SaveDialog` class that is derived from PyUI's `Dialog` class. Listing 14.4 shows the code for the `SaveDialog` class.

Listing 14.4 SaveDialog class

```python
class SaveDialog(pyui.dialogs.Dialog):
    """Dialog to accept a filename entered by the user.
    """
    def __init__(self):
        pyui.dialogs.Dialog.__init__(self, w=300, h=100, title="Save
File")
        self.setLayout(pyui.layouts.GridLayoutManager(2,2))
        self.label = pyui.widgets.Label("Filename:")
        self.edit = pyui.widgets.Edit("stuff.stk", self.onEnter)
        self.okButton = pyui.widgets.Button("OK", self.onOK)
        self.cancelButton = pyui.widgets.Button("Cancel",
self.onCancel)

        self.addChild(self.label)
        self.addChild(self.edit)
        self.addChild(self.okButton)
        self.addChild(self.cancelButton)
        self.pack()

    def onEnter(self, edit):
        self.close(self.edit.text)
        return 1

    def onOK(self, button):
        self.close(self.edit.text)
        return 1

    def onCancel(self, button):
        self.close(0)
        return 1
```

This class is a simple dialog that prompts the user to enter a name to save the current set of strokes as. It uses the PyUI's grid layout manager to position the four interface elements into a grid (see Figure 14.6).

The last piece of the stroke application is the main Application object and the startup code. This is very similar to the game examples in previous chapters (see Listing 14.5).

FIGURE 14.6 SaveDialog screenshot.

Listing 14.5 Stroke application main loop.

```
class Application:
    def __init__(self, width, height):
        self.width = width
        self.height = height
        self.renderer = pyui.desktop.getRenderer()

        self.cf = CanvasFrame()

    def run(self):
        running = 1
        frames = 0
        counter = 0
        lastFrame = pyui.readTimer()
        endFrame = pyui.readTimer()

        while running:
            pyui.draw()
            if pyui.update():
                interval = pyui.readTimer() - endFrame
                endFrame = pyui.readTimer()
            else:
                running = 0

            # track frames per second
            frames += 1
            counter += 1

            # calculate FPS
            if endFrame - lastFrame > 1.0:
                FPS = counter
                counter = 0
                lastFrame = endFrame
                print "FPS: %2d" % (FPS )

def run():
    width = 800
```

```
        height = 600
        pyui.init(width, height, "p3d", 0)
        app = Application(width, height)
        app.run()
        pyui.quit()

    if __name__ == '__main__':
        run()
```

The stroke application demonstrates using PyUI to perform common GUI tasks such as menus and event handling. It shows how to customize the behavior of PyUI's standard interface elements and how to use some of the built-in dialogs.

 The full source code to the stroke application is in the file chapter14/ strokeMain.py on the accompanying CD-ROM.

14.5 INTERACTING WITH THE SIMULATION

UIs must be able to display information about the game world, and be able to update when the state of the world changes. One method of achieving this is the observer design pattern. In this pattern, UI elements become observers of game objects so that changes in the state of the game world can be reflected in the UI. This strategy leads to a clean separation of game code and UI code, as the loose coupling between game objects and UI elements doesn't require the game code to be dependent on UI code.

Listing 14.6 is an implementation of a class that can be observed by multiple observer objects. It allows observers to be added and removed, and provides a method to notify observers that the object has changed. Observers that use this system must have a signal method that accepts the observable object.

Listing 14.6   Observable interface.

```
class Observable:
    def __init__(self):
        self.dirty = 0
        self.observers = []

    def addObserver(self, observer):
        self.observers.append(observer)
        self.dirty = 1

    def removeObserver(self, observer):
```

```
        self.observers.remove(observer)
        self.dirty = 1

    def notify(self):
        for o in self.observers:
            o.signal(self)
        self.dirty = 0

    def setDirty(self):
        self.dirty = 1
```

For game objects to be observable, they implement this observable interface. This functionality is general enough to be added to the Entity class. This is done by using multiple inheritance with the Observable class as a *mixin*. This results in an Entity class that is derived from the existing SimObject class and the Observable class. Listing 14.7 shows how this is done.

Listing 14.7   Entity class with observation.

```
from hoop.sim import SimObject
from hoop import eventManager
from hoop import entityManager
from hoop.observer import Observable

class Entity(SimObject, Observable):
    """Game Entity.
    """
    def __init__(self, category, drawCallback = None):
        SimObject.__init__(self, category, drawCallback)
        Observable.__init__(self)
        self.gid = entityManager.nextGID(self)

    def isSame(self, other):
        if isinstance(other, Entity):
            return self.gid == other.gid
        else:
            return 0

    def postEvent(self, action, *args):
        args = (self.gid, action) + args
        apply(eventManager.postEvent,args)

    def update(self, interval, world):
        if self.dirty:
            self.notify()
        return SimObject.update(self, interval, world)
```

Notice that the constructors of both the parent classes are invoked explicitly in the constructor of the GameObject class. This is because Python doesn't invoke constructors of parent classes implicitly—the code must call these constructors or the object will not be properly created.

In this example, if the object's dirty flag is set, the update method of the Entity class calls the notify method of the Observable mixin class to inform observers that it has changed.

The other side of the Observable pattern is the class that is notified when a change occurs, the Observer. The interface for the observer is a single method that is invoked to signal that the observed object has changed state. Since this interface is so simple, we won't create a mixin class for it. In some languages, an Observer mixin class would be required so that the signal method could be bound at compile time. However, Python's dynamic typing allows methods to be discovered at runtime so that simple interfaces like this don't require the creation of entire classes. The observer interface is shown here:

```
def signal(self, subject):
    """the subject has changed state
    """
```

To demonstrate observers in action, we will create a UI window that is attached to a simulation object. This window follows the object around the screen and displays the object's physical information. In the example, the UI window is an observer of the simulation object. Each time the simulation object moves, it sets itself to be dirty, which causes the notify method to be called and the observers to be signaled. Figure 14.7 shows this InfoPanel in action.

FIGURE 14.7 InfoPanel screenshot.

The InfoPanel is a PyUI FormPanel that implements the observer interface described previously. Listing 14.8 shows the code for the InfoPanel.

Listing 14.8   InfoPanel.py.

```python
class InfoPanel(pyui.widgets.FormPanel):
    """Panel to display data about a sim.
    """

    setup = [
        ("int",   "gid",      "Game Id:",   1, None),
        ("float", "posX",     "X Position:", 1, None),
        ("float", "posY",     "Y Position:", 1, None),
        ("float", "velocityX","X Velocity:", 1, None),
        ("float", "velocityY","Y Velocity:", 1, None),
        ("float", "facing",   "Facing:",    1, None)
        ]

    def __init__(self):
        pyui.widgets.FormPanel.__init__(self, InfoPanel.setup)
        self.subject = None

    def signal(self, subject):
        (screenX, screenY) = engine.worldToScreen(subject.posX,
subject.posY)
        self.window.moveto(screenX, screenY)
        self.populate(subject)
```

The list of tuples called setup is the data used to initialize and process the form shown in Figure 14.7. Each tuple in the list describes a single line on the form, including its type, the member variable to map the value to, and the form label. This information is used to generate the form shown in Figure 14.7, without the programmer setting up the widgets and layout manually.

The signal method of the InfoPanel is invoked every frame by the Entity object's call to notify. This method converts the simulation object's position from world space to screen space and moves the window that contains the panel to that position. This makes the window follow the simulation object around the screen.

Each time signal is called, the populate method of the FormPanel is called to update the information the form displays. The populate method is part of PyUI's FormPanel class that updates the values in the form fields from attributes of the object that is passed to it. It extracts data by referring to the names specified in the setup data with which the form was constructed. In this case, the posX, posy, velocityX, velocity, facing, and gid attributes are read from the simulation object and updated in the form.

There are a couple of helper classes for this example. The UCategory is a category class used to create the SimObjects, and the Updater class extends the Entity class to make sure that it is dirty every frame. This ensures that the UI window is refreshed each frame. The code for these classes is shown here:

```
class UCategory:
    def __init__(self):
        self.name = "gob"
        self.mobile = 1
        self.collide = 1
        self.threshold = 0
        self.life = 0
        self.image = "basic.png"
        self.source = "sourceQuad.py"

class Updater(Entity):
    """make sure notify is called every frame.
    """
    def update(self, interval, world):
        self.dirty = 1
        return Entity.update(self, interval, world)
```

While this is convenient and requires little code, it is not very efficient. Each frame, the form is being recreated and redrawn, and the subject object is being queried for data via named attribute lookups. A faster but less generic information display would be more appropriate, but this InfoPanel or something like it could be useful for debugging simulations in real time.

To make the InfoPanel more interesting, we will give it the ability to switch to another simulation object when the mouse moves over that object. This functionality is implemented in the main portion of the example program. First, a handler is added for mouse movement messages in the constructor of the Application object.

```
pyui.desktop.getDesktop().registerHandler(
                pyui.locals.MOUSEMOVE,self.pickObject)
```

Next, the pickObject method is implemented on the Application object.

```
def pickObject(self, event):
    (worldX, worldY) = engine.screenToWorld(event.pos[0], event.pos[1])
    sim = self.world.checkPoint(worldX, worldY)
    if sim:
        self.selected.removeObserver(self.infoPanel)
        sim.addObserver(self.infoPanel)
        self.selected = sim
        self.selected.notify()
```

This method transforms the position of the mouse move into world coordinates, and then uses the collision system to determine if it collides with a `simulation` object. If an object is found, it removes the InfoPanel observer from the currently selected object and adds it to the newly selected object. This makes the InfoPanel switch from its current target and follow the new object around the screen instead of the old one.

ON THE CD

The full code to this example application is in chapter14/simObserver.py on the accompanying CD-ROM.

14.6 DRAWING TEXT

Drawing fonts can be one of the most difficult parts of UI development for games. Unlike non-game applications, games cannot rely on the OS's built-in font drawing functionality, as it is usually too slow and cannot draw to game window surfaces.

Bitmap Fonts

Bitmap fonts are a technique for font rendering that uses a static image containing all the drawable characters for each font. This image is loaded as a texture, and when the engine draws text, it uses offsets into texture to draw each character. Figure 14.8 is an example of a bitmapped font texture.

FIGURE 14.8 Bitmapped font.

While bitmapped fonts are relatively efficient to draw, they do have some limitations. For every font that the game uses, a character texture must be created. This also applies to each variation of the font. Variations such as italics, bold, and underlining each require an independent image that includes the characters drawn in that particular style. The other varying aspect of fonts is their point size, and this can also require independent images. Although it is possible to scale fonts from source images as they are rendered, the visual quality suffers with this approach, especially if the source image or rendered font is small. Therefore, it might be necessary to have character textures for different-sized text. All of these combinations make bitmapped fonts difficult to manage if complex text drawing is required for a game.

In addition, bitmapped fonts usually have to be proportional. This means that all of the characters take up the same amount of horizontal space. Some fonts such as Courier are built to work like this, but most modern fonts are nonproportional. The different characters take up different amounts of space. For example, the character "i" takes up much less space than the character "W" in a nonproportional font. This is necessary, as the characters in the source image are aligned in columns whose positions can easily be calculated during rendering.

Bitmapped fonts can take up large amounts of texture memory. Large-sized fonts especially can require very large textures to hold all of their renderable characters, so games must be careful to limit the number of font variations that are active at any time, and have ways to free font resources that are no longer in use.

Dynamic Fonts

Another text-rendering solution is to use a font-rendering engine to build font textures dynamically, and use these textures as source images for text rendering. This approach is more complicated to implement, but provides a much more flexible solution than bitmapped fonts do.

In this technique, a font-rendering engine such as the built-in GDI font system in Windows, or a third-party library such as FreeType, is used to render characters onto textures to create source images that can be used in a similar way to bitmapped fonts. Fonts created in this fashion usually have font metrics available that enable the application to determine the width and height of each character. This information can be used to build texture coordinates for the source images that allow proportional fonts to be drawn.

While this technique allows fonts to be built dynamically, it still requires a texture in memory for each font and each font variation. The memory usage concerns of bitmapped textures still apply.

PyUI includes an OpenGL True Type font renderer that can be used for text drawing. This font renderer uses the FreeType font-rendering engine that is built into PyGame to render text to OpenGL textures.

Because fonts are usually used for UI drawing, the method on the PyUI renderer to draw fonts expects the renderer to be in screen space. If an application needs to draw text in world space or outside of a PyUI interface element, it becomes a little complicated. Calling the PyUI `drawText` method in these cases causes the text to appear upside down and in the reverse Y position of where it should be. This is because the OpenGL projection matrix is set up for world space rather than screen space. To safely draw text outside of UI elements with PyUI, an addition flag can be passed to the `drawText` method to force it to switch back into screen space just for that particular draw call. The following code shows drawing a flipped PyUI font.

```
pyui.desktop.getRenderer().drawText("text!!!",
            (50,50), pyui.colors.white, self.font, flipped = 1)
```

SUMMARY

This chapter was a discussion of UI concepts and implementation issues for game development. It described general issues with UIs in game development, the PyUI library for game interface development, integrating UIs with game simulations, and font rendering.

As examples, this chapter included a simple drawing application written with PyUI, and a simulation example that attached an observing UI window to objects in the physical simulation.

The observer code developed in this chapter is applicable in many situations and will be added to the hoop library. It is integrated into the `Entity` class so that all game objects are observable by the UI.

15 Artificial Intelligence

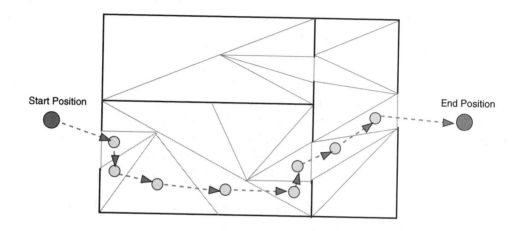

The term *artificial intelligence* is used in games to refer to the techniques involved in controlling the behavior of nonplayer entities. Although the academic field of artificial intelligence is very broad, artificial intelligence in game development is constrained to a more limited scope. Two of the most common artificial intelligence topics are state machines and pathfinding.

Artificial intelligence, and in particular entity behavior, is one of the most common areas of game development where Python is used. Python's flexibility and dynamic language capabilities make it a good candidate for artificial intelligence programming in games. In addition, Python's accessibility to nonprogrammers and game designers makes it a good choice for scripting behavior in games.

This chapter examines the artificial intelligence topics of state machines and pathfinding. Sections 15.1 and 15.2 discusses state machines and show implementations of state machines in Python. Section 15.3 talks about pathfinding concepts, Section 15.4 talks about the A^* pathfinding algorithm, and Section 15.5 shows an implementation of the A* algorithm in Python. Finally, Section 15.6 is a sample application that shows the pathfinding algorithm working in real time.

15.1 BASIC STATE MACHINES

State machines, sometimes called *finite state machines* (FSMs), are a technique to track the behavioral states of game entities, and to control how they transition from one behavioral state to another. They are a simple concept that can be used to create powerful functionality without introducing a lot of complexity into the application code. The game mode system presented in Chapter 12, "Game Simulations," was an example of a state system.

State machines can operate at low levels, such as controlling whether a player is crouching, standing, or lying down, or operate at high levels, such as controlling the strategies of an enemy general. They are a very flexible technique that can be applied to many situations in game development.

One defining characteristic of state machines is that they can only be in a single state at a time—the set of states that they can be in are mutually exclusive. This important characteristic mirrors many situations that exist in the real world, and many situations that are useful for game simulations to model. For example, a character can be running, walking, or standing, but not more than one of these at the same time. A state machine could be created that restricts the character to be in one, and only one of these states.

When implementing a state machine, it is useful to be able to execute code when an object transitions into a state and when an object transitions out of a state. The code that performs this functionality is often called *enter* methods and *leave* methods. As their names suggest, enter methods are invoked when a state is entered, and leave methods are invoked when a state is left to enter another state.

The objects that state machines are used to control are often called *actors*. In games, actors can be avatars, monsters, vehicles, or any other type of game object that requires some form of complex behavior. Figure 15.1 shows the relationship between actors and states.

Listing 15.1 shows an implementation of an actor class that has three states to control its movement. This is the first state machine implementation in this chapter and is relatively simple. We will introduce more functionality to this actor class as we progress through the chapter.

Listing 15.1   Actor class.

```
class SimActor(Entity):
    """an entity that is able to move in a controlled way
    in the physical simulation.
    """
    def __init__(self, category):
        Entity.__init__(self, category)
```

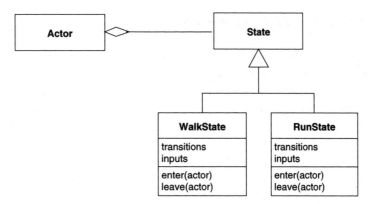

FIGURE 15.1 Actor/state relationship.

```
    self.states = {
        "stop":StopState(),
        "turn":TurnState(),
        "walk":WalkState()
        }
    self.currentState = self.states["stop"]

def setMoveState(self, newStateName):
    newState = self.states.get(newStateName, None)
    if not newState:
        return 0
    self.currentState.leave(self)
    self.currentState = newState
    self.currentState.enter(self)
    return 1
```

The three movement states of this class are stop, turn, and walk. The actor can only be in one state at a time, so the current state of the actor is kept in the member variable currentState. Each of the states that the actor can be in has a corresponding state class. These classes are named StopState, TurnState, and WalkState, and their implementations are shown in Listing 15.2.

Listing 15.2 State classes.

```
class StopState:
    def enter(self, actor):
        actor.velocityX = 0
        actor.velocityY = 0
```

```
                actor.turnRate = 0

        def leave(self, actor):
            pass

    class TurnState:
        def enter(self, actor):
            actor.velocityX = 0
            actor.velocityY = 0
            actor.turnRate = 200

        def leave(self, actor):
            pass

    class WalkState:
        def enter(self, actor):
            actor.turnRate = 0
            actor.setState(
                actor.posX,
                actor.posY,
                actor.facing,
                200)

        def leave(self, actor):
            pass
```

Each of these classes implements an `enter` method and a `leave` method. Although in this case, the `leave` method does nothing, the `enter` methods of each of these classes set the physical state of the avatar to correspond with the behavior of the state. The `setState` method of the actor that is invoked by these classes is the method of the simulation class from which the actor class is derived. The *stop* state makes the actor stand still, the *turn* state makes the avatar turn to the left, and the *walk* state makes the avatar move forward.

This simple code could be used to implement game objects that move around the world in more realistic ways than the bouncing blocks of previous chapters, but there is one major problem with it. This code creates an instance of each state for each actor that is created. This causes many Python objects to be created and uses an unnecessary amount of system memory. One way to deal with this problem is to use the *singleton* pattern to ensure that there is only one instance of each state. Notice that the state classes in Listing 15.2 don't keep any local data. Their methods operate on the actor passed into them, but don't access any member variables of the `self` object. This also fits well with the strategy of making the states into singleton objects.

A convenient way to implement singletons in Python is to use modules instead of classes. As modules are only ever loaded once, and can be accessed easily with the `import` statement, they provide much of the same functionality of singleton classes that must be created in some other languages. We will use this strategy to implement each of the state classes as singletons to improve the memory usage of this example.

The following code shows how the actor class must be modified to deal with the state modules instead of state classes.

```python
from states import stop, turn, walk

class SimActor(Entity):
    """an entity that is able to move in a controlled way
    in the physical simulation.
    """
    def __init__(self, category):
        Entity.__init__(self, category)
        self.states = {
            "stop":stop,
            "turn":turn,
            "walk":walk
            }
        self.currentState = self.states["stop"]
```

The main difference from the previous version of this is that the `self.states` dictionary contains modules rather than instances. This means that no new state objects are created for each actor instance. This dramatically reduces the amount of memory used by this system.

The state modules themselves reside in a module called *states* and are imported by the actor module. These modules are very similar to the state classes presented previously. The code for the walk module is shown here:

```python
# Walk state module
name = "walk"

def enter(actor):
    actor.turnRate = 0
    actor.setState(
        actor.posX,
        actor.posY,
        actor.facing,
        200)
```

```
def leave(actor):
    pass
```

Notice that the functionality of the walk module is identical to the corresponding walk class shown previously, but the methods are implemented as top-level module methods rather than class methods.

The following code shows a simple example of using the actor class implemented here. It creates an actor and makes the actor change states, and then return to the stop state.

```
category = SimCategory("actor", 1, 0, 1, 0, "sourceQuad", None)
actor = SimActor(category)
actor.setMoveState("turn")
actor.setMoveState("walk")
actor.setMoveState("stop")
```

15.2 STATE MACHINE ENHANCEMENTS

There is much more to the topic of state machines than the simple state machine presented in the previous section. This section discusses some more advanced features of state machines including transition validation, inputs, and parallel state machines.

Transition Validation

It can be useful to build rules into the state system to govern the transitions between states. One of the most useful places this can be used is in controlling the posture of characters. Consider a humanoid character in a game that can be in one of a number of posture states. These states include lying down, sitting, crouching, standing, mounted, and potentially others. The character can only be in one of these states at a time, and the states it can transition to from each of the states are different. To animate the character smoothly, it might be impossible to go directly from lying down to standing without going to the crouching state first. These types of rules can be added to the state system by specifying the states that can be transitioned to from each state.

To implement state transition validation, the actor must check if it can perform a transition before it begins each transition. The check must be made before leaving the current state, or the actor could be left with no state at all! The following code shows how transition validation can be added to the actor class from the previous section of this chapter.

```
def setMoveState(self, newStateName):
    # check for valid transition
    if not newStateName in self.currentState.transitions:
        return 0
    # get the new state
    newState = self.states.get(newStateName, None)
    if not newState:
        return 0
    # leave old and enter new
    self.currentState.leave(self)
    self.currentState = newState
    self.currentState.enter(self)
    return 1
```

The line in this code that performs the transition validation uses the transitions variable of the state module to check if the new state is allowed. The transitions variable contains a list of the valid states that can be transitioned to from that state. The following code shows how this could be implemented in a *crouch* state module. Although there might be a *walk* posture in the same set of states, it would be impossible to transition to the walk posture from the crouch state. The character would have to stand before it could walk.

```
# Crouch state

name = "crouch"
transitions = ("liedown", "stand")

def enter(actor):
    # crouch code

def leave(actor):
    pass
```

State Inputs

Another characteristic of state machines is the concept of inputs. The state machine can be set up with a mapping between input events and states. When the state machine receives an input event, it can then automatically perform the transition to the appropriate state. In the case of a game, this would trigger game-specific code. This mechanism can be used to make game objects that can respond to situations in a data-driven way.

Inputs can be driven by data in a similar way to transition validations. To implement state inputs, each state module has a dictionary that maps inputs to the state to be transitioned to. The following code is the crouch state module, including input mapping data.

```
# Crouch state

name = "crouch"
transitions = ("liedown", "stand")
inputs = {
    "up":"stand",
    "down":"liedown"
    }

def enter(actor):
    # do crouch code

def leave(actor):
    pass
```

In this example, the inputs that can be accepted are *up* and *down*. These inputs make the character transition to the *stand* and *liedown* states respectively. For a different state, such as the stand state, the results of the inputs would be different, but the general mechanism remains the same. This arrangement of states could be used in a game where the player presses keys to change a character's posture up and down. The posture of the character could be changed by this state system in response to the user's requests.

The other piece of implementing state inputs is the code in the actor to accept inputs. In this example, this is implemented as a method called moveInput that finds the correct transition and then calls the setMoveState method that already exists on the actor class. The moveInput method is shown here:

```
def moveInput(self, input):
    newStateName = self.currentState.inputs.get(input)
    if newStateName:
        return setMoveState(newStateName)
    else:
        return 0
```

Parallel State Machines

It is often necessary for game entities to have more complex behavior than can be implemented with a single state machine. These entities might require both high-level and low-level behaviors that cannot be represented as mutually exclusive states. Trying to squeeze too many states into a single state machine is a bad idea that leads to an explosion of states that are impossible to manage. Imagine trying to integrate behavior such as walking and turning into the same state machine that controls reactions to the proximity of voices or the type of light that the entity is in. This would lead to many convoluted states with ridiculous names like `walk_novoices_shadow` and `turn_voices_shadow`.

One solution to this problem is to group the states into manageable and mutually exclusive layers, and to use a state machine to handle each layer. This technique is sometimes referred to as *parallel state machines*. Figure 15.2 shows how states can be grouped into layers.

Figure 15.2 shows three layers of states: a movement layer, a posture layer, and a higher-level action layer. These layers each contain a set of mutually exclusive states, even though the total set of states is not mutually exclusive.

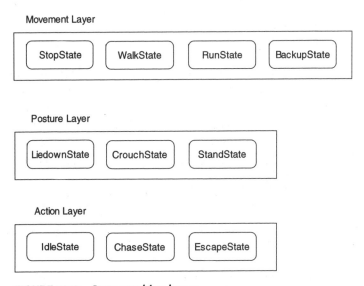

FIGURE 15.2   State machine layers.

Having this many different states makes managing them more difficult. module level, this could lead to a large set of state modules in the state mod rectory that could even have name conflicts. If two layers both have an *id* then where would the module go? One solution to this is to use a directory/ for each layer of states. This would lead to a directory structure like:

```
movementstates/
    __init__.py
```

```
stop.py
    walk.py
    run.py
    backup.py
 posturestates/
     __init__.py
    liedown.py
    crouch.py
    stand.py
actionstates/
     __init__.py
    idle.py
    chase.py
    escape.py
```

h of the directories movementstates , posturestates, and actionstates are
modules because of the __init__.py files that exist in each directory. Each
es in the directories are also modules.
tate modules would then be immune to name conflicts between layers and
easily partitioned for management. Using these state modules would then
uch as:

```
ovementstates import stop, walk, run, backup
sturestates import liedown, crouch, stand
```

 state modules handled, the other side of this problem is managing the
tes at runtime for the actor objects. One method of managing multi-
tates is to introduce a StateManager class. This class has both global
evel responsibilities. The responsibilities for the StateManager class

 state layers as singletons
 set of state modules for each layer as singletons
r, hold the current state in each layer
o be set for actors in each layer
o be sent to actors for each layer

At the
ule di-
e state,
module

 Python implementation of a StateManager class.

eManager class.
_____

tion(Exception):

```python
class StateManager:
    """ I keep the set of global states and layers. Instances
    of me are responsible for tracking states of actors.
    """

    layers = {}

    def __init__(self, actor):
        self.actor = actor
        self.currentStates = {}

    def setInitialState(self, stateName, layerName):
        """Set the initial state of a layer.
        """

        layer = StateManager.layers.get(layerName, None)
        if layer:
            state = layer.get(stateName)
            if state:
                self.currentStates[layerName] = state
                return 1
        raise StateException("No state %s or layer
%s"%(stateName,layerName))

    def setInput(self, input, layerName = None):
        """Send an input event. May be directly to a layer.
        """

        if layerName == None:
            # try each of the current states
            for key in self.currentStates.keys():
                state = self.currentStates[key]
                newStateName = state.inputs.get(input)
                if newStateName:
                    return self.gotoState(newStateName, key)
            return

        # use the specified layer / currentState
        currentState = self.currentStates.get(layerName)
        if not currentState:
            raise StateException("No layer %s" % layerName)
        newStateName = currentState.inputs.get(input)
        if newStateName:
            return self.gotoState(newStateName, layerName)

    def gotoState(self, newStateName, layerName):
        """Set a layer to a state.
        """

        layer = StateManager.layers.get(layerName)
        if not layer:
```

```
            raise StateException("No layer %s" % layerName)
        currentState = self.currentStates.get(layerName)
        if not currentState:
            raise StateException("No curreState for layer  %s" %
ayerName)
        newState = layer.get(newStateName, None)
        if not newState:
            raise StateException("New state %s doesnt exist" %
 vStateName)
        currentState.leave(self.actor)
        self.currentStates[layerName] = newState
        newState.enter(self.actor)
        return 1

    lef getState(self, layerName):
        """Get the state name for a layer.
        """
        state = self.currentStates.get(layerName)
        return state.name
```

ss has a dictionary of layers that is a class-level variable. This dictionary
with the layers and states for the game application. The class-level
propriate, as it maintains the singleton status of the layer and state ob-
ayers variable of the class is a class variable, it exists on the class as a
han on a particular instance of the class. This means that for all in-
tate manager, there will still be only one layers variable.

here is a potential problem with this implementation. What if the
lifferent types of actors that have different state layers? Since the lay-
n the StateManager class itself, the different types of actors using
inager class must use the same set of states! This problem can be
ring classes that are derived from the StateManager class for each
ctors. With this configuration, each type of actor has its own
, and therefore its own set of layers, and the different types of ac-
t with each other.

code shows how a class can be derived from the StateManager
with layers and states. It creates movement and posture dictio-
ers, and adds these layers to the CharacterStateManager class.
ation code should only be executed once by the application
n.

```
es import stop, turn, walk, run
s import liedown, crouch, stand
 import StateManager
```

```
class CharacterStateManager(StateManager):
    pass

movementStates = {
    "stop":stop,
    "turn":turn,
    "walk":walk,
    "run":run
    }

postureStates = {
    "liedown":liedown,
    "crouch":crouch,
    "stand":stand
    }

CharacterStateManager.layers["movement"] = movementStates
CharacterStateManager.layers["posture"] = postureStates
```

In addition to the class-level functionality, an instance of the StateManager
is created for each actor instance. The state manager then tracks the state o
actor in each of the layers that it contains with the currentStates dictionary. T
states are controlled by the gotoState and setInput methods of the state man
These methods are similar to the corresponding methods on the actor class
the previous section. The gotoState method differs, as it requires a layer to be
plied in addition to a state so that the changes can be made to the appro
layer. This version of the setInput method optionally takes a layer also. If n
is specified, the method tries to apply the input to each of the layers in turn
finds a layer in a state that has a use for the input. This allows inputs to be
to actors without knowing which of the actor's internal state layers care ab
particular input.

To use the state manager, the actor class must undergo some changes.
ified actor class is shown here:

```
class SimActor(Entity):
    """an entity that is able to move in a controlled way
    in the physical simulation.
    """
    def __init__(self, category, stateManager):
        Entity.__init__(self, category)
        self.stateManager = StateManager(self)
        self.stateManager.setInitialState("stop", "movement")
        self.stateManager.setInitialState("stand", "posture")
```

```
def setInitialState(self, stateName, layerName):
    self.stateManager.setInitialState(stateName, layerName)

def setInput(self, input, layerName = None):
    return self.stateManager.setInput(input, layerName)

def gotoState(self, stateName, layerName):
    return self.stateManager.gotoState(stateName, layerName)
```

most of the state code moved into the StateManager class, the actor be-
simpler class. It enters into default states when it is created, and has two
ugh methods to apply inputs and states to layers in the state manager. No-
that the setInput method can be invoked without a layer parameter. Fig-
ows the relationships between the actor, state manager, and state classes.

class
the
hese
ager.
from
sup-
priate
layer
until it
posted
but the

A mod-

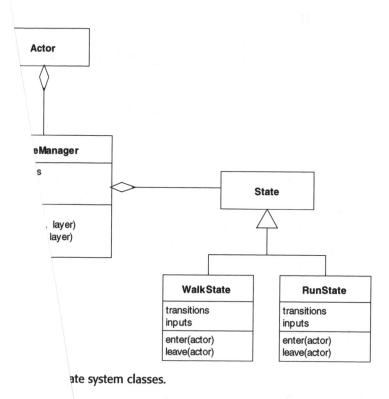

ate system classes.

Externally, this enhanced actor class is used in a very similar way to the actor class from the previous section. The only difference is that state changes require the layer name to be supplied. The following example sends the *faster* input to the actor.

```
class Character(SimActor):
    def __init__(self, category):
        cm = CharacterStateManager(self)
        SimActor.__init__(self, cm, category)

category = SimCategory("actor", 1, 0, 1, 0, "sourceQuad", None)
character = Character(category)
character.gotoState("crouch", "posture")
character.setInput("faster")
```

15.3 PATHFINDING CONCEPTS

Pathfinding is an element of game development that is also considered to be under the umbrella of artificial intelligence. In addition to state machines, it is another method of controlling the behavior of entities in game worlds in ways that make these entities appear to be acting with intelligence and purpose. There are many ways that pathfinding is applied in different types of games. In real-time strategy games, it is used to help vehicles navigate the map and follow waypoints. In first-person shooters, it helps enemies hone in on the player and move around the level, and in some role-playing games that use a point-to-move interface; it can be used to control the movement of the player's avatar. In general, pathfinding is used to help game entities move around in their environment. Figure 15.4 shows an example of finding a path around some obstacles.

There are two main aspects of implementing pathfinding in games. The first is representing the environment in a way that can be used for pathfinding, and the second is the process of finding paths in an efficient and correct way within this context.

World Representations for Pathfinding

A representation of a game environment for pathfinding must meet certain requirements. For correctness, it must include representations of all the objects that can block the path of pathfinding entities, and this must constantly be updated as objects move within the environment. This is very similar to the collision system discussed in Chapter 7 "Collision Detection." Often in games, the pathfinding

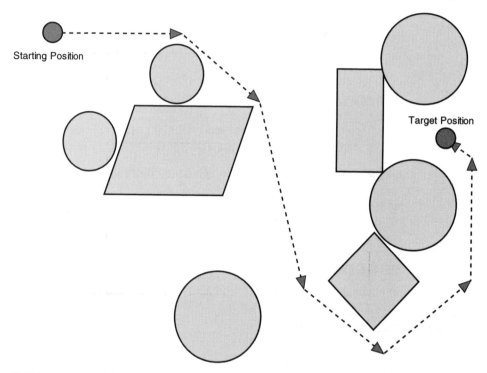

FIGURE 15.4 Pathfinding example.

system uses the collision systems heavily. For performance, the pathfinding representation of the world must allow certain types of collision tests to be performed
very quickly. This is important because pathfinders tend to perform many collision
tests as they find their way around obstacles in the world.

There are a number of common types of world representation used for
pathfinding in games. The simplest is a grid—similar to the collision grid from
Chapter 7, but usually at the level of granularity that corresponds to the size of
moving objects in the game. Objects in the world *stamp* a mask onto the grid at
their location. This mask could take up multiple squares and can be rotated based
on the facing of the object. When objects move, they unstamp and restamp the
mask on the grid. Figure 15.5 shows an object and its mask on a collision grid.

Another type of world representation is waypoints. This is a higher-level representation of the world that must usually be handcrafted for each area of the
world. In this representation, the world contains special objects called *waypoints*
that are located in important places for path finding. These can then be used to navigate around the world in a more abstract way than a collision grid. For example, a

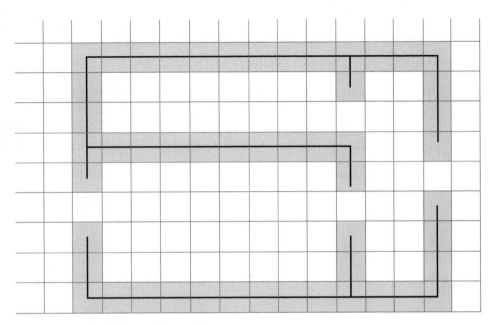

FIGURE 15.5 Collision grid stamping.

house might have waypoints at doorways, and in the center of rooms. This allows the pathfinding algorithm to use these waypoints with the assumption that they are already in appropriate places. This technique is sometimes used in conjunction with more sophisticated techniques such as avoidance and line-of-sight checking that handle the lower-level details of movement between waypoints. Figure 15.6 shows an example of waypoints on a map.

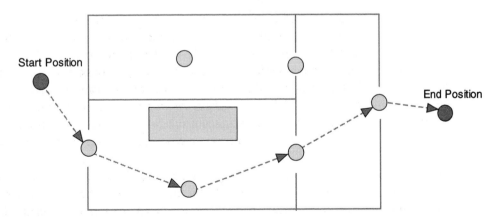

FIGURE 15.6 Waypoints.

Another type of world representation is *navigation meshes*. This is conceptually similar to the collision grid, but instead of being a grid of tiles, the surface that pathfinding is performed on is a collection of triangles of arbitrary sizes. Instead of navigating the tiles in a grid, the pathfinding algorithm navigates the triangles in the navigation mesh. This type of system can be integrated with the art pipeline so that levels or pieces of the environment created by artists can have navigation meshes automatically generated for them by a tool. In a 3D game, this technique can be used to constrain pathfinding to 2D by creating 2D navigation meshes for the 3D objects and levels in the world. Figure 15.7 shows an example of a navigation mesh.

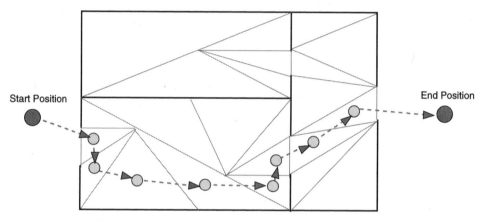

FIGURE 15.7 Navigation mesh.

15.4 THE A* ALGORITHM

The most common pathfinding algorithm for games is known as the A* (*A-star*) algorithm. There has been a large amount of literature written about this algorithm and ways to enhance it for speed, and for more natural-looking paths. It was originally created for use in grid-based worlds, but the algorithm can be applied to other world representations. This section discusses how the A* algorithm works and shows a number of examples. The next section shows how to implement the algorithm in Python.

Figures 15.8, 15.9, 15.10, and 15.11 are some examples of A* pathfinding at work. They show a simple path with no obstructions, a path around a simple obstruction, a path into a concave object, and a path into a complex object, respec-

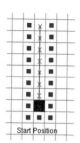

FIGURE 15.8 Path-finding example 1.

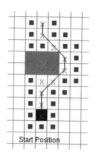

FIGURE 15.9 Path-finding example 2.

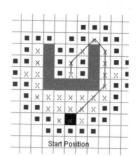

FIGURE 15.10 Path-finding example 3.

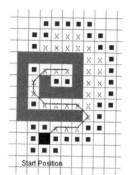

FIGURE 15.11 Path-finding example 4.

tively. Although the problem in each of these cases might appear to be subtly different, the A* algorithm can be used to solve all of these paths.

In Figures 15.8 through 15.11, the filled tiles are blocked by obstacles, and the black line shows the path from the start position to the goal. Two more pieces of information in these diagrams show some of the internal workings of the pathfinder. The Xs show tiles that have been explored by the algorithm, and the tiles with smaller squares in them have not been explored by the algorithm. These are the first clues to how the algorithm works.

The A* algorithm operates on *nodes*. In the case of a grid like the one in Figures 15.8 through 15.11, each node is a grid square, but the nodes could be waypoints, or some other type of world representation. As it runs, the algorithm must be able to find out certain pieces of information about each node. In the simplest case, it must be able to tell if a node is blocked, how expensive it is to reach the node from the starting point, and how expensive it is to reach the goal position from the node.

Blocked nodes are nodes that the pathfinder cannot enter or cross. This is usually because some game object is occupying the associated space in the game world. The functionality to check if a node is blocked is sometimes separated from the pathfinder to reduce dependencies. Often, a method is passed into the pathfinder that it will call to determine if a particular node is blocked.

The cost to reach a node from the starting position is not just the simple distance from the starting position to the node position. This cost must take into account all of the nodes that must be traversed to reach the node location. In some cases, such as Figures 15.10 and 15.11, this path can be far from straight. The cost is usually built incrementally as the algorithm processes nodes. The cost to any node can be calculated as the cost to its parent node plus the cost to the node's location from the parent node. This sometimes uses a callback-based system similar to blocked nodes. If nodes have differing costs, then the pathfinder must call back into the application to discover the traversal costs as the algorithm runs. This particular technique can be used for terrain systems that effect movement speed. This cost is sometimes referred to as the *g* value of the node.

The cost to reach the goal position cannot use node traversal, as the nodes to the goal position haven't been discovered yet. This cost is just the distance to the goal position from the node position. As an optimization, the distance squared is sometimes used instead of the actual distance to avoid performing expensive square root operations. The performance of the function that calculates this cost can have a significant impact on the performance of the pathfinder, as it might be called many times during a single path-find operation. This cost is sometimes referred to as the *h* value of the node.

With this information, the pathfinder can assign a *fitness* to each node. The fitness of a node is the cost from the starting position, plus the cost to the goal (f = g + h).

The pathfinder keeps two lists of nodes. The *open list* contains nodes that have not been explored yet, and the *closed list* contains nodes that have already been explored. When the pathfinder begins a task, it pushes the starting node into the open list, and the closed list is empty. It then begins a loop of finding the fittest node in the open list, exploring each of the adjacent nodes of the fittest node, and pushing unblocked nodes onto the open list, until it finds the goal.

In a grid-based system, adjacent nodes are the grid tiles that touch the current tile. The algorithm might use all eight adjacent tiles, including the diagonal tiles, or it might just use the four tiles that are not on the diagonal directions. In other types of world representations, adjacent nodes might be calculated in another way, such as visibility from the current node, or touching in a mesh.

When the pathfinder finds the goal node, it is not quite finished. To find the actual path, it must construct a path back through the nodes until it reaches the starting position.

This section describes a basic version of A* algorithm. There are enhancements to it to produce more accurate paths and for optimizations that are not included in this description.

15.5 IMPLEMENTING A* IN PYTHON

This section shows how to implement the A* algorithm in Python. Python might not be the ideal language for the iteration intensive task of pathfinding, but it can be sufficient for medium-sized pathfinding tasks if used wisely. The idea of allowing callbacks for certain aspects of the task such as checking the blocked status of nodes, and calculating the cost of traversing nodes, can be used to keep the pathfinder separate from game code so that it could potentially be replaced with an optimized version in another language if that becomes necessary.

The pathfinder uses a Node class to represent nodes in the pathfinding algorithm. Listing 15.4 shows a simple implementation of a node.

Listing 15.4 The Node class.

```python
class Node:
    """A node used by the pathfinder.
    """
    def __init__(self, x, y):
        self.x = x
        self.y = y
        self.parent = None
        self.children = []
        self.f = 0  # "fitness" - total cost
        self.g = 0  # cost of getting to this point
        self.h = 0  # distance from the goal

    def initialize(self, distance):
        self.h = distance
        self.f = self.h + self.g

    def __cmp__(self, other):
        return cmp(self.f, other.f)

    def setParent(self, parent):
        self.parent = parent
```

This class has the attributes g, h, and f that were discussed in the previous section, and some utility methods. The __cmp__ method is included so that Node classes can be kept in a sorted list managed by Python's built-in bisect module. As this method helps to ensure that nodes in a list are sorted by their fitness, this is an optimized way of keeping track of the *best* node found so far.

The following code shows the beginning of a Pathfinder class in Python.

```python
class Pathfinder:
    """Pathfinder that works on a grid.
    """
    directions = [(-1,0),  (1,0),
                  (0,-1),  (0,1),
```

```
                       (1,1),   (-1,-1),
                       (1,-1),  (-1,1) ]

    COST = 1

    def __init__(self, cbValid):
        self.startX = 0
        self.startY = 0
        self.goalX = 0
        self.goalY = 0
        self.cbValid = cbValid
        self.running = 0
        self.clearNodes()

    def clearNodes(self):
        self.openSet = []
        self.closedSet = []
        self.best = None

    def setupPath(self, startX, startY, goalX, goalY):
        """setup the pathfinder to find a path.
        """
        if self.cbValid(goalX, goalY) == 0:
            return 0

        self.startX = startX
        self.startY = startY
        self.goalX = goalX
        self.goalY = goalY
        self.clearNodes()

        startNode = Node(startX, startY)
        distance = (goalX-startX)**2 + (goalY-startY)**2
        startNode.initialize(distance)

        self.openSet.append(startNode)
        self.running = 1
        return 1
```

As discussed in the previous section, the pathfinder keeps a list of open nodes and a list of closed nodes. To begin a pathfinding operation, the setupPath method is called with the locations of the starting position and the goal. This method clears the pathfinder's internal node lists and creates a starting node that is pushed onto the open list. Notice that the distance calculation is optimized to not use the square root of the calculated distance. This method does not actually perform the pathfinding operation; it just makes sure that the pathfinder is in the correct state for it to happen.

In this class, the iterative piece of executing a pathfinding operation has been exposed to the application so that it can be controlled by the application. This aspect of this class is used later in this section when the sample application uses it to make pathfinding visible in real time.

Therefore, instead of a method to run the pathfind operation to completion, the Pathfinder class has a iteratePath method that is called by the application until it returns 1 to indicate the goal has been found. The iteratePath method is shown here:

```python
def iteratePath(self):
    """Run a single iteration of the path finder.
    """
    if self.running == 0:
        return 0
    if len(self.open) == 0:
        return 0

    # get the fittest node
    self.best = self.openSet.pop(0)
    self.closedSet.append(self.best)
    if not self.best:
        return 0

    # check if we found the goal
    if self.best.x == self.goalX and self.best.y == self.goalY:
        return 1

    # explore the new node
    for d in self.directions:
        x = self.best.x + d[0]
        y = self.best.y + d[1]
        if  self.cbValid(x, y):
            self.processAdjacent(self.best, x, y)
    return 0
```

The iteratePath method finds the fittest node from the open list by popping the first element. This works because the open list is already sorted by the fitness of nodes. It loops through each of the directions from the directions set and calculates the adjacent tile positions. If the cbValid method tells it that the tile is not blocked, it goes ahead with processing that adjacent position. The processAdjacent method is where much of the work of the algorithm is performed. This method and its helper method findNode are shown here:

```
def processAdjacent(self, parent, x, y):
    """calculate the costs and parent for a node.
    """
    g = parent.g + self.COST
    checkNode = self.findNode(self.openSet, x, y)
    if checkNode:
        # update node with better route
        parent.children.append(checkNode)
        if g < checkNode.g:
            checkNode.setParent(parent)
            checkNode.g = g
            checkNode.f = g + checkNode.h
    else:
        checkNode = self.findNode(self.closedSet, x, y)
        if checkNode:
            # update the cost of this node
            parent.children.append(checkNode)
            if g < checkNode.g:
                checkNode.setParent(parent)
                checkNode.g = g
                checkNode.f = g + checkNode.h
        else:
            # unknown node. create it
            newNode = Node(x,y)
            newNode.setParent(parent)
            newNode.initialize((self.goalX-x)**2 + (self.goalY-y)**2,
g)
            bisect.insort_right(self.openSet, newNode)

def findNode(self, checklist, x, y):
    """check if a node is in the list"""
    for node in checklist:
        if node.x == x and node.y == y:
            return node
    return None
```

The processAdjacent method of the pathfinder performs a number of different operations depending on the status of the node that was passed to it. If the position has never been seen before, a new node object is created and added to the open list. If the node is already in the open list or closed list, the cost of the node is compared with the cost of the reaching the node through the current parent node. If the new parent node path is cheaper, then the node is updated to use the cost of the new, most efficient path to that location. This is demonstrated in Figure 15.12.

The dark line in Figure 15.12 shows a path that was found to the target location that is more efficient than the previously found path that is shown with a dotted

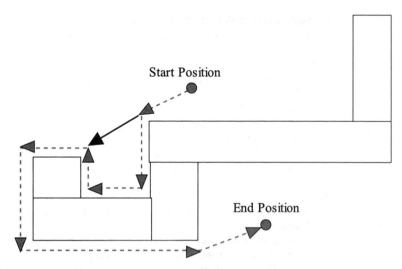

FIGURE 15.12 Finding a better path.

line. In this case, the cost of the node at that location is updated to reflect this new more efficient path.

Finally, the pathfinder has a method to traverse the set of nodes backward from the goal location to find the optimal path through the nodes to the starting position. This is the final step of the process, and in this case, the finishPath method must be called by the application after the iteratePath method returns a zero value.

```
def finishPath(self):
    """traverse backwards to build the correct path
    """
    node = self.best
    path = []
    while node:
        path.insert(0, (node.x, node.y) )
        node = node.parent
    self.running = 0
    return path
```

The full code to the pathfinder class is on the accompanying CD-ROM in
ON THE CD chapter15/path/pathfinder.py.

15.6 VISUALIZING THE PATHFINDER

Now that we have a working pathfinder in Python, this section develops a sample application to show the pathfinder working in real time. This application was used to generate Figures 15.8, 15.9, 15.10, and 15.11 from earlier in this chapter. It allows the user to block tiles on a grid with the mouse, and then to execute pathfinding operations from the starting position to any location on the grid. Figure 15.13 is a screenshot of the application performing a complex pathfinding operation.

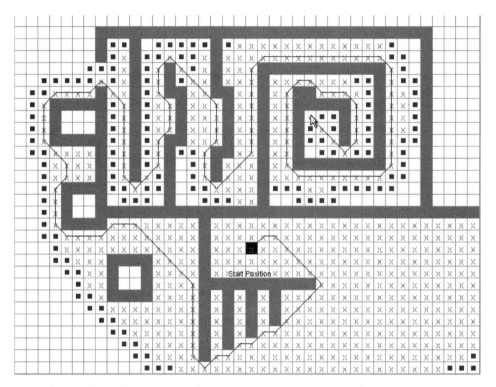

FIGURE 15.13 Pathfinder application.

This application shows how the pathfinder can be controlled by an external application and how the callback method for determining blocked nodes can be implemented. The start of the PathGame class is shown here:

```
tileSize = 20

class PathGame:
    def __init__(self, width, height):
        self.width = width
        self.height = height
        self.path = []
        self.blocked = []
        self.startX = 20
        self.startY = 10
        self.path = None
        self.drawing = 0
        self.pathfinder = Pathfinder(self.isBlocked)
        desktop = pyui.desktop.getDesktop()
        desktop.registerHandler(pyui.locals.LMOUSEBUTTONDOWN,
                                self.onLeftClick)
        desktop.registerHandler(pyui.locals.RMOUSEBUTTONDOWN,
                                self.onRightDown)
        desktop.registerHandler(pyui.locals.RMOUSEBUTTONUP,
                                self.onRightUp)
        desktop.registerHandler(pyui.locals.MOUSEMOVE,
                                self.onMouseMove)
```

The initialization of this class registers mouse handlers, and creates a pathfinder object. Notice that the pathfinder is passed the isBlocked method as its validation method. This method is shown here:

```
def isBlocked(self, x, y):
    if (x,y) in self.blocked:
        return 0
    if x < 0 or y < 0:
        return 0
    if x >= self.width/tileSize or y >= self.height/tileSize:
        return 0
    return 1
```

The isBlocked method checks the list of blocked tiles and checks that the position passed from the pathfinder is not outside of the bounds of the screen. Remember that this method will be called by the pathfinder many times as it processes nodes. The handlers for the mouse operations are shown here:

```
def onRightDown(self, event):
        self.drawing = 1
        return 1

    def onRightUp(self, event):
```

```
                self.drawing = 0
                return 1

        def onMouseMove(self, event):
            (posX, posY) = engine.screenToWorld(event.pos[0], event.pos[1])
            if self.drawing:
                tile = (posX / tileSize, posY / tileSize)
                if not tile in self.blocked:
                    self.blocked.append(tile)
            return 1

        def onLeftClick(self, event):
            (posX, posY) = engine.screenToWorld(event.pos[0], event.pos[1])
            self.pathfinder.setupPath(self.startX, self.startY,
    posX/tileSize, posY/tileSize)
            self.path = None
```

These methods allow the player to block tiles when holding down the right mouse button, and the initiate a pathfinder operation by clicking the left mouse button.

The PathGame class has an update method that is called every frame by the main application. This method calls the iteratePath method of the pathfinder 10 times each frame so that the path and nodes being processed can be seen unfolding across the screen. The update method is shown here:

```
def update(self, interval):
    for i in range(0,10):
        result = self.pathfinder.iteratePath()
        if result:
            self.path = self.pathfinder.finishPath()
```

If the iteratePath method returns a nonzero value to indicate that it has found the goal, the update method calls the pathfinder's finishPath method to complete the process and retrieve the path that has been calculated.

The final piece of the PathGame class is the code to draw the status of the pathfinder as it runs. The draw methods are shown here:

```
def draw(self, width, height):
    # draw grid
    for i in range(0,40):
        ii = i*tileSize
        engine.drawLine(0, ii, width, ii, pyui.colors.grey)
        engine.drawLine(ii, 0, ii, height, pyui.colors.grey)
    for x,y in self.blocked:
```

```
            engine.drawRect( x*tileSize, y*tileSize,
                             tileSize, tileSize, pyui.colors.red)

        if self.pathfinder.openSet:
            # draw the open nodes
            for node in self.pathfinder.openSet:
                self.drawTile(node.x, node.y, pyui.colors.blue)

            # draw the closed nodes
            for node in self.pathfinder.closedSet:
                self.drawTile(node.x, node.y, (110,110,50,255), "X")

            # draw the path if there is one
            if self.path:
                oldX, oldY = (self.startX,self.startY)
                for (x,y) in self.path:
                    engine.drawLine( oldX*tileSize+10,
                                     oldY*tileSize+10,
                                     x*tileSize+10,
                                     y*tileSize+10,
                                     pyui.colors.black)
                (oldX, oldY) = (x,y)

        # draw starting location
        engine.drawRect( self.startX*tileSize,
                         self.startY*tileSize,
                         tileSize, tileSize,
                         pyui.colors.black)
        engine.drawText( "Start Position",
                         (self.startX*tileSize-30, self.startY*tileSize-
50),
                         pyui.colors.black)

def drawTile(self, x, y, color, letter = None):
    if letter == None:
        engine.drawRect(x*tileSize+6,
                        y*tileSize+6,
                        tileSize-12,
                        tileSize-12, color)
    else:
        engine.drawText( letter, ( x*tileSize+5, y*tileSize-10), color)
```

This code draws all of the entries from the pathfinder's open list and closed list, and if there is a currently active path, it draws a line that follows the path.

 The full code for the pathfinder application can be found on the companion CD-ROM in chapter15/path/pathMain.py.

SUMMARY

This chapter described two major aspects of artificial intelligence programming commonly used in games. The topics of state machines, world representations for pathfinding, and the A* algorithm were discussed in detail, including implementations in Python of each of these components.

This chapter included the pathfinding visualization example that showed how the A* algorithm works and allows the user to experiment with the algorithm in many different ways.

The topic of artificial intelligence is not restricted to game development. There is a large amount of academic interest in this subject that extends to cover additional areas such as genetic algorithms, neural nets, cellular autonoma, flocking behaviors, and artificial life simulations. While research from the academic world sometimes seeps into games, there is usually a large gap between the types of work being done in these two camps. However, game developers have produced a large amount of material related to artificial intelligence topics in books and magazines.

16 Procedurally Generated Game Content

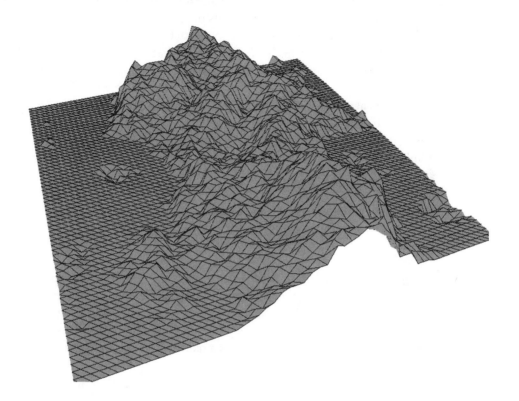

As fantastic virtual worlds, part of the appeal of games is the new realms that they show us, and the amazing locations and creatures that reside in them. These things must be painstakingly created by developers, artists, and designers, and are often referred to as *game content*. Game content must be carefully crafted to provide a balanced and consistent play experience and must fit within constraints set by designers and the technical limitations of the game engine. For these reasons, game content is time consuming and expensive to produce, and the scope of games is often limited by the amount of content that can be produced for them.

As described in Chapter 6, "Data-Driven Simulations," data-driven systems are often used to help alleviate this limitation, and to provide larger sets of content for games. Another technique used to increase the scope of the content in games is *procedural content generation*. This technique can be used in conjunction with data-driven systems to create systems that generate game content. This content can be made to fit the very specific requirements of game designers and can automatically be constrained to work within the scope of the game's technological constraints. The procedural aspect of this technique means that many variations of the content can be created. This can expand the scope of games and increase their replayability.

In role-playing games, this technique is used to generate huge varieties of weapons and armor for players to equip their characters with, and to generate variations of a basic set of monsters for players to battle against. In strategy and simulation games, this technique is used to generate landscapes for games to be played on and to randomize the behavior of enemy generals. In action games, it is used to vary the placement of enemies in maps, and the actions of these enemies during battles. All of these techniques give a game greater depth and give players more play time for their money.

Python has a built-in module for generating random numbers. This module provides a variety of useful functions that can be used for procedural content generation.

This chapter examines predictable random number generation and some topics in game development that used this technique. Section 16.1 discusses Python's random module and how to use it, Section 16.2 discusses terrain generation, and Section 16.3 implements a terrain generator in Python. Section 16.4 discusses random name generation and implements a name generator in Python.

16.1 PREDICTABLE RANDOM NUMBERS

All of these uses of procedural content generation use random numbers at their core. Random numbers are a deep mathematical topic that has been the subject of much research due to its applications in cryptography and security. In game development, the chaotic qualities of random numbers that make them important for cryptography are less relevant, but random numbers are still an important topic that has many uses.

The Python distribution includes a random module for generating random numbers. It provides a diverse set of randomization functions that can be used for procedural content generation. In addition to being able to generate random numbers, Python's `random` module can perform some other useful tasks, such as shuffling lists, and choosing a random element from a list.

Random Number Distributions

The `random` module can generate random numbers in a number of different distributions, including exponential, uniform, and Gaussian distributions. Figure 16.1 shows random lines generated in each of these distributions.

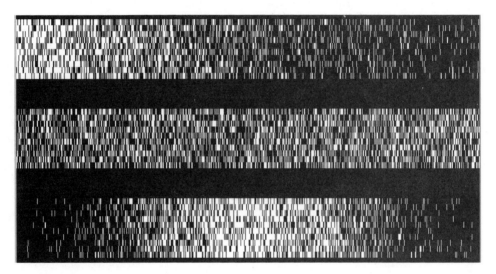

FIGURE 16.1 Random distributions.

The first set of random lines is an exponential distribution. The grouping of lines are thicker at the left and becomes exponentially thinner further to the right. The second set of random lines is uniformly distributed. Although the lines are randomly placed, the distribution of lines within the set is the same in all areas. The third set of random lines is in a Gaussian distribution. At the center of the set, called the *mean*, the lines are densely clustered, but farther out, the density of lines decreases with a steep curve. Random numbers in a Gaussian distribution like this follow a bell curve based on the *standard deviation* of the set. Both the exponential and Gaussian distributions can be used to generate game content where the rarity of particular items in the set, such as powerful magic items, is different from more common items.

Predictable Random Numbers

Sometimes, it is desirable for random numbers to be truly chaotic and random, but in other cases, it is desirable for random numbers to actually be predictable. In game development, it can be useful to be able generate random numbers from a *seed* and have the set of random numbers be the same for that seed every time it is used. For example, if an application sets the random seed to be a certain value, and then generates 10 random numbers, it should be able to reset the seed at any time and generate those same 10 numbers. In addition, another machine running the same application should be able to produce the same results from the same seed! Although these numbers are random, they are predictable and reproducible. This property can be very useful in game development.

The most common use of predictable random numbers in games is in the generation of game worlds. Being able to generate a guaranteed set of random numbers from a single seed value can act as a type of compression of game data. Instead of storing thousands of different maps, a game could use an algorithm that creates viable game maps from a set of random numbers. This technique can be applied to the creation of many types of game worlds, including terrain, dungeons, and galaxies. It allows games to expose very large worlds that would have been impossible to craft by hand and that would never be able to fit on the distribution media. Later in this chapter is an example of generating terrain using predictable random numbers.

Another use of predictable random numbers is in multiplayer games. If all of the participating machines in a multiplayer game have the same random number generator and the same seed, they can produce random results that are guaranteed to be the same. For example, instead of sending all of the terrain data of a level to each participant in a game, each client could be sent just a seed value and then could generate the terrain data themselves. This technique greatly reduces the volume of network traffic required for the game.

Using the random Module

The random module has been used trivially in some of the previous examples in this book. This section examines it in more detail. The functionality of the random module is implemented by the Random class. Although many of the methods of the module can be invoked on the module directly, these versions of the methods are actually accessing an internal instance of the Random class kept by the module.

When creating a Random instance, a seed can be supplied. The following code shows how to create a random instance.

```
import random
r = random.Random(42)
print r.random()
```

The random method is the core of Python's random module. It returns a floating-point number in the range of 0.0 to 1.0. Most of the other functionality in the module is implemented in terms of this method.

Listing 16.1 shows how the random module can be used to generate numbers of different distributions. This code was used to generate Figure 16.1.

Listing 16.1   Random distributions.

```
class GaussDistribution:
    def __init__(self, numValues, min, max):
        self.rand = random.Random()
        self.values = []
        average = (min+max)/2
        for i in range(0,numValues):
            self.values.append( self.rand.gauss( average, average/3) )

class UniformDistribution:
    def __init__(self, numValues, min, max):
        self.rand = random.Random()
        self.values = []
        for i in range(0,numValues):
            self.values.append( self.rand.uniform(min, max) )

class ExpoDistribution:
    def __init__(self, numValues, min, max):
        self.rand = random.Random()
        self.values = []
        average = (min+max)/3
        for i in range(0,numValues):
            self.values.append( self.rand.expovariate( 1.0/average) )

class NumApp:
    def __init__(self, width, height):
        numValues = width*5
        min = 0
        max= width
        self.distributions = []
        self.distributions.append( GaussDistribution(numValues, min,
max) )
        self.distributions.append( UniformDistribution(numValues, min,
max) )
        self.distributions.append( ExpoDistribution(numValues, min,
max) )

    def draw(self, width, height):
        y = 100
```

```
for d in self.distributions:
    count = 0
    for v in d.values:
        engine.drawRect(v, y, 1, 10, (255,255,255,255) )
        count += 1
        if count % 400 == 0:
            y += 10
    y += 50
```

Each of the distribution classes `GaussDistribution`, `UniformDistribution`, and `ExpoDistribution` generates a list of random numbers between a minimum and maximum range as the member variable `values`. These random numbers are used by the `NumApp` class to draw lines showing their distribution.

The full listing of the random number distribution example can by found on the accompanying CD-ROM in chapter16/numbers.py.

ON THE CD

16.2 TERRAIN GENERATION

One common application of predictable random numbers is in the generation of terrain. This section discusses terrain generation using the mid-point displacement. It implements a height field generator in Python.

Terrain is an important element of many games. In real-time strategy games, terrain is a critical part of each map, as it impacts where and how units can move, and the location of bases and raw materials. In flight simulators and other combat sims, terrain is part of the realistic backdrop used to create immersion, and in strategy games such as *Civilization*® and *SimCity*™, coping with the strengths and weaknesses of the map's terrain is a huge part of the games' challenge.

Terrain differs from the simulation objects discussed in previous chapters, as it is generally static and is much larger than individual simulation objects. It also doesn't fit into the collision system described in Chapter 7, "Collision Detection." Different types of collision detection are required for terrain than are required for simulation objects. In general, terrain differs from simulation objects in terms of creation, storage, collision detection, and rendering.

Height Maps

In games, terrain is often represented as a height map. This consists of a 2D grid of points, with each point having a height. Connecting the points into a mesh creates a contiguous landscape that looks and plays like real terrain. In addition to height, the points can also have other information associated with them, such as texture or terrain type. Sometimes, the type of terrain is derived from the height of the point. For example, heights of less than a certain value might be considered water, other heights considered land, and the highest points considered mountains. This type of categorization of the terrain by height can lead to terrains mapped with textures in realistic ways. Figure 16.2 shows a 3D height map drawn with quads and lines.

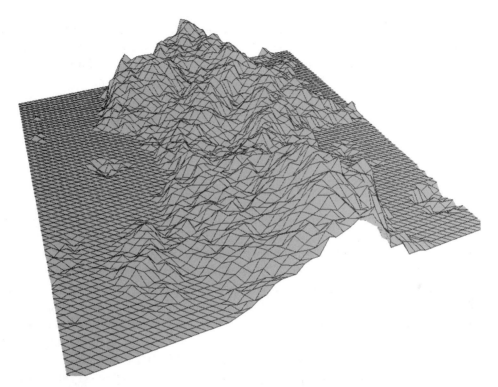

FIGURE 16.2 Height map.

The height map has flat areas at the sides, and a long mountain range that runs through the center. Although this is just a randomly generated set of points connected by lines, it exhibits recognizable natural landscape-like features. This similarity between generated terrain and real terrain is a great trick for game developers!

Mid-Point Displacement

Mid-point displacement is a technique of modifying a flat height map in an iterative fashion to create a set of terrain that resembles terrain in the real world. Although height maps in games are usually two-dimensional, it is easy to demonstrate the concept of mid-point displacement with a one-dimensional line. Figure 16.3 shows how mid-point displacement can be used to modify a line into a silhouette of a mountain range.

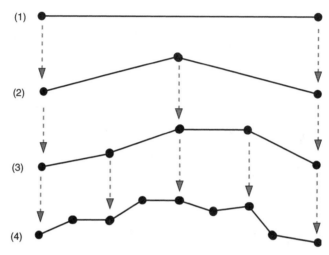

FIGURE 16.3 One-dimensional height map.

Figure 16.3 begins with a straight line (1) between two points. The second line (2) includes the points from the first line (shown by arrows), but adds another point in the center of the space between the two points. This new point is moved a random amount up or down—in this case up, hence the name "mid-point displacement." This process is repeated through two more steps so that more points are added and displaced, but the higher-level structure of the line remains constant. By the fourth iteration (4), the line has transformed into something that could be seen as the silhouette of a mountain range.

This same technique can be applied to a grid of lines in three dimensions to produce realistic looking 3D terrain. One algorithm for implementing mid-point displacement on dimensional height maps is the *Diamond Square* algorithm. This algorithm starts with a grid of points that all have the same height. It then runs an iterative process of displacing points, similar to the one-dimensional line shown previously. Each iteration displaces increasingly more points, but with a smaller displacement value. This leads to the first iterations creating large-scale features, and the further iterations modifying these features to add detail. The actual displacement of points in each iteration uses a two-stage process of displacing a square-shaped set of points and a diamond-shaped set of points.

Figure 16.4 shows the points displaced on the first iteration.

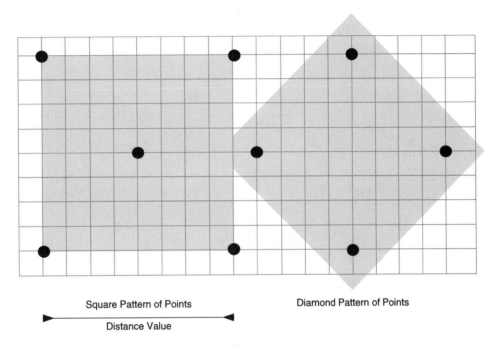

FIGURE 16.4 First iteration of point displacement.

Notice that in the first iteration, the size of the diamond and the square are the same as the size of the grid itself. This means that the first iteration will create large-scale terrain features. As successive iterations become smaller, they will create smaller features and variations on the larger theme. For this technique to work, the grid size must be a power of two plus one. The example grid shown in Figure 16.4 is a 9x9 grid, but sizes of 33x33, 65x65, or 129x129 are also valid.

As each point is displaced, it is not just displaced from the starting value of all the points; it is displaced from the average value of the points around it. This ensures that the points form a continuous curve instead of a jagged landscape. Calculating the average value of the neighboring points is a little more complex than it would initially appear. This value cannot be the average of the point's immediate neighbors, as those points might not have been displaced yet. At each iteration, the algorithm uses a `step` value to specify how far apart the points are that it is displacing. To correctly calculate neighbor locations, it must also use this `step` value to find the neighboring points to use for the calculation of the average height of a point. Figure 16.5 shows the second iteration of the diamond square algorithm.

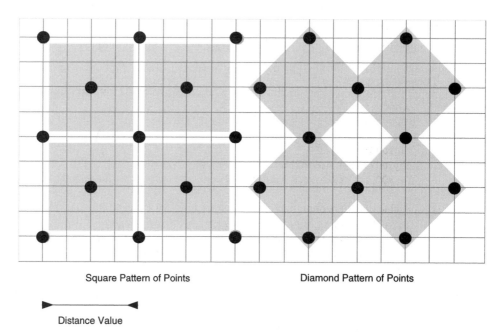

Square Pattern of Points   Diamond Pattern of Points

Distance Value

FIGURE 16.5   Second iteration of point displacement.

For this iteration, the `step` value has been halved so the points being displaced are closer together. This process of halving the `step` value and displacing points continues until the grid is fully shaped into a piece of terrain.

A random number generator determines the actual amount that each of the points is displaced. If this is a predictable random number generator, then pieces of terrain can be recreated at will from specific seeds.

16.3 TERRAIN GENERATION IN PYTHON

This section implements a terrain generator in Python that uses the concepts described in the previous section. This terrain generator uses a 129x129 grid of points and creates terrain that wraps around the edges of the map. This is achieved by masking the coordinates used to calculate average point heights so that they wrap at the edges of the map.

Listing 16.2 shows the start of the terrainGenerate class.

Listing 16.2   Terrain generator.

```
import random
import math

regionSize = 128
regionMask = regionSize - 1
INVROOT2 = 1.0 / math.sqrt(2.0)

class terrainGenerator:
    def __init__(self, seed):
        self.seed = seed
        self.rand = random.Random(self.seed)
        self.tiles = []

    def getHeightMasked(self, x, y):
        bx = x & regionMask
        by = y & regionMask
        return self.tiles[ regionSize * by + bx ]

    def setHeight(self, x, y, value):
        self.tiles[ regionSize * y + x ] = value

    def displacePointSquare(self, x, y, step, displacement):
        averageHeight =(self.getHeightMasked(x-step,y-step) +
                    self.getHeightMasked(x+step,y-step) +
                    self.getHeightMasked(x-step,y+step) +
                    self.getHeightMasked(x+step,y+step)) * 0.25
        self.setHeight(x, y, averageHeight + displacement)

    def displacePointDiamond(self, x, y, step, displacement):
        averageHeight =(self.getHeightMasked(x,y-step) +
                    self.getHeightMasked(x+step,y) +
                    self.getHeightMasked(x-step,y) +
                    self.getHeightMasked(x,y+step)) * 0.25
        self.setHeight(x, y, averageHeight + displacement)
```

The methods getHeightMasked and setHeight are helper methods to access tiles in the grid by their X and Y coordinates. Notice that the getHeightMasked method masks the coordinates before using them to offset into the tile's grid. The two displacePoint methods calculate the average height of a point based on its neighbors at a specified distance, and change its height by a specified amount. These methods are all used by the main generateTerrain method shown in Listing 16.3.

Listing 16.3 Terrain generation main function.

```
def generateTerrain(self, minVal, maxVal):
    """Generate the terrain heightmap for this region.
    """
    avgHeight = (minVal+maxVal)/2
    self.tiles = [avgHeight] * (regionSize * regionSize)
    fDisplacement = 100.0
    step = regionSize / 2

    while step > 0:
        # displacement on centers
        for y in xrange(step, regionSize, step * 2):
            for x in xrange(step, regionSize, step * 2):
                displacement=self.rand.uniform(
                        -fDisplacement, +fDisplacement)
                self.displacePointSquare(x, y, step, displacement)

        # additional displacement on corners
        for y in xrange(0, regionSize, step * 2):
            for x in xrange(0, regionSize, step * 2):
                displacement = self.rand.uniform(
                        -fDisplacement, +fDisplacement)
                self.displacePointSquare(x, y, step, displacement)

        fDisplacement = fDisplacement * INVROOT2

        # displacement on diamonds
        y = 0
        while y < regionSize:
            for x in xrange(step, regionSize, step * 2):
                displacement = self.rand.uniform(
                                -fDisplacement, +fDisplacement)
                self.displacePointDiamond(x, y, step, displacement)
            y = y + step

            for x in xrange(0, regionSize, step * 2):
                displacement = self.rand.uniform(
                                -fDisplacement, +fDisplacement)
```

```
                    self.displacePointDiamond(x, y, step, displacement)
              y = y + step

          fDisplacement = fDisplacement * INVROOT2
          step = step >> 1

      # scale height values to specified min and max
      currentMin = min(self.tiles)
      currentMax = max(self.tiles)
      scale = (maxVal - minVal) / (currentMax - currentMin)
      offset = minVal - currentMin
      self.tiles = map(lambda t: int((t+offset)*scale), self.tiles)
```

This code might look a little daunting, as it implements many of the concepts described in the previous section. It is explained in detail in this section.

The setup code at the start of the method populates some variables that are used during the main iteration loop. The setup code is shown here:

```
avgHeight = (minVal+maxVal)/2
self.tiles = [avgHeight] * (regionSize * regionSize)
fDisplacement = 10.0
step = regionSize / 2
```

The `avgHeight` variable is the average height of the minimum and maximum values passed into the function. This is used to populate the initial list of grid tiles. The member variable `self.tiles` is the list of grid tiles that make up the terrain. This is effectively the height map data. It is initialized to a list containing the initial height value for each tile. The Python syntax of:

```
[variable] * number
```

creates a list of the size of `number`, where each element has the value of `variable`. This is a convenient way to initialize lists with specific values. The variable `fDisplacement` is the magnitude that points will be displaced. This value will be reduced at each iteration so that the flow of large-scale features is maintained. The `step` variable is used to determine the distance between points to be displaced, and the location of neighboring points when averages are calculated.

Once these variables are set up, the method enters its main loop. Each iteration of this loop modifies the terrain at a level of detail that is determined by the value of `step`. Once this value reaches zero, the loop is finished.

The loop is divided into two sections: the modification of square areas, and the modification of diamond areas. The square areas are processed first with the following code:

```
# displacement on centers
for y in xrange(step, regionSize, step * 2):
    for x in xrange(step, regionSize, step * 2):
        displacement=self.rand.uniform(
            -fDisplacement, +fDisplacement)
        self.displacePointSquare(x, y, step, displacement)

# additional displacement on corners
for y in xrange(0, regionSize, step * 2):
    for x in xrange(0, regionSize, step * 2):
        displacement = self.rand.uniform(
            -fDisplacement, +fDisplacement)
        self.displacePointSquare(x, y, step, displacement)

fDisplacement = fDisplacement * INVROOT2
```

The first loop calculates the positions of the centers of squares whose size is derived from the current value of step. The second loop calculates the positions of the corners of squares of the same size. In both loops, a random displacement is acquired from the object's random number generator, and the displacePointSquare method is called to perform the actual displacement. Notice that the current step value is passed into that method so that it can calculate neighbor tiles' positions appropriately. The last line reduces the displacement value for the next section of code.

Once the square areas are displaced for the iteration, the diamond areas are displaced. The code for the diamond areas is shown here:

```
y = 0
while y < regionSize:
    for x in xrange(step, regionSize, step * 2):
        displacement = self.rand.uniform(
                    -fDisplacement, +fDisplacement)
        self.displacePointDiamond(x, y, step, displacement)
    y = y + step

    for x in xrange(0, regionSize, step * 2):
        displacement = self.rand.uniform(
                    -fDisplacement, +fDisplacement)
        self.displacePointDiamond(x, y, step, displacement)
    y = y + step

fDisplacement = fDisplacement * INVROOT2
```

The outer while loop moves the value of Y from the top to the bottom of the set of tiles. At each Y value, the two inner loops calculate the corner locations of diamonds using the step value to size them appropriately. Similar to the previous section code, the displacePointDiamond method is called to perform the actual displacement. Finally, the value of fDisplacement is reduced again for the next iteration of the loop.

At the end of each iteration through the outer while loop, the step value halved. The line:

```
step = step >> 1
```

uses a binary shift operator to perform this operation in an optimized way.

Once the outer while loop is finished, the values in self.tiles are transformed to correspond to the range of requested values passed into the method. This last portion of the method is show here:

```
# scale height values to specified min and max
currentMin = min(self.tiles)
currentMax = max(self.tiles)
scale = (maxVal - minVal) / (currentMax - currentMin)
offset = minVal - currentMin
self.tiles = map(lambda t: int((t+offset)*scale), self.tiles)
```

Python's built-in min and max functions can operate on lists directly, so currentMin and currentMax are calculated without having to iterate through the set of tiles manually. The last line in this section looks a little daunting, but is an efficient way to modify the contents of the tiles list to correspond to the specified range. The built-in map function accepts two arguments: a function, and a list. The function is applied to each of the elements in the list, and a new list is constructed from the resulting values. In this case, the list is the set of tiles, and the function is a *lambda* function. Lambda functions in Python are a shorthand way of defining small functions for use in operations like this map function. The lambda function shown previously could have been defined as:

```
offset = 10
scale = 1.5

def scaleFunc(inValue):
    return int( (inValue+offset) * scale )
```

An advantage of the lambda function is that it executes in the same scope as the scope it is called, so that in this case, the scale and offset variables are available inside the function without having to make them globals.

Therefore, at the end of the generateTerrain method, the member variable self.tiles contains a 128x128 height map of a flowing piece of terrain.

To see the results of all this work, the next section of code shows how to render the terrain as a texture in OpenGL with colors mapped to different height ranges. Figure 16.6 shows a sample of the output of this example.

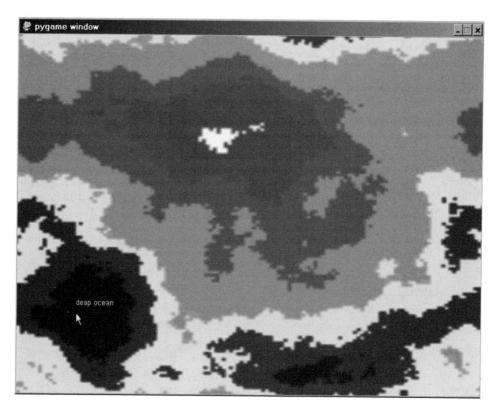

FIGURE 16.6 Terrain texture screenshot.

To map terrain heights to colors, this example uses a table of color ranges, as shown here:

```
terrains = (
    [(0,0,100,255),      "deap ocean", 5],
    [(0,20,200,255),     "ocean",      5],
    [(100,240,240,255),  "coastal",    3],
    [(230,230,88,255),   "sand",       2],
    [(180,160,95,255),   "shore",      1],
    [(10,185,10,255),    "grass",      8],
```

```
[(40,120,40,255),    "forest",     6],
[(125,90,20,255),    "mountain",   4],
[(100,90,60,255),    "montain top",4],
[(235,250,244,255),  "snow",       3]
)
```

The columns of the table are a color tuple, the terrain type name, and a range value. The range value specifies the relative amount of the total terrain that is of that particular type of terrain. These table entries are in order from the lowest terrain to the highest terrain.

The TerrainApp class is responsible for creating textures, generating terrain, and rendering the terrain. The start of this class is shown here:

```
class TerrainApp:
    def __init__(self, width, height):
        self.seed = 28
        self.displayList = 0
        pyui.desktop.getDesktop().registerHandler(pyui.locals.KEYDOWN,
self.onKey)
        self.buildLookups()
        self.generateTerrain()

    def buildLookups(self):
        self.terrainTotal = 0
        self.colorLookup = []
        self.nameLookup = []
        for color, name, value in terrains:
            self.terrainTotal += value
            for i in range(0, value):
                self.colorLookup.append(color)
                self.nameLookup.append(name)

    def onKey(self, event):
        if event.key == pyui.locals.K_SPACE:
            self.generateTerrain()
            return 1
        return 0

    def generateTerrain(self):
        self.generator = terrainGenerator(self.seed)
        self.generator.generateTerrain(0,self.terrainTotal-1)
        self.seed += 1
        self.createTexture(self.generator.tiles, self.colorLookup)
```

The interesting portions of code are the method that builds the lookup table of colors, and the method that calls the terrain generator. The buildLookups method constructs two lists that make it efficient to find the terrain height value and the color value for an offset into the terrain. As the color table shown earlier is specified in relative range amounts, it isn't possible to use it directly accessing absolute values. The colorLookup and nameLookup variables are lists that can be used to look up the corresponding color or name of an absolute offset.

The generateTerrain method creates a terrainGenerator object and uses the current seed value to generate terrain. It calls the createTexture method to create an OpenGL texture for the terrain height map that was generated. The createTexture method is shown here:

```
def createTexture(self, tiles, lookup):
    engine.flushTextures()
    data = array.array('B')
    for tile in tiles:
        color = lookup[tile]
        data.append(color[0])
        data.append(color[1])
        data.append(color[2])
        data.append(color[3])
    data = data.tostring()

    # Create the OpenGL Texture
    texture = glGenTextures(1)
    glBindTexture(GL_TEXTURE_2D, texture)    # 2d texture (x and y size)
    glPixelStorei(GL_UNPACK_ALIGNMENT,1)
    glTexImage2D(GL_TEXTURE_2D,0,4,128,128,0,GL_RGBA,GL_UNSIGNED_BYTE,
data)
    glTexParameterf(GL_TEXTURE_2D, GL_TEXTURE_MAG_FILTER, GL_LINEAR)
    glTexParameterf(GL_TEXTURE_2D, GL_TEXTURE_MIN_FILTER, GL_LINEAR)

    # add the texture to global dictionary
    engine.gTextures["terrainTexture"] = texture
```

This method iterates through the set of terrain points and populates the array data with the color values from the color lookup list. The array data is an array of bytes. Similar to the graphics engine's loadTexture function, an OpenGL texture object is created from the array. This texture object is pushed into the graphics engine with the name "terrainTexture" so it can be used for rendering.

Finally, TerrainApp has a draw method that renders the terrain as a texture, and draws the name of the current terrain under the mouse cursor. This method is shown here:

```
def draw(self, width, height):
    engine.drawImage(0,0,width,height, "terrainTexture")
```

```
# calculate terrain position
(mouseX, mouseY) = pyui.desktop.getRenderer().mousePosition
terrainX = int((mouseX/float(width)) * 128)
terrainY = int((mouseY/float(height)) * 128)
offset = int(terrainY * 128 + terrainX)

# lookup name
value = self.generator.tiles[offset]
name = self.nameLookup[value]
engine.drawText(name, (mouseX+1, height-mouseY-1),
       pyui.colors.black)
engine.drawText(name, (mouseX, height-mouseY), pyui.colors.white)
```

Drawing the terrain texture itself is trivial. A single quad that fills the screen is mapped with the texture. Since the resolution of the terrain texture is 128x128 and the resolution of the screen is 800x600, the terrain texture is stretched to fit the screen by OpenGL. Finding the terrain type under the mouse is a little more work. First, the mouse's position is transformed into a range of zero to 128 to correspond to the dimensions of the terrain grid. Then, an offset into the contiguous set of terrain tiles is calculated. The value of the terrain at that location is found, and a lookup is performed in the name lookup list that was generated earlier to find the name of that type of terrain.

The full source code to the terrain viewer application is on the accompanying CD-ROM in chapter16/terrainView.py.

ON THE CD

16.4 NAME GENERATION

Another use for predictable random number generators is the creation of names. Games with large worlds can have so many nameable locations or characters in them, that naming each one individually can be unfeasible. In games with dynamic or procedurally generated worlds, it might not even be possible to assign names to every piece of game content, as the content might not exist until the player encounters it. One solution to this problem is to use a name generator based on the predictable random number generator technique discussed in this chapter.

Name generators can operate from a seed in a similar way to the terrain generator. When using a predictable random number generator, this means that the same name can be generated from a particular seed each time. For a procedurally generated world, the same seed, or a derived seed, can be used for terrain generation and name generation to make the names of terrain features, location, or inhabitants consistent.

Name generators often use a technique called *Markov Chains*. In this technique, a set of input is processed to determine the frequency at which each of the input tokens follow previous input tokens. In some uses of Markov Chains, the tokens are words and the technique is applied to rearrange the content of stories or articles. In the case of a name generator, the tokens are characters and the technique is applied to rearrange letters to form new words.

Having a set of input for a name generator can be very useful in games. With different sets of inputs, different name generators can be made to create names with different flavors and accents. For example, one name generator could be configured to create names of elves, and another the names of dwarves. Or, one generator could create the names of stars, and another the names of cities or planets. With varying sets of input data, name generators can be very powerful.

Listing 16.4 is a set of names commonly used in stars and constellations. This set of input will be used for the name generator developed in this section.

Listing 16.4   Space names.

```
Draco Perseus Ursa Major Gemini Aquila Pegasus Andromeda Cepheus Taurus
Leo Virgo Corona Borealis Bootes Serpens Libra Ophiuchus Lyra Hercules
Cygnus Draco Hercules Canes Venatici Ursa Major Auriga Andromeda Draco
Ursa Minor Camelopardalis Pisces Austrinus Aquarius Lepus Orion
Eridanus Corvus Libra Scorpius Lupus Triangulum Astrinus Ara Centaurus
Centaurus Crux Tucana Pavo Achernar Aldebaran Algenib Algieba Algol
Alioth Alkaid Alphard Alphecca Alpheratz Altair Andromeda Antares
Aquarius Aquila Arcturus Aries Auriga Bellatrix Betelgeuse Bootes
Cancer Canes Venatici Canis Major Canis Minor Canopus Capella
Capricornus Carina Cassiopeia Castor Cepheus Cetus Cor Caroli Corona
Borealis Corvus Cursa Cygnus Deneb Deneb Algedi Denebola Draco Eltanin
Enif Eridanus Fomalhaut Gemini Hamal Hercules Hydra Izar Kochab Leo
Lepus Libra Lyra Markab Merak Mirfak Mizar Nunki Ophiuchus Orion
Pegasus Perseus Pisces Pisces Austrinus Polaris Pollux Porrima Procyon
Rasalhague Rastaban Regulus Rigel Sadr Sagittarius Saiph scheat
Scorpius Serpens Shaula Sheratan Sirius Spica Tarazed Taurus Ursa Major
Ursa Minor Vega Virgo Zubenelgenubi Zubeneschamali
```

The name generator shown in this chapter uses a token of two characters as its source. As it reads the input text, it keeps track of each unique combination of two characters as a token. For each of these tokens, it counts the number of occurrences of each character that follows it. For example, the input word *Taurus* creates the mapping:

```
ta: { u = 1 }
au: { r = 1 }
```

```
ur: { u = 1 }
ru: { s = 1 }
```

If we add the input word *Ursa* to this mapping, we get:

```
ta: { u = 1 }
au: { r = 1 }
ur: { u = 1, s = 1 }
ru: { s = 1 }
rs: { a = 1 }
```

Since there have been two occurrences of the token *ur*, there are two possible letters to follow that token. This mapping is implemented with the class LetterMap whose code is shown in Listing 16.5.

Listing 16.5   LetterMap class.

```
alphabet = "abcdefghijklmnopqrstuvwxyz"

class LetterMap:
    """utility class used by NameGenerator to track
    mapping between tokens and letters.
    """
    def __init__(self, token):
        self.token = token
        self.totalSize = 0
        self.letterMap = {}

    def addLetter(self, toLetter):
        """collect an instance in the sample data of
        a character after this token
        """
        if not toLetter in alphabet:
            return

        self.totalSize += 1
        value = self.letterMap.get(toLetter, 0)
        self.letterMap[toLetter] = value + 1

    def getLetter(self, random):
        """get a random letter based on my
        statistics
        """
        i = random.randint(0, self.totalSize)
        pos = 0
        for letter, number in self.letterMap.items():
```

```
            if i > pos and i <= pos + number:
                return letter
            pos += number
        return None
```

The addLetter method is where individual letter instances are added to the map. The dictionary letterMap keeps track of which letters have been found, and the value for each key is the number of times the letter has been added. This code also includes the getLetter method that is used later when actually generating random words.

The NameGenerator class itself uses instances of the LetterMap class to manage its statistics. In addition to tracking the content of words, it also tracks the sizes of words and calculates the standard deviation of the word sizes. This extra information is used to be able to generate random words whose size corresponds to the words in the input set. Listing 16.6 shows the input portions of the NameGenerator class.

Listing 16.6 NameGenerator class.

```
class NameGenerator:
    """class to generator random names from a seed and
    a set of input data.
    """
    def __init__(self, seed):
        self.nameMap = {}
        self.numNames = 0
        self.numCharacters = 0
        self.random = random.Random(seed)
        self.wordSizes = []

    def inputFile(self, fileName):
        """read a set of words from an input file"""
        f = open(fileName)
        text = f.read()
        f.close()
        words = text.split(" ")
        self.input(words)

    def input(self, inputNames):
        """collect statistics from a set of words in a string
        """
        for name in inputNames:
            for i in range(0, len(name)-2):
                # extract the token and next character
                fromToken = name[i:i+2]
                nextChar = name[i+2]
```

```
            if not fromToken[0] in alphabet:
                continue

            # add to letter map
            letterMap = self.nameMap.get(fromToken,
LetterMap(fromToken))
                letterMap.addLetter(nextChar)
                self.nameMap[fromToken] = letterMap

            # update statistics
            self.numNames += 1
            self.numCharacters += len(name)
            self.wordSizes.append(len(name))

        self.calcStandardDeviation()

    def calcStandardDeviation(self):
        """calculates the standard deviation of the size
        of words in the input set.
        """
        self.mean = self.numCharacters / self.numNames
        variance = 0
        for size in self.wordSizes:
            variance += (self.mean-size)**2
        self.standardDeviation =
math.sqrt(variance/float(self.numNames))
```

The most interesting part of this code is the `input` method that processes a set of input to extract statistics. The outer `while` loop in this method iterates through the input words and collects the word sizes for calculating the standard deviation. The inner `while` loop iterates through the letter tokens in each word and collects statistics about the word. The lines:

```
fromToken = name[i:i+2]
nextChar = name[i+2]
```

use Python's string slicing capability to extract the letter token and the next character in the word. The line:

```
letterMap = self.nameMap.get(fromToken, LetterMap(fromToken))
```

uses the built-in `get` method of the dictionary class to find the `LetterMap` instance that corresponds to the token. The second parameter to this method will be returned if the key value is not found in the dictionary. This is a shorthand way of checking for the existence of the key value in a single step. This code is equivalent to:

```
if self.nameMap.has_key(fromToken):
    letterMap = self.nameMap[fromToken]
else:
    letterMap = LetterMap(fromToken)
```

but only performs a single lookup in the dictionary and fits on a single line of code. Notice that the letterMap object must be added or replaced in the dictionary after the value has been manipulated, as it might be a new instance that does not already exist in the dictionary.

The name generator has a random number generator instance as a member variable. This object is initialized with the seed value of the name generator so that names can be generated in a predictable way.

Finally, the name generator has a method to create a new, random name based on the statistics it has collected. Listing 16.7 shows the code for the makeName method.

Listing 16.7 NameGenerator class makeNames method.

```
def makeName(self):
        """makes a new random name based on the statistics
        collected from the sample data.
        """
        size = self.random.gauss(self.mean, self.standardDeviation)
        output = self.random.choice(self.nameMap.keys() )
        for i in range(0,size):
            lastChar = output[-2:]
            letterMap = self.nameMap.get(lastChar, None)
            if letterMap:
                newChar = letterMap.getLetter(self.random)
                if newChar:
                    output += newChar
        return string.capwords(output)
```

This method uses the random module's gauss method to determine the size of the new word. This makes the size of the new words fit the size distribution of words in the input set. It uses the random module's choice method to choose a random starting token for the word, and then iterates from that position using the letterMap objects to find the next character each time. Listing 16.8 is a list of words generated by this class from the input set shown in Listing 16.4.

Listing 16.8 Randomly generated names.

```
Gollux Beneban De Rpenatz Ici Cyon Turustries Cyo Rici Rvustrican Vuseu
Inorvuse Sustrius Qua Ilatani Aze Adron Uben Rgolar Gies Igenisce
Astrinischus Lgiesces Cance Uilaric Unki Gnus Natici Ebard Hariustaur
```

While these names don't make any sense, they are credible names for game objects in a science fiction universe. While this is only a small set of names, this algorithm can be used to generate hundreds or even thousands of names for a game.

This basic algorithm can easily be extended by adding suffix, prefix, hyphenation, or compound naming functionality. The variety of names that can be generated is almost endless!

ON THE CD
The full source code to the random name generator is on the accompanying CD-ROM in chapter16/names.py.

SUMMARY

This chapter described the concept of procedural content generation and how it can be used in game development. It included discussions of predictable random numbers, Python's `random` module, terrain generation using the mid-point displacement algorithm, and name generation using the Markov Chain algorithm.

As examples, this chapter included a visual representation of different random number distributions, a terrain generator and viewer, and a random name generator for creating science fiction names. Each of these examples used Python's `random` module.

This chapter described techniques that can be used to expand the scope of games, and to automate the content creation process. While there will always be a role for world building and carefully crafted content, these techniques can be used to raise the level at which designers and programmers work. Instead of worrying about the micro-level details of each piece of game content, procedural generation of content allows developers to focus on the algorithms and data that are used to create content. This can allow more content to be created and can enforce consistency and attention to detail across the entire spectrum of game items.

V Multiplayer Games

17 | Network Concepts

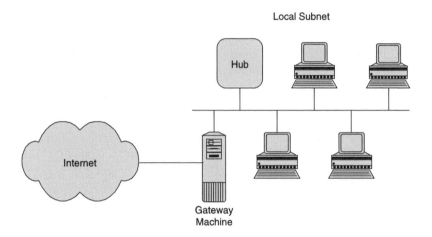

Local Subnet

Hub

Internet

Gateway
Machine

Multiplayer games are built on a foundation of network technology. Understanding the underlying infrastructure of networking and the Internet is vital for the development of multiplayer games. To be competitive, modern multiplayer games must be able to operate over the Internet and over private LANs. The challenges introduced by an unpredictable and chaotic system like the Internet are many, but it is possible to create games that provide a rewarding multiplayer experience using the Internet as the network backbone. This chapter discusses network technologies that are used in multiplayer and online games, and is a background for the more game-specific topics in the next chapters.

While this chapter includes some Python-specific information, it is mainly devoted to the network concepts and infrastructure required for online games. We discuss specifics of network programming with Python in later chapters.

The core topics of networking covered in this chapter include network identification with IP addresses and ports, the *Transmission Control Protocol* (TCP), and the *User Datagram Protocol* (UDP). In addition, we discuss the concepts of bandwidth, latency, and byte ordering in relation to online game development.

17.1 NETWORK IDENTIFICATION

Every node in a network must have an address to identify it. This section covers how network nodes are identified with names and IP addresses, and the concept of port numbers to further identify connections between network nodes.

Network identification is an important topic for multiplayer games. Before a multiplayer game begins, the participants must locate each other on a network, or communicate through a central service. Both of these tasks require the participating machines to have valid network identities. While games are running, the identities of the participants are used for purposes such as packet filtering, security, and player identification.

Internet Names

The names of machines on the Internet are organized into a hierarchical structure. Each level in the hierarchy is separated by a period in the name, with the top of the hierarchy being on the right, and more specific portions of names to the left. The structure of Internet names are familiar to many people from the *Uniform Resource Locators* (URLs) used on the World Wide Web, but the meaning of the structure of network names is not as widely know.

Each level of the name hierarchy represents a logical partition in the structure of the Internet. These levels are sometimes referred to as *domains*. The rightmost portion of a network name is the upper-level domain. There are a fixed number of these domains that are strictly managed by the domain registration services. The upper-level domains include:

- **.edu**—Educational institutions
- **.gov**—United States federal government agencies
- **.com**—Commercial organizations
- **.net**—Internet service organizations
- **.org**—Nonprofit organizations
- **.mil**—United States military usages
- **.us**—United States, state and local government
- **.****—Country codes (.au = Australia .uk = United Kingdom)

This original partitioning of the Internet namespace has faced some muddying with the Internet's massive growth, but the general structure of it remains. The following are some examples of valid Internet names:

- *www.yahoo.com*
- *my-machine.accounting.my-company.org*

- *ftp.sourceforge.net*
- *gameserver4.heat.net.uk*

The leftmost portion of a network name is the *hostname* of the particular computer that exists at that address. This name is configured locally on each machine and must be unique within the node's local domain. Sometimes, this name is a virtual name that can be used as an alias to another machine or even a set of machines. This is a common practice with the *www* prefix for Web sites.

The remaining levels of the name hierarchy represent logical partitions of the naming space that can be configured by organizations that use the Internet. Generally, these names are kept to a few levels so users can easily remember them. Figure 17.1 shows how Internet names are divided.

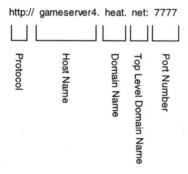

FIGURE 17.1 Structure of an Internet name.

The hostname of a particular machine can usually be found by running the `hostname` command. On Microsoft Windows machines, the hostname can also be found on the Network Identification tab of the System Settings control panel.

IP Addresses

In addition to a descriptive name, each node on the Internet has an *Internet Protocol (IP) address*, which is a 32-bit integer. This amount of address space allows a maximum of 2^{32} possible addresses (4,294,967,296, or just over 4 billion addresses). The actual maximum number of address is not quite this high, as some ranges of IP numbers are reserved for special purposes.

IP addresses are divided into four 8-bit values and are usually represented in a format called *dot notation*. Each of the four values is a number in the range 0 to 255.

Numbers in dot notation are easier to read and remember than the long numeric of the actual IP address value. The following are some examples of IP addresses shown in dot notation:

- 192.168.1.22
- 44.55.123.89
- 204.22.122.151

Certain IP addresses have special meanings. The address 127.0.0.1 is reserved to be always the address of the local machine. It is known as the *loopback address*, and network traffic sent to this address never actually leaves the local machine. Other addresses are assigned specifically as private networks that are not connected directly to the Internet. These addresses are used in many different places as internal company networks or private home networks. Although addresses in these ranges can be used many times throughout the world, there are no conflicts, as they are hidden behind private gateways and routers. The private, reserved IP address ranges are:

- 10.0.0.0–10.255.255.255
- 172.16.0.0–172.31.255.255
- 192.168.0.0–192.168.255.255

As IP addresses are the most efficient way of storing a network address, they are the preferred format for use in multiplayer games.

In addition to regular IP addresses, a new standard called IPv6 exists to extend the address of the Internet to include many more possible locations. This standard is not yet in wide use and is not expected to have a significant impact on online games for some time.

Name Translation

Each node on a network has both a descriptive network name and an IP address. It is sometimes necessary to convert between these two formats. There are a number of ways to do this.

Some systems keep a *hosts* file that contains a table of direct mappings between network names and IP addresses. Hosts files are good for small networks, but do not scale effectively enough for large organizations. A hosts file for all of the machines on the Internet would be huge! Here is an example of a hosts file:

```
127.0.0.1          localhost
192.168.1.1        gameplayer42 gameplayer42.mynet.com
```

```
192.168.1.2          otherguy otherguy.mynet.com
                     gateway gateway.mynet.com SR: ??
56.44.12.12          fred.companyX.com
```

Note that even if an IP address is included in a hosts file, there is no guarantee that that address is actually accessible from the current machine's network location. In the preceding example, the machine *fred.companyX.com* would not be accessible without the assistance of a router.

To cope with the huge number of names and addresses on the Internet, the *Domain Name System* (DNS) database is used. This is a distributed database that contains the name-to-address translation information for every node on the Internet. It is a hierarchical system where responsibility of ownership for domains is delegated to the organizations that control those domains.

The DNS system is accessed automatically by many programs, including Web browsers, file-sharing programs, e-mail clients, and almost any other networked application. This important piece of Internet infrastructure is usually invisible, but developers of multiplayer games need to be aware of it.

Any time a name is translated into an IP address using the DNS service, a network message is sent and the application must wait for a response. Often, a message such as "looking up host" is displayed while this happens. This delay is often hidden inside of system calls, so it can be overlooked by developers. With their stringent performance requirements, multiplayer game servers must be careful not to perform DNS lookups when they are not absolutely required.

Port Numbers

Although machines on a network can be identified by their name or IP address, it is often a requirement to be able to identify a particular connection on a machine. This is handled by port numbers. A port number is a 16-bit number within the range 0 to 65536, and each network connection on a machine has a unique port number. There are sets of ports for UDP/IP protocol traffic and TCP/IP protocol traffic. We discuss these protocols later in this chapter.

Similar to IP addresses, some port numbers are reserved for special purposes. The port numbers below 1024 are reserved on Unix systems for the root user, and many common network applications have standard port numbers that they assume to use unless specifically told otherwise. Examples of *well-known* ports include:

- **Port 21**—File Transfer Protocol
- **Port 23**—Telnet Protocol
- **Port 25**—Simple Mail Transfer Protocol
- **Port 53**—Domain Name Service

- **Port 80**—World Wide Web

When specifying a network identity with a port number, the port number is shown after the name or IP address and is separated by a colon character. The following are examples of network names with port numbers:

- www.yahoo.com:8080
- 192.168.1.33:7788

Port numbers are significant for multiplayer games, as game servers often run on specific ports to which clients connect, and peer-to-peer communication between game clients must occur on correspondingly well-known ports.

Subnets

Subnets are the subunit of the network that defines the boundaries of where machines can communicate with each other directly. Communication between network nodes on different subnets requires the assistance of a router or gateway. This is significant for game development, as traffic within subnets can be substantially faster than routed traffic, and subnets are a good unit for broadcasting the existence of game servers or requests for multiplayer games. Figure 17.2 shows how subnets are architected.

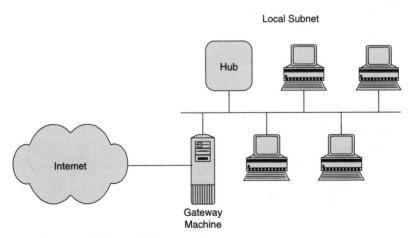

FIGURE 17.2 Subnet architecture.

Subnet partitioning is reflected in the IP addresses of machines in the network. The partitioning is usually done at the byte boundary of the IP address so that the final eight bytes of the IP address represent the system address, and the next eight bytes of the address represent the subnet address. This partitioning can be modified with the *subnet mask*, but the configuration described is the most common. Figure 17.3 shows how IP addresses are partitioned into subnets.

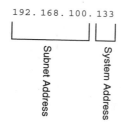

FIGURE 17.3   Subnet mask on IP address.

17.2 TCP/IP

TCP/IP is one of the most common protocols in use on the Internet. It is used by many common network applications such as e-mail clients and Web browsers as the basis for higher-level, application protocols. Many online games use TCP/IP, but it is not the exclusive game network protocol. For performance-critical and low-latency games such as first-person shooters, the UDP/IP protocol is often used.

TCP/IP is a connection-based stream protocol that guarantees that all sent packets are received at their destination in the order in which they were sent. This means that every time a packet of information is sent across the network using the TCP/IP protocol, it will absolutely arrive at its destination in the correct order. Although the underlying Internet infrastructure might drop packets and introduce other failures, the TCP/IP protocol ensures packet delivery by a complex system of acknowledgments and packet identifiers. It uses internal buffers to store network packets until they are confirmed by their destination, which allows troublesome packets to be re-sent when required. The receiving end of a TCP/IP connection ensures that packets are received by the application in order by keeping internal buffers and only supplying data to the application when the sequence of packets is complete.

As a connection-based protocol, TCP/IP establishes connections between source and destination addresses. Once a connection is established, packets sent on a connection are implicitly routed to the connection's destination.

To perform all of these functions, each TCP/IP packet has a header of 40 bytes. Half of the size of this packet header is for the underlying IP protocol, and the other half is for TCP/IP's protocol management functionality. This is a relatively large header in relation to other protocols. The size of TCP/IP packets is determined by the protocol; the application has no direct control over the actual size of packets and the frequency at which they are sent.

These characteristics make TCP/IP an easy protocol to use, and allow developers to focus on the application level, rather than the specifics of the network transport layer. However, these characteristics do not match the requirements of all online games. Games that send a large number of small but frequent messages do not fit into the TCP/IP model. This is especially true when the game doesn't care if some of the messages arrive out of order, or do not show up at all. The protocol management functionality in TCP/IP becomes a major overhead in these cases, as it adds its large header to each message for no useful purpose.

The classic example in online games of a type of message that should not use TCP/IP is *movement messages*. Movement messages are very small, are sent rapidly, and dropped messages or out-of-order messages can be handled quite easily at the receiving end. Movement messages are a case that leads many online games to use the UDP/IP protocol instead of TCP/IP for at least part of their network solution.

17.3 UDP/IP

UDP/IP is a simple protocol that is also commonly used on the Internet. This protocol provides less functionality than TCP/IP, and has correspondingly less associated overhead. The header on UDP/IP packets is only 28 bytes, in comparison to 40 bytes for TCP/IP packets. UDP/IP is often used in performance-critical networking areas of online games.

UDP/IP is a connectionless protocol. Each packet sent through this protocol must have its destination address and port specified individually. This is different from the TCP/IP model where a connection is established, and packets are sent through connections.

Also unlike TCP/IP, UDP/IP does not guarantee that packets arrive at their destination, and does not guarantee that the packets that do arrive are in the same order in which they were sent. Each packet sent via the UDP/IP protocol is an independent entity that traverses the Internet with no regard to other packets. This means that UDP/IP packets have smaller header overhead than TCP/IP packets do.

The lightweight nature of UDP/IP makes it useful in situations where the overhead of TCP/IP cannot be supported. In particular, UDP/IP is well suited for sending movement packets in online games. Many high-performance online games such as *Quake* and *Unreal Tournament* use the UDP protocol as their networking infrastructure.

17.4 BLOCKING AND NONBLOCKING I/O

An important concept for network programming, and system programming in general, is the concept of blocking and nonblocking I/O. This concept will be relevant in the next chapters that cover network programming and architectures, so it is covered here as necessary background material.

Any time an application performs an operation involving a network connection or a file system, there is a choice to be made. The application can wait for the requested operation to complete, or it can go about its other responsibilities and check on the status of the operation at a later time. The first of these two cases is known as *blocking I/O* or *synchronous I/O*. In this case, the application suspends its execution until the requested operation is finished regardless of how long the operation takes. The second case is known as *nonblocking I/O*. In this case, the application does not wait for network operations to complete; it continues performing other tasks and checks the status of the request later.

In network programming, certain types of operations can block. Examples of these operations include reading data from a network connection, writing data to a connection, and establishing a new network connection. It is important to be aware of which operations block and which do not block, so that code can be structured to deal with the timing issues involved.

Although it is unavoidable that certain network operations take time, the blocking effect can be avoided by explicitly setting network connections to nonblocking. The practical effect of this in Python is that any time a potentially blocking call is made on a nonblocking network object, an exception is raised. This exception can be caught by the application so that execution can continue.

17.5 BANDWIDTH

In network programming, and online games in particular, bandwidth is an important issue. In general, *bandwidth* is the measure of how much data can be passed through a communication channel over a period of time. Specifically in game development, bandwidth is often used to refer to as the number of bytes per second that can be transferred between network participants, usually a client and a server.

Games must be very careful to keep their bandwidth usage below the bandwidth available to the network participants. If a game uses more bandwidth than the users are capable of processing, their play experience will suffer, as the game will fail to respond to user input, and the player's version of the world will not be synchronized with other players. Bandwidth is a very sensitive area of multiplayer game development.

In some applications, bandwidth is not a real-time issue as it is in online games. For example Web browsers have no time constraints on downloading images and text for Web pages. They use the maximum amount of bandwidth they can get from the Web server all the time. The Web would be a very different place if Web pages were restricted in the amount of data they consist of, and had strict time requirements for pages to complete loading. Games place very different requirements on bandwidth than most other networked applications do.

When comparing bandwidths, be sure that the measurements are in the same format. Some situations measure bandwidth in kilobits per second (Kbps), while others measure it in kilobytes per second (KBps). Both of these measurements are sometimes abbreviated as Kbps, which can make comparisons of bandwidths incorrect in some situations.

Modems that use the telephone network typically have speeds of 28.8 , 33.8 , or 56 Kbps. The *56K* bandwidth that is often used to refer to modem speeds is in Kbps. These numbers translate into practical bandwidth capabilities of approximately two to five KBps. This gives some indication of the type of bandwidth restrictions under which online games must operate. Although broadband connections like cable modems and DSL lines are becoming more common, the majority of computer users in the world are still on regular modems that have relatively low bandwidth capabilities.

17.6 LATENCY

Latency is a topic that is closely related to bandwidth. Any operation across a network incurs some delay before a response is received. In network programming, this amount of time is referred to as latency. Latency is often measured as the number of milliseconds that it takes to receive a response to a network message. In online games, this is sometimes known as a *ping time*.

Latency is bad for online games. It adds a delay between when the user requests an action, and when the response to that request is received. It can give the user the impression that the game is nonresponsive, or even broken when latency is high. Latency is the bane of real-time games that are played across the Internet. When the exact timing of firing a weapon can be the difference between life and death for a virtual character, unpredictable latency is a strong negative force.

Latency is affected dramatically by bandwidth. The closer the bandwidth usage of a game is to the communication channel's bandwidth capacity, the more latency will be injected into the system. This occurs because the spikes in bandwidth cause queuing of data at the protocol level that delay some of the data from immediate transmission. This is especially bad with TCP/IP, as congested networks tend to drop more packets, which causes more packet resends and buffering at the protocol level.

Telephone-line based modems introduce considerable latency in their translation of network signals from digital format to the analog format required to travel over the telephone network. Latencies of 200 to 500 milliseconds for modems are not uncommon. Broadband connections such as cable modems and DSL lines have lower latency values that range upward from a best case of about 20 milliseconds. The lowest latency is achieved over direct LAN connections. In this case, latencies of less than 10 milliseconds are a reality, and multiplayer games are very smooth.

17.7 BYTE ORDERING

Byte ordering is an issue of which network programmers must be aware. Historically, different hardware platforms have stored data in two formats: *big-endian* and *little-endian*. The difference between these formats is the order in which bytes are stored for multibyte values such as integer numbers. The diagram below demonstrates these two data formats for a 16-bit integer. Figure 17.4 shows the decimal number 4000, which is 0x0FA0 in hexadecimal. As a 16-bit integer, the two binary bytes are *0001111* (or 0x0F) and *10100000* (or 0xA0).

In the little-endian format, this number is represented with the *least significant bits* on the left-hand side, and the *most significant bits* on the right-hand side. The in-memory binary representation is 10100000-00001111, or 0xA00F. In big-endian format, the order of the bytes is reversed to 00001111-10100000, or 0x0FA0. This applies to all data types that take up more than one byte of data. *Integers, longs, floats, doubles,* and *shorts* must all conform to the byte order of a situation. Strings are immune to byte ordering, as each of their characters is a single byte that does not require any manipulation.

This is significant for network programming because different machines on a particular network might use different byte orders. To deal with this issue, there is

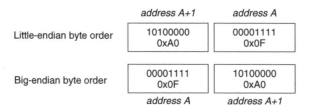

FIGURE 17.4   Byte ordering.

a specified *network byte order* that is used for all network traffic. Since machines know their own byte order and the network byte order, this allows them to communicate correctly with other machines regardless of the other machines' native byte order. Network byte order for IP protocols is big-endian, and the native byte order for Intel-based computers is little-endian. The native byte order for a particular platform is called its *host byte order*.

There are functions available to convert between network and host byte order. The implementation of these functions on each platform performs the correct operation to make the data available in the correct format for the platform. In Python, these functions are implemented in the socket module. Table 17.1 lists some of these functions.

TABLE 17.1   Byte Switching Functions

Name	Size	Function
ntohl()	32-bit	Switch from Network to Host byte order
htonl()	32-bit	Switch from Host to Network byte order
htons()	16-bit	Switch from Host to Network byte order
ntohs()	16-bit	Switch from Network to Host byte order

The multiplayer game examples in this book use the External Data Representation (XDR) protocol. This protocol has built-in byte switching in its *pack* and *unpack* functions, so the application code does not have to deal with byte order issues at all.

SUMMARY

This chapter described network concepts relevant to the development of online games. We discussed the ways in which network identification works across the Internet, including IP addresses, ports, and subnets. We also discussed the TCP/IP and UDP protocols and their characteristics that are relevant to game development, and the concepts of bandwidth and latency.

The information in this chapter was background that will be built upon in the next chapters as we discuss network programming with Python and multiplayer game programming. The concepts from this chapter are a solid foundation of networking theory for online game development.

18 Network Layers

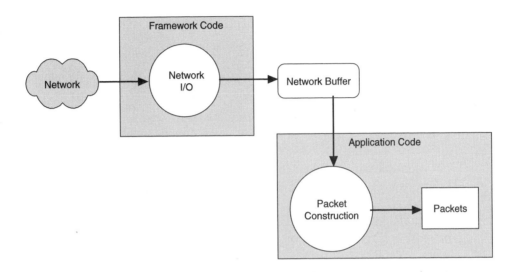

In multiplayer game architectures, the network layer provides the interface between the game application and the low-level networking services provided by libraries or the OS. This component has some impact on the implementation of other game systems, as they must rely on it to transport events, object state, and actions between the participants of multiplayer games.

In games, network programming almost exclusively uses the *socket* application interface to the TCP/IP and UDP/IP protocols. The socket interface is available on most game platforms and is the standard way of interacting with low-level network services. It is widely used in game development in addition to other types of application development, and can be accessed from many languages, including Python. Figure 18.1 shows the layers of multiplayer game network architecture and the relationships between them.

Built on the socket interface are *network layers* that expose functionality to game application code. Some of the responsibilities of network layers are connection management, managing incoming and outgoing data on network sockets, and protocol packing and unpacking. These responsibilities are best kept out of the ap-

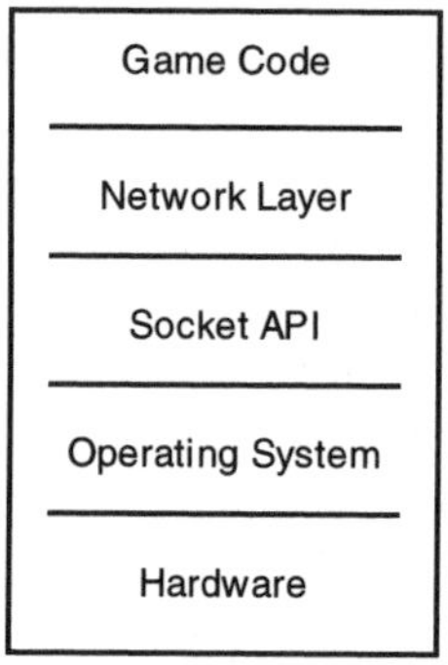

FIGURE 18.1 Network layers.

plication domain, and kept invisible to application programmers. The network layer provides an interface that allows a separation between application code and network code.

At a higher level, there are a number of ways to architect network layers and network servers. Different requirements in terms of the number of simultaneous users, scalability, and throughput have led to varying server implementations that have different resource and performance characteristics, and varying levels of difficulty of implementation. As these server models are quite mature, applications and frameworks exist that provide implementations of them, and additional functionality. The *Twisted* framework is a Python-based server framework that implements the asynchronous, concurrent server model that we describe later in this chapter. It can be used for multiplayer game development and is used for the example application in this chapter and the next.

This chapter discusses networking topics that are necessary for building network layers for multiplayer games. Section 18.1 discusses the basics of socket programming with Python, and Section 18.2 discusses how to read and write data using the socket programming interface. Section 18.3 discusses different types of TCP/IP server models that can be built on the socket layer, Section 18.4 is an introduction to the Twisted network/server framework, and Section 18.5 discusses implementing network protocols for games. This section uses the Twisted framework so it can concentrate on the specifics of protocol design rather than server framework implementation and interfacing with low-level OS network services.

18.1 SOCKET BASICS

Python's standard distribution includes a socket module that provides access to the socket programming interface. Python's socket module is a thin layer around the OS's socket services. It has module-level methods that implement a number of utility functions, and a `Socket` class that implements an interface similar to the standard Unix socket interface. It also includes constants that are used when configuring network options, and three exception types for error handling. It provides access to TCP/IP and UDP functionality, and allows both blocking and non-blocking operations to be performed.

`Socket` objects are used to access the core functionality of the socket programming interface. The constructor for `socket` objects takes two constants as arguments. These constants specify the socket *family* and the socket type. The family for sockets is always the constant `AF_INET`. The second constant determines whether the socket is a TCP/IP, with the value `SOCK_STREAM`, or a UDP socket with the value `SOCK_DGRAM`. The following code shows how a TCP/IP socket object is created.

```
import socket
mySock = socket.socket(socket.AF_INET, socket.SOCK_STREAM)
```

In the socket model, there are two ways for connections to be established. A socket can actively connect to a known socket address, or it can passively wait for another socket to connect to it. In the language of the socket model, the active connect is performed by *clients*, and the passive method of waiting for another socket to connect is performed by *servers*.

Actively connecting to a known server socket is a technique used by many common network applications. For example, Web browsers connect to Web servers, e-mail clients initiate connections to mail servers, and file transfer clients connect to file transfer servers. The following code shows how to connect a TCP/IP socket to a server address with Python.

```
import socket
mySock = socket.socket(socket.AF_INET, socket.SOCK_STREAM)
address = ("gameserver.mynet.org", 5555)
try:
    mySock.connect( address )
except socket.error, e:
    print "Error:", e, "connecting to ", address
```

The address passed to the `connect` method is a tuple of a hostname or IP address, and a port number. The `connect` method raises an exception if it cannot resolve the address, or if it cannot establish a connection to the address and port number. The `try`/`except` block around the `connect` method allows these potential exceptions to be trapped in this piece of code. Note that the `connect` call is a blocking call. By default, the application's execution is suspended until this call returns.

Setting up a connection to passively wait for incoming connections is a little more complicated. There are three stages to the process. First, a socket is created in the same way just described. Next, the socket is bound to a local address that becomes the address that other sockets use when connecting to the socket, and finally, the socket is set to *listen* for incoming connections. The following code shows how to set up a server socket with Python that listens to a specific port.

```
mySock = socket.socket(socket.AF_INET, socket.SOCK_STREAM)
address = ("localhost", 7777)
try:
    mySock.bind( address )
    mySock.listen(5)
except socket.error, e:
    print "Unable to setup server socket:", e
```

Similar to the `connect` method of the active socket, the `bind` method accepts a tuple of name or IP address and port number. The `bind` method might raise an exception if the address is invalid, so again, a `try`/`except` block is used around this code to trap the potential exception.

The argument to the `listen` method is the size of the connection queue. This queue determines how the socket behaves when many clients attempt to connect to it simultaneously. When more clients connect to a socket than the application can handle, the incoming sockets are placed in the listen queue until the application is ready to process them. If the queue is full, any remaining clients are turned away with a connection failure.

Although the preceding code creates a server socket, this is not enough to actually accept incoming connections from clients. To receive incoming connections, servers use the `accept` method of the `socket` class. This is a blocking method that can be called on listening sockets to return the next incoming connection that is queued for that socket. In Python, the `accept` method returns a tuple containing the new client socket and the address the client connected from. It is often called in a loop that continues to accept connections and pass them off to other code for processing. The following code shows the `accept` call in use.

```
try:
    (clientSocket, fromAddress) = mySock.accept()
    print "Client connected from:", fromAddress
    # process the connection here
except socket.error, e:
    print "Unable to accept connections:", e
```

The different methods of handling client connections once they are accepted fall under the TCP/IP server model and are described in Section 18.3 of this chapter.

Finally, when an application is finished using a connection, the connection should be closed to free any resources it was using, and to release the port number. There are a limited number of ports on any machine, so it is important to close sockets when they are no longer required. Python's `socket` class has a `close` method that closes a socket. Note that any operations attempted on a closed socket will fail. The following code shows how to close a socket with Python.

```
mySock.Close()
```

18.2 SENDING AND RECEIVING DATA

This section shows how applications use sockets to send and receive data across networks. This process is more complex than it initially appears because of the unpredictable nature of the underlying transport layer.

Using TCP/IP, the `send` method is used to actively transmit data across a socket connection, and the `recv` method is used to passively accept data from a socket connection. With UDP's connectionless interface, there are corresponding methods called `sendto` and `recvfrom` that send data to, and receive data from, specific network addresses rather than connections.

With UDP sockets, the data to each `sendto` call becomes a discrete packet that is dispatched across the network immediately. This packet will be either received or not received in its entirety at the packet's destination address. With TCP/IP, the data to `send` calls is cached in internal buffers until the protocol determines it should actually be sent.

With Python socket objects, each call to the `send` method takes a string as its argument. In most socket interfaces, the `send` call takes a size in bytes as an additional argument, but Python can determine the size of the data string automatically, so this is not required. Note that Python strings can include null characters; they are not necessarily terminated by a null value. Unlike strings in some other programming languages, they can be used as data that includes these characters.

The `send` call does its best to transmit the data passed to it, but sometimes it is unable to transmit all of the data. To allow the application to deal with this situation, the send call returns the size of the data it actually transmitted. This unpredictable behavior of the transport layer requires applications to track the amount of data sent in each call, and if the application wants all of a particular piece of data sent, it must loop over the send call until it is finished. The following code shows a send loop that guarantees that all of the specified data is sent.

```
dataSize = 100
    data = "*" * dataSize
    current=0
    try:
        while current < dataSize:
            current += mySock.send(data[current:])
    except socket.error, e:
        print "Send failed:", e
```

This code begins with the variable current at zero, and increments its value with each send call. Python's string slicing functionality is used to isolate the portion of untransmitted data that is passed to the send call each iteration through the loop. When the value of current is the same as the size of the piece of data, the send loop is finished.

Receiving data behaves the same way as sending data. Each call to the recv method returns a string of data that was available from the network, but does not guarantee that any particular size of data is returned. The following code shows a receive loop that guarantees that the specified number of bytes is received.

```
def recvData(mySock, dataSize):
    data = ""
    current = 0
    try:
        while current < dataSize:
            data += mySock.recv(dataSize - current)
            current = len(data)
    except socket.error, e:
        print "Recv failed:", e
    print data
```

The current method acts in a similar way in this method as it does in the send loop. Its value is incremented in each iteration of the loop until all the data is received. Note that both the send loop and the receive loop can contain multiple blocking operations, so they take an unpredictable amount of time.

This level of interaction with the network is usually abstracted away from application code by the concepts of message packets, connections, and other higher-level classes. However, understanding the lower levels of networking is vital to multiplayer game development.

18.3 TCP/IP SERVER MODELS

The TCP/IP protocol covers establishing and closing connections, and sending data and receiving data, but does not specify how server applications manage multiple connections. There are a number of well-known server models for managing multiple TCP/IP connections. This section describes some of these server models in the context of game server development.

Connection Management

Servers that allow connections from multiple clients simultaneously must be able to keep track of each connection, process incoming and outgoing data for each connection, and allow additional connections to be created. These tasks must be performed so they appear to clients to be concurrent rather than serial. In addition, there should be a fair allocation of processing time between tasks and connections, so that no connection is favored over others. This is especially important in interactive real-time systems such as game servers.

Network and server developers have dealt with connection management issues for many years. During that time, a number of architectures have been developed that are commonly used as models for developing new servers. These models use variations of blocking and nonblocking I/O, different numbers of threads, different numbers of processes, and different OS services. The background from Chapter 17, "Network Concepts," and the previous sections of this chapter are required reading for understanding these server models.

The `SocketServer` module of the standard Python distribution is used in this chapter to implement example servers of each of the models. This simplifies the development of network servers in Python by providing a flexible interface for creating and operating different types of servers that use blocking I/O. Each of the example servers in this chapter that use the `SocketServer` module use the `GameRequestHandler` class shown in Listing 18.1.

Listing 18.1   GameRequestHandler class.

```
import os
import thread
import SocketServer

class GameRequestHandler(SocketServer.BaseRequestHandler):
    """Handler for game server
    """
    def handle(self):
        data = self.request.recv(100)
```

```
        data = "ECHO: <%s>" % data
        total = len(data)
        current = 0
        while current < total:
            current += self.request.send(data[current:])
        print "(PID:%s:THREAD:%s) Processed Request from %s:%s" % (
            os.getpid(), thread.get_ident(),
            self.client_address[0],
            self.client_address[1])
```

This class is derived from the `BaseRequestHandler` class in the `SocketServer` module. The `BaseRequestHandler` exposes a number of methods for derived classes to override, but our handler only overrides the `handle` method to perform simple request handling. This method is invoked by the `SocketServer` framework when a network request is ready to be processed. The information printed by this method includes the process ID and thread ID of the execution path that is processing the request. This will be used to demonstrate how the different server models use different combinations of threads and processes.

Simple Iterative Server

This is the simplest TCP/IP server model, and is really only appropriate for demonstration purposes. In this model, only one client can be handled at a time, and the client must be dealt with as a single, discrete processing unit. Any client connections that are requested while the server is busy are queued until the server finishes completing its current request.

This server model uses blocking I/O for reading, writing, and accepting connections. It has a single thread that handles network activity and request processing. The core part of this server model is a loop that blocks to accept a client connection, performs a synchronous dialog with the client, closes the connection, and returns to wait for the next connection. This server model is simple enough that the code for an iterative server written using only the `socket` module can be developed quite quickly. Listing 18.2 shows the code for an iterative server.

Listing 18.2 Iterative server using sockets.

```
import socket

class IterativeServer:
    def __init__(self, hostname, port):
        self.address = (hostname, port)
        self.sock = socket.socket(socket.AF_INET, socket.SOCK_STREAM)
        self.sock.bind(self.address)
```

```
            self.sock.listen(5)
            self.running = 0
            self.count = 0

    def run(self):
        self.running = 1
        print "Server Running."
        while self.running:
            try:
                (client, fromAddress) = self.sock.accept()
                self.processClient(client, fromAddress)
            except socket.error, e:
                print "ERROR: Unable to accept connection:", e
                self.running = 0
            if self.count == 5:
                self.running = 0
        print "Processed %d requests. Exiting." % self.count

    def processClient(self, client, fromAddress):
        """Echo data back to the client.
        """
        try:
            data = client.recv(100)
            data = "ECHO: <%s>" % data
            total = len(data)
            current = 0
            while current < total:
                current += client.send(data[current:])
        except socket.error, e:
            print "ERROR: processing client", e
        self.count += 1
        client.close()
        print "Processed connection from ", fromAddress

server = IterativeServer("localhost", 7777)
server.run()
```

This server reads data from the incoming client connection and echoes that data back to the client. The act of processing a connection is handled by the processClient method. This method blocks on the receive and send operations, so the entire process is synchronous. Notice that the processClient method is very similar to the handle method of the GameRequestHandler class shown previously.

After processing five requests, the server exits. The following output is from running this server.

```
$ python server1.py
```

```
Server Running.
Processed connection from  ('127.0.0.1', 1202)
Processed connection from  ('127.0.0.1', 1207)
Processed connection from  ('127.0.0.1', 1212)
Processed connection from  ('127.0.0.1', 1217)
Processed connection from  ('127.0.0.1', 1222)
Processed 5 requests. Exiting.
```

Notice that the port number in the connecting address is different in each connection. IP connections implicitly allocate a local port when a connection is made. This port is used as the address to route data back to the connecting application.

This server can be connected to with the standard *telnet* program that is available on most computer systems. The following output shows the data echoed back to the telnet session.

```
$ telnet localhost 7777
 Trying 127.0.0.1...
 Connected to athlon1100.
 Escape character is '^]'.
 testing hi there!!
 ECHO: <testing hi there!!
 >Connection closed by foreign host.
```

Notice that the trailing ">" character is on a new line from the rest of the echoed message. This is because the data echoed back includes the return character that triggered the telnet program to send the current line that was entered. In addition, notice that the address *localhost* was transformed into the local loopback address *127.0.01* when the telnet client connected to the server.

This server can also be created with the SocketServer module. The following code creates an iterative server using the SocketServer module and processes five requests before exiting.

```
# Simple Iterative Server
server = SocketServer.TCPServer(address, GameRequestHandler)
for i in range(0,5):
    server.handle_request()
```

This code uses one of the built-in server classes of the SocketServer module. The TCPServer class is a blocking, single-threaded, single-process server class that passes requests to the specified handler class. Each client connection is considered a single request, and an instance of the handler class is created for it—in this case, the GameRequestHandler class. The handle_request method of the server blocks until a client connects to the server. To process each request, the series of methods setup, handle, and `finish` are invoked on the `handler` object. As the `GameRequestHandler` implements the `handle` method, its version of that method is invoked. Only one request can be processed at a time, and the default implementations of these methods do nothing. The output of this server is:

```
$ python socketserver.py
  (PID:564:THREAD:936) Processed Request from 127.0.0.1:1662
  (PID:564:THREAD:936) Processed Request from 127.0.0.1:1667
  (PID:564:THREAD:936) Processed Request from 127.0.0.1:1672
  (PID:564:THREAD:936) Processed Request from 127.0.0.1:1677
  (PID:564:THREAD:936) Processed Request from 127.0.0.1:1682
```

Notice that the process IDs and thread IDs are the same for all of the requests. All the requests are processed in the main (and only) thread of the only thread that makes up the server.

This server model can be appropriate for some situations, such as a login server that authenticates users and returns them a ticket. However, its blocking, synchronous nature means that it does not take advantage of the parallelism between the network and the computer's CPU, and will not scale to handle many requests. If many clients attempt to connect to this server, the listen queue will become full, and clients will receive an error that the connection was refused.

For multiplayer game development, this server model is only suitable for the simplest games, or possibly for simple network infrastructure services used by online games.

Concurrent Forking Server

The concurrent forking server model handles multiple client connections by spawning or forking an OS process to handle each client. This new process is then responsible for all communication between the client and the server. When spawning a new process, a new program is executed to handle the client. When forking a new process, the current process is copied and the new copy follows a new path of execution to handle the client while the original continues running the `accept` loop.

Having a separate process for each client allows the application to have independent paths of execution to handle each client. These client processes operate concurrently, and in isolated environments. Usually, the server will limit itself to a certain number of active child processes at any time. Clients that connect when all of the processes are in use are queued for later processing, or rejected outright.

A variant of this model is to *pre-fork* a number of processes and keep those processes in a pool of *worker processes* to handle clients. This variant avoids the cost of starting a process for each client, but introduces some different complications. It requires processes to be used for multiple clients in a serial fashion. When a process finishes a dialog with a particular client, it is assigned a new client with which to work. This reuse of processes is more complicated in some ways than starting a fresh, new process for each client, as the application must be very careful to clean up all state and remove all references to previous clients before working with a new client. Some common Unix servers such as database servers and Web servers use this model.

This server model does not restrict client interactions to be discrete events. The iterative server discussed previously requires that a client connect, communicate, and disconnect in a single operation within a short period of time. However, since this server model has a dedicated process for each client, it allows clients to stay connected and perform multiple communications over any period of time.

Figure 18.2 shows the architecture of this server model.

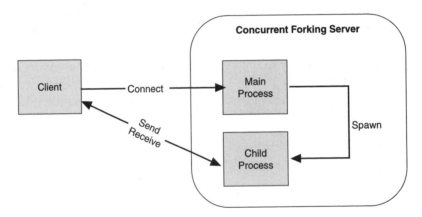

FIGURE 18.2 Concurrent forking server.

In this model, the main process of the application is just an entry point and management facility for the child processes. Similar to the iterative server, the main process operates an accept loop that is usually a blocking accept call. When a client connection is received, a new process is created (or drawn from a pool of existing processes) and assigned to handle the new client.

During operation, this type of server must keep track of the child processes it has spawned, and be aware when any of those processes exit. In general, in systems programming, parent processes that spawn children processes must clean up those processes to free the resources that those children own. As a parent process, the main process of servers of this model falls into this category. The server must perform a *wait* or *join* for each child process that exits to ensure it is finalized correctly by the OS. These operations are OS calls that exist specifically to release the resources of child processes.

Servers of this type must provide a way for information to be communicated between the parent and child processes. If the child process is spawned, this can be done with command-line arguments. A custom command line can be generated for each client process and used when that process is started. In addition, there are other interprocess communication mechanisms that can be used between parent and child processes, including pipes, inherited file descriptors, and shared memory. However, these methods are not as efficient as local operations within processes and are much more difficult to use.

Implementation of this type of server is further complicated by the differences between the process models of Windows-based and Unix-based OSs. Python's os modules exposes the necessary process operations to implement this type of server on Unix, but the lack of availability of certain functionality on Windows makes cross-platform implementations of this type of server difficult with the base Python distribution.

The SocketServer module can be used to implement a version of the concurrent forking server. It provides a ForkingTCPServer class that implements the forking functionality of spawning a process to process each request. The code for this server is shown here:

```
# Concurrent Forking Server
server = SocketServer.ForkingTCPServer(address, GameRequestHandler)
for i in range(0,5):
    server.handle_request()
```

This code is very similar to the iterative server discussed previously, and the results are also very similar. The main difference is that multiple requests can be processed simultaneously, as there is a process to handle each request. The following output shows each request with a different process ID. Note that this class only works on Unix, *not* on Windows.

```
$ python socketserver.py
 (PID:565:THREAD:936) Processed Request from 127.0.0.1:1662
 (PID:566:THREAD:936) Processed Request from 127.0.0.1:1667
 (PID:567:THREAD:936) Processed Request from 127.0.0.1:1672
 (PID:568:THREAD:936) Processed Request from 127.0.0.1:1677
 (PID:569:THREAD:936) Processed Request from 127.0.0.1:1682
```

Multiprocess servers are among the most heavy-weight of the server models. They require a relatively high amount of system resources, as data might have to be duplicated between the memory spaces of different processes. They can be slow to handle client connections if processes are spawned each time, but this can be alleviated to some degree with careful application of a pool of worker processes. They also require interprocess communication, which introduces an additional level of complexity to the application.

On single processor systems, multiprocess servers can suffer from the overhead of *context switching*, which is the time it takes the CPU to switch between the executions of different processes. If the application performs many units of small work in different processes, the impact of context switching can be considerable for multiprocess servers.

Concurrent Threaded Server

The concurrent threaded server model handles multiple clients simultaneously by assigning a thread to each client connection. The thread is then responsible for all network operations between the client and the server. Usually, application-specific logic or processing is performed in the main thread, and only network specific operations are performed in the client's threads. This model is similar to the concurrent forking server model described earlier, but it uses the lighter-weight implementation of threads instead of processes.

Similar to the forking server, each thread is an independent path of execution that is dedicated to a single client connection. However, unlike processes, threads exist in the same memory as the main thread, so they are not in an isolated environment. This enables easier communication between the different paths of execution, but introduces potential data sharing issues, as multiple threads can access the same piece of data at the same time.

Similar to the forking server, it is possible to have a pool of *worker threads* that handle client connections, and to limit the number of connections based on the number of available threads, or some application-specific maximum.

In this model, the main thread of the application is an entry point and management facility. The main thread is usually the owner of the major application objects, such as the game world, and performs all of the game logic and simulation operations. Having this thread as the central executor of logic reduces the number of potential cases of data being used by multiple threads simultaneously.

In this model, client threads perform network I/O and transform the data into game messages, events, or requests, which are pushed into thread-safe holding queues. When the main thread is ready, it reads the data from these queues and performs the required processing. In a similar way, outgoing events and messages directed at clients are pushed to a thread-safe queue that is read by the client thread, and transformed into data that is sent to the appropriate client. Figure 18.3 shows this model.

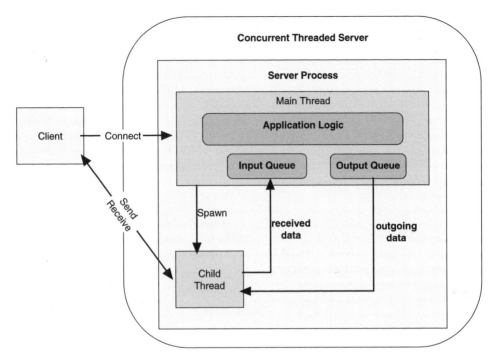

FIGURE 18.3 Threaded server.

Python's standard distribution includes thread support with the `thread` and `threading` modules that use the OS's underlying thread support. It also includes the `mutex` module for mutually exclusive access to shared data. These facilities can be used to build multithreaded servers in Python, but true multithreaded capabilities are restricted in Python due to the *global interpreter lock*. Since Python's core is not completely thread safe, there is a global lock that is kept by the active thread so that it can safely access Python data.

The `SocketServer` module can be used to implement a version of the concurrent threaded server. It provides a `ThreadingTCPServer` class that implements the functionality of spawning a thread to process each request. The code for this server is shown here:

```
# Concurrent Threading Server
server = SocketServer.ThreadingTCPServer(address, GameRequestHandler)
for i in range(0,5):
    server.handle_request()
```

This code is very similar to the concurrent forking server, and the results are also very similar. The main difference is that each request is handled in a thread instead of in a separate process. The following output shows each request with the same process ID and a different thread ID. Note that this class works on Unix and Windows.

```
$ python server3.py
 (PID:784:THREAD:1196) Processed Request from 127.0.0.1:1095
 (PID:784:THREAD:1204) Processed Request from 127.0.0.1:1100
 (PID:784:THREAD:1196) Processed Request from 127.0.0.1:1105
 (PID:784:THREAD:1204) Processed Request from 127.0.0.1:1110
 (PID:784:THREAD:1196) Processed Request from 127.0.0.1:1115
```

Multithreaded servers use fewer resources than multiprocess servers do, but they are still not the most efficient of the server models. Threads themselves take up OS resources, and the locking objects that provide exclusive access to shared data do also. Multithreaded servers also suffer from the overhead of context switching between the threads of the application. Although less than the overhead of switching between processes, it does take some time for applications to switch their active thread.

Multithreaded programming is a complex topic that can be more difficult than it initially appears. Issues such as exclusive access to data, dead-locks, and thread starvation can make the development of multithreaded servers much more difficult than the development of single-threaded applications. The impact of introducing multithreaded issues into a project can be high, so this server model should only be chosen if these issues are well understood by the development team.

Concurrent Asynchronous Server (Reactor Pattern)

This server model uses nonblocking I/O to enable it to handle multiple client connections concurrently in a single-threaded, single-process application. It provides the benefits that come with concurrent client connections, without the problems of multithreaded or multiprocess programming.

This model uses the *select* OS service to check for the availability of *waitable* objects. In this context, waiting objects are sockets, and their availability means that data can be sent or received with a guarantee that the operation will not block. This enables the server to perform network operations in a predictable timeframe, something that the other server models are unable to do with their blocking I/O strategies.

In this model, the application responds or *reacts* to events from the network. In a similar way to how the iterative server requires the entire dialog with a client to be a single, discrete operation, this server model requires each reaction to a network event to be a discrete operation that completes in a bounded amount of time. This server model is sometimes called the *reactor pattern* because the application reacts to events from the network. Figure 18.4 shows the architecture of this server model.

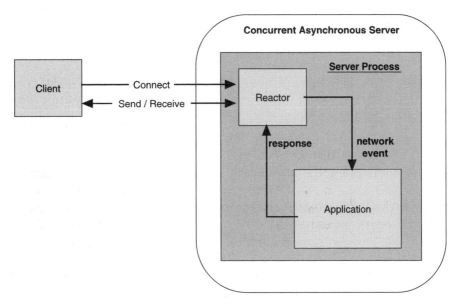

FIGURE 18.4   Concurrent asynchronous server model.

The implementation of concurrent asynchronous servers is quite complex. Python's standard distribution includes the select module that exposes functionality that can be used to implement the reactor pattern. Select works by accepting sets of waiting objects from application code, and returning subsets of these sets of objects that can be processed without blocking. The key to the select module is that it allows nonblocking I/O to be performed on multiple sockets.

The select method is sometimes called within a select loop in a similar way that accept loops work. The order of operations for a select loop is:

1. Build the set of readable sockets.
2. Build the set of writable sockets.
3. Build the set of exceptional objects.
4. Call select with the sets of sockets.
5. Receive the sets of sockets that will not block.
6. Perform network operations on the nonblocking sockets.

This strategy ensures that the application never blocks on network I/O. The CPU can stay busy performing simulations, or application logic, and can invoke this set of operations at convenient times knowing that it will not block.

The SocketServer module does not provide asynchronous I/O capabilities, so it cannot be used to write servers of this type. The Twisted server framework described in the next section is used for developing asynchronous server applications.

Developing the infrastructure for a server that can perform asynchronous network operations is a nontrivial task. In some ways, it is more complex than developing the infrastructure for a multiprocess or multithreaded server. However, once this infrastructure is in place, the application code that uses this infrastructure is more flexible and less constrained than any of the other server models. Of the server models discussed, this server model is the least intrusive into application code.

As a single process, single-threaded application, servers of this model use a low amount of resources in comparison to the other server models. As they do not require locking objects, thread objects, or process objects to operate, these servers don't require management mechanisms for these types of objects. Context switching is also not an issue for concurrent asynchronous servers, as they exist within a single thread of a single process.

The Twisted network framework is an open-source project that provides a server that falls under this model. This server will be used for some of the examples in this book and is discussed in detail in the next section.

18.4 INTRODUCTION TO TWISTED

Twisted is a framework written in Python for building networked applications. It provides a large suite of services that range from low-level system services, to high-level application services. Some of the functionality that Twisted provides is extremely useful for multiplayer game development. Twisted actually began its life as a game server, and it continues to be appropriate as a platform for building online games. Twisted is being described here as it is used in the example code in this chapter, and is also used in the examples in the remaining multiplayer chapters in this book.

Twisted uses an asynchronous, concurrent server model and uses the reactor pattern. It conveniently manages the low-level details of asynchronous I/O and socket management with classes that provide clean and simple interfaces to application code. This means that applications written with Twisted never have to perform direct socket operations or interact directly with the network layer of the OS. They can use the interfaces provided by Twisted, and be sure that error handling is being performed correctly at the OS level. This separation from the low-level network layer allows for faster application development, and less platform-specific or nonportable code.

Twisted is an open-source project with a distributed community of developers. The hub of development is Twisted Matrix Labs, which can be found online at *www.twistedmatrix.com*. There are mailing lists and IRC channels that can be accessed from the Web site that are devoted to the development and use of Twisted. The full source code to the Twisted project can be downloaded from the site, including documentation, examples, and a suite of unit tests.

The example code in this book only uses a small portion of Twisted. The entire Twisted package includes application-level functionality such as a Web server, an FTP server, a chat server, a distributed object system, and a relational database interface. This book's example code use none of these high-level components; it uses some of the lower-level components that perform application-neutral services.

The Twisted Reactor

The core piece of Twisted asynchronous framework is the `Reactor` class. This class implements support for managing multiple network connections and processing network operations for these connections in a reactive manner. It is this component that implements the concurrent asynchronous server model described previously. In applications that use Twisted, the reactor is in *control* of the application. It is told to run, and it takes over the application and calls user code when appropriate to react to events. In the example game code in this book, the reactor is used in a less intrusive manner. As games have their own `main` loop and prefer to remain in control of its execution, instead of passing control to the reactor, the example code initializes the reactor, and then calls an `update` method on it each iteration through the `main` loop. The code used to perform this update is shown here:

```
from twisted.internet import reactor

# update the network
reactor.runUntilCurrent()
reactor.doSelect(0)
```

This code will be seen in the client and server example later in this book. The `runUntilCurrent` method processes any pending application events, and the `doSelect` method processes pending network events.

Twisted Protocols

The other main component of Twisted used in this book is the protocol class. This class provides an abstract interface to a network connection and allows application code to interact with the network layer. The protocol class is a base class from which user classes are derived. It has methods that are invoked by the Twisted framework when network events occur, and when data is available to read on the connection. Methods are called on the protocol class from within the doSelect method of the reactor, and only one such call is active at a time. This conforms to the single-threaded reactor model that Twisted uses and means that application code does not need to deal with thread-related issues.

The protocol class has a data member that is its *transport*. This file-like object is responsible for the actual data transmission functionality of the protocol. When application code sends data on the protocol's connection, it writes to the transport object.

The details of using the Twisted protocol class are included in the coming sections as the details of game protocol design are discussed.

18.5 GAME PROTOCOL DESIGN

Protocols are standard procedures for regulating data transmission between computers. In multiplayer games, the participants communicate with each other using predefined protocols. The design of multiplayer game protocols is a topic that has a large impact on the bandwidth usage, stability, performance, and development time of games. This sections discusses game protocols, and develops a protocol for client/server game architectures.

Static and Dynamic Protocols

There are two broad categories of protocols used for network communication in games: *static* and *dynamic*. One of the key differences between these types of protocols is the location of the information that specifies the contents of each message.

In static protocols, the types of messages that can be sent using the protocol are specified in the protocol description. The types of message are fixed for that version of the protocol. Both sides of a connection using a static protocol are aware of all the possible messages that can be used and understand how to process them. Because of this shared knowledge, static protocols only require a small amount of auxiliary information to be transmitted. Usually, it is enough to specify a *message type* that both ends of the connection understand. Many traditional network applications and most multiplayer games use static protocols.

For dynamic protocols, messages can be built as the program is running. Messages have type information encoded in them so they can contain arbitrary sets of data. Messages can be processed by using the type information encoded in them. Dynamic protocols require more bandwidth to account for their embedded type information, and require more processing resources to encode and decode the dynamic messages. Moreover, developing the infrastructure for a dynamic protocol can be difficult, especially in languages with static typing such as C++. However, dynamic protocols provide a much greater level of flexibility and can increase the speed of game application development. Dynamic protocols are a platform on which higher-level network constructs such as distributed object systems can be built. When used in this way, they can provide a network layer that is very unobtrusive to the game application code. Some examples of dynamic protocols in use on the Internet are XML-RPC, CORBA, and Twisted's Perspective Broker. In addition, some massively multiplayer online games use distributed object systems built on dynamic protocols.

The discussions of protocols in this chapter are focused on static protocols. Figure 18.5 shows messages in static and dynamic protocols.

Static Protocol Message   Dynamic Protocol Message

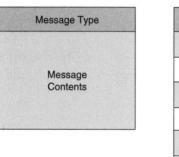
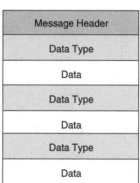

FIGURE 18.5   Static and dynamic messages.

Streams and Packing

The format of data that is sent over a network connection is very specific. Both ends of the connection must be in agreement about the format of data, or communication is impossible. Most network protocols use binary stream formats, as they pack the most information into the smallest amount of bandwidth and are most efficient to read and write. Some protocols that are not intended for real-time use such as XML-RPC use text format streams, but this is not recommended for game development.

Binary protocols must have conventions for processing all of the low-level data types that the protocol supports. Usually, these include types such as 32-bit integers, 16-bit shorts, 8-bit characters, 32-bit floating-point numbers, and 64-bit double precision floating-point numbers. Some protocols extend this basic set with higher-level constructs such as lists, strings, Booleans, or even dictionaries.

In Python where the socket module requires network buffers to be strings, it is not immediately obvious how to pack binary data into string buffers. Python strings are immutable, which further complicates the process. It is better to use the Python array module rather than strings for network buffers. As arrays are mutable, they do not have to be reallocated or copied each time they are changed by application code. Listing 18.3 shows how to pack and unpack a 32-bit integer into a Python array.

Listing 18.3 Integer packing and unpacking.

```python
import array

def pack_int(intValue, buffer):
    """pack an integer value to the buffer
    """
    for i in range(3,-1,-1):
        byteValue = (intValue >> (i*8) ) & 0xff
        buffer.append(byteValue)

def unpack_int(buffer, pos):
    """unpack an integer value from the buffer
    """
    intValue = 0
    pos = pos+3
    for i in range(3,-1,-1):
        byteValue = buffer[pos-i]
        intValue += (byteValue << (i*8) )
    return intValue

buffer = array.array('B')
pack_int(7777, buffer)
print unpack_int(buffer,0)
```

This code iterates through each of the four bytes of the 32-bit integer to read them from, or write them to, the buffer array. The array is created with a type specifier of `'B'` to make it an unsigned byte array. Each entry in the array is an unsigned 8-bit integer value, so a 32-bit integer is packed into four bytes of the array. If this were a text format stream, an integer number could take up a varying number of bytes. For example, a small number such as 213 takes up three bytes, which is less than the packed binary format, but a large number such as 1,000,000,000 (1 billion) takes up 10 bytes. Because of this, text protocols usually require extra length information or separators to define the end points of individual items. Binary protocols are more predictable and efficient.

Although this code works, performing this type of low-level operation in Python is not optimal. It is also problematic for floating-point numbers. Decoding the binary format of Python floating-point numbers with Python code is a tricky process. Python's standard distribution includes the `struct` module and the `xdrlib` module for packing binary data. The example code in this chapter uses the `xdrlib` module to pack data. This module uses an internal buffer to build streams of data, and provides methods to pack most of the common Python data types. The module exposes `Packer` and `Unpacker` classes that perform the actual data manipulation. Some of the methods on the `Packer` class of `xdrlib` module include:

- `pack_int( intValue )`— packs a 32-bit integer
- `pack_float( floatValue )`— packs a 32-bit floating-point number
- `pack_string( stringValue )`—packs a variable length string

The corresponding methods of the `Unpacker` class of the `xdrlib` module are:

- `unpack_int()`—returns an unpacked 32-bit integer
- `unpack_float()`—returns an unpacked 32-bit floating-point number
- `unpack_string()`—returns an unpacked string

These methods are used later in this chapter when we develop a protocol.

Network Packets

Almost all protocols are comprised of network messages or *packets*. Each packet has a specified size, some information that specifies which packet type it is, and a payload of data. In static protocols, the packet type specifies the contents of the packet payload, so the protocol code can have specific code to read and write the contents of each packet type. Figure 18.6 shows an example of the structure of a packet.

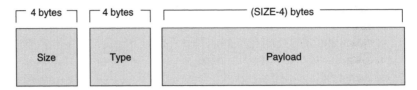

FIGURE 18.6 Packet structure.

In the Figure 18.6, the first four bytes of the packet are a 32-bit size value for the remaining portions of the packet. The next four bytes are a 32-bit packet type value, and the next (size – 4) bytes are the payload of the packet. This structure shows how packets are read from the network. First, the protocol reads the initial four-byte size information, and then uses this value to determine how many more bytes must be read for the packet to be complete. Once all the data is received, it can extract the packet type from the data, and assume that the remaining portion of data is the complete payload. As static protocols usually have specific code for reading each packet type, this code can then be invoked to process the packet payload.

A naive Python implementation of a network packet reader could look like:

```
# read the size and type
sizeData = socketRead(4)
typeData = socketRead(4)

# unpack the size and type
packetSize = unpack_int(sizeData)
packetType = unpack_int(typeData)

# read the payload using the size
payload = socketRead(packetSize)

# find the handler and invoke it
packetHandler = lookupHandler(packetType)
packetHandler(payload)
```

This code reads four bytes for each of the packet size and the packet types. Once it has these values and unpacks them, they are used to read the payload and to pass it off to a registered `handler` method. This code assumes that the `socketRead` method blocks to retrieve the specified number of bytes.

There is a serious problem with this piece of code: it requires three separate network `read` operations to obtain all the data for a single packet, and each of these network `read` operations causes the application to block. This code could not be used in a concurrent asynchronous game server, as it would stop the entire server while it waits for the three pieces of data to arrive.

The solution to this problem is to isolate the network I/O from the packet encoding and decoding. This isolation is achieved by using `buffer` objects that hold network data. Packet processing is performed from the `buffer` object rather than from the network stream directly. This technique allows nonblocking network operations to populate the `buffer` objects in a single step, and allows packets to be read from the buffer only when they are complete. Figure 18.7 shows this process.

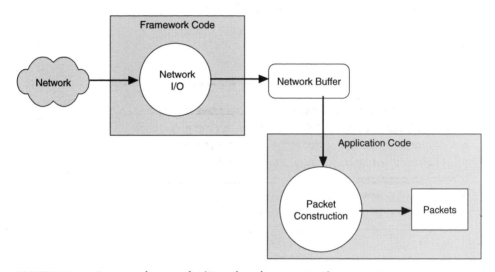

FIGURE 18.7 Separated network I/O and packet construction.

In Figure 18.7, the direct network I/O is performed by the network framework, and writes into a buffer. Packets are then constructed from this buffer by application code asynchronously.

The Twisted framework provides a `protocol` class that implements this type of functionality. This framework class calls application code when network events occur, and when data is available on the connection. The interface to Twisted's `protocol` class that invokes application code is shown here:

```
def connectionMade(self):
    """Called when a connection is established.
    """
```

```
def dataReceived(self, data):
    """Called when any data is received on the connection
    """

def connectionLost(self, reason=connectionDone):
    """Called when the connection is shutdown
    """
```

The `dataReceived` method is the key to the separation of network I/O and packet construction. The application-specific implementation of this method is responsible for managing the contents of the network buffer. The following code shows a portion of a `protocol` class derived from the `Twisted` `protocol` class that can read a packet from the network without blocking.

```
import xdrlib
import struct
from twisted.internet.protocol import Protocol

MSG_ERROR = -99

class GProtocol(Protocol):
    """A Protocol for game messages.
    """
    def connectionMade(self):
        """ (called by Twisted framework)
        """
        self.packetBuffer = ""
        self.packetSize = 0
        self.errorMsg = ""
        self.errorId = 0
        self.msgMap = {}

    def dataReceived(self, data):
        """ (called by Twisted framework)
        this method received data from the network. It has two states,
            - receiving a packet size
            - receiving the rest of a packet
        """
        self.packetBuffer += data

        # process all the packets in the data.
        while self.packetBuffer:
            if self.packetSize == 0:
                # reading the size
                if len(self.packetBuffer) < 4:
                    return
```

```
            else:
                    self.packetSize=struct.unpack('i',
self.packetBuffer[:4])[0] + 4
                    print "Got packet size of :", self.packetSize

        if len(self.packetBuffer) >= self.packetSize:
            # we have a full packet
            packetData = self.packetBuffer[4:self.packetSize]
            self.packetBuffer = self.packetBuffer[self.packetSize:]
            self.packetSize = 0
            self.processPacket(packetData)
        else:
            print "Read %d bytes.. waiting." %
len(self.packetBuffer)
            return
```

In the dataReceived call, the data passed in is immediately appended to the object's packetBuffer data member. A loop is then entered to read data from this buffer until no more full packets can be found. If this loop was not present, the code would only process one packet each time it is invoked. If multiple packets happened to arrive in the same network read, all but the first would be delayed at best.

Note that *reading* in this context is not actually reading from the network, but is reading from the network buffer. This type of read operation is entirely in-memory and will never block.

The packet-processing loop has two states. It can be reading the size of the next packet, or reading the payload of a packet. When it completes reading the size of a packet, it unpacks the size value from the four bytes read, and switches to reading the payload of that specified size. When it completes reading a full packet payload, it calls the processPacket helper method to dispatch the packet to application code. This method is shown here:

```
def processPacket(self, data):
    """Process a packet from the connection. Sends an error
    if the handler method fails.
    """
    unpacker = xdrlib.Unpacker(data)
    msgId = unpacker.unpack_int()
    handlerMethod = self.msgMap.get(msgId)
    if handlerMethod:
        try:
            if not handlerMethod(unpacker):
                self.sendError()
        except:
            print "Exception in msg handler"
            raise
```

```
    else:
        print "Unknown network message", msgId
```

This method uses an `Unpacker` object from the `xdrlib` module. It first unpacks the packet type, and then uses that type to find a registered handler for the packet type. The handler is then invoked and passed the `unpacker` object so that it can perform whatever unpacking operations it requires. Handler methods are added to this protocol with the `registerHandler` method shown here:

```
def registerHandler(self, msgId, handler):
    self.msgMap[msgId] = handler
```

The following is an example of using this method to set up a handler for the `CS_JOIN_GAME` message.

```
self.registerHandler(CS_JOIN_GAME, self.onJoinGame)

def onJoinGame(self, unpacker):
    name = unpacker.unpack_string()
    self.app.joinGame(name, self.player)
    return 1
```

This handler unpacks a single string from the `unpacker` object and calls into application code with the string value. This system is used in the next chapter when an example multiplayer game is implemented.

There are two more methods on the `GProtocol` class. The `writePacker` method is a utility for writing the contents of a `xdrlib` packer object to the network. It prepends the packer's contents with a size value to conform to the protocol. The `sendError` method sends an error message to the connection. Both methods use the *transport* data member that provides access to data writing, and querying parameters of the connection associated with the protocol. These two methods are shown here:

```
def writePacker(self, packer):
    """Helper method for writing the contents of a packer"""
    buffer = packer.get_buffer()
    sizeBuffer = struct.pack('i', len(buffer))
    self.transport.write(sizeBuffer)
    self.transport.write(buffer)

def sendError(self):
    """Helper method for sending errors to the client
    print "Error:", self.errorId, self.errorMsg
    packer = xdrlib.Packer()
```

```
packer.pack_int(MSG_ERROR)
packer.pack_int(self.errorId)
packer.pack_string(self.errorMsg)
self.writePacker(packer)
```

This code assumes that the TCP/IP protocol is being used. Protocols for UDP are different due to the connectionless nature of the protocol. It is possible to write UDP protocols that are extremely simple by just passing discrete packets, but the lack of guaranteed delivery of UDP packets makes implementing a full game application with UDP quite complex. Functionality for resending lost packets, managing packet priorities, and managing virtual connections that are overlaid on the connectionless UDP sockets must be dealt with. For applications or games, using TCP/IP is much simpler in most cases.

SUMMARY

This chapter described components of network layers that are used in multiplayer game development. It included the basics of socket programming with Python, reading and writing data with sockets to network connections, a number of TCP/IP server models, an introduction to the *Twisted* server framework, and a discussion and implementation of a network protocol for games.

The code in this chapter is relatively general and could be used in multiple networked game applications. Sharing of network layers between applications is common, as it allows them to communicate easily and efficiently, and reduces the amount of code required. Sharing a network layer implementation is even better than just sharing a network protocol between applications. It helps to ensure that all participants have the same version of the protocol in place, and that their assumptions on its use are identical.

The infrastructure discussed and developed in this chapter can be used as the basis for the network layer for a multiplayer game. In Chapter 19, "Clients and Servers," a generic client server architecture for multiplayer games is developed using this network layer. It includes the capability to run multiple game instances on a single server, and a lobby for players to view and join games. In Chapter 20, "Multiplayer Game Example," a multiplayer version of the classic Tic-Tac-Toe game is developed using this infrastructure.

19 Clients and Servers

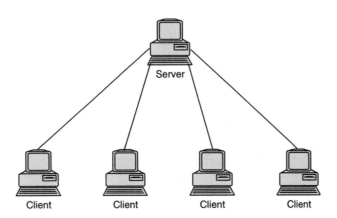

M ultiplayer games employ a number of network architectures that include the peer-to-peer network model, the client/server network model, and the complex massively multiplayer network model. The client/server model is probably the most common architecture for online games, and is the architecture with the most parallels in non-gaming application development.

Game servers and game clients communicate with each other using specific protocols and often share code that implements protocols and other low-level network functionality. Some elements of game clients and servers are general enough to be isolated into framework code that is application neutral. This type of framework code can be reused for different game applications and used as a stable platform to increase the speed at which new multiplayer games can be developed.

Python's excellent support for network programming makes it possible to develop multiplayer game applications quickly. As networked applications are often event driven, Python's functional nature makes it a good language for implementing the message processing and routing components of a network layer.

This chapter discusses some of the common game architectures and describes the implementation of a general-purpose game server and client. This set of applications provides a game lobby and the ability to join and leave game instances on the server. Section 19.1 discusses multiplayer game architectures, and Section 19.2

discusses code organization for multiplayer games. Section 19.3 shows how a general-purpose game server can be implemented using the Twisted framework, and Section 19.4 shows how to develop a corresponding client for the game server.

19.1 MULTIPLAYER GAME ARCHITECTURES

There are a number of well-known multiplayer architectures used by games. These architectures describe the roles of the participating machines, the relationships between them, and the nature of the data that each machine possesses. The common multiplayer game architectures are *peer-to-peer*, *client/server*, and *massively multiplayer*.

Peer-to-Peer Architecture

In the peer-to-peer game architecture, each participant establishes a network connection to each of the other participants. The machines involved in the game communicate with each other directly, forming a type of star network. Although one machine might be a coordinator, for most purposes, each machine in the network is equal with all of the others.

From a network perspective, all of the participants in this model are both clients and servers. As each participant accepts connections from each of the other machines, it must listen for incoming connections like a server. As each participant connects to the other machines, it must actively make connections like a client (see Figure 19.1.)

In this model, all of the machines have a complete copy of the game's data. There is no partitioning of game data for individual users. Games that use this model often run a *lock-step* simulation. This means that the simulation advances at a fixed rate on every machine simultaneously, but only when every machine in the multiplayer game is ready for the simulation to advance. This ensures that the data sets on all of the machines are up to date at all times.

This game architecture is commonly used by strategy games. Many of the popular real-time strategy games such as *Starcraft®* and *Age of Empires®* use the peer-to-peer architecture for multiplayer games.

An advantage of this architecture is that there is no single point of failure. If a machine leaves the game for any reason, the other participants can continue, as they each have a full copy of all the game data. Even if the coordinator machine leaves, a new coordinator can be chosen, and the game can continue.

The basic peer-to-peer game architecture cannot scale to handle large numbers of players, as the number of required network connections and data duplication

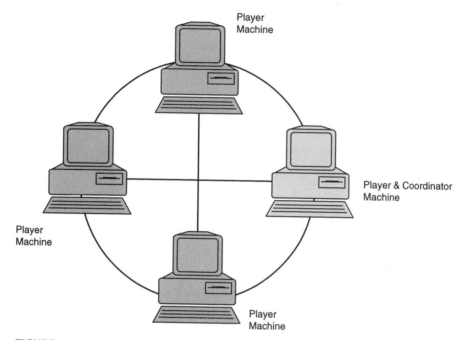

FIGURE 19.1   Peer-to-peer game architecture.

grows exponentially as the number of players increases. Since every player connects to every other player, the number of network connections required for a peer-to-peer game rises at a more than linear pace as the number of player increases. Figure 19.2 shows this.

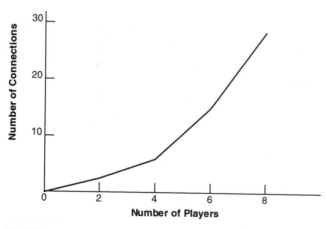

FIGURE 19.2   Number of connections in peer-to-peer games.

Peer-to-peer games are also limited in the size of the game world and amount of activity that can occur in them. As all the game data is resident on every machine and state changes for all portions of the game world are propagated to every machine, the bandwidth requirements for this model grow for every player as the number of players increases.

There are also security issues with peer-to-peer games across the Internet, as they require machines to expose their IP address to the other participants. Moreover, as all the players have access to all the information in the game world, they are susceptible to *map hacks* and other client-side cheating mechanisms.

Client/Server Architecture

In the client/server architecture, one machine is the designated server, and all the other participants are the clients. Communication occurs between the clients and the server with no communication happening between clients directly. In some cases, one of the client machines is also the server, and in some cases, there is a machine that is a *dedicated* server and not a client.

From a network perspective, this architecture fits easily into the definition of the TCP/IP client/server model described in the previous chapter. The server listens for and accepts incoming connections, and the clients actively connect to the server.

In this model, the server is the authoritative owner of all the game data and the sole decision maker for game events. Clients are usually only sent the portions of the world data that are relevant to the player at the current time. Therefore, at any time, the client only knows about its local surroundings, not the entire state of the game world. In this model, the master simulation runs on the server, and clients run their own simulations using the data available to them. The server simulation is not locked in any way to the simulation that runs on client machines.

This architecture is commonly used by action games, and games that require security. First-person shooters such as the action-oriented *Quake* and *Unreal* use this model, as well as online card and gambling games. Figure 19.3 shows the client/server architecture.

The client/server architecture allows games to handle larger numbers of players and larger game worlds than peer-to-peer games. Since communication occurs between the client and the server, the number of players has less impact on the total bandwidth used by the network. Moreover, additional players have no direct impact on the bandwidth used by each individual player's machine.

Since the players in the game do not have a full copy of the game world's data set, the data state updates required for each player require less bandwidth. This tactic is used with great effectiveness in first-person shooters who perform aggressive culling of networked objects based on visibility and proximity to players. It also al-

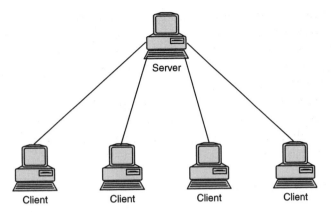

FIGURE 19.3 Client/server architecture.

lows complex simulations to be run on the server that are completely opaque to players. This technique means that the workings of the simulation are completely secure. The memory space that runs the simulation is not available for players to read or modify.

The multiplayer game example developed in this chapter uses the client/server game architecture.

Massively Multiplayer

In the massively multiplayer game architecture, there is a set of servers that run a huge game world or set of game worlds, additional servers for management and monitoring, and many clients that are routed through this set of servers as they play the game. This is the most complex of the server models, but also the model that scales to handle the largest game worlds and the most players.

From a network perspective, this model is made up of different types of servers that perform different functions, and many clients. The servers communicate with each other over private, secure networks, and the clients communicate to some of the servers over the Internet.

In this model, the game data is distributed among a set of servers, and can even be persisted to a secondary storage medium such as disk or a relational database. This architecture allows huge game worlds to exist, as the memory and processing power of multiple physical machines can be used to store and run it. This is enhanced by running multiple clusters of servers that are sometimes called *shards*. Each shard runs a separate instance of the game world in a partitioned space so that scalability issues with individual game worlds are bypassed.

This architecture is used for the massively multiplayer role-playing games such as *Ultima Online™* and *Everquest®*, and other large online games with persistence such as *Diablo®*. Figure 19.4 shows an example of a massively multiplayer game architecture.

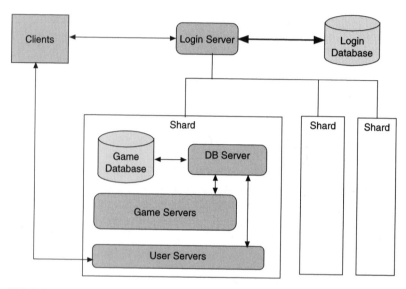

FIGURE 19.4 Massively multiplayer game architecture.

This model is an extension of the basic client/server model and shares many of the same characteristics. Secure simulations exist on the server, and data is sent to clients on a need-to-know basis. The processing for the simulation is hidden from the client in a similar way to the client/server model, but in this model, the processing is distributed over multiple server machines. This allows even large simulations to be created and even more players to be handled.

Note that developing a massively multiplayer game architecture is a difficult task involving many issues of network programming that don't exist in smaller multiplayer games. Considering the small number of games that have been built on this scale, using this model is truly only for those with quality technical expertise and large budgets.

19.2 CODE ORGANIZATION

When developing a multiplayer game, there are a number of distinct types of code. Some code is used exclusively by the server, some code is used exclusively by the client, and some code is shared by both the server and the client. These types can be further broken down into sub-areas that deal with functionality, but for the purposes of code organization, they form a useful and convenient categorization system.

Using these categories, code can be placed into Python modules that have particular responsibilities. The directory structure for the code of a multiplayer game might look like this:

■ Root game directory
  ● Client directory
  ● Shared directory
  ● Server directory

For the demonstration purposes of this chapter, the code for the generalized client/server framework resides in the hoopnet directory. This directory forms the root directory of the directory tree. Listing 19.1 shows the directories and files that exist within this directory.

Listing 19.1 Multiplayer game directory structure.

```
hoopnet/client/application.py
    hoopnet/client/protocol.py
    hoopnet/client/ui.py
    hoopnet/client/__init__.py
    hoopnet/server/gameserver.py
    hoopnet/server/protocol.py
    hoopnet/server/__init__.py
    hoopnet/shared/gprotocol.py
    hoopnet/shared/messages.py
    hoopnet/shared/player.py
    hoopnet/shared/__init__.py
    hoopnet/__init__.py
```

Note that this structure includes files named __init__.py in each directory. Remember that these files designate the directory as a Python module and allow files within it to be imported. To use this structure, the directory above the hoopnet directory must be added to the PYTHONPATH environment variable. Once this is in place, code can be imported from anywhere in the tree by specifying its location relative to the root path. The following import statements demonstrate this:

```
from hoopnet.shared.gprotocol import GProtocol
from hoopnet.shared.messages import *
from hoopnet.client.ui import LobbyFrame
```

This explicit importing technique is often used by Python library distributions. It prevents name conflicts between modules in different directories and classes in different modules. Notice that the coding convention of uppercase letters for the first letter of class name, and lowercase letters for module names allows the reader to distinguish between imports of classes and modules.

19.3 A GAME SERVER

This section describes how to build a game server using the Twisted framework. The portions of the game server described in this section are general enough that they could be applied to many different games. This server infrastructure is used in the next chapter where the Tic-Tac-Toe specific game logic is developed.

This game server has the capability to handle multiple clients, and to run multiple games simultaneously. The generic functionality allows clients to create, join, and leave games. This meta-game functionality acts as a lobby where players can see active games, and choose which games to enter.

This code is structured for the core of the game logic to be implemented on the server. In client/server multiplayer games, the server is the authoritative owner of the true game state and game rules. This is an important security consideration, as it helps to prevent clients from cheating and disrupting the game for others.

The major, generic components of the game server are the main GameServer class, the GameProtocolFactory class, and the ServerProtocol class. There is also a small ServerGame class that is a stub for user-defined game classes to derive from. Figure 19.5 shows the classes in the game server and their relationships.

In Figure 19.5, the shaded boxes are classes that belong to the game server framework, and the unshaded boxes are classes from the Twisted framework from which the framework classes are derived.

The core of the server is the GameServerApp class. There is a single instance of this class while the application is running, and it is responsible for tracking the players, games, and connections that exist. It has a main loop that could update a physical simulation, but for this particular game, there is no physical simulation to update. Listing 19.2 shows the code for the GameServerApp class.

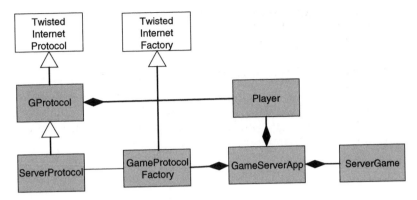

FIGURE 19.5 Game server class diagram.

Listing 19.2 GameServerApp class from gameserver.py.

```python
class GameServerApp:
    """GameServerApp is the central management class of the server.
    Tracks all of the connected players, and the active games.
    """
    def __init__(self, port, protocolClass, gameClass):
        self.port = port
        self.gameClass = gameClass
        self.factory = GameProtocolFactory(self, protocolClass)
        reactor.listenTCP(port, self.factory)
        self.players = []   # currently connected players
        self.games = []     # currently active games
        self.running = 1

    def run(self, delay):
        """Run the server until the game ends.
        """
        self.lastFrame = time.time()
        self.beginFrame = time.time()

        print "Server Running."
        while self.running:
            self.iterate()
            time.sleep(delay)

    def iterate(self):
        """Execute a single iteration of the server.
        """
        now = time.time()
```

```
        interval = now - self.beginFrame
        self.beginFrame = now

        # update the network
        reactor.doSelect(0)

        # update the games
        for game in self.games:
            game.update(interval)

    def login(self, name, player):
        """Player login message
        """
        player.name = name
        player.protocol.sendGameList(self.games)
        return 1

    def addPlayer(self, protocol):
        print "Adding player"
        newPlayer = Player(protocol)
        self.players.append(newPlayer)
        return newPlayer

    def removePlayer(self, player):
        print "Removing player"
        if player.currentGame:
            player.currentGame.removePlayer(player)
        player.destroy()
        self.players.remove(player)

    def createGame(self, name, player):
        """Create a new game instance.
        """
        for game in self.games:
            if game.name == name:
                # game already exists.
                player.setError(11, "Game %s already exists" % name)
                return 0

        newGame = self.gameClass(name, self)
        self.games.append(newGame)

        # tell all the players about the new game
        for p in self.players:
            p.protocol.sendNewGame(name)

        return self.joinGame(name, player)
```

```
def joinGame(self, name, player):
    """A player joins a game by its name.
    """
    if player.currentGame:
        player.setError(12, "Already playing a game")
        return 0

    # find the game
    for game in self.games:
        if game.name == name:
            result = game.addPlayer(player)
            if result:
                player.currentGame = game
            return result

    player.setError(13, "Game %s does not exist" % name)
    return 0

def leaveGame(self, player):
    if not player.currentGame:
        player.setError(15, "Not in a game!!!")
        return 0

    print "player leaving game"
    player.currentGame.removePlayer(player)
    player.currentGame = None

def removeGame(self, game):
    self.games.remove(game)
    for p in self.players:
        p.protocol.sendRemoveGame(game.name)
```

This class and the GameProtocolFactory and ServerProtocol classes work closely together when a new connection is made. The game server associates the factory with a port, and the factory creates protocol objects when clients connect. This process might seem complex, but in practice it is very flexible, and the abstractions of factories and protocols are very unobtrusive into application code. The sequence of events when the server is started is:

1. The server creates a factory with a protocol class.
2. The server registers the factory for a specific port.
3. The server listens on the port.
4. The server's main loop is run.

This startup process occurs in the constructor of the GameServerApp class. Once this process is complete, clients are able to connect to the server.

The game server class acts as a factory for game objects. The class is constructed with a gameClass argument that specifies the type of game object to create when a player requests a new game. This game class should have an interface that conforms to the simple base ServerGame class. It has methods that are invoked by the server when players enter or exit the game for any reason. They allow the game class to perform application-specific functionality to handle these cases. A game-specific class derived from the ServerGame class is shown later in this chapter. Listing 19.3 shows the code for the ServerGame class.

Listing 19.3 ServerGame class.

```
class ServerGame:
    def __init__(self, name, application):
        self.name = name
        self.application = application

    def addPlayer(self, player):
        pass

    def removePlayer(self, player):
        pass
```

Within the main loop of the game server, the doIterate method of the Twisted reactor is invoked. Within this call, Twisted performs asynchronous I/O and invokes application-level code to handle network events and data. The protocol methods such as connectionMade are invoked during this stage.

When a connection is received from a client, the sequence of events is:

1. The factory for the port is found by the framework.
2. The buildProtocol method of the factory is invoked by the framework.
3. A new protocol object is created of the protocol class specified previously.
4. The connectionMade method is called on the new protocol object.

Listing 19.4 shows the GameProtocolFactory class.

Listing 19.4 GameProtocolFactory class.

```
class GameProtocolFactory(Factory):
    """ Factory to pass the game server instance to protocol
    instances when they are created.
    """
```

```
def __init__(self, app, protocolClass):
    self.app = app
    self.protocolClass = protocolClass

def buildProtocol(self, addr):
    p = self.protocolClass(self.app)
    p.factory = self
    return p
```

This `factory` class creates protocol instances of the class that the factory was constructed with, and constructs them with a reference to the game server. When the framework invokes the `buildProtocol` method, the new `protocol` object that is created is able to interact with the game server.

The game server `protocol` class itself has a number of responsibilities. When network events occur, it calls methods on the game server that allow it to track the players that are online. The `addPlayer` and `removePlayer` methods shown in Listing 19.3 are used for this purpose. The `protocol` class is also responsible for receiving network messages. When a network message arrives, the `protocol` class invokes the appropriate `handler` method to unpack the data and process it. The final responsibility of the `protocol` class is to provide application-specific methods to send network messages. These methods perform the network layer packing of data for specific messages so they can be unpacked by `handler` methods.

As this game server has the built-in functionality of managing game instances and allowing players to join and leave games, it has a set of built-in network messages to handle this functionality. The start of the code for the `ServerProtocol` class is shown here:

```
import xdrlib

from hoopnet.shared.gprotocol import GProtocol
from hoopnet.shared.messages import *

class ServerProtocol(GProtocol):
    """Server side of game protocol
    """
    def __init__(self, app):
        self.app = app

    def connectionMade(self):
        """Create a player for this connection.
        """
        GProtocol.connectionMade(self)
        self.player = self.app.addPlayer(self)
```

```
        # setup message handlers
        self.registerHandler(CS_CREATE_GAME, self.onCreateGame)
        self.registerHandler(CS_JOIN_GAME, self.onJoinGame)
        self.registerHandler(CS_LOGIN, self.onLogin)
        self.registerHandler(CS_LEAVE_GAME, self.onLeaveGame)

    def connectionLost(self, reason):
        """Remove the player from the game.
        """
        self.app.removePlayer(self.player)
```

This code shows the methods that are invoked by the framework on network events. In the connectionMade method, the handler methods for network messages are registered. In this particular application, the prefix *CS* designates a message from the client to the server. The reverse prefix *SC* designates a message from the server to the client.

The following code shows the message handler methods of the ServerProtocol class. These are the methods that are registered in the connectionMade method shown previously.

```
    def onLogin(self, unpacker):
        name = unpacker.unpack_string()
        return self.app.login(name, self.player)

    def onCreateGame(self, unpacker):
        name = unpacker.unpack_string()
        print "Creating new game", name
        return self.app.createGame(name, self.player)

    def onJoinGame(self, unpacker):
        name = unpacker.unpack_string()
        self.app.joinGame(name, self.player)
        return 1

    def onLeaveGame(self, unpacker):
        self.app.leaveGame(self.player)
        return 1
```

These methods call into the game server application object so that it can manage game instances. They also allow the server to manage which players are involved in which games. The final part of the protocol code is the methods to send messages to the client. As each protocol instance is associated with a particular client, these methods don't require an address or socket. They call the writePacker method of the GProtocol class that was defined previously, to write the data to the transport

object for the connection. The code for the message-sending methods of the
ServerProtocol class is shown here:

```
def sendReady(self, gameName, numPlayers):
    packer = xdrlib.Packer()
    packer.pack_int(SC_GAME_READY)
    packer.pack_string(gameName)
    packer.pack_int(numPlayers)
    self.writePacker(packer)

def sendPlayerLeave(self, playerName):
    packer = xdrlib.Packer()
    packer.pack_int(SC_PLAYER_LEAVE)
    packer.pack_string(playerName)
    self.writePacker(packer)

def sendGameList(self, games):
    packer = xdrlib.Packer()
    packer.pack_int(SC_LIST_OF_GAMES)
    packer.pack_int( len(games))
    for game in games:
        packer.pack_string(game.name)
    self.writePacker(packer)

def sendRemoveGame(self, gameName):
    packer = xdrlib.Packer()
    packer.pack_int(SC_REMOVE_GAME)
    packer.pack_string(gameName)
    self.writePacker(packer)

def sendNewGame(self, gameName):
    packer = xdrlib.Packer()
    packer.pack_int(SC_NEW_GAME)
    packer.pack_string(gameName)
    self.writePacker(packer)
```

This set of messages informs the client of changes that occur on the server.
Connected clients keep a list of the games that exist on the server. When they connect, the full list of games is sent to them, and when a new game is created or an existing game is removed, a message is sent to the client to update its list. Notice that this code is entirely independent of any specific game and could be used to manage any type of client server multiplayer game.

The set of network messages used by this application framework are defined in the file hoopnet/shared/messages.py. This separation keeps the set of framework messages small, so it is more readily usable for other game applications. The messages are divided into client-to-server messages, and server-to-client messages. Each of these categories has a prefix; *CS* for client-to-server messages, and *SC* for server-to-client messages. These messages are shared between the server and the client. Listing 19.5 shows the messages.py file.

Listing 19.5   Framework message types.

```
# server to client messages
    SC_GAME_READY    = 1000
    SC_NEW_GAME      = 1001
    SC_LIST_OF_GAMES = 1002
    SC_PLAYER_LEAVE  = 1003
    SC_REMOVE_GAME   = 1004

    # client to server messages
    CS_LOGIN         = 2000
    CS_CREATE_GAME   = 2001
    CS_JOIN_GAME     = 2002
    CS_READY         = 2003
    CS_LEAVE_GAME    = 2004
```

Having specific message types for client-to-server and server-to-client reduces potential conflicts and makes the message handlers more explicit. Since servers only have handlers for client-to-server messages, if clients send messages of the wrong types, the server will ignore them.

This completes the generic portions of the server for this example application. This section showed how to build a server application using the Twisted framework. The client is implemented in the next section.

19.4 A GAME CLIENT

This section describes the construction of a game client to communicate with the game server from the previous section. It also uses the Twisted framework, the game protocol class that was defined in the previous chapter, and some other code from the *shared* section of the code tree created in Section 19.2. This client is not for any particular game; it is a generic client that could easily be modified or extended to be used for different types of games.

The game client connects to a single server at a time and can participate in a single game at a time. Unlike the server, it does not have to manage the details of multiple connections, players, and games; so it is much simpler than the server. It does keep a list of the games that exist on the server so that the player can choose games to join. The main classes of the client are `GenericClientApp`, `GameClientFactory`, and `ClientProtocol`. For interactivity and display, there is also a user interface class that uses PyUI. Figure 19.6 shows the classes in the client.

In Figure 19.6, the shaded boxes are classes that belong to the game server framework, and the unshaded boxes are classes from the Twisted framework from which the framework classes are derived.

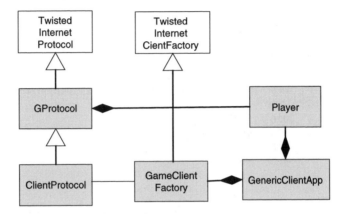

FIGURE 19.6 Client class diagram.

The game client has a main application and main loop that are very similar to the other examples in this book. The most significant difference from the previous examples is that in the `main` loop, it updates the network as well as the graphics engine. The start of the code for the main client `application` class called `GenericClientApp` is shown here:

```
import random
import time
import pyui

from twisted.internet.protocol import Protocol, ClientFactory
from twisted.internet import reactor

from hoop import engine

from hoopnet.shared.player import Player
from hoopnet.client.protocol import ClientProtocol
from hoopnet.client.ui import LobbyFrame
```

```
class GenericClientApp:
    def __init__(self, width, height, clientFactoryClass):
        self.clientFactoryClass = clientFactoryClass
        self.playerName = "Player%d" % random.randint(0,1000)
        self.gameNames = []
        self.currentGame = None

    def update(self, interval):
        """Update the network via the Twisted Reactor.
        """
        reactor.runUntilCurrent()
        reactor.doSelect(0)

    def onConnected(self, protocol):
        self.player = Player(protocol)
        self.lobby = LobbyFrame(self, self.playerName)
        self.requestLogin()
        return self.player

    def exit(self):
        self.running = 0

    def connect(self, hostname, port):
        print "Connecting to:", hostname, port
        reactor.connectTCP(hostname, port,
self.clientFactoryClass(self))
        reactor.running = 1

    def addPlayer(self, protocol):
        self.player = Player(protocol)
        self.lobby = LobbyFrame(self, self.playerName)
        self.requestConnect()
        return self.player

    def removePlayer(self, player):
        pass
```

The main application creates a single instance of this class that exists for the lifetime of the application. When the connect method is called, this application object connects to a server whose network address is passed to the method. Similar to the way the game server uses a factory to create protocol objects, this class uses a client factory to manage its connection to the server. The GameClientFactory object passed to this object when it is created manages details of the connection. The code for this class is shown here:

```
class GameClientFactory(ClientFactory):
    def __init__(self, app):
        self.app = app

    def startedConnecting(self, connector):
        print 'Started to connect.'

    def buildProtocol(self, addr):
        print 'Connected.'
        return ClientProtocol(self.app)

    def clientConnectionLost(self, connector, reason):
        print 'Lost connection.  Reason:', reason

    def clientConnectionFailed(self, connector, reason):
        print 'Connection failed. Reason:', reason
```

This class is derived from Twisted's ClientFactory class. It allows the application to respond to network events and to customize the way in which protocol classes are created. In this case, informational messages are printed when events occur, and the ClientProtocol object is created with a reference to the client application object.

The update method of the GenericClientApp class is called each frame during the main loop. This invokes the Twisted framework to process any network data or events that have occurred since the last time it was invoked. Under the covers, the reactor object performs asynchronous I/O, buffering, and management of callbacks into application code during this call. Message handlers and factory events are invoked during this phase. It should be noted that the handlers and application code invoked is called in a serial manner. A single thread is used for all of these calls, so there is no need to deal with thread-safe synchronization objects, thread-specific data, or other issues associated with multithreaded programming.

The onConnected method of the GenericClientApp class is invoked via the protocol object when a connection has been established with the server. This starts the sequence of login events between the client and the server. Figure 19.7 shows this sequence.

Figure 19.7 includes the events for logging into the server, and creating a game. It shows the messages between the client and server, and the handlers that are invoked on each side for each message.

The low-level operations for this sequence of events are carried out by the ClientProtocol class. Like the ServerProtocol class, this class is derived from the GProtocol class from the previous chapter. In the next chapter, a class for a specific client protocol for the Tic-Tac-Toe game is created that is derived from this class.

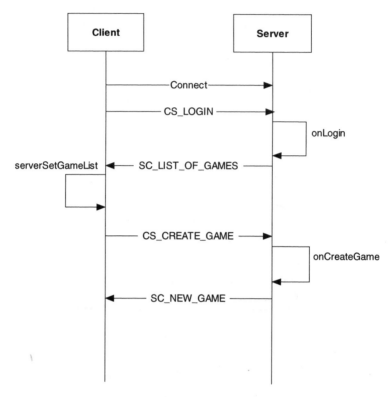

FIGURE 19.7 Event sequence.

The ClientProtocol class contains general functionality for logging on to the server, and for creating and joining games. Listing 19.6 shows the code for the ClientProtocol class. It is quite long, as it handles a number of different messages from the server.

Listing 19.6 ClientProtocol class.

```
import xdrlib

from hoopnet.shared import gprotocol
from hoopnet.shared.messages import *

class ClientProtocol(gprotocol.GProtocol):
    """Client side of GProtocol
    """

    def __init__(self, app):
```

```
        self.app = app

    def connectionMade(self):
        gprotocol.GProtocol.connectionMade(self)

        # setup message handlers
        self.registerHandler(gprotocol.MSG_ERROR, self.onError)
        self.registerHandler(SC_GAME_READY, self.onReady)
        self.registerHandler(SC_NEW_GAME, self.onNewGame)
        self.registerHandler(SC_LIST_OF_GAMES, self.onListOfGames)
        self.registerHandler(SC_PLAYER_LEAVE, self.onPlayerLeave)
        self.registerHandler(SC_REMOVE_GAME, self.onRemoveGame)

        self.app.onConnected(self)

    ### Message handler methods ###

    def onError(self, unpacker):
        errorId = unpacker.unpack_int()
        errorMsg = unpacker.unpack_string()
        print "ERROR [%d] %s" % (errorId, errorMsg)
        return 1

    def onReady(self, unpacker):
        """Game is ready to play"""
        name = unpacker.unpack_string()
        numPlayers = unpacker.unpack_int()
        self.app.serverReady(name, numPlayers)
        return 1

    def onNewGame(self, unpacker):
        name = unpacker.unpack_string()
        self.app.serverAddGame(name)
        return 1

    def onRemoveGame(self, unpacker):
        name = unpacker.unpack_string()
        self.app.serverRemoveGame(name)
        return 1

    def onPlayerLeave(self, unpacker):
        name = unpacker.unpack_string()
        self.app.serverPlayerLeave(name)
        return 1

    def onListOfGames(self, unpacker):
        numGames = unpacker.unpack_int()
```

```
                    gameNames = []
                    for i in range(0,numGames):
                        gameNames.append(unpacker.unpack_string())
                    self.app.serverSetGameList(gameNames)
                    return 1

                ### Message sender methods ###

                def sendLogin(self, name):
                    packer = xdrlib.Packer()
                    packer.pack_int(CS_LOGIN)
                    packer.pack_string(name)
                    self.writePacker(packer)

                def sendCreateGame(self, gameName):
                    packer = xdrlib.Packer()
                    packer.pack_int(CS_CREATE_GAME)
                    packer.pack_string(gameName)
                    self.writePacker(packer)

                def sendJoinGame(self, gameName):
                    packer = xdrlib.Packer()
                    packer.pack_int(CS_JOIN_GAME)
                    packer.pack_string(gameName)
                    self.writePacker(packer)

                def sendLeaveGame(self):
                    packer = xdrlib.Packer()
                    packer.pack_int(CS_LEAVE_GAME)
                    self.writePacker(packer)
```

This code contains `handler` methods for messages from the server and methods to send messages to the server. The message handlers in the client `protocol` class invoke code in the client application class once the data from the network has been unpacked. It encapsulates the low-level network functionality for the client application. The following is the code for the message handlers of the `GenericClientApp` class that are invoked by the `protocol` class.

```
        def serverSetGameList(self, gameNames):
            """accept list of games from server"""
            self.gameNames = gameNames
            print "list of games:", gameNames
            self.lobby.setGameNames(gameNames)

        def serverAddGame(self, name):
            """accept new individual game from server"""
```

```
            self.gameNames.append(name)
            self.lobby.addGameName(name)

    def serverRemoveGame(self, name):
        """remove individual game from server"""
        self.gameNames.remove(name)
        self.lobby.removeGameName(name)

    def serverReady(self, gameName, numPlayers):
        print "Ready:", gameName
        self.currentGame = gameName
        self.lobby.setShow(0)

    def serverPlayerLeave(self, playerName):
        pass
```

These methods perform tasks related to the lobby window that inform the player of the games that exist on the server. They are application-level methods rather than network-level methods. Notice that they are all prefixed with the text *server* to show that they process network events from the server. Some of these methods are overridden by the game application in the next chapter to perform game-specific operations when players enter and exit games.

The final piece of the GenericClientApp class is the methods to send messages to the server. These methods are all prefixed with the text *request* to designate that they send requests to the server. The code for the server request methods of the Client class is shown here:

```
    def requestLogin(self):
        self.player.protocol.sendLogin(self.playerName)

    def requestCreateGame(self, gameName):
        self.player.protocol.sendCreateGame(gameName)

    def requestJoinGame(self, gameName):
        self.player.protocol.sendJoinGame(gameName)

    def requestLeaveGame(self):
        self.player.protocol.sendLeaveGame()
        self.lobby.setShow(1)
        self.lobby.getFocus()
```

These methods access the protocol object that is associated with the player to send messages. The protocol object is an instance of the ClientProtocol (or later, the `TicTacClientProtocol`) class that implements the send methods for each of these requests.

The `LobbyFrame` class

The `lobby` variable referenced in the previous code is an instance of the user interface class `LobbyFrame`. This class is derived from the PyUI `Frame` class and displays the set of active games on the server. Figure 19.8 is a screenshot of this class in action.

FIGURE 19.8 The game lobby.

The Create Game button allows a new game to be created. This sends a CS_CRE-ATE_GAME message to the server. The Join Game button is only active when a game is selected on the right-hand side. This sends a CS_JOIN_GAME message to the server. The Exit button calls the `exit` method of the client object to make the application shut down. Listing 19.7 shows the code for the `LobbyFrame` class.

Listing 19.7 The `LobbyFrame` class.

```
import pyui
from tictac.shared.messages import *
from tictac.shared.tictacmsgs import *

class LobbyFrame(pyui.widgets.Frame):
    def __init__(self, client, playerName):
        self.client = client
        self.playerName = playerName
        pyui.widgets.Frame.__init__(self,200,200,300,300,"Lobby for %s"
% playerName)
```

```
        self.createBox = pyui.widgets.Edit("testGame#1", 12,
self.onCreate)
        self.createButton = pyui.widgets.Button("Create Game",
self.onCreate)
        self.joinButton = pyui.widgets.Button("Join Game", self.onJoin)
        self.exitButton = pyui.widgets.Button("Exit", self.onExit)
        self.gameList = pyui.widgets.ListBox(self.onSelected)

        self.joinButton.disable()
        self.setLayout(pyui.layouts.TableLayoutManager(2,7))

        self.addChild(self.createButton, (0,0,1,1) )
        self.addChild(self.createBox,    (1,0,1,1) )
        self.addChild(self.joinButton,   (0,2,1,2) )
        self.addChild(self.exitButton,   (0,5,1,2) )
        self.addChild(self.gameList,     (1,1,1,6) )
        self.pack()

    def onCreate(self, widget):
        if len(self.createBox.text) > 0:
            self.client.requestCreateGame(self.createBox.text)
        return 1

    def onSelected(self, item):
        if item:
            self.joinButton.enable()
        else:
            self.joinButton.disable()
        return 1

    def onJoin(self, widget):
        item = self.gameList.getSelectedItem()
        if not item:
            return 1
        self.client.requestJoinGame(item.name)
        return 1

    def onExit(self, button):
        self.client.exit()
        return 1

    def setGameNames(self, names):
        self.gameList.clearAllItems()
        for name in names:
            self.gameList.addItem(name, None)
```

```
def addGameName(self, name):
    self.gameList.addItem(name, None)

def removeGameName(self, name):
    self.gameList.removeItem(name)
```

This class uses a PyUI table layout to position the interface elements, and provides a number of methods that are called by the application when network messages are received. The lobby object is created by the main client application and remains in existence for the duration of the application. When the player is actually in a game, it is hidden by the client application so that the game board is visible.

SUMMARY

This chapter described some network architectures and the types of games that use these architectures. It focused on the client/server architecture, as it is the most common architecture and the most appropriate for online games that run across the Internet. It included implementations of both a generic game server and a generic game client that communicate with each other using a message-based protocol, that could be used as the basis for developing an online game. The example code in this chapter used low-level network functionality provided by the Twisted framework, and used the game protocol class that was described in the previous chapter.

Although this chapter included a great deal of code, it did not include a functional example application. The next chapter builds on the generic framework from this chapter to develop a playable multiplayer game.

The code developed in this chapter is contained in a module called the hoopnet module. This module can work in conjunction with the hoop library code developed throughout this book. The hoopnet module is used as a library in the next chapter where an example multiplayer game is developed.

20 Multiplayer Game Example

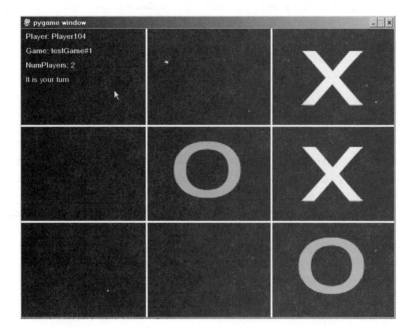

The actual game code of multiplayer games depends heavily on the network infrastructure and interacts with the network layer to generate and process game events. This is the code that implements the game logic, game rules, user interface, and any other pieces specific to the particular game. Compared to the game code for single-player games, the game code for multiplayer games is usually more event-driven. It tends to operate in more discrete actions that have defined inputs and outputs that can be transmitted across the network.

Chapter 12, "Game Simulations," discussed how Python is a good language for game simulations, and how to use Python to develop game systems. Python is also a good language for developing multiplayer game code for many of the same reasons. In addition, Python's module system is useful for managing the large amount of code and complex dependencies that multiplayer games require.

This chapter discusses application-level game programming for multiplayer games. Section 20.1 discusses organizing the application code and framework code in a consistent and scalable way, and Section 20.2 introduces the game logic for the example Tic-Tac-Toe game that is developed in this chapter. Section 20.3 describes the Tic-Tac-Toe game server, including the game logic and rules, and Section 20.4 discusses the game client including the user interface for playing the game.

20.1 CODE ORGANIZATION

Section 19.2 of the previous chapter discussed code organization for the framework components of a multiplayer game. As this chapter continues to build an actual playable game using that infrastructure, it requires additions to the directory structure that was defined previously.

Large game projects can have enormous amounts of source code, and it is usually necessary to partition that code into manageable pieces. The categories of client, server, and shared code were used in the previous chapter to partition the code. Since the game code and the framework code for the example built in this chapter both include client, server, and shared code, it would be possible to cram the new application code into the existing set of directories. However, this would mix framework and application code in the same places, which makes it more difficult to isolate the framework code for reuse, and could cause name conflicts. Instead, the application code is placed in its own directory that is parallel to the hoopnet directory and partitioned into client, server, and shared directories within that directory. Since the example game is Tic-Tac-Toe, the directory for the application code is *tictac*. This complete directory structure is shown here:

- root
  - tictac
    - client
    - server
    - shared
  - hoopnet
    - client
    - server
    - shared

This arrangement conveniently fits with the existing Python path setting. Since the root directory above the hoopnet directory was already placed in the Python path in the previous chapter, the `tictac` module should now be importable in the same manner as the `hoopnet` module. For example:

```
from hoopnet.client.ui import LobbyFrame
from tictac.client.ui import TicTacWindow
```

Notice that there can be files of the same name in each of the directory tree without conflicts, and that the syntax for importing is consistent in both framework and application code.

20.2 THE TIC-TAC-TOE GAME

This section describes how the Tic-Tac-Toe game works without explicit references to code. The implementation of the functionality described here is implemented later in the chapter.

When a player first creates a game, it is empty of players. The creating player is immediately entered into the game so it has one player. When another player joins the game, it is deemed *ready* and the first turn begins. Each turn is for a specific player to make a move. Only the designated, active player can make a move during a particular turn.

When a player requests a move, it is performed on the server and the results are sent to each of the participating players. Notice that the move is only *requested* by the client and is processed on the server. This allows secure validation of moves to be performed on the server so that players cannot cheat or disrupt the game. The server rejects invalid move attempts by players, and valid moves are broadcast to the clients. Each turn, a message sent to clients contains the status of all the squares on the game board.

Once a player makes a move, the server checks for a winner. If a player has won the match, it tells each of the players and finishes the game. No more moves can be performed once the game is finished, and the players are able to leave the game and return to the lobby.

This entire sequence of events is shown in Figure 20.1. Figure 20.1 shows the network message IDs associated with each step of the process.

While this sequence is specific to the Tic-Tac-Toe game the general flow is very similar to how many online games work. This example could be adopted to support more complex games with little modification to its architecture.

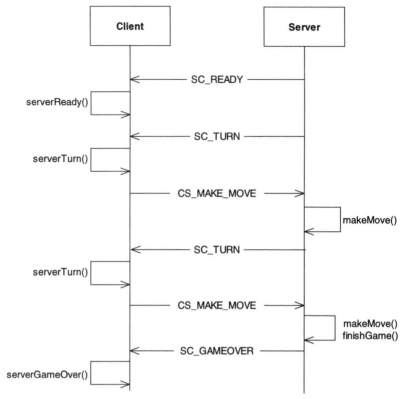

FIGURE 20.1   Tic-Tac-Toe game sequence.

20.3 THE GAME SERVER

This section describes the implementation of a multiplayer Tic-Tac-Toe game server. This is a very simple game, but it demonstrates extending the generic server infrastructure that was developed in the previous chapter.

The Tic-Tac-Toe game uses classes that are derived from the classes defined in the previous chapter. The new server classes and their parent classes are listed in Table 20.1.

This is shown in Figure 20.2.

TABLE 20.1   Tic-Tac-Toe Classes

Parent Class	Tic-Tac-Toe Class	Responsibilities
`ServerProtocol`	`TicTacServerProtocol`	Handles and sends game-specific messages on the server
`GameServerApp`	`TicTacServer`	Handles game-specific network operations on the server
`ServerGame`	`TicTacGame`	Game rules and logic, player management

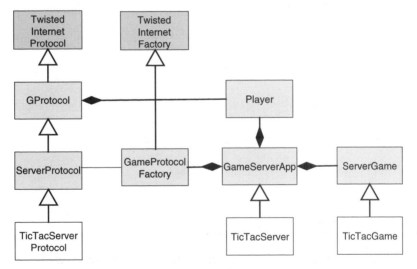

FIGURE 20.2   Tic-Tac-Toe game server classes.

The TicTacGame **Class**

This class is the core of the Tic-Tac-Toe game on the server and is derived from the stub ServerGame class. It implements the actual game rules and logic, and manages the players who enter and leave the game. Notice that the game rules and logic do not exist on the client at all. This is an important point for the security and stability of online games. Giving clients access to the code for the game rules can facilitate cheating and hacking by malicious players.

Listing 20.1 shows the code for the TicTacGame class.

Listing 20.1 TicTacGame class.

```
from hoopnet.server.gameserver import ServerGame
from tictac.shared.messages import *

class TicTacGame(ServerGame):
    """A game of TicTacToe. Has two players
    """

    winners = [
        (0,1,2),
        (3,4,5),
        (6,7,8),
        (0,3,6),
        (1,4,7),
        (2,5,8),
        (0,4,8),
        (2,4,6)
        ]

    def __init__(self, name, application):
        ServerGame.__init__(self, name, application)
        self.players = []
        self.ready = 0
        self.finished = 0
        self.count = 0
        self.playerTurn = 0
        self.squares = [SQUARE_EMPTY] * 9

    def addPlayer(self, player):
        if len(self.players) >= 2:
            player.setError(14, "Game is full!")
            return 0

        if self.finished:
            player.setError(15, "Game is finished")
            return 0
```

```
        print "Adding player to game", player.name

        self.players.append(player)
        player.currentGame = self

        # send the ready msg with the number of players
        for player in self.players:
            player.protocol.sendReady(self.name, len(self.players))

        if len(self.players) == 2:
            self.players[0].symbol = SQUARE_CIRCLE
            self.players[1].symbol = SQUARE_CROSS
            self.ready = 1
            self.playerTurn = 0
            for player in self.players:
                player.protocol.sendTurn(
                    self.players[self.playerTurn].name,
                    self.players[self.playerTurn].symbol,
                    self.squares, 0)
        return 1

    def removePlayer(self, player):
        # remove this player.
        self.players.remove(player)

        self.squares = [SQUARE_EMPTY] * 9
        self.ready = 0

        # tell the others
        for p in self.players:
            p.protocol.sendPlayerLeave(player.name)

        if len(self.players) == 0:
            print "removing game"
            self.application.removeGame(self)


    def makeMove(self, position, player):
        if player != self.players[self.playerTurn]:
            player.setError(11, "Not your turn!!")
            return 0

        if self.squares[position] != SQUARE_EMPTY:
            player.setError(11, "Square is not empty")
            return 0

        # set the actual square position
```

```
            self.squares[position] = player.symbol

            # go to next turn
            if self.playerTurn:
                self.playerTurn = 0
            else:
                self.playerTurn = 1
            for p in self.players:
                p.protocol.sendTurn(
                    self.players[self.playerTurn].name,
                    self.players[self.playerTurn].symbol,
                    self.squares, 0)

            # check for winners
            for a,b,c in TicTacGame.winners:
                if self.squares[a] != SQUARE_EMPTY:
                    if self.squares[a] == self.squares[b] and \
                        self.squares[a] == self.squares[c]:
                        # we have a winner!
                        self.finishGame(player)

            # check for end of game
            self.count += 1
            if self.count == 9:
                self.finishGame(None)

    def finishGame(self, winningPlayer):
        self.finished = 1
        if winningPlayer:
            name = winningPlayer.name
        else:
            name = ""
        print "Winning player is <%s>" % name
        for player in self.players:
            player.protocol.sendGameOver(name)

    def update(self, interval):
        pass
```

The squares on the game board are numbered from left to right and from top to bottom from zero to nine. This setup is shown in Figure 20.3.

The winners class variable stores the sets of squares that make up winning rows. This data is used in the makeMove method to check if a player has won the game. The squares list stores the state of each of the squares on the board. It contains one of the constants SQUARE_CIRCLE, SQUARE_CROSS, or SQUARE_EMPTY for each square. These

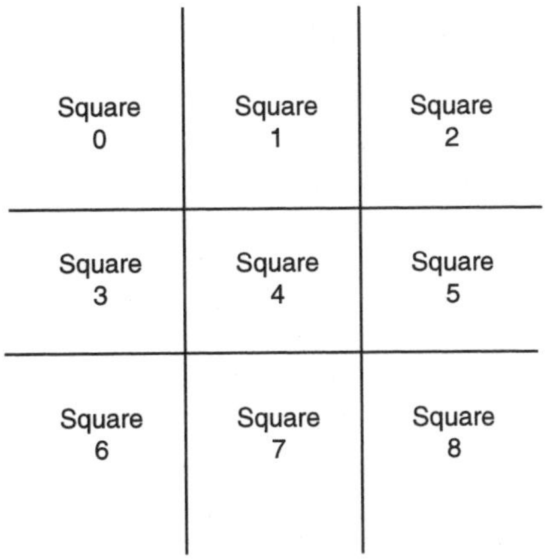

FIGURE 20.3   Tic-Tac-Toe board squares.

constants and the message constants for the game are defined in tictac/shared/tic-tacmsgs.py. Listing 20.2 shows this code.

Listing 20.2   Tic-Tac-Toe game constants.

```
# server to client messages
SC_TURN        = 1104
SC_GAMEOVER    = 1105

# client to server messages
CS_MAKE_MOVE   = 2104

# shared constants
SQUARE_EMPTY    = 0
SQUARE_CROSS    = 1
SQUARE_CIRCLE   = 2
```

The most interesting portion of the TicTacGame class is the makeMove method. This method performs validations on each move request, and then updates the game's squares with the new move. It broadcasts the new game state to each of the players using the sendTurn method, and then checks for a winner. If the latest move has won the game for the player, or the game is a tie, it broadcasts this to the players using the sendGameOver method and sets the game to be finished.

Notice that the class has an update method. The game server framework invokes this periodically, but for this particular game it does nothing, as the Tic-Tac-Toe game has no real-time requirements. This could be used to implement turn timeouts or other types of real-time functionality on the server, such as collision detection or a physical simulation.

The TicTacServerProtocol **Class**

The TicTacGame class uses the TicTacServerProtocol class for network communication. This class implements message handlers for the game-specific messages from the client, and send methods for the game-specific messages that are sent to the client. It is derived from the ServerProtocol class that was defined earlier in this chapter. Listing 20.3 show the code for this class.

Listing 20.3   TicTacServerProtocol class.

```
class TicTacServerProtocol(ServerProtocol):
    """Protocol for tictactoe game.
    """
    def __init__(self, app):
        ServerProtocol.__init__(self, app)

    def connectionMade(self):
        ServerProtocol.connectionMade(self)
        self.registerHandler(CS_MAKE_MOVE, self.onMakeMove)

    ### Message Handler Methods ###
    def onMakeMove(self, unpacker):
        position = unpacker.unpack_int()
        self.app.makeMove(position, self.player)
        return 1

    ### Message Sender Methods ###
    def sendTurn(self, playerName, symbol, squares, finished):
        packer = xdrlib.Packer()
        packer.pack_int(SC_TURN)
        packer.pack_string(playerName)
        packer.pack_int(symbol)
        for s in squares:
            packer.pack_int(s)
        packer.pack_int(finished)
        self.writePacker(packer)

    def sendGameOver(self, playerName):
        packer = xdrlib.Packer()
        packer.pack_int(SC_GAMEOVER)
        packer.pack_string(playerName)
        self.writePacker(packer)
```

This class holds a reference to the game server instance and uses this to invoke methods on the game object when messages are received. The most interesting method is the sendTurn method. It builds a network message that contains the state of the game board, the name of the player whose turn it is, the player's symbol, and a flag for whether the game is finished. This data comes from the game object that invokes this function.

The TicTacServer **Class**

This class is the container of all of the game instances and manages all of the players who are online. It is derived from the GameServer class that was defined previously and implements functionality and doesn't add much additional functionality. Listing 20.4 show the code for this class.

Listing 20.4 TicTacServer class.

```
class TicTacServer(GameServer):
    def __init__(self, port):
        GameServer.__init__(self, port, TicTacServerProtocol,
TicTacGame)

    def makeMove(self, position, player):
        if not player.currentGame:
            player.setError(15, "Not in a game!!!")
            return 0
        return player.currentGame.makeMove(position, player)
```

The constructor passes application-specific classes to the game server base class so that the correct types of objects are constructed by it. The makeMove method is invoked by the TicTacServerProtocol class. It routes move messages to the player's current game. Notice that the particular game for a move is not specified by the player; it is inferred from the player object on the server. This is a common technique that prevents the player from sending move message for games they are not part of.

Running the Server

The final part of the server is a Python script to start and run it. This is used to execute the server from a command line. Listing 20.5 shows the code for the file server.py.

Listing 20.5   Main code for server.

```
from tictac.server.tictacserver import TicTacServer

def run():
    port = 7777
    delay = 0.1
    serverInstance = TicTacServer(port)
    serverInstance.run(delay)

if __name__ == '__main__':
    run()
```

This file resides in the root directory above the hoopnet and tictac directories. It can be executed from the directory above that directory with the command line:

```
$python server.py
```

Remember that the root directory must be in the PYTHONPATH so modules can be imported from the tictac and hoopnet packages.

20.4 THE TIC-TAC-TOE GAME CLIENT

This section describes the client for the Tic-Tac-Toe game. This client corresponds to the server developed in this chapter and uses the generic client functionality that was developed in the previous chapter.

The client does not have an implementation of the game itself, as that functionality exists on the server. The client has a protocol class, a client application class, and a user interface class to display the game board when a game is being played. The classes in the client and their relationships to the framework classes are shown in Figure 20.4.

The Client Protocol

The TicTacClientProtocol client protocol class is derived from the ClientProtocol class from the previous chapter. This class handles the SC_TURN and SC_GAMEOVER messages from the server and has a send method for the CS_MAKE_MOVE message. These methods correspond to methods on the TicTacServerProtocol class that was defined previously. Listing 20.6 shows the code for the TicTacClientProtocol class.

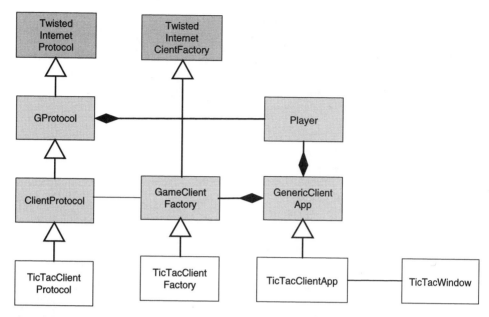

FIGURE 20.4   Tic-Tac-Toe client classes.

Listing 20.6   `TicTacClientProtocol` class.

```
import xdrlib

from hoopnet.client.protocol import ClientProtocol
from tictac.shared.messages import *

class TicTacClientProtocol(ClientProtocol):
    def __init__(self, app):
        ClientProtocol.__init__(self, app)

    def connectionMade(self):
        print "connectionmade..."
        ClientProtocol.connectionMade(self)
        self.registerHandler(SC_TURN, self.onTurn)
        self.registerHandler(SC_GAMEOVER, self.onGameOver)

    def onTurn(self, unpacker):
        playerName = unpacker.unpack_string()
        symbol = unpacker.unpack_int()
        squares = []
        for i in range(0,9):
            squares.append(unpacker.unpack_int())
```

```
            finished = unpacker.unpack_int()
            self.app.serverTurn(playerName, symbol, squares, finished)
            return 1

    def onGameOver(self, unpacker):
        playerName = unpacker.unpack_string()
        self.app.serverGameOver(playerName)
        return 1

    def sendMakeMove(self, position):
        packer = xdrlib.Packer()
        packer.pack_int(CS_MAKE_MOVE)
        packer.pack_int(position)
        self.writePacker(packer)
```

The Client Application

The `TicTacClientApp` class is derived from the `GenericClientApp` class from the previous chapter. This class manages the game board user interface and passes events from the network to the user interface so that the results of events are visible to the player. Listing 20.7 show the code for this class.

Listing 20.7 `TicTacClientApp` class.

```
from hoopnet.client.application import GenericClientApp,
GameClientFactory
from tictac.client.protocol import TicTacClientProtocol

from tictac.client.ui import TicTacWindow

class TicTacClientApp(GenericClientApp):
    """Specific game client for the tic-tac-toe game.
    """
    def __init__(self, width, height):
        GenericClientApp.__init__(self, width, height,
TicTacClientFactory)
        self.tictacWindow =
TicTacWindow(width,height,self.playerName,self)

    def requestMakeMove(self, value):
        self.player.protocol.sendMakeMove(value)

    def serverTurn(self, playerName, symbol, squares, finished):
        self.tictacWindow.turn(playerName, symbol, squares, finished)
```

```
def serverGameOver(self, playerName):
    self.tictacWindow.gameOver(playerName)

def serverReady(self, gameName, numPlayers):
    self.tictacWindow.activate(gameName, numPlayers)
    return GenericClientApp.serverReady(self, gameName, numPlayers)

def serverPlayerLeave(self, playerName):
    self.tictacWindow.playerLeave(playerName)
```

In a manner consistent with the GenericClientApp class from the previous chapter, the methods beginning with the prefix *server* in this class pass events from the server to the tictacWindow member variable. Methods that begin with the *request* prefix pass requests from the user interface to the network, which are then passed to the server.

In the construction of this class, the parent class is passed a factory class that is derived from the GameClientFactory from the previous chapter. This factory class differs from the parent class as it constructs a protocol of the TicTacClientProtocol that is specific to this game, rather than the generic ClientProtocol class from the previous chapter. The code for this simple factory class is shown here:

```
class TicTacClientFactory(GameClientFactory):
    """Factory to construct tic-tac-toe protocol classes.
    """
    def buildProtocol(self, addr):
        print 'Connected.'
        return TicTacClientProtocol(self.app)
```

The TicTacWindow Class

This class displays the contents of the game board. It uses the standard three-by-three Tic-Tac-Toe grid and places circles and crosses in the squares in which players have made moves. In addition to just the game board, it displays some additional details about the game, such as the player's name, the game's status, and the number of active players. Figure 20.5 is a screenshot of the game board.

This class uses images to draw the crosses and circles, and PyUI rendering primitives to display the border lines between squares. It has registered message handlers for mouse clicking to accept moves from the players, and keyboard events to detect when the player wants to leave a finished game.

As the code in the TicTacClientApp class shows, methods of this class are invoked when events are received from the network. The activate method is called when a player enters the game, the turn method is called when a new turn begins, the gameover method is called when the game ends, and the playerLeave method is

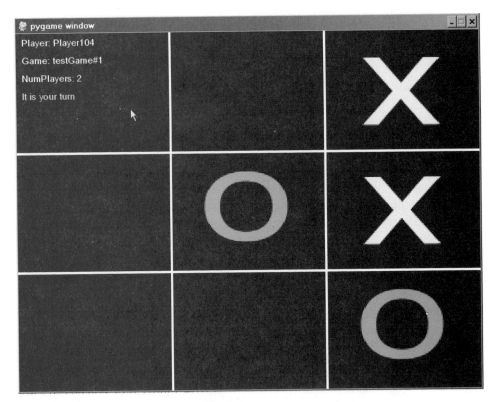

FIGURE 20.5 Tic-Tac-Toe game board.

called when a player leaves the game. Listing 20.8 shows the code for the `Tic-TacWindow` class.

Listing 20.8 The `TicTacWindow` class.

```
import pyui
from tictac.shared.messages import *

class TicTacWindow(pyui.widgets.Window):
    def __init__(self, width, height, playerName, clientApp):
        pyui.widgets.Window.__init__(self, 0,0,width, height)
        self.gameName = ""
        self.clientApp = clientApp
        self.innerX = width/3
        self.innerY = height/3
        self.numPlayers = 0
```

```python
        self.alive = 0
        self.finished = 0
        self.playerName = playerName
        self.msg = ""
        self.yourTurn = 0
        self.symbol = 0
        self.squares = [SQUARE_EMPTY] * 9
        self.registerEvent(pyui.locals.LMOUSEBUTTONDOWN,
self.onMouseDown)
        self.registerEvent(pyui.locals.KEYDOWN, self.onKey)

    def activate(self, gameName, numPlayers):
        """called when a player enters the game.
        """
        self.gameName = gameName
        self.numPlayers = numPlayers
        if self.numPlayers == 2:
            self.alive = 1
        else:
            self.alive = 0
        self.setDirty()

    def playerLeave(self, playerName):
        self.numPlayers -= 1
        self.alive = 0
        self.setDirty()

    def turn(self, playerName, symbol, squares, finished):
        self.squares = squares
        self.symbol = symbol
        if playerName == self.playerName:
            self.yourTurn = 1
            self.msg = "It is your turn"
        else:
            self.yourTurn = 0
            self.msg = "It is your opponent's turn"
        if finished:
            self.yourTurn = 0
            self.msg = "Game Over!!!"
        self.setDirty()

    def gameOver(self, playerName):
        print "gameover:", playerName
        self.yourTurn = 0
        if playerName == self.playerName:
            self.msg = "You Win!!!"
        elif playerName == "":
```

```
                    self.msg = "It is a tie!"
            else:
                    self.msg = "You lost at Tic Tac Toe!!!!"
            self.finished = 1
            self.setDirty()

    def onMouseDown(self, event):
        print "onMouseDown"
        x = event.pos[0] / self.innerX
        y = event.pos[1] / self.innerY
        offset = y*3 + x
        print "Offset:", offset, self.alive, self.squares
        if self.alive and self.yourTurn and self.squares[offset] ==
SQUARE_EMPTY:
                self.clientApp.requestMakeMove(offset)
        return 1

    def onKey(self, event):
        if event.key == pyui.locals.K_SPACE and self.finished:
            self.clientApp.requestLeaveGame()
            self.msg = ""
            self.gameName = ""
            self.finished = 0
            self.squares = [SQUARE_EMPTY] * 9
            self.numPlayers = 0
            self.setDirty()
        return 0

    def draw(self, renderer):
        """Draws the game board
        """

        # draw lines
        for i in range(1,3):
            x = self.innerX*i
            y = self.innerY*i
            renderer.drawRect( pyui.colors.white, (0, y, self.width, 4)
)
            renderer.drawRect( pyui.colors.white, (x, 0, 4,
self.height) )

        # draw grid
        i = 0
        for y in range(0,3):
            for x in range(0,3):
                image = None
                if self.squares[i] == SQUARE_CROSS:
```

```
                        image = "images/X.png"
                elif self.squares[i] == SQUARE_CIRCLE:
                        image = "images/O.png"
                if image:
                        renderer.drawImage((self.innerX*x+4,
self.innerY*y+4,
                                          self.innerX-8, self.innerY-8),
image)
                i += 1

        renderer.drawText("Player: %s" % self.playerName, (10,10),
                                        pyui.colors.white)
        renderer.drawText("Game: %s" % self.gameName, (10,40),
                                        pyui.colors.white)
        renderer.drawText("NumPlayers: %s" % self.numPlayers, (10,70),
                                        pyui.colors.white)
        renderer.drawText(self.msg, (10,100), pyui.colors.green)
        if self.finished:
                renderer.drawText("Press Space to Exit the game.",
(10,130),
                                        pyui.colors.red)
```

The TicTacWindow class is derived from the PyUIWindow class, not the Frame class like the lobby class from the previous chapter. This class doesn't have borders or a Close button; it is just a drawable rectangle that fills the entire screen.

The draw method of this class is where the actual board and status information about the game are displayed. This code uses the squares data that was included in the SC_TURN message to determine what to draw in each square of the board. It iterates through the squares and draws an appropriate image in the ones in which players have made moves.

Running the Client

The final part of the client is the main Python script to run the client. This is used to execute the client from the command line. Unlike the server, which only required a few lines to execute, the client is a graphical application like most of the other example programs in this book and requires a little more support to execute. Listing 20.9 shows the full code for the file to execute the client.

Listing 20.9 Client main code.

```
import time
import random
import pyui
```

```python
from hoop import engine

from tictac.client.application import TicTacClientApp

class Application:
    def __init__(self, width, height):
        self.width = width
        self.height = height
        self.renderer = pyui.desktop.getRenderer()
        self.renderer.setMouseCursor(None)
        engine.initialize(width, height)
        self.client = TicTacClientApp(width, height)
        self.client.connect("localhost", 7777)
        self.renderer.setBackMethod(self.render)

    def render(self):
        engine.clear()
        engine.render()

    def run(self):
        """I am called to begin running the game.
        """
        running = 1
        frames = 0
        counter = 0
        lastFrame = pyui.readTimer()
        endFrame = pyui.readTimer()

        while running:
            pyui.draw()
            if pyui.update():
                interval = pyui.readTimer() - endFrame
                endFrame = pyui.readTimer()
                if self.client.update(interval) == 0:
                    running = 0
            else:
                running = 0

            # track frames per second
            frames += 1
            counter += 1

            # calculate FPS
            if endFrame - lastFrame > 1.0:
                FPS = counter
                counter = 0
                lastFrame = endFrame
```

```
            print "FPS: %2d" % (FPS )

        time.sleep(0.03)

def run():
    width = 800
    height = 600
    pyui.init(width, height, "p3d", 0)
    app = Application(width, height)
    app.run()
    pyui.quit()

if __name__ == '__main__':
    run()
```

This code is very similar to many of the other example applications in this book. One difference is that it connects to the server when it starts. The following line instructs the client to connect to the server running on the local machine on the port 7777.

```
self.client.connect("localhost", 7777)
```

The first parameter to this method could be a host name or an IP address on another machine if the server is not running locally.

Another difference is that this client sleeps for three milliseconds each time through the main loop. Since the Tic-Tac-Toe application is not a real-time simulation, this application doesn't have to update the display frequently, or perform time-based simulation updates. This means that the application does not have to run its main loop as fast as real-time game applications. Sleeping each time through the main loop caps the CPU utilization of the client. This is especially useful when the client and the server are running on the same machine and sharing the CPU. Sleeping allows the other process (the server) some CPU resources to perform its operations. If the client ran at full speed with no sleep or pausing, the server would exhibit sporadic delays as it competes for CPU resources with the always-active client. This technique also allows multiple clients to run on the same machine smoothly.

This client can be invoked with the command line:

```
$python client.py
```

However, remember that the root directory must be in the PYTHONPATH so modules can be imported from the tictac and hoopnet packages.

ON THE CD   The full source code to the client and server from this chapter can be found on the accompanying CD-ROM in chapter20.

SUMMARY

This chapter described the implementation of a very simple multiplayer game using the network framework developed in the previous chapter and the Twisted framework to provide the low-level networking functionality. It included a Tic-Tac-Toe game that could be played by multiple players, a server that allows the creation of games and allows players to join games, and a client with a graphic front end that allowed players to actually play the game.

This example demonstrated sequences of communication between the client and server, message handling, and sending requests. It showed how to organize the code of a multiplayer game application to share code between the client and server, and to isolate framework code from application-specific code as different Python modules.

Although this chapter and the previous chapter concerning multiplayer game development provide a solid foundation, the topic of online games is huge and is constantly growing as the scope and complexity of online games increase. There are many subjects such as security, observation, UDP networking, broadcasting, and databases that are involved in building a large-scale online game. Unfortunately, this book does not have the space to cover these topics.

VI Advanced Topics

21 Using the Python C API

A number of situations in game development require Python code to be integrated with C code. Some examples include:

- To access existing functionality that is only available through C
- To optimize the performance of a particular piece of Python code
- To reduce the resource requirements of a program

This integration is achieved by using the *Python C API*. The Python C API is the programming interface that is used to develop extension modules, extension classes, and for embedding the Python interpreter into other applications. It gives developers access to the Python interpreter through well-defined interfaces that are stable and documented. The Python C API is the foundation for interfaces between Python and the C language, so it is used in almost all game projects that use Python. In addition, knowledge of this interface gives insight into the internals of the Python interpreter that can allow developers to write more efficient pure Python code.

While some applications of the Python C API outside of the game industry are simple wrappers that allow access to existing libraries, use of the Python C API in games tends to be more than just the simple features, and requires programmers to be familiar with the interface and programming model.

This chapter discusses the Python C API and issues related to it for game development. Knowing how this programming interface works is crucial for developing code that interfaces safely and efficiently between Python and the C programming language. Section 21.1 discusses the PyObject type and the abstract object layer, Section 21.2 discusses reference counting with the Python C API, and Section 21.3 discusses exceptions handling with the Python C API. Section 21.4 discusses conversion of data between Python and the C language for argument passing and return values. Section 21.5 discusses the concrete object interfaces for the various concrete Python types.

Applying the Python C API to the development of extension modules, extension classes, and embedding Python is covered in the next chapter.

21.1 THE ABSTRACT OBJECT LAYER

Two of the most important concepts of the Python C API are the PyObject type and the abstract object layer. PyObject is the C data type by which all Python objects are represented in Python C API code. It is an opaque data type that represents Python objects regardless of their underlying implementation. Almost all code that uses the Python C API uses the PyObject type. This data type is used as arguments passed to C functions called from Python, and is the type of the return value of C functions called from Python.

All Python objects have a type and a reference count. The PyObject type encapsulates this functionality. For each of the well-known Python types, there is a macro in the Python C API that checks if the object pointed to by a PyObject pointer is of that type. The format of these macros is Py*TypeName*_Check(p), where *TypeName* is the type being checked against, and *p* is the PyObject pointer. Some examples of these macros are `PyList_Check`, `PyNumber_Check`, `PyString_Check`, and `PyFile_Check`. The reference count of Python objects is discussed in the next section.

Although the Python C API is implemented in the C programming language, which is not known as being object oriented, there is a kind of hierarchy of types derived from the PyObject type. The PyObject type acts as an abstract base class for concrete Python type objects. The concrete types include numeric objects, sequence objects, mapping objects, file objects, and module objects. They are described in a later section of this chapter.

As `PyObject` is a base class, it encapsulates a set of common functionality. To implement this functionality, there is a set of functions that operate on PyObjects known as the *abstract object layer* of the Python C API. This interface consists of functions that can operate on Python objects of any type, or on broad categories or types of Python objects. They use PyObject pointers as their arguments rather than pointers to any of the concrete Python data types.

The abstract object layer is partitioned into groups of functions called *protocols*. This usage of the word *protocol* is not related to networking. In this context, it refers to specific, well-known interfaces. The protocols in the abstract object layer are the object protocol, the number protocol, the sequence protocol, the mapping protocol, the iterator protocol, and the buffer protocol. Each of these groups of functions implements functionality associated with Python objects of a specific type. The full specification of the functions in all of the protocols can be found in the Python C API documentation.

The Object Protocol

The object protocol deals with functionality that is common to almost all types of Python objects. It includes functions to get and set attributes, to check for the existence of attributes, to compare objects with other objects, to interrogate the type of objects, and to invoke callable objects. Some of the functions in the object protocol are shown here:

```
int PyObject_HasAttr(PyObject *o, PyObject *attr);
int PyObject_HasAttrString(PyObject *o, char *attr_name);

PyObject* PyObject_GetAttr(PyObject *o, PyObject *attr);
PyObject* PyObject_GetAttrString(PyObject *o, char *attr_name);

int PyObject_SetAttr(PyObject *o, PyObject *attr, PyObject *v);
int PyObject_SetAttrString(PyObject *o, char *attr_name, PyObject *v);
```

These functions show how to check for the existence of an attribute of an object, and how to get and set the value of an attribute of an object. Each method has two slightly different implementations. The first accepts two PyObject pointers, and the second accepts a PyObject pointer and a character string. The first version of the functions is used when the application code has a Python string object to pass as the second parameter, and the second one when the application has a character string to pass as the second parameter. The equivalent Python code for using these functions is shown here using the corresponding built-in Python functions:

```
i = hasattr(object, "width")   # PyObject_HasAttr
i = getattr(object, "width")   # PyObject_GetAttr
setattr(object, "width", 32)   # PyObject_SetAttr
```

It is common in the Python C API to find functionally equivalent Python code for portions of the API. It is also common to see variations of functions that accept both PyObject pointers and native C data types.

The Number Protocol

The number protocol of the abstract object interface provides functions for dealing with Python objects as numbers. Numbers in this case includes integers, floats, and long integers. The protocol includes the `PyNumber_Check` method to check if a PyObject is a number, and many methods for operating on Python objects as numbers. Some of the methods of the number protocol are shown here:

```
PyObject* PyNumber_Add(PyObject *o1, PyObject *o2);
PyObject* PyNumber_Subtract(PyObject *o1, PyObject *o2);
PyObject* PyNumber_Multiply(PyObject *o1, PyObject *o2);
PyObject* PyNumber_Divide(PyObject *o1, PyObject *o2);
```

These methods operate on two PyObject pointers that point to Python number types. The value returned from these methods is also a PyObject pointer to a new Python object, not a C language numeric variable. The conversion between C data types and Python objects is covered later in this chapter.

The Sequence Protocol

The sequence protocol provides functions for operating on Python objects as sequences. Many Python objects can be interacted with as sequences. Strings, lists, tuples, and arrays all have sequence characteristics and so can be used with this protocol. The protocol includes the `PySequence_Check` to check if a PyObject conforms to the sequence protocol. Some of the methods of the sequence protocol are shown here:

```
int PySequence_Length(PyObject *o);
PyObject* PySequence_GetItem(PyObject *o, int i);
PyObject* PySequence_GetSlice(PyObject *o, int i1, int i2);
int PySequence_SetItem(PyObject *o, int i, PyObject *v);
int PySequence_DelItem(PyObject *o, int i);
```

These methods accept the `sequence` object to be operated on as their first argument. The other arguments depend on the particular operation. The equivalent Python code for these sequence functions is shown here:

```
seq = [1,2,3,4]
i = len(seq)          # PySequence_Length
first = seq[0]        # PySequence_GetItem
slice = seq[1:3]      # PySequence_GetSlice
seq[1] = 14           # PySequence_SetItem
del seq[2]            # PySequence_DelItem
```

The Mapping Protocol

The mapping protocol provides functions for operating on Python objects as dictionaries or *maps*. It allows application code using the Python C API to perform all of the operations that can be performed on dictionaries from Python. It includes the PyMapping_Check method to check if a PyObject points to an object of the dictionary type. Some of the methods of the mapping protocol are shown here:

```
int PyMapping_Length(PyObject *o);
int PyMapping_DelItemString(PyObject *o, char *key);
int PyMapping_DelItem(PyObject *o, PyObject *key);
int PyMapping_HasKeyString(PyObject *o, char *key);
int PyMapping_HasKey(PyObject *o, PyObject *key);
int PyMapping_SetItemString(PyObject *o, char *key, PyObject *v);
```

These methods allow application code to inspect and manipulate Python dictionary objects. Notice that there are two variations of some of the methods for operating on arguments that are Python objects and arguments that are C language character strings. The equivalent Python code for these sequence functions is shown here:

```
dict = {"one":1,
        "two":2,
        "three":3}

result = dict.has_key("one")  # PyMapping_HasKey
dict["four"] = 4              # PyMapping_SetItemString
l = len(dict)                 # PyMapping_Length
del dict["one"]              # PyMapping_DelItemString
```

Other Protocols

In addition to the protocols listed previously, the abstract object interface also includes the less frequently used *iterator* and *buffer* protocols. The iterator protocol is new in version 2.2 of Python and is used to interact with iterator objects. The buffer protocol allows Python code to interact with buffers of native memory that exist in C programs and to convert them to Python strings.

21.2 REFERENCE COUNTING

Memory management is a complex topic that is the bane of programmers who work with languages such as C and C++ that only provide very primitive memory management facilities. Errors in the area of memory management can lead to memory leaks and program failures. Usually, though, Python programmers are protected from the difficulties of memory management by Python's garbage collector. This system allows Python programmers to take memory management for granted in many situations.

The Python language uses reference counting to determine when resources associated with objects can be released, or *garbage collected*. Garbage collection schemes such as Python uses have traditionally had problems with *circular references,* but the technique used by Python enables it to discover circular references and to free their resources. Circular references are sets of objects that contain (possibly indirect) references to themselves. Traditional garbage collection systems cannot free these types of objects, as their reference counts never drop to zero, but the technique used by Python enables it to discover circular references and to free their resources.

When using the Python C API, programmers must be more aware of reference counting than when writing Python code. It is possible to introduce memory leaks and cause program failures, so programmers must explicitly manage the reference counts of objects being used.

Heap vs. Stack Memory

There are two types of memory in applications written in languages such as C and C++: heap memory and stack memory. Heap memory is where long-lived objects are allocated with the `malloc()` or `new` commands. These objects must be managed by the application and must be released with the `free()` or `delete` commands when the application is finished with them. Programmers' failure to comply with this system leads to memory leaks, crashes, and unexpected behavior.

Stack memory is where short-lived or *automatic* objects are created. Local variables and temporary variables are allocated on the stack. These objects are released by the system automatically when the program leaves the scope where they were defined. Using stack allocated variables is much easier than using heap allocated variables, as the programmer doesn't have to manage the lifetime of the objects manually.

Almost all Python objects represented by PyObject pointers exist on the heap. It is not valid for application code to declare PyObject instances on the stack or to declare static PyObject instances, although it is valid to declare local pointers to PyObject instances on the stack. Usually, PyObject pointers are created and destroyed by the Python runtime system, the interpreter, so programmers don't have to worry about where they are allocated, or when they are released. However, when programming with the Python C API, care must be taken to perform correct management of the reference counts of heap-based Python objects.

This is especially important in game development where the number of objects being created and destroyed could be quite large, and the lifetime of the applications can be very long. Even a small memory leak can be fatal to an application eventually if it is happening every frame that a game is running.

Reference Counting Macros

The Python C API includes macros for managing reference counts of Python objects. The Py_INCREF() and Py_DECREF() macros increment and decrement the reference count of a Python object. The Py_DECREF() macro also releases the memory associated with an object if the reference count drops to zero. Releasing is performed through the type object associated with the Python object whose reference count has become zero. Remember from the previous section that every Python object has a reference count and a type.

The argument to these macros is always a PyObject pointer. These macros should only be called in situations where the argument to them cannot be NULL. Passing a NULL value to these macros will cause a crash or other undefined behavior. There are special, but slower, macros that have built-in checking for Null pointers, the Py_XINCREF() and Py_XDECREF() macros.

The Python C API has terminology for describing when these macros should be used. It classifies references to objects as *real* or *new references* and *borrowed references*. Real references indicate that the reference count of the object has been incremented, and the reference is an independent owner of the object. Borrowed references are temporary references that do not imply ownership of the object. These references don't have to be explicitly released by the application.

In practice, some of the Python API functions return real, new references, and some return borrowed references. The documentation for the Python C API includes this information for each function. For example, the PyObject_GetAttr() function shown in the previous section returns a new reference to the attribute. Code that uses this function must be careful to call Py_DECREF() on the value that is returned so that is does not become a memory leak.

If application code using the Python C API needs to keep a PyObject pointer for some period of time—beyond the function where it was created—it should use the Py_INCREF() macro to acquire an independent reference to the object so it is not released by the interpreter. It must also release this reference with the Py_DECREF() macro when it is finished with the object. Attempting to use a PyObject pointer after the interpreter has released the memory that it points to will cause undefined behavior to occur.

21.3 EXCEPTION HANDLING

Similar to reference counting, the use of exceptions when using the Python C API is more explicit and requires more management than when writing pure Python code. Each time a Python C API function is called, the return value should be checked for failure cases. When Python C API functions fail, they return NULL, −1, or false depending on their return type. They also discard any local references and set up the exception information so that the interpreter can be informed of the failure. The exception information is stored outside of the stack in per-thread storage, so it can persist as multiple levels of functions return to unwind the stack. This information consists of the *exception type, the exception value,* and the *trace back.*

Application code that uses the Python C API should pass exceptions back to the interpreter's main loops, but should be careful to release any references that are held. There are methods in the Python C API to aid in identifying exceptions. The `PyErr_Occurred()` function tests whether an error has occurred and returns a PyObject pointer to the exception object. Notice that exceptions are Python objects, so they are represented as PyObject pointers. The `PyErr_ExceptionMatches` function can be used to compare the return value from `PyErr_Occurred()` to static exception type objects to determine the type of exception that has occurred. Some of the static exception type objects include:

```
PyExc_Exception
PyExc_StandardError
PyExc_ArithmeticError
PyExc_LookupError
PyExc_AssertionError
PyExc_AttributeError
PyExc_IOError
PyExc_ImportError
PyExc_ZeroDivisionError
```

The following code shows how the current exception state can be tested.

```
PyObject *attr = PyObject_GetAttrString(pObject, "name");
if (!attr)
{
    PyObject *exception = PyErr_Occurred();
    if (PyErr_ExceptionMatches(PyExc_AttributeError, exception) )
    {
        printf("ERROR: No name for Object!\n");
    }
    else
    {
```

```
        printf("ERROR: Unknown error getting name.\n");
    }
    return NULL;
}
```

This code checks the type of exception returned from the `PyObject_GetAt-trString` function. If it is the known exception type `PyExc_AttributeError`, it knows to print a meaningful message, but doesn't know how to handle other types of exceptions for this operation.

21.4 DATA CONVERSION

Since Python and C are different languages with different in-memory representations of objects, transferring data between the two languages requires the use of specific functions of the Python C API. This process of moving data between languages is called *marshalling*, and in Python there are numerous ways it can be done. There are two places where marshalling is always performed in the Python C API, when extracting parameters passed to extension functions, and when building return values to be passed back from extension functions. This section covers both of these cases.

Extracting Parameter Values

When C functions are called by the Python interpreter, the signature of the functions must conform to the one shown here:

```
PyObject *testFunction( PyObject *self, PyObject *args );
```

The `self` argument is only used when the function implements a built-in method. This is discussed in more detail in the next chapter in the section that deals with *extension types*. The `args` argument is a Python tuple object that contains the values with which the function was called. Since Python is dynamically typed, the function signature for methods cannot be determined at compile time, so this data-driven approach is used.

The Python C API function `PyArg_ParseTuple()` is used to extract the arguments from the tuple into C language data structures. This function takes a PyObject pointer to a tuple, a format specification string, and the addresses of C variables to be populated with data. It returns zero on failure, and a non-zero value on success. The signature of the function is shown here:

```
int PyArg_ParseTuple(PyObject *arg, char *format, ...);
```

The format string contains tokens that represent the data types of the items in the tuple and the corresponding data variables passed to the function. Table 21.1 lists some of the common tokens that can be used in the format string. The full set of format tokens can be found in the Python documentation.

TABLE 21.1   Tuple Parsing Tokens

Token	C Data Type
s	char *
b	char (8 bit)
h	short int (16 bit)
i	integer (32 bit)
f	float
d	double
O	PyObject *
S	PyStringObject *

The tokens can specify to extract data into C data types such as integers and floats, but also to extract data into Python C API data types such as PyObject pointers. This can be useful if the application code must call other Python C API functions on Python objects passed into it, rather than just simple pieces of data. Note that PyObject pointers extracted in this way are *borrowed* references, so they do not need to be decremented when the calling function ends.

The following code shows how PyArg_ParseTuple is used to extract data from a tuple. This code assumes a Python tuple of the format [float, float, string, byte, byte, byte].

```
float      x, y;
char       r, g, b;
const char *text;

if( !PyArg_ParseTuple(args,"ffsbbb ", &x, &y, &text, &r, &g, &b);
{
  PyErr_SetString(PyExc_AttributeError, "Bad attributes !");
  return NULL;
}
```

Notice that the characters in the format string correspond to the data types of the arguments passed to the function after the format string. The arguments are passed with the & (address of) operator so that their value can be modified by the function.

Some special tokens in the format strings have additional functionality above just specifying the data types of the arguments. The pipe (|) character specifies that the tokens to the right of it are optional parameters that can be omitted in the tuple passed to the function. The tokens to the right of the pipe character must still match the specification exactly. The colon (:) character specifies that the format string ends here, and the remaining characters make up the name that should be used when exceptions are built within the function call. The semicolon (;) character also specifies that the format string ends here, but with this token, the remaining characters are used as the error message for exceptions generated by the function call.

The `PyArg_ParseTuple` function is a very powerful tool that can be used in simple ways, like the previous example, or can be used in more complex ways to enable tight integration between C and Python code.

Building Return Values

The other side of data conversion between C and Python is returning values from C functions invoked from Python. All C functions invoked by Python return a PyObject pointer, but this can be any type of Python object; a list, a tuple, a dictionary, or a complex class object. There are methods in the Python C API that can be used to create Python objects to be used as return values of functions.

The Python object returned from C functions should be a real reference, not a borrowed reference. There are methods in the Python C API to create simple Python objects from simple C data types. Some of these methods are shown here:

```
PyObject* PyInt_FromLong(long ival);
PyObject* PyLong_FromLong(long v);
PyObject* PyFloat_FromDouble(double v);
PyObject* PyString_FromString(const char *v);
PyObject* PyFile_FromString(char *filename, char *mode);
```

These methods can be used to create a simple return value for a function and return the value in a single step. For example, the following code:

```
return PyInt_FromLong(55);
```

creates a new Python integer object on the heap from the C language value of 55, and returns the new, real reference to it from the current function.

More complex Python objects can be constructed with the `Py_BuildValue` function. This is the counterpart of the `PyArg_ParseTuple` discussed previously. It allows tuples of Python objects to be created using a specification string, and C language variables. It returns a new Python tuple object suitable for returning from C functions. The format string tokens recognized by the `Py_BuildValue` function are similar to the format specifications for extracting data from tuples, but not exactly the same. The full set of format tokens can be found in the Python documentation.

The following is an example of building a Python tuple from C data types. The format of this tuple is [float, float, string, byte, byte, byte], the same as in the previous example.

```
float x = 100.0f;
float y = 50.0f;
char *text = "My Message.";
char r = 255;
char g = 100;
char b = 255;

return Py_BuildValue("ffsbbb", x, y, text, r, g, b);
```

If the format specification string does not match the arguments passed to the function, a NULL value is returned, and a Python exception is generated. Conveniently, this is the appropriate behavior for the return values from C functions.

21.5 CONCRETE OBJECT LAYER

In addition to the abstract object interface and the `PyObject` type discussed in Section 21.1, the Python C API includes sets of methods for operating on specific types of Python objects, and specific pointers for types of Python objects. These functions and types are arranged in the *concrete object layer*. This layer is used for more advanced types of interactions between Python and the C language.

The objects that make up this layer are fundamental objects, numeric objects, sequence objects, mapping objects, and *other* objects. Notice that the concrete objects correspond to the protocols in the abstract object layer. While the functions in the abstract object layer operate on abstract PyObject pointers, the functions in the concrete object layer operate on concrete Python object instances that are typed, such as the `PyStringObject`, `PyIntObject`, and `PyFloatObject` types. Although the signatures of the functions in these interfaces accept `PyObject` pointers, only pointers to objects of the correct type should be passed to these functions.

Some of the methods in the concrete object layer are actually C macros rather than actual methods. These macros sometimes lack the error-checking functionality of otherwise corresponding functions, but when used in safe circumstances, they offer a performance improvement over those functions. The macros can be identified visually, as a portion of their names are in capital letters. For example, the macro `PyList_GET_ITEM()` in the sequence layer is equivalent in functionality to the function `PyList_GetItem()`, except that it does not perform error checking on the values passed to it.

Fundamental Objects

The fundamental layer represents the lowest layer of types above the `PyObject` abstract base type. It includes two types of Python objects, the `PyTypeObject` and the singleton `Py_None` object.

The `PyTypeObject` represents objects that describe the structure of Python's built-in types. It is used when performing type comparisons between Python objects. These objects are not used very often in Python C API programming for game development. The methods associated with this type can be found in the Python C API documentation. There is a built-in instance of this object for each of the concrete types in the Python C API. These instances are equivalent to the attributes of the `types` module in Python.

The abstract object interface defines the method `PyObject_IsInstance` that uses type objects. This method checks if the type of the Python object passed to it matches a given type. The signature of this function is:

```
int PyObject_IsInstance(PyObject *inst, PyObject *cls)
```

The `inst` argument is the Python object to be checked, and the `cls` argument is a Python type object of the type `PyTypeObject`. This type object is often one of the built-in type instances, as in the following example:

```
if (PyObject_IsInstance(myObject, PyInt_Type) == 1)
{
    printf("MyObject is an integer.\n");
}
```

The built-in type instance objects are defined in each of the following concrete object layers.

The `Py_None` object is a singleton that represents a null value. As a singleton, there is only one instance of this type, and it corresponds to the `None` object in Python code. This object is sometimes used as a return value in C functions called by Python, and to test if the return value of Python C API functions was None.

There are no methods associated with this type of object, but the comparison operator (==) can be used to compare any object against the Py_None singleton.

Numeric Objects

The numeric layer represents the numeric types. The Python types in this layer are the PyIntObject type that represents regular integers, the PyLongObject type that represents long integers, the PyFloatObject type that represents floating-point numbers, and a special structure for complex numbers. These types are used when converting numeric data between C and Python, and when operating on Python numeric objects from the C language.

Table 21.2 lists the type objects and check functions for the types in this layer.

TABLE 21.2   Numeric Types

Type	Type Object	Check Function
PyIntObject	PyInt_Type	PyInt_Check()
PyLongObject	PyLong_Type	PyLong_Check()
PyFloatObject	PyFloat_Type	PyFloat_Check()

As much of the interesting arithmetic functionality for numeric types is implemented in the abstract object layer, the numeric layer does not include very much specific functionality apart from data conversion and type checking.

Sequence Objects

The sequence layer represents objects that are made up of sequences of other objects. The Python types in this layer are the PyStringObject type for representing Python strings, the PyUnicodeObject type for representing Unicode data, the PyBufferObject for representing Python buffer objects, the PyTupleObject for representing Python tuples, and the PyListObject for representing Python lists.

The common functionality of all of these types includes random access to sequence elements, slicing, concatenation, and length counting. This common functionality is implemented in the sequence protocol of the abstract objects layer. The functionality in the concrete sequence layer is specific functionality to the types that are defined in this layer.

Table 21.3 lists the type objects and check functions for the types in this layer.

TABLE 21.3   Sequence Types

Type	Type Object	Check Function
PyStringObject	PyString_Type	PyString_Check()
PyUnicodeObject	PyUnicode_Type	PyUnicode_Check()
PyBufferObject	PyBuffer_Type	PyBuffer_Check()
PyTupleObeject	PyTuple_Type	PyTuple_Check()
PyListObject	PyList_Type	PyList_Check()

Mapping Objects

The mapping layer represents dictionary objects. There is a single Python type in this layer, the PyDictObject type that represents Python dictionary objects.

Similar to sequence objects, some of the common functionality of dictionary objects is implemented in the mapping protocol of the abstract object layer. However, most of the useful functionality of dictionary objects is implemented in the mapping layer.

Table 21.4 lists the single type object and check function for this layer.

TABLE 21.4   Map Types

Type	Type Object	Check Function
PyDictObject	PyDict_Type	PyDict_Check()

Other Objects

A number of other types of objects in the concrete layer don't fit into a larger category. Some of these objects are files, methods, modules, iterators, and slices. These types follow the same pattern as the other types of objects described in this section. They implement type-specific functionality and have corresponding type objects and pointers that are used when dealing with concrete instances of them.

Full documentation on the remaining types of concrete object types can be found in the Python C API documentation.

SUMMARY

This chapter described how to use the Python C API without going into specific applications of it. This topic is important in game development as almost every Python project will have to resort to building cross-language integration at some point.

This chapter included discussions of the abstract PyObject type, and the methods associated with the protocols in the abstract object layer of the Python C API that operate on objects of this type. It discussed the issues of reference counting and exception handling, and converting data in both directions between Python and the C language. Finally, it discussed the concrete object layer that contains functions specific to concrete types of Python objects.

The topics described in this chapter form the foundation of knowledge that the next chapters use to build components that interact between Python and the C language. This foundation is important to ensure that these components adhere to the conventions of the Python C API so they don't leak memory, or crash the Python interpreter. This knowledge will also be useful when looking at automated interface generation tools in later chapters.

The full specification of the Python C API and an excellent tutorial can be found in the Python documentation that is included in the standard distribution.

22 Extending Python

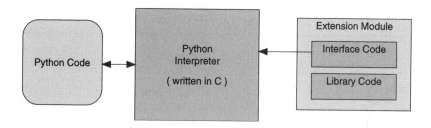

There are three strategies for the integration of Python and C code, all of which use the Python C API that was discussed in the previous chapter. In the first technique, called *extension modules,* components are implemented in C, but have an interface written with the Python C API that allows the Python interpreter to interact with them as if they were regular Python modules. In the second technique, called *extension types*, components are also implemented in C using the Python C API, but they expose new classes or types instead of just having a module interface. This technique is itself an extension of the extension modules technique. In the final technique, called *embedding*, the Python interpreter is embedded in another application and communicates with the host application through the Python C API.

Some tools such as *SWIG* and *Boost* can be used to automate the generation of Python C API code. When used carefully, these tools can significantly reduce the amount of time it takes to develop extension modules. Although these tools can be used to create extension modules, knowing the details of how extension modules work is vital to knowing if the use of these tools is appropriate for a particular application.

This chapter examines the different techniques of extending Python, and shows examples of using these techniques in the context of game development. Section 22.1 discusses writing extension modules with the Python C API, and Section 22.2 discusses enhancing extension modules by developing extension types with the

Python C API. Finally, Section 22.3 discusses using tools to automate interface generation. Embedding Python into other applications as a scripting language is covered in the next chapter.

22.1 WRITING EXTENSION MODULES

As its name suggests, the practice of *extending* expands the functionality of the Python language to include functionality written in other languages (generally the C language). Extension modules use the Python C API to handle the interface between Python and the C language for the module, and the C language code that provides the actual functionality of the module. As this code used is often a library of functionality, this code is referred to as *library* code in this section. The code that is specific to interfacing with Python is referred to as *interface* code.

To use this approach, the interface code and the library code are compiled into a single DLL or shared object that acts as a Python module. On Windows, Python extension modules usually have the extension *.pyd* to designate that they are Python DLLs. On Unix-based systems, extension modules usually have the *.so* extension to designate that they are shared object files. Figure 22.1 shows this architecture.

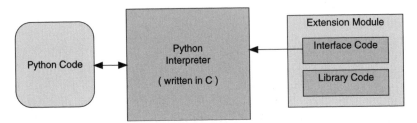

FIGURE 22.1   Extension module architecture.

Of the architectures described in Chapter 3, "Python Game Architectures," the *Python Programming* architecture uses the extending method. Of the types of simulations in Chapter 5, "Simulation Concepts," *Controlled Simulation* and *Parallel Simulation* architectures use the extending method.

Using Extension Modules

To Python application code, extension modules can appear exactly the same as modules written in Python code. This is a very useful characteristic of the Python module system. It can allow Python code to use a Python implementation of a module or an optimized C implementation of a module in different circumstances. Moreover, it can allow projects to defer the development of optimized versions of components until later in the project by first using a pure Python implementation of the module. This helps game projects to become playable and testable earlier, and allows time for module interfaces to stabilize before time is spent optimizing them.

This technique can be demonstrated with the `pickle` module in Python's standard distribution. Usually, the regular `pickle` module is used for serialization of Python objects. This version is written in pure Python. However, when higher performance is required, the `cPickle` module can be used. This is a Python extension module written in C that exposes the same interface as the `pickle` module. The following code shows how to import the `cPickle` module instead of the `pickle` module in a way that is transparent to user code.

```
try:
    import cPickle
    pickle = cPickle
except ImportError e:
    import pickle
```

On some systems or platforms, the `cPickle` module might not be available, so this code wraps the `import` statement in an exception handling block. After this block of code executes, the `pickle` variable is a module that implements the `pickle` interface. In some circumstances, it is a reference to the pure Python `pickle` module, and in other circumstances, it is a reference to the optimized C implementation in the `cPickle` module. Notice that the code:

```
pickle = cPickle
```

assigns the name `pickle` to the `cPickle` module. Remember that in Python, modules are objects, and they can be assigned and referenced in this way like any other type of data. Once this module has been imported, either implementation can be used by Python code without that code being aware of the underlying implementation. The following code uses the `pickle` module in this way.

```
try:
    import cPickle
```

```
        pickle = cPickle
    except ImportError e:
        import pickle

    outFile = open("outFile.dat", "w")
    pickle.dump(myObject, outFile)
    close(outFile)
```

Game applications often have both pure Python modules and extension modules. With a modular architecture, it is possible for modules such as collision detection or graphics to have implementations in both C and Python that can be used interchangeably.

Creating an Extension Module

This section discusses the components of an extension module and demonstrates how to develop an extension module using the Python C API. The example in this section is an extension interface to replace the graphics engine module from Chapter 8, "Graphics." It is developed under the assumption that there is an existing implementation of the graphics engine in C++, so it only implements the interface code, not the full graphics engine. This extension module could be used to swap out the existing graphics engine module that is written in Python for an optimized version written in C that provides the same functionality. Note that the GraphicsObject class that is exposed by the Python version of the engine module is not implemented in this section. It is implemented in the next section of this chapter that deals with extension types.

Each extension module has three significant components that allow it to be accessed by Python: a name, an initialization method, and a function table. In addition, extension modules have code that implements their core functionality. This code might not be related to Python in any way, and is called the *library code* of the module.

The name of an extension module is used for a number of purposes. The binary DLL or shared object that the extension module compiles to, must have a name in the file system that is derived from the module's name. This allows Python to find the matching binary object for the module. The example extension module must correspond to the Python module implemented in the file *engine.py*, so it must be named cEngine to distinguish it from the pure Python implementation. The file name of the compiled binary is *cEngine.pyd* or *cEngine.so*. The name is also the label used by Python to identify the module in Python code. The code to conditionally import this module from Python, and fall back to the pure Python implementation is shown here:

```
try:
    import cEngine
    engine = cEngine
except:
    import engine
```

Note that the names of Python extension modules are case sensitive, even on platforms where the file system is not. The final use of the name is in the construction of the name of the module's initialization function.

The initialization function of an extension module is the entry point that Python uses to load the module when it is imported. This function must be named *initNAME*, where NAME is the name of the extension module. The signature of the initialization function is shown here:

```
void initcEngine();
```

This can be complicated by the need to export symbols from a DLL on Windows platforms, and the need to extern the method from C++ code, so a more realistic signature for an initialization function is:

```
extern "C" __declspec(dllexport) void initcEngine();
```

Sometimes, these additional parameters are encapsulated in C macros for platform portability. The initialization function can perform any module-specific initialization required by the library code, but its real purpose is to initialize the module itself with the Python interpreter. The initialization function must call the `Py_InitModule` method of the Python C API and pass it the name of the module and the module's function table. Listing 22.1 show the code for a simple initialization function.

Listing 22.1   Initialization function.

```
extern "C" __declspec(dllexport) void initcEngine ()
    {
        (void) Py_InitModule( " initcEngine ", EngineFunctions );
    }
```

The function table of an extension module is an array of `PyMethodDef` structures. The Python C API defines this structure, and each instance of it holds the information to enable a C method to be invoked by the Python interpreter. This structure is shown here:

```
struct PyMethodDef {
```

```
      char          *ml_name;
      PyCFunction    ml_meth;
      int            ml_flags;
      char          *ml_doc;
};
```

It contains a method name, a function pointer to the method itself, a set of flags, and a documentation string for the method. This might seem complex, but in practice the layout of the function table is easy to read. Listing 22.2 shows the function table for the example extension module.

Listing 22.2   Extension module function table.

```
#include "Python.h"

static PyMethodDef EngineFunctions[] =
{
  {"initialize",   py_initialize,    METH_VARARGS, "initialize engine" },
  {"shutdown",     py_shutdown,      METH_VARARGS, "shutdown the engine" },
  {"addObject",    py_addObject,     METH_VARARGS, "add graphics object" },
  {"removeObject", py_removeObject,  METH_VARARGS, "remove graphics object"
},
  {"render",       py_render,        METH_VARARGS, "render scene" },
  {"setView",      py_setView,       METH_VARARGS, "set viewport origin" },
  {"getWidth",     py_getWidth,      METH_VARARGS, "get screen width" },
  {"getHeight",    py_getHeight,     METH_VARARGS, "get screen height" },
  {"worldToScreen",py_worldToScreen,METH_VARARGS, "convert coordinates" },
  {"screenToWorld",py_screenToWorld,METH_VARARGS, "convert coordinates" },
  {"getSources",   py_getSources,    METH_VARARGS, "get sources" },
  {"getTextures",  py_getTextures,   METH_VARARGS, "get textures" },
  {"flushSources", py_flushSources,  METH_VARARGS, "flush all sources" },
  {"flushTextures",py_flushTextures,METH_VARARGS, "flush all textures" },
  {NULL,           NULL,             NULL,         NULL }
};
```

This array of `PyMethodDef` objects is statically initialized with some methods, and a NULL structure to designate the end of the array. This NULL structure must exist at the end of the function table so the Python interpreter knows when to stop reading functions from it. Notice that the names in this table correspond to the names of the module-level functions from the graphics engine module from Chapter 8.

The second column in the table is the `PyCFunction ml_meth` attribute of the `PyMethodDef` structure. This is the C function that is invoked when the Python method on the module is called from Python code. The C functions in this example are all prefixed with the string py_ so that they don't cause namespace conflicts with other functions in the C code. Using a prefix like this is not part of the Python C API interface, and is not required, but it is a useful practice that can prevent obscure errors during development.

All of the functions in the function table have the same signature. In fact, all C function invoked by Python must have this same signature. This signature is shown here:

```
PyObject *py_getWidth( PyObject *self, PyObject *args )
```

The first argument is a PyObject pointer to the Python object that the function was invoked on. This is not used for module-level functions. It is discussed in more detail in the next section of this chapter. The second argument is a tuple of the Python arguments with which the function was called. As Python is dynamically typed, the set of variables in this argument list could be different each time the method is called, so it isn't possible to have a static function signature in C for the methods. As these values are passed as a Python tuple object, the data conversion function PyArg_ParseTuple() that was discussed in Chapter 21, "Using Python C API," can be used to extract the values into C variables. The return type is also a PyObject pointer. The Py_BuildValue() function that was discussed in Chapter 21 can be used to construct Python objects to use as return values.

Extension Module Example

In Chapter 8, the Python-based graphics engine module acted as a singleton, and Python's module system ensured that there was only one instance of the module in existence at any time. This allowed methods to be called on it that were routed to a module-level instance of the GraphicsEngine class within the module. The extension module for the graphics engine uses a similar mechanism, but instead of a Python object, the singleton object is a C++ object.

This example assumes that the GraphicsEngine C++ class already existed before the Python C API code was written, so it is a realistic example of wrapping an existing library to conform to the interface of a Python module. Listing 22.3 shows the C++ header for this class.

Listing 22.3 GraphicsEngine C++ class.

```
class GraphicsEngine
{
public:

  GraphicsEngine(int width, int height);
  ~GraphicsEngine();

  bool addObject(GraphicsObject *object, float x, float y, float
facing);
  bool removeObject(GraphicsObject *object);
  void render();
  void setView(int x, int y);
  int getWidth();
  int getHeight();
  void worldToScreen(const float inX,const float inY,float &outX,float
&outY);
  void screenToWorld(const float inX,const float inY,float &outX,float
&outY);
  void flushTextures();
  void flushSources();

protected:

  int m_width;
  int m_height;
  int m_viewPosX;
  int m_viewPosY;
  list<GraphicsObject*> m_objects;
};
```

The public interface of this class is similar to the interface of the Python engine module, but not identical. The interface code must deal with the differences so that the class can be used from Python code.

The first issue the interface code must deal with is creation and destruction of the singleton C++ GraphicsEngine object. Like the Python engine module, the extension module has an internal engine object. In this case, it is a GraphicsEngine pointer called gEngine, as shown here:

```
GraphicsEngine *gEngine = NULL;
```

The Python engine module has an initialize method to explicitly create the engine object within the module. Therefore, the extension module must also have

an `initialize` function. This function creates the global C++ engine object. It also
has a `shutdown` function that deletes the object. Listing 22.4 shows these C functions.

Listing 22.4   Initialize and shutdown functions.

```
/*
** py_initialize()
**
** Params:   width and height
** Returns:  1
*/
PyObject *py_initialize( PyObject *, PyObject *args )
{
  int width, height;

  if( !PyArg_ParseTuple(args, "ii:py_initialize", &width, &height) )
  {
    return NULL;
  }

  if (gEngine)
  {
    PyErr_SetString(PyExc_AssertionError, "Engine already
initialized");
    return NULL;
  }

  gEngine = new GraphicsEngine(width, height);
  if (!gEngine)
  {
    PyErr_SetString(PyExc_AssertionError, "Unable to create Engine");
    return NULL;
  }

  return PyInt_FromLong(1);
}

/*
** py_shutdown()
**
** Params:   none
** Returns:  1
*/
PyObject *py_shutdown( PyObject *, PyObject *args )
{
  if (gEngine)
  {
```

```
      delete gEngine;
      gEngine = NULL;
      return PyInt_FromLong(1);
  }
  else
  {
    PyErr_SetString(PyExc_AssertionError, "Engine not initialized");
    return NULL;
  }
}
```

Notice that these functions are actually called `py_initialize` and `py_shutdown` so they are easily identifiable as Python extension module methods. They also have the function signature of Python C API methods that was shown previously. In addition, the `py_initialize` function uses the `PyArg_ParseTuple` function that was described in the previous chapter to convert the width and height values into C variables.

These methods manage the lifetime of the global engine object. They check for its existence by testing if the value of the `gEngine` pointer is NULL. If the engine is in the wrong state when a function call is made, the calls set the exception state and return a NULL value to pass the exception to the Python interpreter. The following output shows these methods in action.

```
$ python
>>> import cEngine
>>> cEngine.initialize(100,100)
1
>>> cEngine.initialize(100,200)
Traceback (most recent call last):
  File "<stdin>", line 1, in ?
AssertionError: Engine already initialized
>>> cEngine.shutdown()
1
>>> cEngine.shutdown()
Traceback (most recent call last):
  File "<stdin>", line 1, in ?
AssertionError: Engine not initialized
>>>
```

When the module methods are invoked in the wrong order, the module throws the appropriate exception that informs the user of the problem.

The other methods of the engine module rely on the existence of the engine object. They are wrappers around the functionality of the C++ `GraphicsEngine` object.

Each of the functions has a corresponding member function on the C++ class, so the interface code's only responsibilities are data conversion and error checking.

The addObject and removeObject methods of the module tell the engine which graphics objects should be drawn. They accept a pointer to a GraphicsObject instance. As the GraphicsObject class is defined within this module, these methods pose a problem for now. They require a new Python extension type, a topic that is described in the next section of this chapter, so the code for those methods is in the next section. Listing 22.5 shows the code for the remaining function in the interface code.

Listing 22.5 Interface functions.

```
/*
** py_render()
**
** Params:
** Returns: nothing
*/
PyObject *py_render( PyObject *, PyObject *args )
{
  if (!gEngine)
  {
    PyErr_SetString(PyExc_AssertionError, "Engine not initialized");
    return NULL;
  }

  gEngine->render();
  return PyInt_FromLong(1);
}

/*
** py_setView()
**
** Param:   x - view X position
** Param:   y - view Y position
** Returns: 1
*/
PyObject *py_setView( PyObject *, PyObject *args )
{
  int posX, posY;

  if (!gEngine)
  {
    PyErr_SetString(PyExc_AssertionError, "Engine not initialized");
    return NULL;
```

```
    }

    if( !PyArg_ParseTuple(args, "ii:py_setView", &posX, &posY) )
    {
      return NULL;
    }

    gEngine->setView(posX, posY);
    return PyInt_FromLong(1);
}

/*
** py_getWidth()
**
** Param:   none
** Returns: engine width
*/
PyObject *py_getWidth( PyObject *, PyObject *args )
{
  if (!gEngine)
  {
    PyErr_SetString(PyExc_AssertionError, "Engine not initialized");
    return NULL;
  }

  int width = gEngine->getWidth();
  return PyInt_FromLong(width);
}

/*
** py_getHeight()
**
** Param:   none
** Returns: engine height
*/
PyObject *py_getHeight( PyObject *, PyObject *args )
{
  if (!gEngine)
  {
    PyErr_SetString(PyExc_AssertionError, "Engine not initialized");
    return NULL;
  }

  int height = gEngine->getHeight();
  return PyInt_FromLong(height);
}
```

```
/*
** py_worldToScreen()
**
** Param:   world X
** Param:   world Y
** Returns: (screenX, screenY)
*/
PyObject *py_worldToScreen( PyObject *, PyObject *args )
{
  float worldX, worldY;
  float screenX, screenY;

  if (!gEngine)
  {
    PyErr_SetString(PyExc_AssertionError, "Engine not initialized");
    return NULL;
  }

  if( !PyArg_ParseTuple(args, "ff:py_worldToScreen", &worldX, &worldY)
)
  {
    return NULL;
  }

  gEngine->worldToScreen(worldX, worldY, screenX, screenY);

  return Py_BuildValue("ii", screenX, screenY);
}

/*
** py_screenToWorld()
**
** Param:   screen X
** Param:   screen Y
** Returns: (worldX, worldY)
*/
PyObject *py_screenToWorld( PyObject *, PyObject *args )
{
  float worldX, worldY;
  float screenX, screenY;

  if (!gEngine)
  {
    PyErr_SetString(PyExc_AssertionError, "Engine not initialized");
    return NULL;
  }
```

```
  if( !PyArg_ParseTuple(args, "ff:py_screenToWorld", &screenX,
&screenY) )
  {
    return NULL;
  }

  gEngine->screenToWorld(screenX, screenY, worldX, worldY);

  return Py_BuildValue("ii", worldX, worldY);
}

/*
** py_getSources()
**
** Params:
** Returns: nothing
*/
PyObject *py_getSources( PyObject *, PyObject *args )
{
  if (!gEngine)
  {
    PyErr_SetString(PyExc_AssertionError, "Engine not initialized");
    return NULL;
  }

  PyErr_SetString(PyExc_NotImplementedError, "getSources not
available");
  return NULL;
}

/*
** py_getTextures()
**
** Params:
** Returns: nothing
*/
PyObject *py_getTextures( PyObject *, PyObject *args )
{
  if (!gEngine)
  {
    PyErr_SetString(PyExc_AssertionError, "Engine not initialized");
    return NULL;
  }

  PyErr_SetString(PyExc_NotImplementedError, "getTextures not
available");
  return NULL;
```

```
    }

    /*
    ** py_flushSources()
    **
    ** Params:
    ** Returns: nothing
    */
    PyObject *py_flushSources( PyObject *, PyObject *args )
    {
      if (!gEngine)
      {
        PyErr_SetString(PyExc_AssertionError, "Engine not initialized");
        return NULL;
      }
      gEngine->flushSources();
      return PyInt_FromLong(1);
    }

    /*
    ** py_flushTextures()
    **
    ** Params:
    ** Returns: nothing
    */
    PyObject *py_flushTextures( PyObject *, PyObject *args )
    {
      if (!gEngine)
      {
        PyErr_SetString(PyExc_AssertionError, "Engine not initialized");
        return NULL;
      }
      gEngine->flushTextures();
      return PyInt_FromLong(1);
    }
```

These methods show a number of variations of C functions that can be called from Python, and use various portions of the Python C API code. Although this is a lot of code, if we draw on the knowledge from the previous chapter that covered the Python C API, all of these functions are very simple. Their only functions are to perform error checking, and to act as intermediaries between the incoming arguments from Python, and the C++ graphics engine object.

Two methods in this code are special. The py_getSources and py_getTextures methods raise an exception to show that they are not implemented. These methods give access to internal data of the module, which was fine when the module was implemented in Python. However, when the module is an extension module implemented in C++, the internal data might not be in a format that is useful or accessible to Python code. Raising the exception informs user code that the methods are not available with this particular implementation.

Therefore, apart from the unimplemented methods, and the methods for management of graphics objects, the interface to the graphics engine module now conforms to the original Python module.

22.2 WRITING EXTENSION TYPES

This section builds on the concept of extension modules and shows how to develop Python extension types. Extension types allow new Python types to be developed in C. Similar to the way extension modules can act like pure Python modules, these new types can act like regular Python types to application code. Extension types can be used as wrappers around existing types or classes in C or C++, or can be used to provide alternate and optimized implementation of pure Python types. This is an advanced topic that requires quite a lot of C code to implement.

Depending on the amount of functionality desired, extension types range from very simple to extremely complicated. Extension types are derived from the very lowest level of the Python types, the *fundamental* Python object. By default, the only functionality they have is a reference count and a type. While it is possible to make extension types behave like some higher-level types to a degree, in general, the programmer must implement all of the functionality of the type with the Python C API. For this reason, extension types can take a lot of effort to develop.

In this section, we develop an extension type to wrap the GraphicsObject C++ class in the cEngine module. This class corresponds to the GraphicsObject class from the Python engine module from Chapter 8. The example will also show how to use the extension type in methods of the extension module.

Listing 22.6 show the C++ header file for the GraphicsObject class. This is the class that the extension type will expose to Python.

Listing 22.6 GraphicsObject C++ class.

```
class GraphicsObject
{
 public:
  GraphicsObject(const char *source, bool mobile, const char *image =
NULL);
  ~GraphicsObject();
```

```
        void getSimData(float &centerX, float &centerY,
                        float &width, float &height);
        void setState(float x, float y, float facing);
        void setFrame(int frame);
        void nextFrame();
        void destroy();

    protected:

        bool m_mobile;
        const char *m_source;
        const char *m_image;
    };
```

Notice that the public interface of this class corresponds to the methods of the Python `GraphicsObject` class from the engine module in Chapter 8.

The Python C API provides the interface for creating extension types. This interface requires a number of pieces to be implemented to create a working extension type. The particular pieces of a type vary based on its functionality, but the components of the example type in this section are:

- An object instance type structure
- A class type structure
- A static type object
- A creation function
- A deallocation function
- A method table and method functions
- Helper methods

These components are explained in the following sections.

Type Structures

Each extension type requires two C structures. One structure is used to represent the Python type object for the extension type. Remember from Chapter 21 that each type has a type object. For example, Python's integer type has a corresponding type object called `PyInt_Type` in the Python C API and `types.IntType` in pure Python. A new extension type must also have a corresponding type object, just like the built-in classes.

The other structure is used to represent instances of the new extension type. It contains instance specific data members and the functions. The instance type structure is a C structure that contains the basic data for the Python objects of the extension type. The standard `PyObject_HEAD` macro is required at the beginning of all instance type structures. This macro fills the structure with a reference count and a type object, the two components of fundamental Python objects. In addition, application code can add other data members or functions to this structure. The example extension type in this chapter adds a pointer to a `GraphicsObject` instance to this structure so that each instance of the extension type can have an associated `GraphicsObject` instance. Listing 22.7 shows the code for the example instance type.

Listing 22.7   `GraphicsObject` instance type structure.

```
/*
**  structure definition for GraphicsObject wrapper
*/
typedef struct {
  PyObject_HEAD
  GraphicsObject *m_gObject;
} py_GraphicsObject;
```

The type structure for extension types is much more complicated than the instance structure. This structure is of the `PyTypeObject` type that is defined in object.h of the Python C API. Listing 22.8 show a portion of the definition of this type that is used for basic object functionality.

Listing 22.8   Python type object structure.

```
typedef struct _typeobject {
  PyObject_VAR_HEAD
  char *tp_name; /* For printing, in format "<module>.<name>" */
  int tp_basicsize, tp_itemsize; /* For allocation */

  /* Methods to implement standard operations */

  destructor tp_dealloc;
  printfunc tp_print;
  getattrfunc tp_getattr;
  setattrfunc tp_setattr;
  cmpfunc tp_compare;
  reprfunc tp_repr;

  /* Method suites for standard classes */

  PyNumberMethods *tp_as_number;
  PySequenceMethods *tp_as_sequence;
  PyMappingMethods *tp_as_mapping;
} PyTypeObject;
```

This structure can be a little daunting at first. It contains all the information the interpreter requires to operate on objects of this type, so it can be a relatively large and complex structure. There are actually many more members to this structure than are shown here, but the remaining members are optional, so they are not shown.

For each extension type, a static instance of this structure must exist to act as that type's Python type object. The standard `PyObject_HEAD_INIT(NULL)` macro is required at the beginning of all type structures. Listing 22.9 show the code for the static type object for the graphics object extension type.

Listing 22.9 GraphicsObject type object.

```
/*
** GraphicsObject type object
**
*/
static PyTypeObject py_GraphicsObject_Type = {
    PyObject_HEAD_INIT(NULL)
    0,                              /* number of items */
    "GraphicsObject",               /* type name */
    sizeof(py_GraphicsObject),      /* basic size of instances */
    0,                              /* item size */
    py_GraphicsObject_dealloc,      /* deallocation function_dealloc*/
    0,                              /* print function - tp_print*/
    py_getattr,                     /* getattr function - tp_getattr*/
    0,                              /* setattr function - tp_setattr */
    0,                              /* comparison function - tp_compare*/
    0,                              /* repr function - tp_repr*/
    0,                              /* tp_as_number*/
    0,                              /* tp_as_sequence*/
    0,                              /* tp_as_mapping*/
    0,                              /* tp_hash */
};
```

Remember that static structure initializations like this assign the values between the curly braces to the attributes of the structure in the order in which they are declared in the structure definition. To aid in reading this initialization, the names of the structure members that are initialized by each item are shown in comments to the right of the values.

This type object is the single instance of this structure that is used by the interpreter in all cases where it requires type information about Python instances of the GraphicsObject type. For example, when Python code attempts to access a member variable of an instance, it checks the tp_getattr attribute of this structure for a method to access attributes. If that member is NULL, it raises an exception, but if it finds a function there, it calls that function with the Python instance as the first argument, and the method arguments as the tuple in the second argument.

As this structure has many zero values, this particular Python extension type will not act like the built-in Python types in all circumstances. Populating more of the data members of this structure will make extension types appear more like built-in types to pure Python code. However, developing extension types in this way requires a large amount of code.

Instance Creation and Deletion

Two of the values in the static type structure defined previously are the creation function for new instances of the type, and the deallocation function for instances of the type. This section shows how to use these functions to manage the C++ object that is being wrapped by this extension type.

The creation function for extension types is actually an extension module function. As it must be accessed as a member of the extension module that contains the extension type, it must be in the extension module's function table. Listing 22.10 shows the code for the creation function for the graphics object type.

Listing 22.10 GraphicsObject creation function.

```
/*
**   GraphicsObject Creation Function
**
*/
PyObject *py_new_GraphicsObject( PyObject *, PyObject *args)
{
  char *source;
  bool mobile;
  char *image = NULL;

  if (!PyArg_ParseTuple(args, "si|s:GraphicsObject",
          &source, &mobile, &image) )
  {
    return NULL;
  }

  // Create the Python wrapper object
  py_GraphicsObject *gObj = PyObject_New(
                            py_GraphicsObject,
                            &py_GraphicsObject_Type);

  // Create the actual graphics object
```

```
gObj->m_gObject = new GraphicsObject(source, mobile, image);

return (PyObject*)gObj;
}
```

This function parses the arguments it was called with and calls the Python C API function PyObject_New to create a new Python object of the py_GraphicsObject type. Notice that it passes the instance type object and the type object to this function. Once an instance has been created, it creates an actual GraphicsObject instance—the engine object that this extension type is wrapping—and assigns it to the pointer in the Python object instance.

Once this function is added to the function table of the cEngine module, it allows new graphics objects to be created from Python code by invoking this method on the extension module. An example of this code is shown here:

```
import cEngine
gObj = cEngine.GraphicsObject("testing", mobile=1)
```

The Python interpreter controls the deletion of objects. When it determines that the reference count of an object has reached zero, it invokes the deallocation function for the type, and passes it to the object to be deleted. Listing 22.11 shows the code for the deallocation function for the graphics object type.

Listing 22.11   GraphicsObject deallocation function.

```
/*
**   Deallocation function for GraphicsObject
*/
static void py_GraphicsObject_dealloc(PyObject* self)
{
  py_GraphicsObject *gobj = (py_GraphicsObject*)self;
  if (gobj)
  {
    if (gobj->m_gObject)
    {
      delete gobj->m_gObject;
      gobj->m_gObject = NULL;
    }
  }
  PyObject_Del(self);
}
```

This function casts the incoming generic PyObject pointer to the specific py_GraphicsObject type. This allows the member attribute that refers to the internal graphics object to be accessed. It deletes the graphics object and calls the Python C API function `PyObject_Del` to delete the instance of the extension object that wrapped the graphics object instance.

These two functions allow instances of the extension type to be created and deleted from Python code. A more advanced situation related to these functions is the case where an existing graphics object that was created by C++ code, rather than Python code, must be exposed to Python. In this case, the ownership of the object might not be as clear-cut as in this example. The instance structure would have to be extended to include information about the ownership of graphics objects so that *borrowed* instances are not deleted inadvertently. In addition, care must be taken to invalidate Python instances of these objects if the C++ code deletes them directly.

Member Function of Extension Types

So far, the previous sections have shown how to define, create, and delete extension type objects. This section shows how to add member functions and attributes to extension types so they can be used to access the C++ objects they are providing an interface to. This section implements an attribute accessor function for the extension type, and the member functions for the extension type.

The attribute accessor function uses a function table similar to the function table used by extension classes; it is an array of `PyMethodDef` objects. This table contains the set of member functions for the extension type. Listing 22.12 show the code for the function table and accessor function for the example extension type.

Listing 22.12 Attribute access code for graphics object type.

```
/*
** GraphicsObject Method Table
*/
PyMethodDef py_GraphicsObject_methods[] = {
  {"getSimData",   py_getSimData, METH_VARARGS},
  {"setState",     py_setState,   METH_VARARGS},
  {"setFrame",     py_setFrame,   METH_VARARGS},
  {"nextFrame",    py_nextFrame,  METH_VARARGS},
  {"destroy",      py_destroy,    METH_VARARGS},
  {NULL,           NULL,          NULL},
};

/*
**   GraphicsObject getattr function
**
*/
```

```
PyObject *py_getattr(PyObject *self, char *attrname)
{
  py_GraphicsObject *obj = (py_GraphicsObject*)self;
  PyObject *result = Py_FindMethod(py_GraphicsObject_methods,
                                   self, attrname);
  return result;
}
```

Remember that the py_getattr function is included in the type structure as one of the data members. The interpreter invokes it when it requires access to the attribute of an object of this type. This function uses the Python C API function Py_FindMethod to look up the attribute name that it is passed in the function table for the type. If the attribute is not found, it returns a NULL value that becomes a Python exception in the interpreter. If the attribute is found, a method object is returned that can be invoked by the interpreter.

The py_getattr function is an example of a member function of the extension type. When it is invoked, the first argument is the instance of the Python object that it is invoked on, the *self*, and the second argument is the Python argument tuple object. All member functions are invoked in this way.

The member in the py_GraphicsObject_methods table from the preceding code corresponds to the member functions of the GraphicsObject Python class. Listing 22.13 shows the code template for these member functions.

Listing 22.13 GraphicsObject member functions.

```
/*
** GraphicsObject getSimData method
*/
PyObject *py_getSimData( PyObject *self, PyObject *args)
{
  return PyInt_FromLong(1);
}

/*
** GraphicsObject setState method
*/
PyObject *py_setState( PyObject *self, PyObject *args)
{
  return PyInt_FromLong(1);
}

/*
** GraphicsObject setFrame method
*/
```

```
PyObject *py_setFrame( PyObject *self, PyObject *args)
{
  return PyInt_FromLong(1);
}

/*
** GraphicsObject nextFrame method
*/
PyObject *py_nextFrame( PyObject *self, PyObject *args)
{
  return PyInt_FromLong(1);
}

/*
** GraphicsObject destroy method
*/
PyObject *py_destroy( PyObject *self, PyObject *args)
{
  return PyInt_FromLong(1);
}
```

As with all member functions, the first argument to these functions is the Python object they were invoked on. As this example is not a full implementation of the graphics engine, the implementation of these functions is missing, but they demonstrate the interface required for member functions of extension types. In this case, the py_destroy should probably return an un-implemented exception, or just be a nonoperation, as destruction of extension objects is controlled by the deallocation function.

The final piece of code in this section is the code for the module functions that add and remove graphics objects from the graphics engine. These methods were mentioned in the previous section, but their implementation was deferred until here as they deal with extension types. Listing 22.14 shows the code for these two functions.

Listing 22.14   Add and remove functions for graphics objects.

```
/*
** py_addObject()
**
** Param:   object - the graphics object
** Param:   x      - the X position of the object
** Param:   y      - the Y position of the object
** Param:   facing - the object's facing direction
** Returns: 0 or 1
*/
```

```
PyObject *py_addObject( PyObject *, PyObject *args )
{

  PyObject *obj;
  float x, y, facing;

  if (!gEngine)
  {
    PyErr_SetString(PyExc_AssertionError, "Engine not initialized");
    return NULL;
  }

  if( !PyArg_ParseTuple(args, "Offf:py_addObject", &obj, &x, &y,
&facing) )
  {
    return NULL;
  }

  if (!PyObject_TypeCheck(obj, &py_GraphicsObject_Type)  )
  {
    PyErr_SetString(PyExc_AssertionError, "object must be a graphics
object");
    return NULL;
  }

  py_GraphicsObject *gObject = (py_GraphicsObject*)obj;
  gEngine->addObject(gObject->m_gObject, x, y, facing);

  return PyInt_FromLong(1);
}

/*
** py_removeObject()
**
** Param:   object - the graphics object
** Returns:  0 or 1
*/
PyObject *py_removeObject( PyObject *, PyObject *args )
{
  PyObject *obj;

  if (!gEngine)
  {
    PyErr_SetString(PyExc_AssertionError, "Engine not initialized");
    return NULL;
  }
```

```
if( !PyArg_ParseTuple(args, "O:removeObject", &obj) )
{
  return NULL;
}

if (!PyObject_TypeCheck(obj, &py_GraphicsObject_Type)  )
{
   PyErr_SetString(PyExc_AssertionError, "object must be a graphics
object");
   return NULL;
}

py_GraphicsObject *gObject = (py_GraphicsObject*)obj;
gEngine->removeObject(gObject->m_gObject);

return PyInt_FromLong(1);
}
```

These functions require the graphics engine to be initialized, and only work when passed objects of the GraphicsObject type. Unlike previous functions, the PyArg_ParseTuple function is used to extract the argument into a PyObject pointer, not a C variable. This is because the incoming argument is actually a Python object. The Python C API function PyObject_TypeCheck is used to compare the type of the incoming object to the static type object for the graphics object wrapper class. This ensures that only the correct types of Python objects are allowed to be accessed as graphics objects.

This completes the implementation of the interface code for the graphics object extension type. If there was a full implementation of the graphics engine and graphics object in C++, this code could be used to replace the Python-based graphics engine from Chapter 8 with a graphics engine developed in C or C++. This example also shows that extension types involve a lot of code—far more than the equivalent implementation in pure Python.

ON THE CD

The full listing of the code in this chapter can be found on the accompanying CD-ROM in chapter22.

22.3 COMPILING EXTENSION CODE

This section discusses how to compile extension modules from C/C++ code to binary objects that can be used by the Python interpreter. The distutils module in the standard Python distribution is the easiest way to build extension modules. It is a Python-based tool for Python package compilation and distribution. It has many features, including the capability to replace the functionality usually provided by makefiles or project files, so that extension modules can be built very easily.

Building extension modules requires a C/C++ compiler. On Windows, Microsoft's Visual C++ or Visual Studio can be used to build extension modules. In addition, the free compiler GCC can be used to build extension modules on almost every platform that supports Python. In either case, a file called *setup.py* is used to configure the distutils build operation. This file contains compile and link options, and information about the files that make up the extension module. Listing 22.15 show the setup.py file for the graphics engine extension module.

Listing 22.15   `setup.py` file.

```
from distutils.core import setup, Extension

setup(name="cEngine",
      version="0.1",
      description="graphics engine",
      author="Sean Riley",
      ext_modules=[Extension("cEngine",["cEngine.cpp",
                                        "engine.cpp"])]
      )
```

The setup function of the distutils module does all the work of compiling and linking the code into an extension module that is ready to be used by the Python interpreter. It calls the default compiler for the platform on which it is run. By default, for Windows, it uses the Microsoft Visual Studio compiler, and for Linux it uses the GCC compiler. The user can override this by specifying the compiler when the script is executed with the —compiler option.

The first argument to the Extension object is the name of the extension module. The second is a list of the C or C++ files that must be compiled to build the module. There are other options to the extension configuration mechanism that allow include paths, library files, and compiler options to be specified. Table 22.1 lists some of these options.

These options allow the creation process for extension modules to interact with any C libraries or packages that are required for the build process. Note that the Python-related configuration options are added by distutils automatically, so there is no need to specify the include path for Python.h or the Python library directory.

Actually using distutils to build extension modules in a development environment is a two-stage process. The first stage is the compilation of the C code into the binary file, and the second stage is the installation of the binary file into

TABLE 22.1 Additional Extension Module Options

Option Name	Description	Example
include_dirs	Include paths	include_dirs = ["/usr/include"]
define_macros	C macro definitions	define_macros = [("DEBUG","1")]
udef_macros	Undefined C macros	undef_macros = [("DEBUG")]
library_dirs	Library directories	library_dirs = ["/lib", "/usr/lib"]
libraries	Libraries to link	libraries = ["sock32", "mmlib"]
extra_objects	Extra objects to link	extra_objects = ["gobject"]
extra_compile_args	Extra compiler arguments	extra_compile_args = ["02"]
extra_link_args	Extra link arguments	extra_link_args = [""]

Python's installation so that it can be found by import statements. Listing 22.16 shows this process in action using the Visual Studio compiler on Windows.

Listing 22.16 Building an extension module.

```
$ python setup.py build
running build
running build_ext
building 'cEngine' extension
C:\Program Files\Microsoft Visual Studio\VC98\BIN\cl.exe /c /nologo /Ox
/MD /W3 /GX -Ic:\Python22\include /TpcEngine.cpp /Fobuild\temp.win32-
2.2\Relea
se\cEngine.obj
cEngine.cpp
C:\Program Files\Microsoft Visual Studio\VC98\BIN\cl.exe /c /nologo /Ox
/MD /W3 /GX -Ic:\Python22\include /Tpengine.cpp /Fobuild\temp.win32-
2.2\Releas
e\engine.obj
engine.cpp
```

```
C:\Program Files\Microsoft Visual Studio\VC98\BIN\link.exe /DLL /nologo
/INCREMENTAL:NO /LIBPATH:c:\Python22\libs /EXPORT:initcEngine
build\temp.win32
-2.2\Release\cEngine.obj build\temp.win32-2.2\Release\engine.obj
/OUT:build\lib.win32-2.2\cEngine.pyd /IMPLIB:build\temp.win32-
2.2\Release\cEngine.lib

   Creating library build\temp.win32-2.2\Release\cEngine.lib and object
build\temp.win32-2.2\Release\cEngine.exp

$ python setup.py install
running install
running build
running build_ext
skipping 'cEngine' extension (up-to-date)
running install_lib
copying build\lib.win32-2.2\cEngine.pyd -> c:\Python22\Lib\site-
packages

$ python
Type "help", "copyright", "credits" or "license" for more information.
>>> import cEngine
>>> print cEngine
<module 'cEngine' from 'C:\Python22\lib\site-packages\cEngine.pyd'>
>>>
```

As shown in the last step, after these commands have been run, the extension module is available to be imported by Python code. The installation copies it to the *site-packages* directory of the Python installation. The use of the distutils module for package management is covered in more detail in Chapter 24, "Packaging and Delivery."

It is also possible to build extension modules without the help of the distutils module. Both conventional makefiles and Microsoft Visual Studio project files can be constructed to build Python extension modules. In these cases, the Python include paths and library paths must be added manually, and the binary files created by the compiler must be moved manually into a directory accessible with the PYTHONPATH to be available for importing.

22.4 AUTOMATING INTERFACE GENERATION

As the previous sections of this chapter have shown, developing Python extension modules and types involves a large amount of C/C++ code. Since, this code is very similar for each of the modules and functions, and follows specific patterns, it would seem possible that this code could be generated automatically to ease the burden on developers building extension modules. In fact, there are tools that do just this! This section describes some of the tools that can be used to aid in the development of Python extensions.

Table 22.2 lists some of the third-party tools and packages that are available to assist in building extension modules, or even to remove the need to create extension modules. All of these tools have the potential to be used in game development, and each them are covered in this section in more detail.

TABLE 22.2 Extension Module Tools

Name	Description
SWIG	Interface code generator for C/C++ that creates wrappers for Python, Perl, Tcl, and other languages. (*www.swig.org*)
Boost.Python	C++ library for interoperability between C++ and Python (*www.boost.org/libs/python/doc/index.html*)
Psyco	A specializing compiler for speeding up Python code. (*http://psyco.sourceforge.net/*)

These tools make interface development easier by generating code. There are advantages and disadvantages to machine-generated code. The main advantage is that the developer doesn't have to write the code manually, so it can be much faster to develop than code that is written by hand. In addition, it can be possible to make sweeping changes to large amounts of code by changing small, centralized, *interface files*, and regenerating all of the code that uses those files.

However, although developers don't have to write the code, sometimes they have to debug the code. Debugging machine-generated code can be very difficult, as it might not have been generated in a way that is human readable, or fits in with the coding standards and practices of a particular project. Moreover, as machine-generated code tends to be very generalized, it is usually much longer than code written for a specific purpose. This can make debugging even more difficult. Another consequence of the code being generalized is that it is usually slower than code that is written for a specific purpose. Of course, there are exceptions to these cases, but they are important issues to take into account when using machine-generated code in game development where performance is critical, and maintenance and debugging are already hard enough.

Automated interface generation can be a seductive tool. The ability to quickly and easily wrap C++ functionality so that it can be accessed from Python can make developers lose sight of the reasons why the code was written in C++ in the first place. On some game projects, the interface layer between Python and C++ can grow uncontrollably as programmers and designers expose more and more core functionality to Python. Each incremental addition to the interface might seem trivial, but as they compound, the management of the interface code and the overhead of data translation can become crippling for the application as a whole. The tendency of automatically generated interfaces to grow out of control is sometimes called *interface bloat*.

When using automated interface generation, developers should adhere to the principle that interfaces should be minimal and complete. Just because it is easy to expose functionality to Python doesn't mean that you *should* expose that functionality. The consequences of exposing low-level functionality to Python can be that operations that were supposed to be performed in highly optimized C++ are performed in Python code where they might be much less efficient.

SWIG

SWIG, which stands for Simple Wrapper Interface Generator, is a tool for allowing code written in C and C++ to be accessed through other languages such as Python, Perl, and Tcl. It can be found on the Web at *www.swig.org*, and its creator, Mr. Dave Beazley, describes it as an *interface compiler*. It is a quite mature product that has been in existence since 1995 in various forms, and has a large set of users around the world. SWIG is especially good at rapid development of interfaces. Its simple syntax and ability to parse C and C++ code make it very easy to create interface code quickly. SWIG has been used successfully on commercial game projects that use Python.

SWIG uses interface files (*.i files) to define the interface exposed by C/C++ code. These interface files are very similar to C/C++ header files, so it takes very little time to learn how to write them. The SWIG executable parses these interface files, and generates code in C that allows the interface to be accessed by the specified language. In the case of Python, it generates Python C API code that is compiled into extension modules. For extension types, it generates shadow classes in Python code that use the generated extension module.

Listing 22.17 is a very simple SWIG interface file for the graphics object class that was defined earlier in this chapter. Note that SWIG provides much more functionality than this interface file uses.

Listing 22.17   SWIG interface file.

```
/* engine.i */

%module cEngine

%{
#include "engine.h"
%}

class GraphicsObject
{
 public:
  GraphicsObject(const char *source, bool mobile, const char *image =
NULL);
   ~GraphicsObject();

   void getSimData(float &centerX, float &centerY, float &width, float
&height);
   void setState(float x, float y, float facing);
   void setFrame(int frame);
   void nextFrame();
   void destroy();

};
```

This looks very much like the C++ header file for the class, but it only includes the public methods, and includes some extra, SWIG-specific information at the top of the file. The line:

```
%module cEngine
```

tells SWIG the name of the extension module to generate for this C++ code. The command line to process this interface file with SWIG is shown here:

```
swig.exe -c++ -python engine.i
```

This generates two files, a cEngine.py file and an engine_wrap.cxx file. SWIG uses a strategy of generating Python C API code to wrap the library, and then wrapping that code with a Python module that exposes the interface that application code should use to access it. The name of the extension module it creates is prefixed with an underscore to designate that it is an internal module and so it doesn't conflict with the name of the generated Python module. This code can be built with distutils, but remember to prefix the module name with an underscore in the setup.py file.

As SWIG is a general-purpose tool, and supports multiple languages, it generates large amounts of code to achieve its results. The engine_wrap.cxx file generated for the GraphicsObject class contains over 800 lines of C code. In addition, there are about 50 lines of Python code for the wrapper classes. SWIG also adds an extra preprocessing step to the build process, but integrating it with build tools usually hides this step.

To expose classes and structures, SWIG does not use extension types as they were described in Section 22.3. It uses extension module functions for all of the methods of the wrapped classes, and generates Python classes that combine these methods into coherent classes. For object instancing, the Python wrapper classes keep an opaque this pointer that refers to the wrapped object instance. This is similar to the instance type structure described in Section 22.3, but it is done at the Python level rather than at the Python C API level. These wrapper classes are called *shadow classes*, and they introduce an additional level of indirection that can have an effect on the performance of interface code.

Boost.Python

Boost.Python is a C++ library for interoperation between Python and C++ code. As it is targeted at C++ rather than C, it is designed to work with templates, namespaces, class hierarchies, and other C++ language features. It can be found online at *www.boost.org/libs/python/doc/* where it is part of the C++ Boost library, so it is well supported and has a strong user base. Conceptually, the functionality of Boost.Python is similar to SWIG. It allows code written in C++ to be accessed from Python.

Unlike SWIG, which generates Python C API code in a preprocessing phase, Boost.Python is a library written with the Python C API that uses C++ templates and macros to generate code at precompile time. Instead of separate interface files, the definition of the exposed Python interfaces is within the C++ header files, so it does not require a separate parser to read interface definitions. At compilation time, the interface definitions in the header files are converted into code that implements the interface. Listing 22.18 shows the Boost.Python interface definition code for the GraphicsObject class.

Listing 22.18   Boost.Python interface definition.

```
#include <boost/python.hpp>

using namespace boost::python;

BOOST_PYTHON_MODULE(cEngine)
{
```

```
class_<GraphicsObject>("GraphicsObject", init<char *, bool, char
*>())
    .def("getSimData", &GraphicsObject::getSimData)
    .def("setState", &GraphicsObject::setState)
    .def("setFrame", &GraphicsObject::setFrame)
    .def("nextFrame", &GraphicsObject::nextFrame)
    .def("destroy", &GraphicsObject::destroy)
    ;
}
```

This listing shows the code that exposes the public interface of the GraphicsObject class to Python. This is actual C++ code that causes an extension type to be created and populated with the specified methods. The .def entries specify member functions to be exposed, and the init template specifies the constructor of the class.

Boost.Python is part of the larger Boost C++ library. This library includes many sub-libraries that enhance the C++ language, and a build system called *bjam* for compiling C++ projects. The Boost.Python library recommends building extension modules with the bjam tool. Building Boot.Python extension modules with other build tools such as distutils or Visual Studio requires some work, but it can be done.

As a C++ template-based solution, Boost.Python can considerably lengthen compile times for C++ code that exposes interfaces to Python. However, it does not introduce a separate preprocessing step, and the generated code is effectively invisible to the application programmers. Moreover, as most of the work is performed at compile time, Boost.Python's runtime performance is not impacted by the type of indirection that SWIG's shadow classes introduce. Its direct use of Python C API's extension types make its runtime performance excellent.

Psyco

Psyco is a tool that is conceptually very different from SWIG and Boost.Python. Instead of being a way to wrap existing C/C++ code, it is a *specializing compiler* for Python that makes existing Python run faster. It is a kind of *Just In Time* (JIT) compiler that improves the performance of Python code without requiring any changes to it. Psyco is not intended to wrap libraries written in C/C++; it is intended to alleviate the need to write modules in C/C++ by improving the performance of all Python programs. Obviously, this is not useful for the purposes of allowing access to existing libraries that are written in C/C++ or access to OS services, but it can be a viable alternative to rewriting Python modules in C/C++ for performance reasons.

Psyco can be found online at *http://psyco.sourceforge.net/* and is distributed under the M.I.T license. Currently, it works on x86 processors on both Windows and Linux.

In simple terms, Psyco works by inspecting and profiling Python byte code as it is executed, and recognizing functions and methods that are targets for optimization. For these methods, it generates machine code that implements the same functionality as the Python method. When these methods are invoked again with a set of arguments of the same type, the machine code version of the method is invoked instead of the Python version. This basic scheme is enhanced by the capability to produce multiple machine code implementations of methods that correspond to different sets of arguments.

Typically, this machine code is from 2x to 100x faster than the Python code it replaces. This can lead to dramatic increases in the performance of Python programs.

The simplest way to use Psyco is to add the following two lines of code to a Python program.

```
import psyco
psyco.full()
```

This causes Psyco to generate machine code for as much of the program as possible. This is a brute-force approach that uses large amounts of memory, but is useful as a simple test to determine what kind of performance difference to expect from Psyco with a particular program. A more reasonable approach is to use the *profile* function of Pysco, shown here:

```
import psyco
psyco.log()
psyco.profile(0.2)
```

This causes Psyco to only optimize functions that meet a specific criteria of time taken. The constant passed to the profile function is called the *watermark* and the exact meaning of it is specified in the Pysco documentation. The log function causes Pysco to write out a log file of the functions that it optimizes. In addition, it is possible to have Pysco only process particular functions that are known to perform CPU-intensive operations, as shown here:

```
import psyco
psyco.bind(transform)
psyco.bind(update)
```

Using Psyco on the example applications in this book yielded a speedup of approximately 50 to 100 percent. With some tuning and restructuring of code, it would be possible to increase this figure even more. That is a significant improvement for adding a few lines of code to the programs!

In general, games must be careful with Psyco as it increases the memory requirements of Python programs. The compiled versions of functions are kept in memory, so increase the memory footprint of the application. The example programs in this book exhibited a memory size increase of about 20 percent when using Pysco in profile mode.

Psyco does not run on every platform that runs Python. It generates machine code for x86 processors, so it will not run on other processor architectures.

SUMMARY

This chapter described techniques for extending Python to integrate with C and C++ code. It included descriptions of how to write extension modules and extension types, and how to compile them into Python extensions. It also discussed automated interface generation, including the tools SWIG, Boost.Python, and Psyco.

As examples, this chapter used the graphics engine module that was developed in Chapter 8. The interface code for an extension module to replace the engine module was developed with the Python C API, and an extension type to allow access to the `GraphicsObject` class was developed with the Python C API. The sections that discussed SWIG and Boost.Python showed how to specify interfaces to the graphics engine so that code could be automated to interface to it.

The techniques described in this chapter can be used to expose existing libraries to Python, and to develop extension modules in high-performance C/C++ code that replace existing Python modules. In game development, there are many libraries that could require Python access. Fortunately, there are already Python wrappers for many game libraries, but for in-house or new libraries, developers must sometimes develop these wrappers themselves.

23

Embedding Python

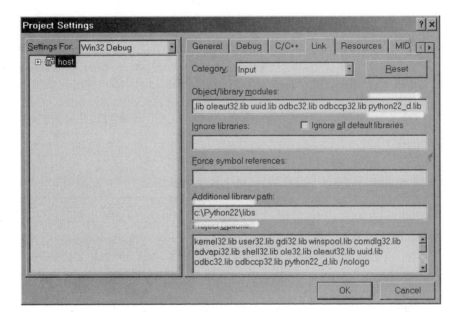

E mbedding Python is different from the practice of extending Python that was
discussed in the previous chapter. It involves integrating the Python interpreter into another program so that a portion of that program can be written
in Python, or to expose a scripting interface for other developers to use to extend
the application. In the game industry, Python is sometimes used in this way as a
scripting language that allows designers and other nonprogrammers to create game
content with less involvement from programmers. Embedding uses a superset of
the functionality of extending Python.

The application in which the interpreter is embedded is called the *host application.* For Python code to communicate with the host application, it can expose functionality in a way similar to extension modules. In this chapter, an example host application is developed that uses embedded Python. It is a simple Windows application that allows Python code to be entered into an edit box. The Python code can be executed by pressing a button, or choosing a menu item, and the resulting output is displayed in another window. The example application also shows how to execute specific Python code in response to user interface events such as menu items.

This chapter discusses how to embed the Python interpreter in another application. It uses an example application to demonstrate the topics discussed. Section 23.1 discusses setting up a project for embedding Python, Section 23.2 discusses the high-level layer of the Python C API for embedding the interpreter, and Section 23.3 deals with communication between the host application and the interpreter.

23.1 EMBEDDING THE INTERPRETER

The code to create and control the Python interpreter is found in a section of the Python C API called the *Very High Level Layer.* This layer contains functions to interact with the interpreter, to execute text as Python code, to execute the contents of files as Python code, and to compile text into Python byte-code. This layer contains a function that must be called to initialize the interpreter before any other calls can be made. The `Py_Initialize()` function must be the first Python C API function called when Python is being embedded in a host application. Corresponding to this function is the `Py_Finalize()` function that shuts the interpreter down.

Once the interpreter is active, other functions can be called to execute Python code. Table 23.1 lists some of these functions.

Whenever Python code is executed, it has a context that consists of a local dictionary and a global dictionary. Some of the functions in Table 23.1 allow this context information to be specified when executing Python code. This technique is useful for interactive applications such as command-line processors. In these cases, each command should modify the local context, and that change should be reflected for subsequent commands. This is achieved by creating or acquiring Python dictionary objects to act as context objects. These objects are then passed as arguments each time Python code is invoked.

Listing 23.1 shows an extremely simple example of starting the Python interpreter, executing some Python code, and stopping the interpreter.

TABLE 23.1   Python Code Execution Functions

Function	Description
int PyRun_SimpleString(char *command)	Execute the Python code in a simple string.
int PyRun_SimpleFile(FILE *fp, char *filename)	Execute the entire contents of the file as Python code.
int PyRun_InteractiveOne(FILE *fp, char *filename)	Execute one Python statement from the specified file.
PyObject* PyRun_String(char *str, int start, PyObject *globals, PyObject *locals)	Execute the string as Python code in the context provided by the dictionaries *globals* and *locals*.
PyObject* PyRun_File(FILE *fp, char *filename, int start, PyObject *globals, PyObject *locals)	Execute the contents of the file as Python code in the context provided by the dictionaries *globals* and *locals*.

Listing 23.1   Simple embedded Python.

```
#include "Python.h"

int main(int argc, char *argv[])
{
  Py_Initialize();
  PyRun_SimpleString("print 'Hello From Python'");
  Py_Finalize();
  return 0;
}
```

For real applications, embedding Python is more complicated. The application must maintain a context for Python code to run in, handle Python exceptions, be aware of output generated by Python code, and be able to communicate between the host application and the Python code. These aspects of embedding Python make it more complex than just extending Python.

The example application in this chapter has three components. First, it includes Windows-specific infrastructure code and user interface code. This code is contained in the file host.cpp. Second, it includes Python-specific code for the embedded interpreter, and communication between the host application and the interpreter. This code is contained in the file extension.cpp. Finally, it has a core application class that would contain the application's critical functionality if this were a real application. If this application was a game, this is where the game rules and logic would reside. These components are shown in Figure 23.1.

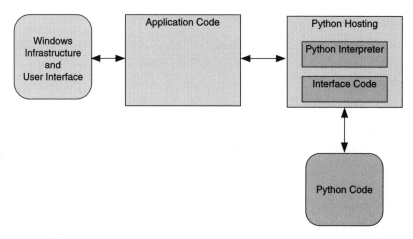

FIGURE 23.1   Application components.

Python Context

Host applications usually require some persistent state between invocations of the Python interpreter. Any state that is created by Python code, such as imported modules and local variables, must be maintained by the application so that it is available to subsequent Python code that is executed. Sometimes, host applications even track multiple contexts for different aspects of the application.

The context information for Python consists of a global dictionary and a local dictionary. These correspond to the dictionaries that can be accessed with the globals() and locals() functions in Python. This is shown here:

```
def test():
  print '-- before --'
  print 'globals:', globals()
  print 'locals:', locals()
```

```
    foo = 99
    print '-- after --'
    print 'globals:', globals()
    print 'locals:', locals()

>test()
-- before --
globals: {'__builtins__': <module '__builtin__' (built-in)>,
'__name__':
'__main__', 'test': <function test at 0x009303D0>, '__doc__': None,
'MyNewValue': 88}
locals: {}

-- after --
globals: {'__builtins__': <module '__builtin__' (built-in)>,
'__name__':
'__main__', 'test': <function test at 0x009303D0>, '__doc__': None,
'MyNewValue': 88}
locals: {'foo': 99}
```

In this example, the locals dictionary is populated with the variable foo that exists in the local scope. The global scope is unmodified by this local variable. For an interactive interpreter such as the Python command-line program, these context dictionaries are created automatically. For an embedded interpreter, they must be created by the host application. Listing 23.2 shows the initialization function of the example application for this chapter, and how it creates these dictionaries.

Listing 23.2   LoadPython function from extension.cpp.

```
PyObject *gLocals = NULL;
PyObject *gGlobals = NULL;

/*
** LoadPython
** Starts the Python interpreter and imports modules.
*/
void LoadPython()
{
    Py_Initialize();

    // aquire context dictionaries
    PyObject *pymodMain = PyImport_ImportModule("__main__");
    gGlobals = PyModule_GetDict(pymodMain);
    gLocals = PyDict_New();

    // initialize host extension module
```

```
PyObject *module = Py_InitModule("host", HostMethods);

// other python initialization
RunPython("import host");
RunPython("import sys");
RunPython("sys.stdout = host");
RunPython("sys.stderr = host");
}
```

This function uses the Python C API to import the built-in __main__ module, and uses its dictionary as the global context dictionary. This ensures that the global context contains the appropriate built-in entries for Python to function correctly. For the local dictionary, it creates a new, empty Python dictionary object.

Executing Python Code

This function also initializes the extension module that defines the host application's external Python interface. This is covered in more detail later in this chapter. Finally, it uses the function RunPython to execute some python code to setup the application. Listing 23.3 shows this function.

Listing 23.3 RunPython function from extension.cpp.

```
/*
** RunPython
** Runs Python code in the application's context and handles
exceptions.
*/
void RunPython(char *cmd)
{
    PyObject *result = PyRun_String(cmd, Py_file_input, gGlobals,
gLocals);
    if (!result)
    {
        PyObject *exceptionType = PyErr_Occurred();
        if (exceptionType)
        {
            PyObject *type, *value, *traceback;
            PyErr_Fetch(&type, &value, &traceback);
            char *out = PyString_AsString(value);
            gApp->write("Python Exception:");
            gApp->write(out);

        }
    }
}
```

This function executes Python code in the application's context and handles any exceptions that occur in the Python code. It uses the `PyRun_String` Python C API function instead of the `PyRun_SimpleString` function that was used previously, so that it can pass the context objects to the interpreter. When an exception occurs, this function extracts the exception object and finds the text message associated with it. It passes this error text to the host application to be displayed on the screen.

In the previous piece of code, the `RunPython` function was used to execute some odd-looking lines of Python that are shown here:

```
RunPython("import host");
RunPython("import sys");
RunPython("sys.stdout = host");
RunPython("sys.stderr = host");
```

This code redirects Python's output and error messages to the host application. In this context, the `host` is the extension module that represents the host application's external interface. The variables `sys.stdout` and `sys.stderr` are Python *file* objects that the interpreter uses when writing output and error messages. As the only method of file objects used in this case is the method called `write` that is invoked to write out data, it is possible for the host extension module to replace the default file objects and have its `write` method called when the interpreter produces output.

23.2 COMMUNICATING WITH THE HOST APPLICATION

For the embedded interpreter to be useful, it must be able to communicate with the host application. The ability to execute Python code and return a value is the simplest possible case of embedding. For real applications, though, this is usually insufficient. Python code running in the embedded interpreter must be able to call into the host application to trigger actions, to set states, and possibly even to control the flow of the application itself.

Communication between the interpreter and the host application occurs through extension modules. However, in this case, the extension modules are in the opposite environment from the extension modules discussed in the previous chapter. Instead of the extension modules being compiled into an external binary object, they are compiled into the host application where they have access to its internal symbols and functionality.

In the example application, there are four methods in the interface of the extension module for the host application. The function table for these methods is shown here:

```
static PyMethodDef HostMethods[] =
{
    {"clear",   py_clear,   METH_VARARGS, "clear fill"},
    {"stripeV", py_stripeV, METH_VARARGS, "vertical stripes"},
    {"stripeH", py_stripeH, METH_VARARGS, "horizontal stripes"},
    {"write",   py_write,   METH_VARARGS, "write"},
    {NULL,      NULL,       NULL,         NULL}
};
```

The write function was discussed previously; it is called to pass text output back to the host application. The other functions in this interface change the background drawing style of the host application's window. Although fairly trivial, they show how application functionality can be invoked from Python. Listing 23.4 show the implementation of these methods.

Listing 23.4   Extension module functions.

```
extern Application *gApp;

PyObject *py_clear(PyObject *self, PyObject *args)
{
    if (!gApp)
        return NULL;
    gApp->fillClear();
    return PyInt_FromLong(1);
}

PyObject *py_stripeV(PyObject *self, PyObject *args)
{
    if (!gApp)
        return NULL;
    gApp->fillVerticalStripes();
    return PyInt_FromLong(1);
}

PyObject *py_stripeH(PyObject *self, PyObject *args)
{
    if (!gApp)
        return NULL;
    gApp->fillHorizontalStripes();
    return PyInt_FromLong(1);
}
```

```
PyObject *py_write(PyObject *self, PyObject *args)
{
    char *text;
    if (!gApp)
        return NULL;

    if( !PyArg_ParseTuple(args, "s:py_write", &text) )
    {
        return NULL;
    }
    gApp->write(text);
    return PyInt_FromLong(1);
}
```

The global variable gApp is a pointer to the single application object of the host application. Apart from use of this application object, this extension module is very similar to the extension modules described in the previous chapter. However, this module does not have an initialization function that is invoked when it is imported for the first time. It is initialized in the LoadPython() function described previously, as shown by the following code:

```
PyObject *module = Py_InitModule("host", HostMethods);
```

For a game, this type of extension module is the interface that Python scripts use to communicate back to the host game application.

23.3 EXAMPLE APPLICATION

ON THE CD

This section describes the remaining portions of the example host application. This is a simple Win32 application written in C/C++ whose code template was generated by Microsoft Visual Studio®. While this application is not a game, it does show how to interact with the embedded Python interpreter and how to associate Python code with user interface elements. It serves as a relatively simple example of how to use the embedded Python interpreter in ways that are similar to how a game would use it. The full source code to this example application can be found on the accompanying CD-ROM. The application is shown in action in Figure 23.2.

The menus allow the background of the window to be switched between clear, vertical stripes, and horizontal stripes. The two menus *Fill* and *Python* allow the background to be switched. The Fill menu calls the application object directly, while the Python menu executes Python code that communicates with the applica-

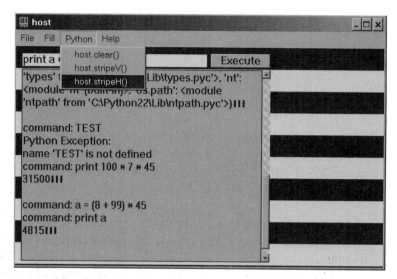

FIGURE 23.2   Example host application.

tion object via the host extension module. Listing 23.5 shows the code in the application's message handler function that controls these menus.

Listing 23.5   Menu handler code.

```
// Regular Menu Handlers
   case ID_FILL_CLEAR:
       gApp->fillClear();
       return 1;
   case ID_FILL_STRIPE_VERTICAL:
       gApp->fillVerticalStripes();
       return 1;

   case ID_FILL_STRIPE_HORIZONTAL:
       gApp->fillHorizontalStripes();
       return 1;

   // Pythyon Menu Handlers
   case ID_PYTHON_CLEAR:
       RunPython("host.clear()");
       return 1;
```

```
case ID_PYTHON_VERTICAL:
    RunPython("host.stripeV()");
    return 1;

case ID_PYTHON_HORIZONTAL:
    RunPython("host.stripeH()");
    return 1;
```

The context of the application contains a reference to the host module as it was imported by the LoadPython function after the interpreter initialized. This allows the snippets of Python code that are associated with the menus to call methods on that module directly.

The other controls within the application's window are an input box, an Execute button and a read-only output box. The user can enter Python code into the input box, and when the button is pressed, the interpreter executes the code, and the command and its results are printed in the output window. This application is a simple Python command-line processor. As the context of the interpreter is persisted between commands, the user can create variables and import modules that will remain available to subsequent Python commands. The code in Listing 23.6 is executed when the user clicks on the execute button.

Listing 23.6   Execute button code.

```
case BN_CLICKED:
    {
        char text[256];
        char output[300];
        GetWindowText(gInputWindow, text, 256);
        sprintf(output, "command: %s", text);
        AddOutputLine(output, true);
        RunPython(text);
        SetWindowText(gInputWindow, "");
    }
```

This code reads the text from the input window, and writes it to the output window with a prefix to show that is it a command. It then calls the RunPython function to execute the code and clears the text from the input window. Python exceptions and output are handled within the RunPython function and are redirected to the output window for the user to see.

23.3 PROJECT SETUP

This section discusses how to configure a project to embed Python. Specifically, it uses a Microsoft Windows application as the host, as this is a common platform for game development with Python, and uses the Microsoft Visual C++ 6.0 development environment.

To embed Python, developers should use the source code distribution of Python and build their own Python binaries. This process creates the Visual Studio files that contain debugging information so that the Python interpreter can be run under a debugger. The source code distribution of Python can be found on the Python Web site at *www.python.org*. The project files for building Python with Visual Studio are located in the PCBuild directory of the source distribution.

The Visual Studio project for the host application should be created as a regular Win32 application. The Python-specific project issues do not have any effect on the creation of the project. In fact, it should be possible to embed Python into any type of project.

On Windows, the files that contain the Python interpreter are python[*version*].dll and python[*version*]_d.dll, where *version* is the major and minor versions of Python currently in use. The _d in the second file designates it as a debug version. The same convention is used by Windows for all Python binaries. For example, an extension module could be called myLib.pyd or myLib_d.pyd for the debug version, and the debug version of the Python executable is called python_d.exe. The DLL files are *dynamic link libraries* that are loaded when the program is started. These files should be in the application's execution path when it is run. In addition, there are library files called python[*version*].lib and python[*version*]_d.lib that are used by the linker when building programs that use Python. All of these files are included in the standard Python distribution for Windows, and in addition, they are all created when Python is built from source code.

To use embedded Python, the host application must link against the Python library files. This is configured in the Link tab of the Project Settings dialog. For the debug build, the library file python[*version*]_d.lib must be added to the set of libraries/modules, and for the release build, the library file python[*version*].lib must be added to the same place. In addition, the directory that contains the library files must be added to the *additional library paths*. Figure 23.3 shows the Visual Studio settings dialog where these options must be entered.

ON THE CD

A working Visual Studio project file for this application can be found on the accompanying CD-ROM.

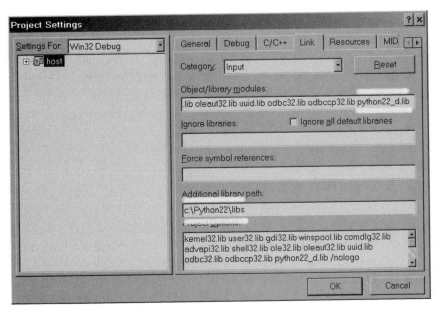

FIGURE 23.3 Linking options for embedding Python.

SUMMARY

This chapter described the process of embedding the Python interpreter in a host application and some of the issues involved with embedding Python. It covered the *Very High Level Layer* of the Python C API that allows Python code to be executed and controls the interpreter's creation and shutdown. It showed how to capture output and exceptions that are generated by Python code, how to maintain an application context for code to execute in, and how to provide an interface for Python code to call back into the host application.

The example in this chapter was a Windows application that embeds the Python interpreter. It acts as a simple Python command processor and prints the output of Python code to a window. In addition, it has menu items that show how to perform functions with Python code. The example application also shows a function that allows safe execution of Python code by checking the interpreter's exception states after code is executed.

The techniques discussed in this chapter can be used to embed the Python interpreter into game applications written in C/C++. This can allow portions of the game to be written in Python to allow greater flexibility, safety, and to allow non-programmers to participate in the game's development in a hands-on way.

About the CD-ROM

INSTALLING AND RUNNING THE SOFTWARE

Running the example programs from the book requires that a number of software packages be installed. First, the Python programming must be installed on the computer. Second, as games have complex infrastructure requirements, the libraries for PyGame, PyUI and PyOpenGL must also be installed. Finally, to run the multi-player example code, the Twisted package must also be installed.

The instructions below explain how to install each of the required components in order. These instructions are for installing on Microsoft Windows machines. It is a good idea to shut down all programs on the machine before continuing with the installation. Some of the installation programs will prompt you for installation locations and other options. For the easiest install, the default locations and installation options should be accepted.

Step 1. Install Python

All of the example programs on the CD require Python to run. The CD includes the installer for the Python standard distribution for Microsoft Windows. To install Python, open the file *Python-2.2.3.exe* or execute it from a command line. Further information about installing Python can be found at *http://www.python.org*. This step may take a few minutes as the full Python distribution is installed.

```
$ Python-2.2.3.exe
```

Step 2. Install PyGame

All of the example programs on the CD-ROM also require PyGame to run. The CD includes the installer for the Microsoft Windows distribution of PyGame. To install PyGame, open *pygame-1.5.6.win32.py2.2.exe* or execute it from a command line. Further information about installing PyGame can be found at *http://www.pygame.org*.

```
$ pygame-1.5.6.win32.py2.2.exe
```

Step 3. Install PyOpenGL

Many of the example programs use the OpenGL graphics library. The PyOpenGL library provides access to OpenGL from Python. To install it, open the file *PyOpenGL-2.0.0.44.win32-py2.2.exe* or execute it from the command line. Further information about installing PyOpenGL can be found at *http://pyopengl. sourceforge.net*.

```
$ PyOpenGL-2.0.0.44.win32-py2.2.exe
```

Step 4. Install PyUI

Many of the example programs also use the PyUI library. The CD-ROM contains the PyUI installer for Microsoft Windows. To install PyUI, open the file *PyUI-1.0.win32-py2.2.exe* or execute it from a command line. Further information about installing PyUI can be found at http *http://pyui.sourceforge.net*.

```
$ PyUI-1.0.win32-py2.2.exe
```

Step 5. Install Twisted

The multiplayer examples in Section V of the book require the Twisted library to run. The CD includes the 1.06 version of the Twisted distribution. To install it, open the file *Twisted-1.0.6.win32.py2.2.exe* or execute it from a command line. Further information about installing Twisted can be found at *http://www.twistedmatrix.com*.

```
$ Twisted-1.0.6.win32.py2.2.exe
```

Step 6. Install Hoop Library

The Hoop library is code that is developed and explained within the book. This code is library is used by the example programs after Chapter 8 in the book, so it must be installed for those example programs to run. To install it, open the file *Hoop-1.0.win32-py2.2.exe* or execute it from a command line. In addition to the installer, the full source code of the Hoop library is also on the CD-ROM.

```
$ Hoop-1.0.win32-py2.2.exe
```

Running Python

Once the software is installed, an interactive Python interpreter can be started by opening the *python.exe* executable. By default, this file resides in the directory *c:/Python22*, which is the default Python installation location. When this file is opened, a window will appear that allows Python code to be entered and executed in an interactive environment. The prompt in the window should look something like the text below.

```
Python 2.2.3 (#37, Oct 14 2002, 17:02:34) [MSC 32 bit (Intel)] on win32
Type "help", "copyright", "credits" or "license" for more information.
>>>
```

This is the Python interactive interpreter. It allows Python commands to be executed, as in the short example shown below.

```
>>> x = 55
>>> y = 100
>>> print x + y
155
>>> l = [x,y]
>>> l.append(101)
>>> print l
[55, 100, 101]
```

The interpreter can be very useful for experimenting with small pieces of Python code, or discovering the exact syntax to perform operations in Python. It can be exited by pressing *Control-Z* and then the return key, or by pressing *Control-Break*.

Running the Example Code

There are two ways to run the example code that comes with this book. The first, and easiest way is to open the Python files with the Windows file explorer by double clicking on them. As the ".py" extension was registered with the operating system when Python was installed, this invoked the Python interpreter and runs the program in the selected file.

The second method is to execute the files from a command line. This method can be preferable if you want to keep the text that was printed by the Python program, or if you wish to maintain settings or an environment across multiple executions of a program. The example below shows the example program *pongMain.py* being executed from its directory on the CD-ROM.

```
D:\chapter12>cd pong
D:\chapter12\pong>pongMain.py
Creating font: arial
Creating font: impact
```

```
FPS: 322 mobiles: 2 statics: 0
FPS: 356 mobiles: 2 statics: 0
FPS: 351 mobiles: 2 statics: 0
D:\chapter12\pong>
```

Most of the example programs can be exited by pressing the *Escape* key. Many of them print status, or informational messages to the windows that they were executed from.

SYSTEM REQUIREMENTS

The following system requirements should be met to run the example code on the CD-ROM:

■ Microsoft Windows 98/2000/ME/XP/NT
■ Pentium II 400mhz or equivalent
■ 64MB physical RAM
■ Video card with 4MB VRAM
■ 60MB disk space

In addition, an OpenGL hardware accelerated graphics card will increase the performance of the graphical example programs, and a 28.8K modem or TCP/IP network connection is required for the multiplayer example programs.

The Python code on the CD-ROM was written for version 2.2.3 of Python. It *may* work with other versions of Python, but it is recommended that the correct version be used.

Index

A

aabb data member, SimObject
    class, 88
A* algorithm
    implementing in Python,
      258–263
    overview, 256–258
abstract object layer, Python C
    API, 392–395
accept method code, 314–315
actor class code
    overview, 240–241, 243
    state manager and, 251–253
    and transition validation,
      244–245
addLetter method defined, 290
addObject method defined, 417
addToWorld method, simulation
    worlds, 48
Age of Empires, 342
algorithms
    A*, 256–263
    Diamond Square, 276–278
AmbientSound class, PyGame
    code, 140
amplitude defined, 134
APIs, 12–13. *See also* Python, C
    API
application class code, 30
apply function, 63
architecture diagram, games, 8–9
architectures, game. *See* games,
    architectures
array module, Python defined,
    332
artificial intelligence, 239

art pipeline in graphics, 100–101
AttractMode code, 179–180
audio systems
    initializing code, 135
    overview, 13–14, 133
    Python suitability for, 14
avatars, 164, 242, 253
avgHeight variable defined, 281

B

bandwidth defined, 305–306
big endian format, 307–308
bind method defined, 314
bitmap fonts, 235–236
blocking I/O, 305
Boost.Python, 436, 439–440
bounding boxes, 78–82
bounding boxes method for
    collision checking, 75
bounding spheres method for
    collision checking, 75–76,
    82–84
BreakBlockCategory classes
    defined, 175–176
breakGame.py code, 178–179
BreakLevel class code, 201–202
BreakModeCategory classes
    defined, 175
breakobjects.py code, 176–177
Breakout game, 174–184,
    189–190
buffer protocol, Python C API,
    395
bullet time, 9
byte ordering, 307–308
byte switching functions, 308

C

calculateVelocity method, 45–46
CanvasFrame class, PyUI code,
    224–227
CanvasPanel class, PyUI code,
    222–224
capabilities defined, 28
C API. *See* Python, C API
Cartesian coordinate system,
    41–42
categoryClass argument,
    Datamanager function, 63
C/C++
    attributes, adding at runtime,
      227
    extension code, compiling,
      432–435
    gEngine code, 414
    graphics and, 100
    initialize and shutdown
      function code, 415–417
    interface functions code,
      417–422
    memory management of,
      395–396
    objects handling in, 169
    and Python, 2, 407–442
    type structures, 423–424
cell method defined, 190
channel object, PyGame code,
    135
channels defined, 134, 135
CharacterStateManager class
    code, 250–251
checkCollideAABB method
    defined, 89–90

checkCollide method defined, 88–89

checkPoint method, AABB class, 81–82

checkPoint module method defined, 94

checkSkip method defined, 91–92

checkWorld method, AABB class, 81

circular references defined, 396

Civilization and terrain generation, 274

class, 64

class code, random, 272–273

class hierarchy, parallel, 61

cleanup, 32–34, 209–211

clearEventsFor method defined, 192

clear method defined, 113

ClientProtocol class, Twisted code, 359–362

clients
construction of, 356–366
overview, 341–342
socket code, 313
Tic-Tac-Toe multiplayer game, 378–388
Twisted, 357–363

client/server game architectures, 344–345

cmp method defined, 190

code, machine generated, 436–437

code organization
multiplayer games, 347–348
Tic-Tac-Toe multiplayer game, 368–369

collision detection. *See also* pathfinding
coordinate spaces, 77–78
methods for checking, 74–77, 82–84
objects, classifying, 70–72
overview, 69–70
partitioning world for, 72–74
system, visualizing, 129–131
unit testing, 157–159

collision grids
implementing, 87–94
partitioning, 72, 73
stamping, 255

CollisionSim Class defined, 130

color depth defined, 29

concrete object layer, Python C API, 402–405

concurrent asynchronous servers, 326–328

concurrent forking servers, 321–324

concurrent threaded servers, 324–326

connect method defined, 313–314

context switching defined, 324

controlled simulations, 39–40

coordinate spaces and collision detection, 77–78

coordinate systems, 214–216

cPickle module, 409

createInstance method, Datamanager function, 65

create Menus method, PyUI defined, 227

createTexture method code, 286

crouch state module code, 246

D

data
attribute defined, 201
conversion, Python C API, 399–402
drivers, 10–11
game levels, 198–202
Python, representation, 22–23
repository, implementing, 58–66
sending/receiving, 315–316, 331–333
sources of, 57
string slicing, 316

databases, relational, 58

data-driven systems
benefits of, 56
data sources, 57–58

and game simulations, 14
overview, 55–56
simulations, 55–67

Datamanager class
Breakout code, 174–175
code, 61–63, 66
initCategory method, 63, 64
label argument, 63
objects, creating, 64
unit testing, 153–155

dataReceived method, Twisted defined, 336–337

desktop, PyUI defined, 218–219

destroyBall method defined, 167

2D graphics
drawing utilities, 104
overview, 11–12
RollerCoaster Tycoon, 101
simulations
properties of, 41
updating, code for, 50–51

3D graphics engines
overview, 12
simulations, properties of, 41

Diablo, 346

dialogs, PyUI defined, 219

diamonds, modification of, 282–283

Diamond Square algorithm, 276–278

Direct3D API, 12, 28

DirectInput library and keyboard polling, 147

DirectSound API, 14

distutils module, 432–435

documentation strings, 32

Domain Name Server (DNS) database, 301

domains defined, 298

doSelect method, Twisted defined, 329

dot notation in IP addresses, 299–300

drawAABB method defined, 130

drawImage method defined, 114

draw method defined, 167

drawStuff method code, 194

drawText method defined, 113–114
dynamic fonts, 236–237

E

Earth & Beyond, 3
embedding in Python. *See* Python, embedding
engine class, code, 107–108
engine module interface, code, 108–109
entity class
    with event posting code, 192–193
    with observation, PyUI code, 231–232
    overview, 185
entityManager.py code, 186
entity.py code, 186–187
eventManager.py code, 191–192
event.py code, 189–190
events
    handling in PyUI, 144–145, 146
    PyUI defined, 221
Everquest, 346
exception handling, Python C API, 398–399
exception states, testing, 398–399
exception type objects, static, 398
execfile function, Python defined, 119
execute button code, 453
ExpoDistribution class defined, 274
exponential distributions, random numbers, 271
extension code, compiling, 432–435
extension modules
    defined, 407
    functions code, 450–451
    initialization function, 411–413
    options, 434
    writing, 408–422, 434–435
extension types
    defined, 407
    member function, 428–432

writing, 422–432
External Data Representation (XDR) Protocol, 308

F

fDisplacement variable defined, 281
findCategory method, Datamanager function, 64–65
findHitdirection method defined, 93–94
finishPath method code, 263
finite state machines (FSMs). *See* state machines
Fly Weight design pattern, example of, 60
fonts
    bitmap, 235–236
    dynamic, 236–237
    PyUI defined, 221
ForkingTCPServer class code, 323
frames, PyUI defined, 219
frames per second (FPS), 32
framework message types, Twisted, 356
Freedom Force, 3
frequency defined, 134
fundamental objects, 403–404

G

gAllEntities variable defined, 187
gameClass argument, Twisted defined, 352
GameClientFactory object, Twisted code, 358–359
Game Object Identifier (GID) defined, 185, 187–188
GameOverMode code, 183–184
GameProtocolFactory class, Twisted defined, 351, 352–353
GameRequestHandler class code, 317–318
games
    architectures
        client/server, 344–345

diagram of, 8–9
        infrastructure components, 7–8
        massively multiplayer, 345–346
        peer-to-peer, 342–344
        Python, 19–24
    class code, 173
    content, procedurally generated, 269–270
    development, 2–3
    events, 188–195
    framework, 27–34
    multiplayer example, 367–388
GameServerApp class, Twisted code, 348–351
game simulations. *See* simulations, game
gApp global variable defined, 451
garbage collector, Python, 33, 396
GaussDistribution class defined, 274
Gaussian distributions, random numbers, 271
generateTerrain method code, 280–281
GenericClientApp, Twisted code, 357–358, 359, 362–363
getSimdata method defined, 106
getSource function, code, 119
global interpreter lock defined, 325
graphics
    art pipeline in, 100–101
    C/C++, 100
    2D, 11–12, 41, 50–51, 101, 104
    3D, 12, 41
    engine interface, code, 103–106
    engines
        defined, 11
        and physical simulation interactions, 106
        Python suitability for, 13
        subcomponents of, 12
    interface, high-speed, 103–106
    object interface, 118–123
    objects, add and remove functions, 430–432

graphics (*cont.*)
  overview, 99–100
  and Python, 101–103, 107–115
GraphicsEngine C++ class code,
  413–417
GraphicsObject C++ class code,
  422–428, 428–432
Graphicsobject class defined,
  104–105
GraphicsObjects interface, 106
GraphicsSource class defined,
  118–119, 120
gsources module variable defined,
  118
glVertex call, OpenGL defined,
  112–113

H

handler function defined, 145
head-up display elements, 15
health bars, drawing, 121–122
heap memory defined, 396
height maps, 274–275
helper class, PyGame defined, 139
hit method, SimObject class, 89,
  90–91
hoop library, construction of, 95,
  196
hostname defined, 299
hosts file defined, 300–301

I

images
  drawImage method defined, 114
  loadImage function, code,
    116–117
  restrictions, 117
InfoPanel, PyUI code, 232–235
initCategory method,
  Datamanager, 63, 64
initialSimCategories, 71–72
input methods, 143, 305. *See also*
    specific method by name
instance creation and deletion,
  426–427
integer packing/unpacking,
    Twisted code, 332–333

interface bloat defined, 437
interface code defined, 408
interface generation, automating,
  435–442
interfaces
  module *vs.* object, 103
Internet names, 298–299
Internet Protocol (IP) addresses,
  299–300
isBlocked method code, 265
iteratePath method code, 261
iterative servers, 318–321
iterator protocol, Python C API,
  395

J

Java programming language, 24
joystick input, 149–150

K

keyboard input, 146–148
keyboard polling defined, 147

L

label argument, Datamanager, 63
lambda functions, Python defined,
  283
latency, 306–307
layout managers, PyUI defined,
  220
LetterMap class code, 289–290
levels
  game
    data, 198–202
    modes, 202–205
    overview, 197–198
  resources, managing, 209–211
libraries. *See also* PyUI library
  audio systems, 14
  hoop library, construction of,
    95, 196
  sound libraries defined, 134
library code defined, 408, 410
life member attribute, simulation
    objects, 45
lines, drawing, 112–113

little endian format, 307–308
loadImage function, code,
  116–117
LoadPython function code,
  447–448
LobbyFrame class, Twisted code,
  364–366
location data member, SimObject
    class, 88
lock step simulation defined, 342
loopback address defined, 300
Lua programming language, 23

M

macros, reference counting, 397
main loop, code for, 31–32
makeMove method defined, 375
makeNames method code, 292
mapping objects, 405
mapping protocol, Python C API,
  395
Markov chains, 288
massively multiplayer game
    architectures, 345–346
Max Payne, 9
memory
  C/C++, management of,
    395–396
  heap *vs.* stack, 396–397
  Python, management of, 2, 396
menu handler code, 452–453
message handler methods, server
    protocol class, 354–355
message handling, 144–146
mid-point displacement, 275–278
mixer.music module, PyGame
    defined, 141
modes
  classes, 172–173
  game, defined, 172
  game levels, 202–205
  post-level, 207–208
  pre-level, 205–206
  window *vs.* fullscreen, 148
modules, 29–30, 94–95
mouse
  handlers, pathfinding, 265–266

input, 148–149, 234
movement messages and TCP/IP, 304
movement states defined, 241
music, 133, 141
mutex module, Python defined, 325

N

name generation
 Markov chains, 288
 overview, 287
 random, 292–293
 seeds, 287–288
NameGenerator class code, 290–291
names, drawing, 121–122
name translation, 300–301
navigation meshes, 256
networks
 concepts
  identification, 298–303
  overview, 297
 engines, 17
 layers
  overview, 17–18, 311–312
  sockets, 313–315
  packets, 333–339
nextlevel attribute defined, 201
Node class code, 259
nodes defined, 257–258
NoiseMaker class, PyGame code, 136–137
nonblocking I/O, 305
number protocol, Python C API, 394
numbers
 distributions, 271
 port, Python C API, 374
 random, 270–271, 272
numeric objects, 404

O

Object protocol, 393
objects
 borrowed references defined, 397

classifying for collision detection, 70–72
finding position from center, 46–47
graphics, add and remove functions, 430–432
identification, 185–188
moving, 84–86, 92, 234
physical attributes of, 9
physical state, setting, 45, 48
Python, serializing, 409
real references defined, 397
removing from world, 48–49
simulation, adding ambient sound to, 140
updating, 140
velocity, computing changes in, 51–52
object space defined, 77
observable interface code, PyUI, 230–231
onConnected method, Twisted defined, 359
onkey method defined, 167
OpenGL
 g1Vertex call defined, 112–113
 and images, 117
 object rendering in, 122
 terrain generation, 284–287
 texture coordinates, 114–115
 textures, 114–115
OpenGL API, 12
OpenGL Contexts, 16, 29
os modules, Python defined, 323

P

Packer class code, 333
packet-processing loop, states of, 337
panels, PyUI defined, 219
parameter values, extracting, 399–401
Pathfinder class code, 259–261
pathfinding. See also collision detection
 efficiency in, 262–263
 mouse handlers, 265–266

overview, 253
Pathfinder class code, 259–261
status, draw methods, 266–267
update methods, 266
validation, 265
visualizing, 264–267
world representation in, 253–256
Pathgame class code, 264–265, 266
peer-to-peer game architectures, 342–344
per pixel method for collision checking, 75
per polygon method for collision checking, 74–75
physical simulations. See simulations, physical
pickle module, 409
ping time, 306–307
Player class code, 203–204
player object defined, 143
play method, PyGame defined, 136
PlayMode code, 180–183
Pongball game, 165–172
pongballgame class code, 165–167
PongPaddle class defined, 169–171
PongPlayer class code, 167–168
port numbers, 301–302
post-level mode, 207–208
postUserEvent method, PyUI defined, 146
pre-level mode, 205–206
prerequisites, user, 4
primitives, drawing methods, 112, 122–123
procedural content generation, overview, 269–270
processAdjacent method code, 261–262
processClient method defined, 319
processPacket helper method, Twisted code, 337–338

protocol class, Twisted code. *See* Twisted, protocol class code

protocol defined, 392–393

protocols, Twisted. *See* Twisted, protocols

Psyco, 436, 440–442

pulse code modulation defined, 135

PyArg_ParseTuple() defined, 399, 400

Py_BuildValue function defined, 402

Py_DECREF() macro defined, 397

PyErr_ExceptionMatches function defined, 398

Py_FindMethod function, Python C API, 429

PyGame

  AmbientSound class code, 140

  capabilities of, 28

  channel object code, 135

  helper class defined, 139

  and images, 117

  joystick input, 149–150

  keyboard polling, 147

  mixer module, 135–138

  mixer.music module defined, 141

  mouse input, 148–149

  NoiseMaker class code, 136–137

  play method defined, 136

  pygame.event.set_grab() defined, 148

  pygame.mouse.get_pos defined, 148

  pygame.mouse.get_pressed defined, 148

  setAmbientProperties method defined, 139

  SoundManager class code, 137–138

  SoundManager with ambient sounds code, 138–139

  sound object code, 135

  source code to initialize, 29

  velocity, calculating, 149

pygame.event.set_grab() defined, 148

pygame.mouse.get_pos defined, 148

pygame.mouse.get_pressed defined, 148

py_getattr function defined, 429

py_getSources method defined, 421

py_getTextures method defined, 421

Py_INCREF() macro defined, 397

Py_None object defined, 403–404

PyObject class defined, 392

PyObject_HEAD macro defined, 424

PyObject_IsInstance method defined, 403

PyOpenGL library defined, 107

Python

  A* algorithm, 256–263

  applications, 1–2, 3

  array module defined, 332

  audio systems and, 14

  C API

    abstract object layer, 392–395

    buffer protocol, 395

    concrete object layer, 402–405

    data conversion, 399–402

    exception handling, 398–399

    function table, extension module, 411–413

    iterator protocol, 395

    mapping protocol, 395

    number protocol, 394

    object protocol, 393

    overview, 391–392

    Py_FindMethod function, 429

    reference counting, 395–397

    return values, building, 401–402

    sequence protocol, 394

    Very High Level Interpreter, 444

  and C code, integrating, 2, 407–442

  data representation, 22–23

  defined, 1

  embedding

    code execution functions, 445

    executing Python code, 448–449

    host application, communicating with, 449–451

    interpreter, 444–449

    overview, 21, 38, 407, 443–444

    project setup, 454–455

    Windows and, 454

  execfile function defined, 119

  game architectures, 19–24

  garbage collector, 33, 396

  global interpreter lock defined, 325

  graphics and, 101–103

  graphics engine, 107–115

  images, restrictions in, 117

  infrastructure technology, 27–28

  initialization, 28–29

  interface functions code, 417–422

  lambda functions defined, 283

  level data in, 199–202

  memory management of, 2, 396

  modules defined, 29–30

  mutex module defined, 325

  network packets, 333–339

  objects, serializing, 409

  object type structure, 424–425

  OpenGL Contexts drawing calls, 29

  os modules defined, 323

  performance characteristics, 19–20

  programming in, 21

pure, advantages *vs.* disadvantages, 20
random module
  defined, 270–271
  implementing, 272–274
  RunPython function code, 448–449
  as scripting language, 21–22
select module defined, 327
simulations
  game, 15
  implementing, 37, 123–129
  physical, 10
socket module, 313, 317
socket objects defined, 313, 315
source code, 2, 63
string slicing
  data, transmitting, 316
  and name generation, 291–292
terrain generation, 279–287
threading module defined, 325
thread module defined, 325
user interfaces, 17, 213
and Visual Studio, 435
xdrlib module defined, 333
Python source code as data source, 63
PyTypeObject defined, 403
pyui.draw call, 32
PyUI library
  applied, 221–230
  CanvasFrame class code, 224–227
  CanvasPanel class code, 222–224
  createMenus method defined, 227
  desktop defined, 218–219
  dialogs defined, 219
  entity class with observation code, 231–232
  events, handling, 144–145, 146
  events defined, 221
  fonts defined, 221
  frames defined, 219
  InfoPanel code, 232–235

initialization of, 30
keyboard input, 146–148
layout managers defined, 220
and message handling, 144
observable interface code, 230–231
overview, 217–221
panels defined, 219
postUserEvent method defined, 146
pyui.draw call, 32
pyui.locals defined, 144–145
renderers defined, 220
SaveDialog class code, 227–228
setBack method defined, 115
text, drawing, 235–237
themes defined, 220
widgets defined, 219
windows defined, 219
world, drawing, 115
pyui.locals defined, 144–145
PyUnit, 152, 153. *See also* unit testing
Py_XDECREF() macro defined, 397
Py_XINCREF() macro defined, 397

Q
Quake, 344

R
radians defined, 46
random class code, 272–273
random distributions code, 273–274
random module, Python
  defined, 270–271
  implementing, 272–274
random numbers
  distributions, 271
  predictable, 270–271, 272
rawData argument, Datamanager function, 63
reactive simulations, 37–38
reactor pattern servers, 326–328
rectangles, drawing, 113

recvfrom method, UDP/IP defined, 315
recv method, TCP/IP defined, 315, 316
reference counting, Python C API, 395–397
references, weak *vs.* regular, 187
registerHandler method defined, 144, 145, 338
relational databases, 58
relationships, inherited vs compositional, 165
removeCallback member, simulation objects, 47
removeFromWorld method, simulation worlds defined, 48
removeObject method defined, 417
renderbucket class, code, 110, 111–112
renderers, PyUI defined, 220
resources, managing, 209–211
return values, building Python C API, 401–402
RollerCoaster Tycoon, 101
RunPython function code, 448–449
runUntilCurrent method, Twisted defined, 329

S
Sample DirectMedia Library API, 13, 14, 144
sample rate defined, 134
SaveDialog class, PyUI code, 227–228
scripting languages, 58
seeds in name generation, 287–288
select module, Python defined, 327
self argument defined, 399
self.tiles variable defined, 281
sendError method, Twisted defined, 338–339
sendGameOver method defined, 375

send method, TCP/IP defined, 315–316

sendto method, UDP/IP defined, 315

sequence objects, 404–405

sequence protocol, Python C API, 394

ServerGame class, Twisted code, 352

ServerProtocol class, Twisted defined, 351, 353–354

servers
  concurrent asynchronous, 326–328
  concurrent forking, 321–324
  concurrent threaded, 324–326
  game, 344–345, 348–356
  overview, 341–342
  simple iterative, 318–321
  socket code, 314
  TCP/IP models, 317–328
  Tic-Tac-Toe multiplayer game, 370–378

setAmbientProperties method, PyGame defined, 139

setBack method, PyUI renderer defined, 115

setState method defined, 106

setstate method defined, 126

setup.py file, 433

setView method, graphics interface defined, 104

shards defined, 345

shootBall method defined, 168

SimCategory class, code, 59–60

Sim City and terrain generation, 274

SimObject class, 72

SimObject constructor, code, 60

simulation objects, PongBall game, 169–171

simulations
  base class, 44–47
  category, code, 124–126
  controlled, 39–40
  conventions, general, 41–43
  data-driven, 55–67

defined, 35–36

2D graphics
  properties of, 41
  updating, code for, 50–51

3D graphics, 41

game
  avatars defined, 164
  defined, 9, 36
  overview, 14–15, 163–164
  Python suitability for, 15
  implementing with Python, 37, 123–129
  interacting with, 230–235
  objects in, 36, 45, 123–124
  parallel, 40–41

physical
  components of, 36–37
  defined, 9, 36
  and graphics engines interactions, 106
  and player experience, 9
  Python suitability for, 10

PongBall game objects, 169–171

Python
  game, 15
  implementing, 37, 123–129
  physical, 10

reactive, 37–38

removeCallback member, simulation objects, 47

removeFromWorld method, simulation worlds defined, 48

rules for defined, 36

unit testing, 155–159

updating, 49–52

world, 47–49

singletons, implementing, 243

sockets, 313–315
  application interface defined, 311
  code, client, 313
  code, server, 314
  iterative server using, code, 318–319
  objects defined, 313, 315

Python socket module, 313, 317

SocketServer module
  asynchronous I/O capabilities and, 328
  code, 320, 323
  and concurrent threaded servers, 325

SoundManager
  with ambient sounds, PyGame code, 138–139
  class, PyGame code, 137–138

sound object, PyGame code, 135

sounds
  ambient in games, 133, 138–140
  cards, 134, 135
  effects, stereo, 136
  libraries defined, 134
  looping code, 136
  stopping automatically code, 136

squares, modification of, 282

stack memory defined, 396

Starcraft, 342

Star Trek: Bridge Commander, 3

State classes code, 241–242

state inputs, 245–246

state machines
  applications, 240
  enhancements, 244–253
  parallel, 246–253

state machines, parallel, 246–253

StateManager class code, 248–250

state modules, management of, 246–248

step variable defined, 281

string slicing
  data, transmitting, 316
  and name generation, 291–292

stroke application main loop, code, 228–230

subnets, 302–303

SWIG, 436, 437–439

synchronous I/O, 305

sys.stderr variable defined, 449

sys.stdout variable defined, 449

T

Tcl programming language, 23–24
TCP/IP (Transmission Control
        Protocol/Internet Protocol)
    connection management,
        317–318
    overview, 303–304
    server models, 317–328
TCPServer class defined, 320–321
telnet and TCP/IP, 320
TerrainApp class code, 285–287
terrainGenerate class code,
        279–280
terrain generation
    generateTerrain method code,
        280–281
    height maps, 274–275
    mid-point displacement,
        275–278
    OpenGL, 284–287
    overview, 274
    in Python, 279–287
    TerrainApp class code, 285–287
    terrainGenerate class code,
        279–280
text
    drawing in PyUI, 235–237
    drawText method defined,
        113–114
    files as data sources, 57
texturebucket class, code, 110–111
textures
    createTexture method code,
        286
    GraphicsObjects interface and,
        106
    and line drawing, 113
    OpenGL and, 114–115
    py_getTextures method
        defined, 421
    resource management and,
        210–211
    texturebucket class, code,
        110–111
TheguiEvent class defined, 145
themes, PyUI defined, 220
The Sims and 2D graphics, 101

threading module, Python
        defined, 325
ThreadingTCPServer class code,
        325–326
TicTacClientApp class code,
        380–381
TicTacClientProtocol class,
        378–380
TicTacGame class code, 371,
        372–375
TicTacServer class code, 371, 377
TicTacServerProtocol class code,
        371, 376–377
Tic-Tac-Toe multiplayer game
    client code, 378–388
    code organization, 368–369
    overview, 367–368, 369
    server code, 370–378
TicTacWindow class code,
        381–385
tiles method for collision
        checking, 76–77
toRadians utility function and
        rotation direction
        conversions, 42
transformation defined, 77
transitions variable defined, 245
transition validation, 244–245
Transmission Control
        Protocol/Internet Protocol
        (TCP/IP), 303–304,
        317–328
transport, Twisted defined, 330
transport data member, Twisted
        code, 338–339
try/except block defined, 314
tuple parsing tokens, 400
Turner event class code, 193–194
Twisted
    ClientProtocol class code,
        359–362
    dataReceived method defined,
        336–337
    doSelect method defined, 329
    framework message types, 356
    gameClass argument defined,
        352

GameClientFactory object
        code, 358–359
game protocol design, 330–339
GameProtocolFactory class
        defined, 351, 352–353
GameServerApp class code,
        348–351
GenericClientApp code,
        357–358, 359, 362–363
integer packing/unpacking
        code, 332–333
LobbyFrame class code,
        364–366
message handler methods,
        server protocol class,
        354–355
onConnected method defined,
        359
overview, 312, 328–329
packet-processing loop, states
        of, 337
processPacket helper method
        code, 337–338
protocol class code, 335–336,
        353, 363–364
protocols
    binary, 332, 333
    dynamic, 331
    static, 330
reactor, 329
runUntilCurrent method
        defined, 329
sendError method defined,
        338–339
ServerGame class code, 352
ServerProtocol class defined,
        351, 353–354
transport data member code,
        338–339
writePacker method defined,
        338
Twisted Matrix Labs, 329

U

UDP/IP (User Datagram
        Protocol/Internet
        Protocol), 304–305

Ultima Online, 346
UniformDistribution class
    defined, 274
uniform distributions, random
    numbers, 271
unit testing
    collision detection, 157–159
    Datamanager class, 153–155
    overview, 151–152
    setup, 152–154
    simulations, 155–159
Unpacker class code, 333, 338
Unreal, 344
update methods
    code for, 50, 52
    pathfinding code, 266
    updateState method code,
        204–205
updateState method code,
    204–205
User Datagram Protocol/Internet
    Protocol (UDP/IP),
    304–305
user interfaces
    and coordinate systems,
        214–216
    desktop, limitations of, 16

drawing of, 214
game, purpose of, 16
head-up display elements, 15
OpenGL Contexts, 16
optimizations, 217
overview, 15–16, 213–214
Python suitability for, 17, 213
requirements, 16, 102
translation functions code, 216

V
validation, 244–245, 265
variable rate updating, 43–44
velocity
    calculateVelocity method,
        45–46
    objects, computing changes in,
        51–52
    PyGame, calculating, 149
Visual Studio and Python
    extension modules, 435

W
walk module code, 243–244
watermark defined, 441
waypoints defined, 254–255
widgets, PyUI defined, 219

windows, PyUI defined, 219
Windows and Python embedding,
    454
world class, unit testing, 153–154
worlds
    and collision detection, 72–74
    drawing, 115
    generation of, 272
    navigation meshes, 256
    objects, removing from, 48–49
    pathfinding in, 253–256
    PyUI library, 115
    simulations, 47–49
    unit testing, 153–154
    updating, 126
    waypoints, 255–256
world space defined, 77
writePacker method, Twisted
    defined, 338

X
XDR (External Data
    Representation) Protocol,
    308
xdrlib module, Python defined,
    333
XML, 57